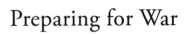

Preparing for War

J. P. CLARK

Preparing for War

The Emergence of the Modern U.S. Army, 1815–1917

Harvard University Press

CAMBRIDGE, MASSACHUSETTS, AND LONDON, ENGLAND · 2017

Library of Congress Cataloging-in-Publication Data
Names: Clark, J. P., author.
Title: Preparing for war : the emergence of the modern U.S. army, 1815–1917/J. P. Clark.
Description: Cambridge, Massachusetts : Harvard University Press, 2017. | Includes
   bibliographical references and index.
Identifiers: LCCN 2016004678 | ISBN 9780674545731
Subjects: LCSH: Military art and science—United States—History—19th century. | Military
   art and science—United States—History—20th century. | United States. Army—Officers—
   Attitudes—History. | United States. Army—Officers—Training of—History. | Military
   education—United States—History—19th century. | Military education—United States—
   History—20th century.
Classification: LCC U43.U4 C55 2016 | DDC 355.00973/09034—dc23
LC record available at http://lccn.loc.gov/2016004678

To Kelly, Faith, and Abigail

Contents

Preface

THIS BOOK BEGAN as an investigation into the Root reforms of the early twentieth century. During my early research, a small band of officers emerged as critical figures in the implementation of those seminal changes, arguably the most far-reaching in the history of the U.S. Army. I soon became curious as to whether this group was representative of, or somehow different from, their peers in the larger officer corps. If the latter, was it possible to identify some feature in their education or experience that had made them atypically open to change? Thus, in its primordial state, this project was a search for distinct groups of "reformers" and "conservatives."

That focus changed one day when a misrouting of materials led me to take up a well-worn copy of reports written by American observers of the Russo-Japanese War. In that volume, I found two starkly different accounts of the same assault, one written by an attaché with the Japanese, the other by one with the Russians. Indeed, they were so different in their interpretation of events that it took some time before I realized that the two reports were describing the same action. Conditioned by my methodology to correlate outlook with an officer's background, I was at first perplexed, then intrigued, and eventually excited, to see that the two observers were as identical in age and professional experience as I could reasonably hope to find.

Explaining the intellectual divergence of these two individuals from a seemingly common base was far more interesting than my original project.

Yet even then, I remained hobbled by my classification of reformers and conservatives. Though no longer looking for distinct groups set apart by schooling, branch, or combat experience, I was still looking for individuals who fit neatly into one or the other category. All the while, my subjects in their diaries, letters, and memoirs stubbornly refused to conform to my labels. "Reformers" sometimes seemed reactionary, while "conservatives" sometimes seemed progressive. As I learned more about these individuals, I often came to understand what element of their earlier career led to these departures from my typology.

As my imagined pattern crumbled, another began to emerge. The new pattern was not one of consensus—there was little of that within the army on any subject of significance. Instead, I began to understand that the confusing mosaic of disagreements that divided the officer corps in sometimes surprising ways was not something for a historian to put in order, but rather that untidy mass was what I had been seeking all along. These quarrels were a map to the officer corps, for what individuals chose to dispute revealed much about the military profession at any given period. As assumptions about the nature of war changed, questions that seemed urgent faded and were replaced by other concerns, while once daring ideas (and those who held them) came be to seen as commonplace or even old-fashioned.

This was a disorienting realization for one raised in the ahistoric belief in a singular military profession, a fixed entity governed by normative values equally applicable to all eras. I struggled with the mutability evident in the records before me; it was as if officers of one era were members of a profession entirely different from those of a different period. Or, as I eventually would come to understand, they were members of the same profession—shared heritage and enduring institutions provided continuity—but they were divided into distinct generations, each deriving a unique identity from the ideas of their contemporary society, individual experiences in peace and war, and the manner in which the army was then organized. When these conditions changed, so too did the officer corps.

Once I began to look through this "generational lens," the origins of the confusing cross-currents that I had found in the Root era reformers became clear. They had been commissioned during a professionally bewildering time. Most had been too young to serve in the Civil War but were nonetheless profoundly influenced by that epic conflict. Yet even while the scope, scale, and intensity of the Civil War mesmerized professional soldiers, those same factors made it an anomaly in the nineteenth-century American military experience. Daily life in the decades afterward resembled far more that of the antebellum period than of the Civil War. This generation led not corps or divisions in pitched battle but companies and batteries patrolling the frontier or guarding the coast. Torn between dreams of grand campaigns and the reality of leading small, dusty detachments, that generation was further buffeted by the social, cultural, and technological dislocations that marked the transition from the nineteenth to the twentieth century. Like others of the Gilded Age, they were on the cusp of great change but not ready to abandon old notions.

This new understanding at last brought my scholarship in line with my own experiences as an officer. Absolute designations of reformers and conservatives assumed an intellectual consistency among officers of the past that I had not found in myself or my contemporaries. The prism of generations also granted insight into today's army. I have been struck by the great gulf of perception, understanding, and experience that separates the senior officers commissioned in the 1970s and 1980s from the junior officers commissioned since 2000. The generals are baby boomers who served a decade or more during the Cold War and who experienced Afghanistan and Iraq only as senior officers. The captains and lieutenants are millennials whose professional experiences are entirely encompassed by those wars, which they experienced at the small-unit level. Bridging the gaps between these quite different frames of reference is not impossible, but it is unlikely because the bureaucratic artifacts that give an army substance—doctrine, regulations, training plans—rarely make explicit the assumptions on which they are based. This allows the old and the young to talk past each other, not realizing their different views. The result is confusion, discord, and mistrust. The most insidious divides are those that go unnoticed. With this realization, I came to a better understanding of the army of a century ago and of the one today.

Preparing for War

Prologue

IN 1815, THE United States was agrarian, candlelit, and horse drawn. On the battlefield, the army arrayed itself in linear formations bristling with flintlock muskets and smoothbore cannon of the Napoleonic era. Pageantry still had a place in warfare; officers inclined to display went into battle adorned with gold braid and plumed hats. The regular army had not yet established its monopoly over military leadership; the common expectation was that in any significant conflict, the regulars would comprise only a portion of the national army that would include considerable numbers of militiamen or volunteers fighting under their own officers and retaining their local identities.

By 1917, the country was industrial, electric powered, and engine driven. The change in the army was just as marked. Soldiers went to war with magazine-fed rifles, steel artillery, machine guns, tanks, and airplanes. Officers and soldiers alike wore olive drab uniforms that while infinitely more practical than those of the century before also suggested a loss of individuality within an undifferentiated mass. The regular army was still too small to fight a major war with just its peacetime strength, but it had become the vessel into which citizen-soldiers were poured in times of crisis. This gave the twentieth-century officer corps far greater (though by no means complete) control over how those citizen-soldiers were organized, led, and equipped.

Even venerable state units were stripped of their local flavor. For instance, upon entering federal service in World War I, the 2nd "Stonewall" Virginia Infantry became the 116th Infantry Regiment, an anodyne label suggesting that units, like individuals, had become interchangeable parts of a machine.

Coincident with these changes in weapons, uniforms, and organization was an equally significant shift in the way that regular officers thought about the profession of arms. The army went from a mode of informal direction grounded in the personality of the commander to a system of formal control using impersonal staff procedures. This change was the methodological equivalent of the sartorial change from gold braid to olive drab. Though undeniably more functional, an element of personality was lost in the transition. Individuals lost autonomy as they were subsumed within standardized organizational structures. Paradoxically, this surrender of individual discretion helped win greater collective freedom. The phenomenon of nineteenth-century "political generals" was, in part, a manifestation of the public's well-founded skepticism that regular officers possessed a form of unique expertise in high command.[1] If "military genius" was a largely innate quality residing within the individual, then a talented amateur was likely to be more successful than a plodding regular. The emergence of institutions like the war college and a general staff gave substance to the regulars' claims to superior expertise. Coincident with that change was the disappearance of political generals, the most telling sign of increasing civilian deference to the regulars in matters military. How and why this transformation occurred is the subject of this book.

More specifically, the narrative will focus on the changing notion of what it meant to prepare for war, which throughout this period was regarded as the central activity of the regular army. In the early nineteenth century, aside from physical preparations such as fortifying key locations and stockpiling materiel, preparing for war entailed little more than a regimen of close-order drill meant to instill the habit of obedience in soldiers; there was no pretension that this training replicated war or prepared officers to make decisions under fire. War Department inspectors were concerned primarily with enforcing fiscal and administrative standards; commanders were allowed to train their subordinates and units as they saw fit. Conventional wisdom held that military competence was a product of character, common sense, and natural aptitude; these innate qualities might be refined through experience or study but were largely beyond the ability of the institution to manufacture.

There was consequently little effort to train officers in anything but the technical skills of engineering and gunnery.

By the early twentieth century, the U.S. Army prepared for war in an entirely different manner. War was no longer regarded as an inscrutable realm so far apart from normal existence that little useful work could be done in peacetime. The new consensus was that the military profession was a body of expert knowledge that could be codified, imparted, and regulated. Whereas not long before schooling had been considered an imposition to be inflicted only upon cadets and the most junior lieutenants, ambitious officers of all ages now regarded army schools as a place to earn distinction. The acknowledgment that at least some elements of war could be replicated in peacetime allowed the possibility of more vigorous and realistic training. Thousands of regulars and national guardsmen came together for grand maneuvers that were as much for the benefit of generals and their staffs as for the common private.

In hindsight, the military benefits of this evolution are so clear that one might conclude that it was the product of design; but the actual process was incremental, organic, and often resisted by elements of the officer corps. Like blacksmiths and telephone switch operators, older officers regretted developments that threatened ways of life that might appear quaint from our perspective but to them seemed essential elements of military service. Umpired field training, professional education, and tactical doctrine: these and other activities associated with modern military professionalism are based on the premise that the army can shape the manner in which officers think and act. Most officers of 1815—steeped in a romantic view of warfare and with that era's overwrought individualism—would have found that notion misguided and offensive. Instead, they subscribed to a guild-like conception of professionalism that granted all members some degree of deference and left those at the middle or higher ranks largely unfettered in how they practiced their trade. By contrast, soldiers of the early twentieth century were products of the Industrial Age; accustomed to mechanical metaphor, they were more inclined to think of the army as a machine for producing military power and themselves as mere components of that larger apparatus. This is not to say that the older generations were indifferent to organizational imperatives or that members of the younger generation unreservedly sacrificed their interests for the sake of the system. Rather, the change was a more nuanced shift in how individuals conceived of their relationship to the institution. This development had a number of implications, but the most important was a general acceptance of professional indoctrination as a necessary component of military effectiveness.

This change in military professionalism coincided with similar shifts within civilian professions because both were driven by the same societal and cultural trends. The intuitive notion that military institutions develop in tandem with their parent societies is supported by a rich literature that includes works by Michael Howard, Geoffrey Parker, John Lynn, and Walter Millis.[2] When armies are viewed against the vista of eras and centuries, it is obvious that they are swept along by the same currents that affect all human institutions: political, economic, demographic, technological, and intellectual forces.

We can acknowledge the primacy of these grand trends without sacrificing the role of contingency. Within the broad channels set by these powerful but blunt external forces, the peculiar characteristics of military institutions and the efforts of individuals were able to alter the course of change, particularly in those small units by which armies typically evolve—revisions of doctrine and regulations, modifications to unit organizations, new training directives and school curricula. Political, economic, social, and cultural factors undoubtedly influenced these military activities, but strategic considerations, bureaucratic politics, organizational culture, and the personalities and desires of key individuals typically played an even greater role. Studies of military adaptation, such as the works of Barry Posen, Stephen Peter Rosen, MacGregor Knox, Williamson Murray, and David Johnson, explore the myriad ways in which conditions within the organization dictate the reaction to a new strategic challenge or the emergence of a new technology. In contrast to the epochal studies of war and society, these works examine smaller periods of time, usually measured in years.[3]

The intermediate scale of generations is an ideal vantage point from which to combine the best of each of these two approaches; it provides sufficient granularity to recognize the contingency associated with the dynamic and unpredictable inner workings of complex institutions while permitting sufficient perspective to see those developments against the sweep of history. This approach will be applied to the U.S. Army from 1815 to 1917, a period in which there were four professional generations, each defined by a distinct method of preparing for war.

The generational approach differs from much of the contemporary literature on military professionalism, which tends to focus on the identification of a fixed set of attributes—organizational characteristics, expertise, and values—that a group must possess in order to be "professional."[4] When applied to history, such a normative standard often is used to determine whether an army was professional at a given time.[5] This kind of analysis has its merits, but the purpose here is not to judge whether one generation was more or less professional than another. Instead, it is to understand how the context of each generation imparted a unique professionalism. As such, this study adopts the minimal definition of a profession as an identifiable body of practitioners bound by a common purpose. By 1815, the officer corps of the U.S. Army had become a relatively stable group of long-serving individuals dedicated to preparing for war and so met that requirement. Hence, in these pages *professionals* will refer to commissioned officers of the regular army. That group will often be set in contrast to *citizen-soldiers,* a term encompassing militiamen, guardsmen, volunteers, and draftees. But while the corporate body of the profession remained fixed, what it meant to be *professional* and the qualities of *professionalism* varied over time, bound up as these terms were in the changing notion of what it meant to prepare for war.

That malleable definition recognizes that the various approaches to preparing for war were not greater or lesser shades of an ideal professionalism but were collective reactions to a specific cultural and military milieu. That context was what gave each generation its distinct character. Just as is true today, individuals in the past understood and were influenced by their world in different ways; generations were not uniform in their views. Indeed, disagreements often defined a generation as much as points of consensus. But while a generation's context did not dictate a single set of views, it did provide a common pool of ideas, values, and experiences that bounded its diversity. As historian Daniel T. Rodgers notes, because most individuals are "users rather than shapers of ideas," our thoughts and actions are defined by "the constellation of live, accessible ways of looking at society" that surrounds us.[6] Each generation of army officers was similarly defined by its own particular "constellation" of ideas that provided the raw material from which its members assembled their own method of preparing for war. When this encompassing milieu changed, so did the outlook of new officers; and so a new professional generation was born.

In practice, however, historians find it difficult to draw meaningful generational boundaries. The gradual and uneven nature of change across populations makes neat delineations based upon date of birth unsatisfactorily arbitrary, giving that single moment marking the passing of one year, decade, or century to the next undue significance. For that reason, this book classifies generations not on their year of birth or commissioning but by their experiences. This atypical method is made possible by the Civil War, which was a sharp, traumatic departure from the past and a defining moment for the officer corps. It also was unlike anything that followed in the decades immediately after. That break created three natural generations: those who completed their service before the war, those who experienced it firsthand, and those who entered the profession in its aftermath. They will be referred to as the foundational, Civil War, and composite generations, respectively. Only the fourth generation—the progressive generation—lacks such a clear definition. It was the product of several factors, the most important of which were the end of the frontier campaigns, advances in military education, and the beginning of the Progressive Era. These conditions tended to have their greatest effect on those commissioned after 1889; but because of the gradual nature of these changes, that boundary is only a tentative guide.

To give life to these groups and to avoid unfounded generalization, this narrative focuses on individuals as they reconciled the disparate influences of society, the army, and their own experiences. Though no officer was wholly representative of his time, when viewed alongside some of their contemporaries, their collective stories reveal the contours of the generation. This understanding expands when generations are compared, for in the transitions we catch glimpse of old assumptions being challenged, previously radical ideas becoming conventional, and new points of dissension emerging. Indeed, one might trace the evolution of the army by plotting the evolution of its defining controversies over time.

Before delving into these individual stories, a brief overview of the larger narrative will help place all that follows in context. The American military profession began with the foundational generation, which was built upon the veterans of the War of 1812, with others—mainly West Pointers—joining them throughout the antebellum period. The most important influences over this first generation were the army's dispersion into small detachments spread across great distances, the glacial rate of promotion, and the nature of linear tactics; all of these factors meant that there was little need for elaborate systems of professional training or education. Officers serving for decades in essentially the same role were capable of handling the army's small units without the benefit of advanced theory. Even during the Mexican-American War, the separation of regulars and volunteers into distinct forces meant that the average regular waged war in much the same capacity as he had served during peace.

The Civil War abruptly changed this pattern. Though there were again distinct regular and volunteer forces, many regulars served as individuals within the volunteer armies, an experience that would forever alter the officer corps and how it prepared for war. During the Mexican-American War, officers with one or two decades of experience typically commanded nothing more than companies, and only a handful of senior officers served as general officers; in that context, the antebellum method of preparing officers through the simple accumulation of experience was sufficient. This was not the case during the Civil War, when individuals with just a few years of commissioned service commanded regiments, while hundreds of regulars were promoted to general officer rank. The deficiencies of Civil War generalship convinced some veterans of the war, most notably Emory Upton, that all officers should be trained in high command and staff duties to prepare them for another war of national scale. But this was not the consensus. Claiming that such training was essential to professional competence was an admission that what had been the defining moment of their professional lives had been fundamentally flawed; that they were not fully equal to whatever role they played in the war. This was particularly true for that large segment of officers who had entered the service as volunteers and then elected to remain in the regular army after the war, for they had received no preliminary training at all. But while the method of preparing for conflict changed little, the scale at which the officer corps thought about war had been forever expanded. Even though the regular army soon shrunk back to a force less than thirty thousand strong, the memory of serving in (and for some commanding) armies, corps, and divisions remained vibrant.

The legacy of the Civil War also weighed heavily on the third cohort—the composite generation—made up of those commissioned from the end of the war through approximately 1889. Officers of this generation were nearly all graduates of West Point, and a significant proportion had been cadets while Upton had been the commandant in the 1870s. Perhaps for this reason, many accepted his argument that the army should reform its methods. But after leaving West Point, the generation went into an army widely dispersed geographically, deeply divided by corps and regimental affiliations, and torn between dreaming of hypothetical conflict on the scale of the Civil War and the quite different reality of daily life that was not much different than conditions in the antebellum army. So while many thought that professional reform was necessary, there was no consensus on the particular forms it should take. Some were content with improving the relatively simple systems of education that were adequate to the needs of a frontier constabulary. Others remained true to Upton's vision of educating every officer in the art of generalship, even though few could articulate a convincing reason why this was necessary. The debate smoldered for years within the tiny professional education establishment but was suddenly brought to the fore in the early twentieth century, when Secretary of War Elihu Root embarked on an aggressive reorganization of the army's internal structures. The composite generation had since risen to all but the army's most senior ranks but had never reconciled their diverging notions of how to prepare for war. Thus, the officers responsible for implementing the Root reforms often worked at cross purposes, each shaped by his quite different professional experiences.

The progressive generation—roughly encompassing those commissioned in 1890 and later—conceived of preparing for war quite differently than their predecessors; they adopted a more regulated professionalism that was more coherent, more energetic, and more willing to tolerate the coercive aspects of professional indoctrination. To some extent, this was the result of internal conditions, such as the post-frontier geographic consolidation and the centripetal effects of the Root reforms, however imperfect they were in initial execution. But the more important factor was the societal influence, for such aggressive centralization and bureaucratization, horrifying as they were to older officers, reflected the essence of the Progressive Era. The acceptance of formalized systems was thus not the product of reformers' designs but a natural byproduct of the entry into the service of a new cohort of officers who simply understood the world differently than their seniors.

From this summary, it should be evident that the understanding of war, and consequently how best to prepare for it, has not been static. Thus, we should be skeptical of the claims made by military institutions as to their ability to inculcate allegedly timeless values and standards across generations. West Point, for instance, prides itself on the "Long Gray Line" of graduates stretching from 1802 to the present, all bound by a common devotion to an ideal exemplified by the motto of "Duty, Honor, Country." But even the academy's intense four years of socialization is insignificant in comparison to the pervasive influence of society. This is proven by a simple comparison. In terms of values and outlook, the early graduates of West Point had more in common with their civilian contemporaries than they do with the cadets of today. If brought into today's classrooms, the early cadets would be bewildered by policy discussions about how the United States can best underpin the global order and shocked by the presence of women, minorities, and openly homosexual cadets. Likely, many of those antebellum graduates would refuse to serve alongside these most recent additions to the Long Gray Line. If so, then "Duty, Honor, Country" is more contextual than some might like to admit. This thought experiment illustrates the degree to which the vertical ties of continuity within the military are less important than the horizontal ties across society. Therefore, each professional generation is more a product of its time than a creation of military institutions. That is why when we look at the pictures, letters, and diaries from each era in American history, the soldiers look and sound much like their contemporaries rather than some unchanging American military archetype. This is illustrated by the contrast between two of the most extraordinary officers of the first and last generation under consideration in this study: Winfield Scott and George C. Marshall. As will be seen, Scott resembled more the Virginia gentlemen of the antebellum period and Marshall more the college-educated managerial elite of the Progressive Era than they did each other. This suggests that we must understand the contemporary society if we are to untangle the inner workings and character of an army.

CHAPTER ONE

A Profession Born in War

FOR A COUNTRY conceived in conflict, the United States began with a notably inadequate framework for organizing the military. In the years immediately after the American Revolution, the political and military leaders of that war, who had only recently struggled with the practical problems of creating and sustaining military force, debated the issue in surprisingly impractical terms; perhaps this was inevitable in a post-revolutionary society where the paramount problem was political rather than military: how to distribute power and ensure individual liberties. Military policy—the method by which the country raises and organizes its armed forces in peace and war—was reduced to two impractical alternatives, each distorted to a caricature by ideology.

The Federalists advocated a professional military organized by a central government. Such an army would advance the Federalists' political goal of centralizing power. But many of the former officers of the Continental Army were Federalists, and they sincerely believed that the American Revolution had demonstrated that professional soldiers were more capable than military amateurs. Though reasonable, it was not yet clear whether the public would tolerate a military establishment or a central government competent enough to make such a force effective.

In opposition were the Antifederalists, who wanted to rely upon the militia for national defense. This bolstered their political aim of keeping powers with the states. The Antifederalists were far less sanguine about the benefits of a standing army; they associated professional soldiers more with King George's redcoats than with Washington's Continentals. But many also drew quite different conclusions from the Revolution. There was a popular belief that the militia had won the war, a notion grounded in the conviction that men fighting as a matter of republican duty and patriotism were better soldiers than professionals fighting out of mercenary interests. Though a highly selective and quite flattering interpretation of the military record of the militia, that view was initially the ascendant. In 1783 and 1784, Congress debated whether it even had the authority to maintain a peacetime standing army. Thus, the initial military policy debate pitted a mythical militia against the aspiration of a professional force.[1]

But while a few years of government under the Articles of Confederation created the conditions for pragmatic political compromise that eventually led to the Constitution, the discussion of military policy remained polarized, abstract, and ideological. The Federalists succeeded in creating a standing army and even won constitutional recognition of the federal government's right to regulate the states' militia to ensure some measure of uniformity. But the Antifederalists, fearing that this was a cynical ploy to weaken the militia, won the battle in practical terms; the 1792 Militia Act essentially abrogated federal oversight, leaving the states free to regulate or neglect their soldiery as they saw fit. This established the pattern that would endure until the twentieth century: In peace, the United States would maintain two distinct military systems, federal regulars and state militia, with virtually no coordination or planning as to how they might be used in time of war. Because neither element was sufficient to provide for the national defense, this elusion left the practical problems of raising and maintaining armies to later generations who would have to improvise in times of crisis.[2]

It was an extravagantly inefficient system for a young republic with scarce military resources. A better policy would have been to draw upon the various levels of government to cooperatively mobilize, organize, and administer armies, each according to its own capabilities. Only the central government could provide a national framework enabling cooperation among the states. It was also the logical sponsor for specialist capabilities and functions that were impractical for the states to maintain, such as fortifications, depots, and arsenals. The states were better suited to mobilizing the raw human and material resources necessary for war. This was essentially the point made by Washington in his treatise "Sentiments on a Peace Establishment."[3] But his advice was ignored amid the bitter ideological struggle, which made military policy an adversarial competition between federal and state activists rather than a collaborative enterprise making best use of the comparative advantages inherent to each level of government.

Prior to the War of 1812, the regular army was buffeted by multiple reorganizations and upheavals as it alternated between failure and triumph. In the early 1790s, two successive veterans of the American Revolution, Josiah Harmar and Arthur St. Clair, were routed by Native American tribes on the Northwest frontier. These embarrassments led to an authorization for a larger army of 5,424 officers and men and the appointment of a commander equal to the task, "Mad" Anthony Wayne, another hero of the War for Independence. Through sheer force of will, Wayne instilled competence and discipline in the newly christened "Legion of the United States." Though many of the officers were veterans, he believed that they had grown lax in their duties. Through exacting discipline, realistic training, and the organization of flexible combined arms "sub-legions" suited to frontier conditions, Wayne brought the Legion to a high state of proficiency. Less than three years after St. Clair's defeat, he won a decisive victory at Fallen Timbers in 1794. The victory was a dramatic demonstration of the benefits of a standing army and so helped end the debate over whether the federal government should have such a force.[4]

Yet in victory, the effectiveness built by Wayne began to dissipate. With his death in 1796, the army lost its animating spirit, and he had left no institutional framework that might fill the void. There was no comprehensive set of regulations and procedures; training and discipline were largely left to the discretion of the local commander. With a general condition of peace across the Northwest after Fallen Timbers, the army was scattered in small detachments across the frontier. Senior officers rarely inspected these far-flung commands. With few external pressures to impel work and discipline amid the quiet routine of garrison life, the excellence of Wayne's legion disintegrated by increments.[5]

The Quasi-War with France (1798–1800) brought another pulse of vigor to the army, though it was one that occurred more on paper than in camp. The war itself was largely a maritime conflict, but for a time it seemed that a large army—several times larger than the one then in existence—would be necessary. President John Adams entrusted the work of organizing this force to the venerable Washington, who in turn left much of the work to his two major generals, Alexander Hamilton and Charles Pinckney. Though Hamilton continued to practice law in New York, he imagined a well-organized army and then sought to give that vision life through correspondence. His proposal for a staff organization with components for supply, administration, medical, and inspectorate became law in March 1799. He also issued directives mandating everything from unit organizations to details of uniforms. Hamilton had even greater ambitions for the creation of a military academy and the establishment of a comprehensive set of tactics and regulations to replace the "Blue Book" of Friedrich Wilhelm von Steuben. Those projects, however, were not complete when the crisis ended, and the "New Army," along with Hamilton, was mustered out of service.[6]

Hamilton's staff never had the chance to set down its bureaucratic roots, as Thomas Jefferson's election brought to power a Republican administration that was skeptical of federal bureaucracy. The 1802 Military Peace Establishment Act eliminated the system of inspectors and much of the War Department's capacity to ensure that its policies and directives were properly executed. The legislation also did away with the quartermaster general, for Republican ideology emphasized the use of private contractors to conduct government business whenever possible. Oversight and accountability quickly suffered, as the secretary of war and his handful of assistants were unable to ensure that contractors consistently provided satisfactory rations on schedule. The act also cut the authorized strength of the army by nearly a third, eliminating the expensive cavalry altogether. From the standpoint of the regulars, the only positive aspect of the legislation was the creation of the United States Military Academy. In 1794, Congress had established a Corps of Artillerists and Engineers to foster technical expertise, and the Adams administration later hired a mathematics instructor for the younger officers of this corps located principally at West Point. But it was Jefferson who gave military education a permanent place within the army. With this exception, however, military effectiveness suffered under the Jefferson administration. The emasculation of the War Department bureaucracy was followed by years of zealous economy enforced by Secretary of War Henry Dearborn, who retained the authority to approve any expenditure over fifty dollars.[7]

In contrast to the changing fortunes of the regular army, the trajectory of the militia remained fairly constant. Without federal oversight, most states allowed their military capacity to deteriorate. The exception to this was the western states, which could field effective forces such as those used by Governor William Henry Harrison in his 1811 victory at Tippecanoe. Yet even the western militia required logistical support, capable leaders, and could face well-organized European armies only under favorable conditions. These nuances and the disparity between the citizen-soldiers of the frontier states and the militia from more settled areas were largely lost on the ideological successors to the Antifederalists, the Democrat-Republican party (hereafter referred to as Republicans) led by Thomas Jefferson and James Madison. As president, Jefferson was particularly prone to overestimating the effectiveness of the militia, even while pursuing a bellicose foreign policy that risked war with Spain and Great Britain.[8]

Thus, when the British warship *Leopard* seized the USS *Chesapeake* in 1808—the last full year of Jefferson's administration—the army was small and poorly administered. As the prospect of war loomed, though Jefferson still preferred the militia, he agreed to a substantial increase of the regular army to three times its previous strength. The regulars, however, lacked both a Wayne to give them steel and a Hamilton to organize them. Instead, the army had the misfortune to have as the senior officer Brigadier General James Wilkinson, perhaps the most unprincipled figure in American military history. During the American Revolution, Wilkinson had been twice forced to resign: first for taking part in the Conway cabal to unseat then-General Washington from command and then later for irregularities in his account as Clothier General. Yet after the war, President Washington had been so desperate to appoint prominent figures from Kentucky to posts within his administration that he made Wilkinson a brigadier general. Wilkinson was soon unhappy in his role as the second-ranking officer and set his sights upon unseating Wayne from the army's senior position. Wilkinson took every opportunity to eliminate officers loyal to Wayne and spread rumors about his senior's unfitness for command in the hope of forcing a congressional investigation. Wayne survived the plots of "that worst of all bad men," but in 1796 gout succeeded where conspiracy had failed.[9] With Wayne's death, Wilkinson became the army's senior officer, a post that he would hold until 1812 except for a period during the Quasi-War when he was superseded by Washington, Hamilton, and Pinckney. Though Wilkinson showed some interest in training and readiness, he mainly devoted his considerable talents to advancing his own interests, including conspiring in filibustering schemes against the Spanish for whom he was also a paid agent. His genius for duplicity culminated with the trial of former Vice President Aaron Burr for treason in 1807; during that affair, the general betrayed his country, the Spanish, and his coconspirators, yet somehow retained his commission.[10]

Yet politics caused more damage to the officer corps than just the appointment of Wilkinson. During quiet periods, both Federalist and Republican administrations seem to have attempted to grant commissions on merit, though both parties likely gave some additional consideration to those of their own political inclinations. But during the crisis-fueled expansions—1798 for the Federalists, 1808 for the Republicans—the party in power abandoned even-handed moderation for frenzied patronage. The War Department lacked the capability to carefully vet the thousands of applicants for hundreds of positions, even if that had been the intention. The problems created by the influx of officers selected for their partisan affiliation rather than military experience or aptitude were made worse by the practice of associating commissions with specific regiments. Regiments quickly created in a crisis could easily be disbanded in calmer times as happened after the Quasi-War, and so officers already in the service—particularly those of the political opposition—were reluctant to surrender their position in an established unit. This meant that the colonel of a new regiment might have no military experience, while a lieutenant in an older regiment might have years of service. With little job security and no meaningful link between performance and rank, there was little incentive for officers to develop expertise. With only sporadic active campaigning in the first decade of the nineteenth century, training degenerated. Most often, it consisted of little more than half-hearted repetition of rudimentary drill with a few dozen men. Poor pay, miserable conditions, and the insecurity of the boom-and-bust cycle of expansion and neglect led most officers to regard the army as only a temporary occupation to be abandoned as soon as a better opportunity presented itself. Many of the most energetic devoted their energy to private enterprise rather than military affairs. The most common pursuit was land speculation, particularly for those on the frontier, but others were more creative. The officers at one fort created a partnership for the manufacture of maple sugar; others owned distilleries.[11] Winfield Scott, who entered the army during Jefferson's expansion of 1808, described the senior officers as having "very generally, sunk into either sloth, ignorance, or habits of intemperate drinking," while the junior officers with only a few exceptions were "positively bad, and a majority of the remainder indifferent."[12]

Though Scott would go on to become one of the most distinguished soldiers in American military history, his entry into military service was emblematic of the problems of the early army. At the time, he was twenty-one-years old and had no qualifications aside from a few weeks of service as a corporal in a militia cavalry troop the previous year. Yet a senator from his hometown of Petersburg, Virginia, arranged an interview with the president that led to the young man's commissioning as a captain of artillery. Thus, Scott was instantly senior to the first thirty-three graduates of West Point, a school that Jefferson had founded upon the theory that engineering and gunnery were too complex to be left to those without technical training.[13]

Scott's battery, along with many of the other units created during the 1808 expansion, was sent to New Orleans, a vulnerable strategic prize. The still-barely-American city had the army's largest garrison—over two thousand men or nearly a quarter of the total strength—and at the time it was customary for the senior officer to command the greatest concentration of troops. Wilkinson arrived in New Orleans after his men, for he had taken the opportunity of an informal diplomatic mission to the Spanish in Cuba to also engage in illicit trade. By the time he joined his command, disease and dissipation had already put a third of the army on the sick list. Wilkinson decided to move the army to a site outside of the city, though as with many things related to the general his motivations were open to question. The site may have been selected because of corruption or due to its convenience for Wilkinson to carry on his various business or romantic affairs. A few weeks after the garrison moved outside of the city, Scott, realizing that war and glory were increasingly unlikely, submitted his resignation and returned to Virginia. Meanwhile in Louisiana, the summer of 1809 was unusually wet and the camp became a disease-ridden quagmire. The inexperienced officers—"imbeciles and ignoramuses!" according to Scott—failed to ensure proper drainage and sanitation, and the medical service was poor, even by the standards of the time. Adding to the suffering, the system of contracting for provisions imposed by the Jefferson administration failed; soldiers grew weak from short or spoiled rations of moldy, worm-ridden flour and rancid pork. Wilkinson resisted suggestions from Washington to relocate the army inland, perhaps because the army was already too burdened with the sick or maybe because he did not want to leave his personal and romantic interests.

Eventually, Secretary of War William Eustis ordered Wilkinson to move the army to Natchez, Mississippi, but even in the midst of disaster he wanted it done on the cheap. Able to bring together only a few boats for the sickest members of the command, the march was as hellish as the experience in New Orleans. The sick died from exposure and lack of care, while those marching were poorly sheltered and fed. Overall, the New Orleans garrison lost over nine hundred men to death and desertion.[14]

Scott was fortunate to miss the ordeal but eventually returned to the army to answer charges that he had pilfered his soldiers' pay. Though the captain successfully cleared his name on the original charge, he was tried and convicted for denouncing Wilkinson as "a liar and a scoundrel." The truth of the statement was no defense but might have mitigated the punishment to only a year's suspension. Scott returned once more to Virginia, where he had access to a library well provided with books on military theory, history, and biography. Thus, his time on suspension might have been of more professional benefit than if he had remained with his company, a telling indicator of the state of the army.[15]

· · · · ·

When war came with Great Britain in 1812, the initial American plans were characterized by the same hubris that had guided military policy since the American Revolution. Like Jefferson, President James Madison believed in the military capabilities of citizen-soldiers and intended to rely principally upon state-raised volunteers. In a fit of bellicose optimism, however, Congress voted to increase the regular army to 35,000 officers and men; in comparison, the 1808 expansion had only with difficulty brought the army to a strength of just 9,921. The task of raising such a force far exceeded the capacity of the War Department. At the beginning of the war, Secretary of War William Eustis had a staff of just eleven clerks, none with more than a year of experience in military administration. Unable to appraise the qualifications of so many prospective officers, Eustis left it to Republican congressmen and other party loyalists to select their state's quota of officers from among the potential candidates. More helpfully, Congress also reversed the Jeffersonian policy of privatization by reinstating the Quartermaster Department, but it would take time to create a corps of competent logisticians.[16]

Though the country lacked both trained armies and competent military administration, the plan for 1812 was an ambitious three-pronged invasion of Canada. Supporting columns were to advance from the western and eastern ends of Lake Erie, while the main effort struck at Montreal from Lake Champlain. This diffuse strategy followed the political contours of the pro-war interests rather than strict military logic. The war divided the country along regional lines, and while routes further to the east would have been easier to support and more directly threatened objectives dear to the British, the governors of Massachusetts and Connecticut refused to cooperate. The war, however, was generally popular in the West.[17]

Enthusiasm, however, is a military resource of limited and transitory utility. The force to the far west quickly met disaster. The commander of that column, Brigadier General William Hull, had been a lieutenant colonel in the Continental Army decades before, and the militia accompanying him initially expected that they would prevail over the British in this new war. As they left camp in Ohio, some of the militiamen placed placards in their hats proclaiming "CONQUER OR DIE." But by the time they stood on the threshold of Canada, several hundred refused to cross in supposed deference to the Constitution; they claimed that the militia could be used only to repel invasions and not outside of the country's borders. It was just as well, for Hull no longer had the strength of his youth. He briefly crossed into Canada before retreating, allowing a smaller British army to herd his force into Fort Detroit. Hull, trembling and crouching inside the fort and unheroically soiled by his own tobacco-stained spit, broke under the strain and surrendered the garrison virtually without a fight.[18]

The commander of the main army, Henry Dearborn, was simply lethargic. A former Continental Army officer like Hull, Dearborn's best days were also far behind; his soldiers derisively referred to him as "Granny." After a series of confused skirmishes with the British and their Native American auxiliaries in the northern forests, the ardor of his militiamen also cooled as they, too, suddenly had constitutional objections to venturing into Canada. Dearborn aborted the campaign not far north of the battlefield at Saratoga, where he had played a conspicuous role in the victory thirty-five years earlier.[19]

The final army—the one on the Niagara frontier—was commanded by Major General Stephen Van Rensselaer, a prominent landowner and Federalist but entirely lacking in military experience. The governor hoped to broaden political support, however, by appointing a member of the opposition to a high command. Van Rensselaer commanded a mixed force of approximately 6,000 militia and regulars strung along the Niagara River. By early October, it was apparent that Hull had failed and Dearborn would achieve little; but the impatient militia threatened to return home if there was not an immediate invasion.

Bowing to their wishes, Van Rensselaer resolved to cross the Niagara River near the Canadian village of Queenston. He entrusted command of the first wave to a cousin, Lieutenant Colonel Solomon Van Rensselaer, who was a veteran militiamen with years of service including several frontier campaigns. General Van Rensselaer ordered Brigadier General Alexander Smyth, the senior officer of the regular army in the area, to simultaneously attack the British garrison at Fort George, several miles from Queenston. Smyth, insubordinate and bombastic, refused to follow the orders of a militiaman, even though the War Department had placed him under Van Rensselaer's command. Smyth did dispatch an artillery detachment under the command of recently promoted Lieutenant Colonel Winfield Scott to join Van Rensselaer, but Smyth neglected to tell Scott of the impending attack. Scott's detachment of artillery was camped several miles from the main army when he learned of the assault planned for the next day. Scott hurried to Van Rensselaer's camp but arrived after the plan had been set. The general was unwilling to make any changes so late in preparations; his only concession was an offer that Scott could accompany the leading wave of troops under the command of the younger Van Rensselaer. Scott refused to waive his seniority and so was left to watch the opening hours of the battle from the American bank.[20]

On the opposite side of the Niagara, perched on a high bluff, a force of British regulars and Native American auxiliaries met the first Americans to cross with a hail of bullets that wounded Lieutenant Colonel Van Rensselaer. Nevertheless, a regular captain led the Americans on to the high ground, where they were met by British reinforcements from Fort George—the same garrison that Van Rensselaer had wanted Smyth to fix in place. In the melee, the British General Isaac Brock was killed leading a counterattack. The battle raged on, but due to slipshod preparations and a strong current, even after several hours only several hundred Americans had crossed the river. Weight of numbers began to favor the British. Throughout the day, Scott had made several offers to cross the river and take command; as the battle hung in the balance, General Van Rensselaer finally allowed him the chance.

Scott was equal to the moment. The 6'4" regular was a conspicuous figure dressed in his resplendent uniform, defiantly upright and ignoring those who urged him to take cover. Under Scott, the line held for several more hours; but as the militiamen still on the American bank saw the results of battle-wounded and dead comrades ferried back across the river—they too invoked the Constitution. General Van Rensselaer sent Scott a plaintive note: "I have passed through my camp. Not a regiment, not a company is willing to join you. Save yourselves by a retreat, if you can. Boats shall be sent to receive you."[21] But the oarsmen refused to make any further trips to rescue their comrades, leaving approximately 1,100 Americans dead or captured on the far shore. The British suffered fewer than 100 casualties in return.

Scott blamed his humiliating capture on the "perverse and mischievous" whims of militiamen, and this stoked a natural distrust of citizen-soldiers for the remainder of his life. But many regulars also performed poorly during the campaigns of 1812. Van Rensselaer might have been inept at Queenston, but his attempt to fight at least compared well to Hull's cowardice and Dearborn's inactivity. Neither were the militiamen solely to blame for Queenston. Smyth's arrogance was just as damaging and hardly justified; like Scott, Smyth had entered the service only in 1808. Thus, his haughty attitude was based on just four years of military service. The limits of his superiority were soon demonstrated, as in the months after Queenston Smyth failed miserably in his own effort at command.[22]

In 1813, the performance of the regulars again varied widely in a year with a few triumphs but many failures. After the disasters of the previous year, Madison was no longer willing to trust the cooperation of governors or the discipline of troops not under federal discipline. He sought a vast increase of the regular army to 57,000, even though recruiting had still not yet brought the army to its already authorized strength. To help fill the ranks, Congress voted a cash bounty and higher pay. Other legislation added staff officers and directed the secretary of war to develop a uniform system of regulations to govern the army. The benefits of these improvements would take some time to realize.[23]

The first half of the year went well for Scott. Paroled from British captivity in late 1812, in March 1813 he was promoted to colonel, and in May he returned to the Niagara front. The army there was at that point commanded by General Henry Dearborn, the same commander who had failed to take Montreal in 1812. The old man was alert enough to recognize the talent of his new chief of staff and give him full rein. Scott set about his work with such energy that within three weeks of his arrival, he had planned and led a successful amphibious operation to take Fort George. He might have captured a sizeable British force, but his pursuit was cut short by an overly cautious general who commanded the army while Dearborn remained ill in his bed. The Americans thus lost the opportunity to clear the British entirely from the Niagara peninsula.[24]

Soon thereafter, the secretary of war replaced Dearborn. But the War Department had so little faith in the interim commander that he was ordered to keep the army in its fortified camp until a more capable general came. Unfortunately, the more capable general was James Wilkinson, who was still happily ensconced in New Orleans. Wilkinson had no desire to leave his new wife and comfortable home for the rigors of a Canadian campaign, so he delayed joining the command until September. Even worse, by 1813 Wilkinson was not just a treasonous cad but an ailing one as well. His regimen of opium treatments for a bowel disorder sometimes left him unable to speak audibly or stand unaided; more commonly, he just seemed drunk, breaking into song or telling rambling, repetitious stories.[25]

Ordered to coordinate movements with one of his many rivals, Wilkinson wasted most of the remainder of the campaign season feuding with his superiors and peers. Scott, displaying uncharacteristic self-control, did his best to work with his new chief, but his contempt for the "unprincipled imbecile" only deepened. In November, while Wilkinson was too unwell to command in person, the armies met at the Battle of Crysler's Farm. The American performance there was so bad that afterward Scott complained of the "incapacity, ignorance, [and] imbecility" that pervaded the officer corps.[26] Nonetheless, Wilkinson's tepid on-again, off-again advance continued for a few more months before it ground to a halt at a stout stone mill defended by just a few hundred British troops. That failure led at last to Wilkinson's long-deserved departure from the service.[27]

Not all of the American efforts in 1813 ended so poorly, but the greatest victories were won by the navy on Lake Erie and the volunteers at the Thames. That year the regular army gained some excellent generals in Jacob Brown and Andrew Jackson, but both were appropriated from the state volunteers. Talented younger leaders such as Scott, Zachary Taylor, and Zebulon Pike, the latter killed while leading a successful raid on a British naval yard, demonstrated that the regulars were not entirely inept; but the inconsistent performance of the regular army overall suggests that these successes might have owed more to the talents of those individuals than to the status of their commission.[28]

From these disparate elements, the core of what would become the foundational generation of the American military profession began to coalesce in 1814. Fittingly in a war characterized by muddle and improvisation, this turning point was the result of War Department indecision that brought several thousand troops together at Buffalo under the command of Major General Brown but without orders for several weeks. There Brown and newly promoted Brigadier General Scott had the opportunity to train what was designated as the "Left Division of the Northern Army." They instilled a discipline and precision that allowed the Left Division to stand in open battle when the British staged a counteroffensive along the Niagara front. Though the American victory at Chippawa and the hard-fought draw at Lundy's Lane were ultimately of little strategic consequence, they became touchstones for the regulars of the Left Division. The full dress uniform of West Point cadets today is still patterned off that worn by Brown's division. Scott's war came to a close at Lundy's Lane, where he received a serious wound to the shoulder. The war ended several months later with the Treaty of Ghent.[29]

After returning to duty, Scott directed the effort to develop a manual of tactics. The lack of such an authoritative manual had caused the Americans considerable problems during the war. Some officers still used the old Blue Book that von Steuben had used to train the Continental Army during the American Revolution. Though good for its time, the Blue Book was based on the system of Frederick the Great, which had been rendered obsolete by the more flexible French Revolutionary system that, while still reliant on linear formations, placed a greater use of skirmishers and fast-moving columns. Most American commanders used one of two widely available versions of those new French tactics. The first was the rather conventional translation of the French 1791 regulations by Alexander Smyth—the same officer who was Scott's commander in 1812. That had been the official manual at the start of the war; but after Smyth was fired for a botched campaign in 1813, the War Department switched its endorsement to the competing translation by William Duane, an influential Republican newspaperman and enthusiastic supporter of the French Revolution. Though drawing from the same source as Smyth, Duane filtered his tactics through an ideological commitment to the nation in arms. Duane wanted a manual

that could be quickly learned by new recruits and so ruthlessly cut out anything that he felt was not useful on the battlefield. Most regulars, including
Scott, hated Duane's manual, for it did away with some of the practices that
they regarded as the hallmarks of a professional army: aligned ranks, precise movements, and synchronized action. While training the Left Division
at the Buffalo training camp, Scott used his personal copy of the original
French regulations. This caused difficulties when the unit came together
with the Right Division, which had been trained using Duane's manual.
Other commanders also used what they preferred, or sometimes simply
what they could find, causing similar confusion throughout the field armies.
In response, Congress directed the War Department to produce a new
authoritative version based on the 1791 French system. As president of the
board of officers charged with the work, Scott ensured that the 1815 *Rules
and Regulations for the Field Exercise and Maneuvers of Infantry* followed traditional forms and did away with the informality championed by the radical
Duane.[30]

Scott also played a role in a different kind of postwar assessment, one that
was probably even more important to the future army than tactics: the decision of which officers to retain. The chastening experience of governing
during conflict led the Republicans to approach defense in a less ideological,
more pragmatic fashion. Though they planned to cut the regular army from
its wartime peak of over 45,000 officers and soldiers, it would still be much
larger than during Jefferson's administration. Perhaps more importantly, the
War Department's administrative structure would remain; and an effort was
made to retain the best officers rather than simply those in the oldest regiments or party loyalists, as had been the case during previous drawdowns.
The postwar army had places for just 656 of the nearly 3,500 officers on the
rolls at the end of the war. The secretary of war left the selection of individuals to the army's six general officers, a group that had already undergone
their own meritocratic winnowing. Wilkinson, Hull, Dearborn, and Smyth
had been replaced by more capable leaders like Scott, Brown, Jackson, and
Edmund Gaines. At only twenty-eight years of age, Scott was the youngest,
but collectively they were all in the peak of life. In 1812, the average age of
the general officers was fifty-five years old; by 1814, it was just thirty-seven
years. That group then reviewed assessments of each officer in the army submitted by their commanders.[31]

Inevitably, the recent war cast a long shadow over the deliberations of which officers to retain. According to Scott, the war had been "a touchstone on which the true temper of our army had been thoroughly tried, so that it had now become easy to select the pure metal from the dross."[32] That emphasis on performance in combat, however, meant that the officers selected for retention were drawn disproportionately from Brown's Left Division. It also privileged past deeds over future potential. The generals tended to favor combat experience over education or refinement, a natural tendency after a hard-fought war but one that ensured that for the next several decades the army would still be defined by the deeds of 1814.[33]

* * * * *

In the two decades following the Treaty of Ghent, the foundational generation coalesced into a professional cohort that was reasonably competent in the tactical, technical, and administrative tasks that they faced daily. In the process, they created a smaller, somewhat rustic version of a European professional army. Scott and other veterans of the War of 1812 did much of this work, but it would not have been possible without the great change in the national political climate. The Federalists had traditionally been more willing to support the regular army, but that party had destroyed itself through its opposition to the War of 1812. This left the Republicans supreme during the "Era of Good Feelings." But rather than leave the regulars at the mercy of hostile politicians, it actually allowed a military renaissance because the army was spared the trauma of being caught between warring political parties. Elected in 1816, President James Monroe, a Continental officer during the American Revolution and a secretary of war for several months in 1814 and 1815, was certainly more sympathetic than his predecessors Jefferson and Madison.[34]

There were still some politicians drawn to the militia for ideological reasons. In 1819, Congressman William Henry Harrison, the hero of the battles of Tippecanoe and the Thames, proposed introducing compulsory military training in schools and more frequent drill for the militia. Implicit in these proposals was the concession that without more training the militia was of dubious utility. But Harrison was concerned with more than military effectiveness. He warned that unless military expertise was widely distributed, those in possession of such knowledge would invariably subjugate those who were not.[35] It would be decades before another such prominent figure would advocate for citizen-soldiers in such stark, ideological terms.

Harrison's call went unheeded because it required more than the public was willing to invest in their state forces. The militia system continued to deteriorate, and the traditional monthly muster became a ready target for ridicule. Sometimes, the militiamen even mocked themselves. Abraham Lincoln remembered the final muster in Springfield, Illinois, in which some of the marchers carried the sign "We'll fight till we run, and we'll run till we die." Locality by locality, the pretense of a universal militia was relinquished and replaced by a new model of voluntary organizations that were often little more than uniformed social clubs based on members' class, ethnicity, or trade. Sometimes the militia was an expression of politics. In Boston, Irish immigrants formed units to assert their right to organize and bear arms but were later forced by nativists to disband, as both a sign of the immigrants' secondary status and a practical step toward physical repression if that should become necessary. (After the Civil War, the creation and later dissolution of African-American militia units in the South would follow a similar pattern.) Whatever their identity and purpose, many volunteer companies received official sanction as being part of that state's "organized militia." That distinguished those from the theoretical "unorganized militia," the vestigial universal militia that still encompassed all able-bodied male citizens. Because the purpose of the volunteer organizations was to reinforce some local identity, regimentation was antithetical to their very ethos. The resulting profusion of varying equipment, garish uniforms, and forms of organization undermined what little military utility the volunteers possessed, for they were difficult to aggregate into larger formations that could be effectively supplied and administered. Indeed, the only commonality among these volunteer units was that few were ready for war.[36]

In contrast to the slow withering of the state troops, the federal military establishment steadily improved in effectiveness and efficiency. This improvement owed much to the efforts of Secretary of War John C. Calhoun, who came to the War Department in 1817, when the lessons of the War of 1812 were still fresh and his party was at the peak of its power. As a congressman during the War of 1812, he had witnessed the confusion caused by improvising armies. Seeking to avoid such problems in the future, as secretary of war Calhoun endeavored to build an enduring framework so "that in passing to a state of war, there should be nothing either to new model or to create; and that the difference between [the peace organization] and the war organization, ought to simply be in the magnitude of the latter."[37] The economic

Panic of 1819 and the resulting fiscal retrenchment provided him with the opportunity. Acknowledging the inevitability of a smaller army, the secretary proposed that it be reduced in accord with what he called the "expansible" concept: The army would retain all of its regiments and officers but reduce the enlisted ranks to slightly more than half of the wartime authorization. In a crisis, this cadre force could be quickly filled with recruits.

The idea was not original to Calhoun but had been long advocated by regulars who deplored the disruptive and ineffective practice of creating a "new army" from nothing to fight alongside the existing "old army." Instead, they wanted an army that even after expansion would be a homogenous entity with seasoned leaders throughout. This was important, according to Calhoun, because "war is an art, to attain perfection in which much time and experience, particularly for the officers, are necessary."[38] Aside from this acknowledgement of their claim to be the sole custodians of the country's military expertise, the regulars derived more practical benefits from the expansible system as well. It justified their employment in peace, diminished the militia and volunteers, and reduced the chance that regulars would have to compete with politically influential novices for wartime command. Calhoun even sought explicit congressional recognition that the regular army was the preeminent land force. The militia would be relegated to guarding fortifications or providing scouts and skirmishers for the regulars in the field.[39]

If Harrison's nation-in-arms militia ideal, proposed just the year before, represented one side of the spectrum of American military policy, then Calhoun's expansible army was at the other end. While Harrison's view likely held more intellectual appeal for most Americans, Calhoun's was far more convenient; and personal comfort trumped ideology, even if it could not be fully acknowledged. The House of Representatives explicitly rejected the expansible concept, specifying in its bill that the army should maintain "a due proportion of field and company officers, according to the present organization of companies." The Senate was more amenable, and the final act accepted the broad outlines of Calhoun's plan but in not so drastic a form: The army was reduced to an authorization of just over 6,000 officers and men, but while enlisted strength was cut by half, the officer corps was reduced by only a fifth.[40]

In the short term, this tacit recognition of the regulars' primacy was a victory; but in the long run, the country would suffer for the failure to address the problem of the militia. Even with its top-heavy organization, the regular army could be expanded only so far before the same issues of quality that plagued the regulars during the previous war would once again resurface. Militia reform as ambitious as Harrison's plan was likely impossible politically, but some more modest improvements might have been achieved. By not making the effort, Calhoun effectively wagered that in future wars Congress would grant the federal government all of the power to direct the raising of armies. Subsequent events would prove him wrong.

The ideological dichotomy of standing army or militia had never reflected the reality of American defense needs, but Calhoun's reforms rendered it even more inadequate. Prior to Calhoun, the War Department was too disorganized to realize its potential; but as administration improved, the federal government gained capabilities that the states could never match. If the militia was to operate in any capacity other than as a local home guard, it would necessarily rely on federal administrative and logistical support. Yet the limited federal presence in communities meant that states (or at least local politicians) were still a necessary conduit for mobilizing the population. These complementary capabilities meant that any significant conflict in the future would be a joint effort. Yet Calhoun ignored militia reform in an effort to attain complete federal dominance within the military sphere. When his bid failed, the country was left burdened with the legal structures governing militia and mobilization developed during the 1780s and 1790s. In the short-term, this was of little concern and scarcely affected the War Department; but the neglect left the country with a formal military policy based on the impractical and obsolete ideological struggles of the Federalists and Antifederalists.

Still in the nationalist phase of his career, Calhoun dedicated his eight-year tenure to building an effective federal military bureaucracy. War Department administration had improved somewhat over the course of the War of 1812, but the demands of overseeing a massive expansion while managing several theaters of operations left little time for anything but expedients. In the post-war calm, Calhoun rationalized administration by creating a comprehensive structure of staff departments (also called bureaus), such as the Quartermaster, Subsistence, and Medical. Each bureau had a chief located in Washington who was directly responsible to the secretary of war and available to him as a technical advisor. These chiefs presided over a network of subordinate staff officers, who in time became experts with decades of experience in their functional specialty. Improvements came rapidly, as everything from personnel records to artillery pieces were standardized, and the War Department was able to keep pace with the demands of an expanding country. The military was the most complex and far-flung organization in antebellum America.[41]

Though a vast improvement over the slipshod practices of the early republic, the bureau organization had some flaws. The semi-isolation—both geographic and bureaucratic—of a small number of technical specialists from the rest of the army caused chronic tensions between "the line" and "the staff." Also, the highly centralized system put an enormous load on the secretary of war, for only in his person did all of the operational and administrative functions come together. Calhoun could manage this feat; but few of his successors matched his energy, diligence, and talent, while the organization they managed grew in size and complexity. When these later secretaries were unable or unwilling to exert strong control, the bureaus became autonomous and often unresponsive fiefdoms under the jealous control of their respective chiefs. This often resulted in conflict with the commanding general of the army, a post created by Calhoun in 1821 but one in which he invested no new authorities. The commanding general was essentially an advisor to the secretary of war, but the title implied something much grander and those filling the office were accustomed to command. Thus, commanding generals soon came to regard themselves as equal to the secretary of war and superior to the bureau chiefs, even though those ambitions had no legal standing and their efforts to assert their power were invariably frustrated. The inability of the commanding general to effectively represent the fighting element of the army became one more grievance of line officers against their staff brethren.[42]

Just as Calhoun introduced order to the War Department, Scott complemented that work by standardizing the practices of the line. In the two decades after the War of 1812, Scott literally wrote the books on how the army operated in war and peace: the first comprehensive general regulations and the first widely accepted official drill regulations. In the summer of 1815, he was rewarded for his war service and work on the officer retention and tactics boards with the opportunity to visit Europe in order to broaden his professional horizons. Though already an accomplished soldier, the young brigadier was just twenty-nine years old and had only seven years of military service. Though already familiar with European military thought and attracted to its aristocratic sense of propriety, Scott had an extraordinary opportunity to develop his professional knowledge. The battle of Waterloo was fought while Scott was still crossing the Atlantic; and so during his long stay in Paris, the city was still filled with occupying Allied forces as well as the proud veterans of Napoleon's armies. Scott was thus able to interview some of Europe's best soldiers in the aftermath of one of the most dynamic periods in military history. He brought this knowledge, as well as a large library of European texts, back with him to the United States.[43]

In 1818, Scott offered to distill this knowledge into the first American *General Regulations* but only on the condition that he work alone. Scott earnestly believed that strict observance to detail was the hallmark of a good army and that there was no officer better suited to establish those details than him. President Monroe and Secretary of War Calhoun, who were both vexed by the army's administrative confusion, were happy to allow him that duty. The *General Regulations* dictated procedures for nearly every routine task: breaking new soldiers into marching, marking canteens and knapsacks as public property, fixing the amount of "mathematical instruments" allowed to an engineer officer in the baggage train, establishing the number of privates necessary to prepare a field cantonment, and describing the general method of deploying an army for battle. In each subject, Scott synthesized his own experience with European methods, particularly those of the French and the British. But although very little of the material was original, it none-theless reflected Scott's definite views on how best to adapt European ways to America. After three years of tedious labor, Scott was so fiercely protective of his vision for how the army should operate that he traveled in person to Washington, where he read it aloud to the secretary of war, defending his work point by point. The *General Regulations* was accepted by Congress in 1821, and Scott revised it periodically thereafter, ensuring that his preferences continued to guide daily operations.[44]

Scott sought to similarly dominate the army's methods of fighting. As with the 1815 drill regulations, Scott presided over a board that produced the 1825 edition. Much of the manual was a refinement of the Napoleonic system already in use. The most significant addition was a new section on light infantry developed by William J. Worth, the commandant at West Point. This was particularly important, because the skirmishing tactics of light infantry were better suited to routine conditions in North America than were the massed linear formations that dominated European battlefields.

In 1831, the French replaced the venerable 1791 system that was also the basis for the American tactics. Scott reasserted his control by undertaking the translation alone and "unencumbered with a board [of officers]."[45] The new manual was controversial. Some critics thought that Worth's light infantry tactics were better suited to American conditions than was Scott's adaptation of the new French system. The standard practice in North America since the colonial era had been for armies to form for battle with soldiers arranged in two long lines ("ranks") one behind the other. This two-rank formation was far simpler than a three-rank formation, which required soldiers to master intricate maneuvers so that all three could keep up a sustained fire without interfering with the others. Scott's intention was that the three-rank formation would be used only in wartime. Under normal conditions, the de facto acceptance of Calhoun's expansible army meant that companies with only half of their full complement of enlisted soldiers would have ludicrously short lines if arranged in three ranks rather than two. But the expansible army also meant that in time of war the ranks would be filled with many recruits, who likely would not have mastered the three-rank drill before they were pressed into battle. For similar reasons, critics also considered the three-rank formation to be unsuitable for the militia or volunteer units that would make up much of any future wartime force. Scott might have preferred the three-rank option precisely because it demonstrated the superiority of professional soldiers.[46]

Because Scott was so eager to impose his preferences on the army, we can assume that he considered those topics not addressed by either the regulations or drill manuals to be beyond the limits of what could or should be standardized. For instance, the *General Regulations* specified the thirteen different registers and records to be maintained by a regimental adjutant, the size of these ledgers, and the design of the box that would transport them but was silent about how a colonel should employ the officers and noncommissioned officers of his regiment in garrison. Similarly, the drill regulations described how a regiment should form a line of battle, down to how many paces should separate the commander from the file closers in the back of the formation, but offered little in the way of general tactical principles.[47] There was also no discussion of how battle could be used to advance the objectives of a campaign. Regulations and tactics ensured common procedures among units but left the essence of command to the individual preferences of officers.

· · · · ·

The one place where the army did attempt deliberate professional socialization—a sustained effort to mold the thinking and actions of officers—was the Military Academy. Before the War of 1812, the school was as unstructured and haphazard as the rest of the army. The change from chaos to order was principally the work of Captain Sylvanus Thayer, a taciturn engineer, who, though the fourth superintendent of West Point, is still honored as the "Father of the Military Academy." Already a graduate of Dartmouth, Thayer received his commission as a second lieutenant when he became just the thirty-third graduate of the Military Academy in 1808—the same year that Scott was commissioned.[48]

Also like Scott, Thayer traveled to Europe just after the War of 1812; and he too returned with experiences and materials that would influence the army for many decades afterward. The approximately twelve hundred volumes on engineering, artillery, and general military subjects that Thayer collected would serve as the core of the academy's library and curriculum for decades afterward.

Thayer was still in Europe when he learned that President Monroe had designated him as the next West Point superintendent. Since its inception, the school had been dedicated to technical training, a reaction to the lack of technical specialists such as artillerymen and engineers during the American Revolution. Yet by the time of Thayer's appointment, the academy had already begun a slow reorientation toward producing military generalists for the army's line. Under Thayer, West Point continued this transformation from what a later superintendent described as "in its infancy simply an Engineer School" to "a school for the entire army."[49]

Thayer began by standardizing the curriculum, which to that point had been variable. Indeed, he had been a cadet for only a year before his own graduation in 1808. He also increased academic rigor and enforced the hitherto often ignored entrance requirements. Thayer also oversaw the introduction of civil engineering to the course of study, an addition that he personally opposed. In the superintendent's view, the chief purpose of education was to instill mental discipline and this was best achieved through detailed study of math and sciences rather than broad exposure to many subjects. Congress, however, disagreed and mandated both civil engineering and introductory courses in the humanities. Though Thayer's preferred curriculum was narrow, his aim was broad: He wished to impart traits and habits rather than skills alone so that graduates would be generalists capable of dealing with a variety of problems rather than technicians limited to a defined discipline. Accordingly, he also expanded military instruction and attempted to mold the unruly cadets into gentlemen through strict discipline. Thayer regarded the academic education and military training as vital components with the same end: a complete officer and gentleman with a rational, scientific mind.[50]

Thayer's work thus complemented that of his contemporaries who were standardizing other parts of the army. Calhoun recognized this and codified the practice of granting commissions first to West Point graduates before turning to any other source of candidate. His War Department required well-educated, numerate staff officers, just as Scott's regulations required disciplinarians to enforce them. By the last years of Thayer's superintendence, West Point was already so central to the American military profession that Alexander Macomb, the commanding general, called it "the very foundation of the whole Army."[51]

If Thayer established the school's framework, then Professor Dennis Hart Mahan formed its early intellectual character. Mahan graduated at the head of his class of 1824, one of the first cadets to matriculate entirely under Thayer. An outstanding student, Mahan became an instructor immediately after graduation and spent his entire career at West Point except for a period in the late 1820s, when a medical convalescence allowed him to study military engineering in Europe. Consequently, Mahan had more direct experience with the armies of Europe than with his own, and it is debatable whether he was more influenced by his contact with American officers or with foreign books.[52]

At West Point, Mahan's principal duty was instruction in engineering, and his several works on the subject were significant contributions to the nascent field of civil engineering in America. Yet Mahan had greater ambitions. He adopted the title of "Professor of Military and Civil Engineering, and of the Science of War," even though he had never served in the army outside of West Point. In teaching the "science of war," Mahan surveyed the evolution of warfare since antiquity but only as a prologue to Napoleon, who cadets learned had so mastered the art and science of war that all that was left was to "systematize . . . and imbody [sic] in the form of doctrine" that which had been "largely traced out" by the Emperor.[53]

Despite his pretensions, however, Mahan's signature work said little about grand maneuvers of corps and confined itself to subjects far more appropriate to the instruction of cadets who during their careers would rarely see an entire regiment assembled together. This practical orientation was reflected in the work's laborious title, *An Elementary Treatise on Advanced-Guard, Out-Post, and Detachment Service of Troops, and the Manner of Posting and Handling Them in Presence of an Enemy With a Historical Sketch of the Rise and Progress of Tactics, &c., &c.* The cadets simply called the text *Out-Post,* which more pithily expressed the emphasis on small-unit actions. A comparison of titles with the slightly earlier work *On War,* by Carl von Clausewitz, reflects a difference of intellectual ambition nearly as wide as the Atlantic, despite their common inspiration in the campaigns of Napoleon. *Out-Post,* particularly its earliest editions, was a practical guide for junior officers rather than an all-encompassing philosophy of war, strategy, and generalship like *On War.* It is true that the peculiarities of early nineteenth-century warfare—small battlefields allowing centralized command by a single general with a small staff—made this distinction not so great as it might seem; some elements of *Out-Post* were as applicable to an army of several thousand as to a company of a hundred. The characteristics of a good defensive position, for instance, were not much different whether for a company or a corps. Nevertheless, the book was primarily what its title suggests—a manual for junior officers.

This was clear in Mahan's more specific advice, such as his admonition that an officer in command of forward positions should always have "a good map of the country, a telescope, and writing materials" or that the same officer should allow horses to be watered only singly or in pairs and always with a rider mounted to allow for quick return. Such details are hardly the concern of generals. Even more telling is what Mahan left out of *Out-Post.* In his discussion of the various elements of an army, he declined to discuss the organization of high-level staffs, as it "would lead to no details of importance here." Furthermore, his course on the science of war allowed time for only a cursory introduction to the subject. When the first edition appeared, cadets received a mere nine hours of instruction. In 1854, a fifth year was added to the academy course, allowing Mahan's military science instruction to expand to thirty-three hours. This change was reflected in a new edition of *Out-Post* that was nearly twice as long as the original. The two new chapters, appearing under the head of "Principles of Strategy and Grand Tactics," are the basis for Mahan's reputation as one of "the first American strategic writers."[54] Nevertheless, *Out-Post* began not as a meditation on generalship but as a practical guide for junior officers, a focus appropriate to the needs of both the young cadets and the miniscule army broken into even smaller fragments in which they served.[55]

Mahan was the preeminent American military intellectual of the foundational generation; but in a pragmatic, anti-intellectual army that meant little. He was not even the most influential figure at West Point, for most of the cadets' military development took place outside the classroom. Under the supervision of the commandant and his assistant "tactical officers," the cadets learned how to lead small detachments of infantry, cavalry, artillery, and engineers through drill and field practice. Much of this training took place during the annual summer encampment, but there were numerous drill sessions throughout the academic year as well. Cadets received only a brief exposure to the theories of Antoine-Henri Jomini from Mahan, but they left the academy seasoned drillmasters. In 1838, the West Point Board of Visitors commended the Corps of Cadets for executing "the most difficult [tactical] evolutions" with "striking" accuracy, and noted that they "resembled compact masses operated upon by machinery." Though the entire Corps of Cadets—typically 200 to 250 strong at any time—could replicate only a few companies worth of soldiers, this was not a particularly serious handicap, as the garrison of most army posts was even smaller. Consequently, graduates were well versed in the basics of tactical employment of the companies and battalions that were the mainstay of the army.[56]

After graduation, the professional training of an officer skewed even farther away from formal classroom education and the problems of high command. Any formal "theoretical" training came in one of the "schools of practice," first established in the 1820s. As indicated by the name, those schools had the narrow purpose of improving proficiency through application, not improving general professionalism through broad education. The first and most enduring of these schools was that of the artillery, meant to provide new officers with additional training in technical subjects such as ballistics. Though titled schools, these institutions were sometimes referred to by the more accurate descriptor of *model posts*. Their chief characteristic was an unusually large garrison, which provided better opportunities for practical training and formal classes. In addition to the Artillery School at Fort Monroe, Virginia, there were episodic experiments with similar schools of practice for the infantry and mounted arms. At times, the schools were allowed to lapse entirely; but even at their apogee, they provided limited classroom instruction focused almost entirely on subjects of immediate application for a junior officer.[57]

In an odd twist, the West Point engineering faculty also received the most advanced education in strategy and high-level staff work then available within the U.S. Army. In 1842, the chief of engineers directed Mahan to lead all instructors assigned to the Department of Engineering in a postgraduate course that combined readings in strategy, the military art, and engineering, with the practical application of designing a fortification for a given location, then developing a plan of attack against that design. The Corps of Engineers provided a natural cradle for American strategic thought, due both to its composition and its work. The branch drew most of the top graduates from each class, while planning fortifications naturally led to consideration of larger operational and strategic questions. In time, the postgraduate course gave rise to a seminar open to all officers dubbed the "Napoleon Club." Some of the projects undertaken for that discussion group were quite ambitious; one officer wrote a study of the campaigns of Frederick the Great that was several hundred pages long.[58]

The study of generalship, however, was so far removed from the realities of daily life—even for senior officers in the field ranks—that it was more a hobby than a duty. In 1835, only two of the fifty-three posts in the army had garrisons larger than five hundred men. Most soldiers served in a garrison of fewer than two hundred, which equates to one to three companies with a half dozen to a dozen officers present.[59] The duties of field officers—colonels, lieutenant colonels, and majors—commanding posts were largely administrative. Few officers of the foundational generation ever had the opportunity to command more than a thousand soldiers. Under such conditions, what use was Jomini?

Yet there was little need for formal study of those tasks that the army did carry out on a routine basis. According to regulations, within two years of commissioning, every officer was to have acquired all the administrative and tactical knowledge required to command a company. Because a Military Academy graduate of the Thayer-era could expect to serve twenty-five to thirty years as either a lieutenant or a captain, this implied that the training at West Point and two years of apprentice-style learning in a regiment were all that was necessary to prepare an officer for the first half of his career.

Thus, officers would continue to perform the same functions that they had mastered by the age of twenty-five well into their forties, broken occasionally by a respite on a general officer's staff or other detached duties. Not surprisingly, historian Edward Coffman notes that in his exhaustive research into officers' letters, diaries, and memoirs, *monotony* is one of the most common descriptors.[60] Even if officers could maintain a zeal for training their command, the depleted ranks of the expansible army and the continual demands of maintenance around the fort meant that at most stations only a few dozen soldiers were available for drill on any given day. So while some officers took advantage of the light demands of garrison duty to pursue professional study, that considerable amount of leisure time could just as easily be (and often was) spent with novels, cards, dancing, and drinking. Riding and hunting were other favorite pursuits and arguably of more immediate professional use. Even without some form of advanced professional education, the War Department administered a far-flung series of posts from which operated disciplined and competently led companies. For the time being, that was sufficient.[61]

CHAPTER TWO

Trials on the Frontier and in Mexico

THE EFFORTS OF Scott, Calhoun, Thayer, and others of the foundational generation gave the army an order and regularity that it had lacked prior to the War of 1812. The result was an institution capable of reliably producing military competence—a professional army. Yet it was not without its flaws, and the wars of the 1830s and 1840s would expose some of them. Nonetheless, the military profession was generally well adapted to its habitat, having reached a point of equilibrium with the military demands, political realities, and national culture of the time.

Though early fears of a standing army trampling liberties had faded, a new ideology hostile to the regulars emerged in Jacksonian democracy. Officers, along with other professionals, came under attack from those trumpeting the virtues of the common man. In a number of states, licensing requirements in law and medicine were reduced or eliminated. The Democrats were in the political ascent; while the more class-conscious Whigs, though still a large segment of the population, fought a rear-guard action. But the military was likely subject to harsher scrutiny, for the unapologetic admiration of European methods by soldiers like Scott and Thayer was at odds with the egalitarian and nationalistic spirit of the age. At least for Scott, the preference for aristocratic forms was not limited to professional matters but extended to political and social issues as well. He opposed universal suffrage, the essence of Jacksonian democracy, and wrote longingly of the "love of law & order" that he believed had ruled before Jackson was elected.[1]

To an extent, the rigid hierarchy of the army kept the disorderly ferment of society at bay. Perhaps not incidentally, the first two sections of Scott's *General Regulations* were devoted to establishing the system of rank, precedence, and "military compliments" owed by subordinates to superiors. From their first days as cadets at West Point, officers lived in a world of strict segregation from their subordinates; Thayer led a lively social scene among the faculty, but he and his officers maintained a far remove from the cadets. With graduation, individuals passed through this barrier from exclusion to inclusion. They were now members of the elite and kept their distance from enlisted soldiers, even in the intimate conditions of the smallest posts where maintaining such segregation must have been personally taxing. To an extent, this was a standard imported from aristocratic European armies. But officers' attitudes towards soldiers were likely even more directly derived from the views of servants and laborers held by the American upper and professional classes, attitudes that were reinforced in both the military and civilian settings by ethnic bias: In the late antebellum period, immigrants were well represented among the rank and file. Yet the ferocity with which officers enforced the social order, often with corporal punishment and ritual humiliations, was exceeded only by the vigor with which the racial hierarchy was policed in the South. Indeed, abolitionist William Lloyd Harrison argued that the treatment of both slaves and soldiers was inconsistent with American values.[2]

Yet within their own ranks, officers reproduced the same struggle between elites and the masses that charged the politics between Whigs and Democrats. This was most clearly seen in the continual sparring between the line and staff. These organizational tensions were partly due to the tensions inherent in different functional imperatives. For instance, artillerymen complained that the ordnance officers who designed and produced cannon were not solicitous enough of the user's needs. But in addition to these structural tensions, there existed a host of social prejudices, biases, and resentments. The root of many of these problems was the method of assigning officers to the different branches based on their class standing at West Point. The engineers and ordnance took the best students, the infantry and cavalry the worst, and the artillery fell in between. Because the curriculum was still heavy in mathematics, science, and engineering, the difference between the "gods and demigods" of the scientific branches and the less-exalted mass was usually nothing more than a talent with figures. Though of obvious relevance to engineers, these skills were far less important to the operations of infantry and cavalry. Because the traits that separated them from the elite seemed to be of little practical use to line officers, they came to see the distinction between them and the staff as founded on a questionable and rather arbitrary basis.[3] In Jacksonian America, arrogance was associated with intellectualism and foreign influence. Officers used this same language of grievance when complaining about elitism within their own ranks, a potent if absurd charge in an army modeled so closely on European forms. Artillery Lieutenant Braxton Bragg dismissed ordnance officers as "silk-stocking and boudoir gentlemen" who worked in "carpeted parlors within princely government edifices," evoking a vague sense of class grievance tinged with Europhobia that would have resonated with many in his time.[4] Brigadier General Edmund Gaines was even more direct when he denounced officers "who have acquired distinction only in the mazes of French Books, with only that imperfect knowledge of the French Language which is better adapted to the Quackery of Charlatans, than the common-sense science of war."[5]

As Scott's chief nemesis and antithesis throughout much of the antebellum period, Gaines embodied the resistance to the elitist ideal within the military. The two generals detested each other. Scott was a pretentious Europhile Whig; Gaines was a homespun xenophobic Democrat. By mischievous fate, Scott and Gaines had been promoted on precisely the same day throughout their careers except in two instances: Gaines had entered the army earlier than Scott, and Scott had received a brevet promotion for meritorious service earlier than Gaines during the War of 1812. Throughout most of the 1820s, the two engaged in an obnoxious dispute over which of these distinctions was more important, thus giving them seniority over the other. The conflict was driven by personal ambition, but it incidentally reflected the conflict within an officer corps torn between reverence for and revulsion to foreign practices. On the eve of the Mexican-American War, Gaines was in command of the army's western division, while Scott was the army's senior officer in Washington. Eager to take charge of the war and exclude Scott, Gaines demanded more control over the supply and administrative functions in his region. He criticized the centralized control of the bureaus as "emphatically a monarchical system" borrowed from Europe and wholly unsuited to American conditions, particularly on the frontier.[6] On receipt of this letter, Scott suggested that Gaines should be examined for insanity. Scott disliked the autonomy of the staff as much as any line officer, but charges of being too European made little sense to a Francophile.[7]

Most officers fell somewhere along the continuum between Scott and Gaines, playing out the great struggles of their day within the officer corps: elite versus common man; European versus native practices. Self-interest more than intellectual consistency likely determined which impulse predominated in a given situation. When dealing with outside groups, officers benefited from elitism. The professional diminution of enlisted soldiers, militiamen, and volunteers reinforced regular officers' centrality to national defense, while their disdain for uncouth frontiersmen bolstered their (in some cases tenuous) claim to be an extension of the eastern elite. Not surprisingly, these other groups often found officers arrogant and questioned the legitimacy of their alleged superiority by attacking the regulars as insufficiently American or impractically theoretical. But when as part of internal struggles officers suddenly found themselves in the role of the inferior, they resorted to the same rhetorical attacks against the foreign and pretentious. While self-serving, these expressions were also likely genuinely believed. That officers voiced their resentments using the language of broader society only demonstrates that they were not immune to the contradictions of their contemporary America. In a time of pronounced nationalism, many officers likely resented their dependence on Europe, even while many eagerly crossed the Atlantic to observe all aspects of military life there. So, too, officers were as happy to benefit from exclusion as they were to protest when it worked against them.[8]

The contradictions of society also aided regulars in another manner; despite the often hostile rhetoric directed against the army—aristocrats, dandies, and Indian sympathizers were common epithets—under the administrations of both Jackson and Martin Van Buren, the institution grew in size. The Indian Removal Act of 1830 was central to achieving Jackson's vision for the United States; and he needed regulars to enforce its provisions and defeat resistance to white expansion, such as the Black Hawk War in 1832. In comparison to militia and volunteers, the regulars were capable of the sustained presence that was necessary to support the long-term project of expansion. Less obviously, though no less critically, regulars were also far more reliable instruments of federal power; whereas volunteers and militiamen often acted in accord with local interests, regulars followed orders from Washington. One infamous instance of this dependable discharge of duty was the Cherokee Removal in 1838. Scott was given oversight of the forced dislocation of the Cherokees, what he later termed a "painful duty."[9] Throughout he sought to ensure that the Cherokees under his charge were treated no more harshly than the absolutely heartless terms of the movement required. Regulars often recognized the immorality of government policy, a feeling usually expressed in private condemnation of the rapaciousness of frontier whites. Nonetheless, though many officers expressed unease with the treatment of the Native Americans, few apparently resigned their commissions out of moral objections.[10]

The reliability of regulars was even more critical when federal policy was at odds with local moods. During the Nullification Crisis of 1833, Scott was the Jackson administration's principal representative in Charleston, the epicenter of the controversy. There was some irony that as president, Jackson relied on the responsiveness of Scott and other generals to direction from Washington, when as a general in the late 1810s he had taken advantage of distance from the capital to forge his own policies. The bellicose Jackson nearly brought on a war with Spain in 1818, and his poor example of military subordination encouraged junior officers to act similarly. Before Jackson's departure from the army in 1821, it was not unusual for officers to give tacit approval to filibustering and other activities. In contrast, when New York politicians were willing to give sanctuary to rebellious Canadian "Patriots" in 1837, Scott deftly suppressed a dangerous situation that could have led to war. Though Scott had been a British prisoner of war in the same area during the War of 1812, his efforts to impose order on the American side of the border were credible enough that the British resisted the urge to pursue rebels into the United States, an act that might have led to war.[11]

The regulars' skill and resolution, however, had its limits, as was evidenced during the Second Seminole War, arguably the most frustrating of all frontier conflicts. The war began in December 1835, when the Seminoles ambushed a column led by Major Francis Dade, killing all but 2 of the 108-soldier command. Within days of the disaster, President Andrew Jackson ordered Scott to take command in Florida and punish the Seminoles. Though Jackson's action was swift, Scott's movement southward was not. Confident in his ability to quickly bring the Seminoles to heel, the general took several weeks to reach the theater of operations, carefully directing the stockpiling of rations and the concentration of several thousand regulars, volunteers, and militiamen whom he would command.[12]

Before Scott left Washington, Jackson advised him to find the Native American villages and compel the warriors to defend their homes and families. That had been Jackson's ruthless but successful strategy during the First Seminole War in 1818. Once Scott finally arrived in Florida, John Eaton, the territorial governor and a former secretary of war, also urged Scott to attack the Seminoles' homes. Though the "food fight" strategy had long been used by militia, volunteers, and regulars alike—indeed, it was the only consistently effective strategy for the whites—Scott planned instead to directly pursue the warriors, crushing them in the vise of three converging columns. In theory, this would counter the Seminoles' mobility and bring the Americans' superior organization and firepower to bear. This reflected Scott's poor understanding of both his enemy and the theater of war; what might have worked with a more powerful and agile army, a less capable foe, and more favorable terrain yielded nothing but disappointment in two failed attempts as the Seminoles easily slipped through the gaps in Scott's clumsy cordon.[13]

In an odd passage of his *Memoirs,* Scott seemed to offer an oblique defense of his use of conventional tactics ill-suited to frontier warfare. Scott boasted of his victories during a period of small ambushes and patrols against the British and their Native American auxiliaries in 1813; writing in his characteristic third-person style, he claimed that he then rejected unconventional warfare lest "these successes in *la petite guerre* . . . [fix] upon him the character of a partisan officer, whereas it was his ambition to conduct sieges and command in open fields, serried lines, and columns."[14] It is difficult to see Scott's suggestion that he deliberately decided to stop excelling in unconventional warfare as anything but an end-of-life rationalization of one of his few failures, particularly as Scott eagerly set out for Florida when he still believed that the Seminoles would be easily conquered.[15]

The contempt for "savage warfare" expressed by officers such as Scott has caused some historians to criticize regulars for failing to develop a theory of frontier warfare, even though service as a constabulary was undoubtedly the army's main and most important service throughout most of the antebellum period.[16] It is true that the regulars produced no frontier Clausewitz or Jomini. Even Colonel Philip St. George Cooke, one of the most experienced frontier fighters in the army, focused almost entirely on the clash of European-style armies in his book on cavalry rather than recording his decades of experience on the Plains. But with the exceptions of a few individuals like Dennis Hart Mahan and his protégé Henry W. Halleck, the foundational generation was not generally inspired to literary effort by conventional warfare either. Officers did submit their ideas for better methods of frontier fighting to the War Department and the *Army and Navy Chronicle.* Although these letters did not constitute a grand theory of frontier warfare, they nonetheless reflected an intellectual commitment to improving technique. Undoubtedly, the written record represents only a fraction of the innovations that were simply incorporated into daily practice without being recorded.[17]

Nonetheless, the 1896 treatise on colonial warfare, *Small Wars: Their Principles and Practice,* by British officer C .E. Callwell, provides a model for what an American officer might have produced. *Small Wars* was indeed an impressive and useful work, covering colonial warfare from the general (the objective of small wars) to the very specific (the peculiarities of fighting in "hill country"), illustrated by a seemingly inexhaustible store of examples drawn from every reach of the nineteenth-century British Empire. But while most American officers would likely have welcomed an equivalent native repository of wisdom, it was no more necessary for North American conquest than it was for the British to expand their colonial empire, a project that was largely complete by the time that Callwell chronicled its methods. Even without a written theory, Jackson and Governor Eaton had urged Scott to adopt the proven method of applying superiority in organization and logistics through continual pressure against the Native Americans' shelter and subsistence. Jackson had employed it effectively in the 1810s, and it would be used later by Philip Sheridan against the Plains tribes in the 1860s and 1870s and by Nelson A. Miles against the Apaches in the 1880s.[18]

Throughout his career, Scott demonstrated intellectual ability and agility too often for us to conclude that victory against the Seminoles was beyond his cognitive ability. His deficiency was more elemental. The currency of frontier fighting was not brilliance but resolve. The life of a guerilla is hard, and the life of a successful counter-guerilla is nearly as trying. Scott was unwilling to endure the physical discomfort necessary to defeat an enemy like the Seminoles. In Florida, he violated the regulation that he had written in 1821, which prohibited "luxury . . . during a campaign, and particularly at head quarters[*sic*]." In Florida, Scott burdened the baggage train with wooden furniture for his tent and an excellent collection of wine.[19] In contrast to Jackson, Sheridan, and Miles, Scott lacked the necessary ruthlessness, ambition, and commitment to overcome a formidable enemy fighting to preserve their way of life. Scott could have been victorious, but it would have required him to resort to means that he found morally offensive, professionally unappealing, and personally too demanding.

As the war dragged on and frustration mounted, some of Scott's contemporaries proved more willing to adopt unconventional tactics and test the physical limits of their men. In 1837, Brigadier Thomas S. Jesup violated a flag of truce to capture the warrior Osceola. That same year, Colonel Zachary Taylor won the largest battle of the war at Lake Okeechobee—precisely the kind of battle that Scott had hoped to bring on during his campaign—but Taylor later concluded that the Seminoles could be defeated only by exerting pressure on their livelihood, as Jackson and Eaton had maintained from the beginning. Taylor instituted a system of frequent small patrols across the breadth of their homeland. This strategy was brought to its logical conclusion by a new commander, Colonel William J. Worth, who extended this continuous pressure into the summer months, thereby keeping the warriors from tending their crops. Simple in conception, Worth's strategy required the utmost in determination from the troops patrolling the swamps in the oppressive heat. Scott (like many other officers) had dismissed a summer campaign as impracticable. Even without summer operations for most of the war, no fewer than 14 percent of the regulars serving in Florida died of disease and many more fell ill. But although Worth's aggressiveness ensured that the army's sick list would grow, he realized that this was the price that had to be paid. By 1842, the cumulative effect of over six years of campaigning had worn down both sides to the point that the conflict was allowed to fade away. The War Department withdrew most of the troops in Florida, leaving the Seminoles to what remained of their land.[20]

Even that disappointing result came only at great cost. At its peak, the war in Florida consumed the labor of over 5,000 regulars—a thousand more than had been on rolls when the war began. But even with an increase to the infantry and dragoons, the demand for troops in Florida drove the War Department to take artillerymen from the seacoast defenses and thrust them into the swamps. These "red-legged infantry" (so-called due to the red trousers stripe worn by artillerymen) were particularly bitter; but the hard, frustrating service in a disease-ridden backwater had little appeal for soldiers of any arm. "Active service ought always to be sought after by a soldier," wrote one lieutenant of dragoons, "but in Florida . . . there is neither thanks, profit nor honor to be gained, therefore I confess my positive dislike to the service."[21] Morale sank so low that there was a wave of resignations beginning in 1835 and peaking the next year, when officers quit at six times the normal rate. In a single year, the army lost 18 percent of the authorized commissioned ranks.[22]

The reasons for the great exodus of the mid-1830s remain obscure; the pull of a booming economy was likely more of a factor than the desire to flee the misery of Florida. But at the time, the latter was presumed to be the case. Because West Pointers had secured a monopoly on new commissions and those most likely to resign were young officers, the many ideological opponents of the Military Academy claimed this seeming desertion in a time of war demonstrated that the school produced nothing more than cowardly aristocrats and fops.[23] Even supporters of the academy were troubled; in 1840, the Board of Visitors unfavorably compared the young graduates' unwillingness to serve with that of earlier generations, concluding that the contrast was "humiliating."[24] The academy seemed vulnerable. Cadet Ulysses S. Grant—who remembered his first summer of training as "very wearisome and uninteresting"—read the news of legislation to abolish West Point with delight.[25]

Grant's hopes for an early release were not realized, for the military academy's political position had been strengthened by the steady increase in congressional involvement. Since Calhoun, secretaries of war had by degrees allowed congressmen an increasingly greater voice in who would receive appointments within their state or district. This policy was formalized in statute in 1843, when each member received an allocation of cadetships, a useful form of patronage. This afforded the academy political support, but it also had more subtle implications for the military profession. Ironically, by making the process of selecting candidates political, the officer corps as a whole was rendered safely apolitical. If cadet selection had been centralized in the executive, there would have been a continual temptation to reward only those of the dominant party. Indeed, on those occasions when the formation of new regiments allowed the executive branch to select officers, they often resorted to blatant partisanship. The West Point selection process, in contrast, prevented any single center of power from shaping an entire cohort of officers.[26]

Like West Point, Scott's reputation suffered from the Second Seminole War. After his initial failure, Scott was sent to take charge of the Creek War in Alabama; but there he was also too slow and methodical. By the time Scott had begun to stir, Brigadier General Thomas S. Jesup had already acted on his own initiative and had the matter in hand. Enraged by Scott's ineffectiveness, the president ordered a court of inquiry into the conduct of the Seminole campaign. His aggressive policy of expansion required an equally aggressive army, and holding an officer of Scott's stature to account would undoubtedly have stiffened the spine of other commanders. Moreover, the two men had a long, tempestuous, and often adversarial relationship. Doubtless, Jackson and many others would have delighted in the public humiliation of the arrogant general, but his fellows acquitted him. The conditions in Florida, they found, were too difficult for anyone to have expected success.[27]

* * * * *

Unlike the Second Seminole War, the war in Mexico was the type of conflict for which the regulars had been preparing. The benefits of Calhoun's reforms were apparent in the ability to sustain much of the army on a distant border. Despite some difficulties, particularly in providing transportation, this was a great improvement over the abominable logistics of the War of 1812. But even concentrating half of the army in southern Texas meant that when the war began slightly less than 4,000 officers and men were all that faced the Mexicans in the disputed area. Congress quickly put the expansible concept into effect by authorizing the president to double the enlisted strength of companies and allowed the creation of a regiment of Mounted Riflemen and sundry smaller units in addition, but even with those measures the regulars' authorized strength was still only 17,812 officers and men. Such a small force was only one disastrous battle or even a simple epidemic of disease from disaster.[28]

Despite their wish to the contrary, the regulars required augmentation by citizen-soldiers. Like Madison during the War of 1812, President James K. Polk had a strong ideological preference for citizen-soldiers; his first instinct was to rely as much as possible on volunteers raised by the states. In allocating regiments, Polk sought to build political support for a controversial and politically divisive war. This was successful to an extent, but the president found that the demand for military patronage was greater than the supply; and so the distribution of spoils also created enemies among the disappointed. But in another parallel to Madison, Polk would eventually increase the regular army, not due to any change of political heart but as a matter of expediency; the states were sometimes unreliable partners. Thus, nearly a year into the war, Polk won congressional authorization for ten additional regular regiments. These new units, however, were similar to the volunteer regiments raised by the states in that they were not intended to be maintained after the war was concluded and most of their officers were civilians of the right political hue rather than professional soldiers. Nonetheless, public and political support for volunteers remained high throughout the war. Even politicians who opposed the war often felt compelled to praise the patriotism of volunteers; the battlefield contributions of citizen-soldiers were consistently overstated even though the regulars bore a disproportionate brunt of the fighting.[29]

This bias towards citizen-soldiers was nothing new, but the Mexican-American War volunteer organizations were an evolution of American military policy. Use of the organized militia was constrained by the Constitution, the Militia Act, and custom. Of particular concern were the open questions surrounding the use of the militia outside of the United States. Volunteers, by contrast, were far more flexible in their use. Their legal basis was the general right of Congress to raise armies, and so they could be organized and used in whatever manner authorized by the originating legislation. Yet this flexibility came at a cost, for Calhoun had warned against the creation of new military structures in the fevered political atmosphere of a war in its early stages. Reflecting Polk's overconfidence and inexperience in military affairs, the law authorizing the first 50,000 volunteers gave the states too much discretion in how they raised their quota. Governors could organize units and select officers by whatever means they wished. Their choices were more often governed by political expediency than by military effectiveness. The biggest flaw, however, was in the term of enlistment. Polk had initially proposed just six months, but the final bill provided for a slightly more sensible option of either twelve months or the duration of the war. Naturally, most units elected the option of twelve months, much of which was consumed in organizing, training, and transporting the unit to distant Mexico. Some volunteers never even made it to the theater of war. Of those that did, many refused to reenlist even though the army was in the midst of the campaign far into enemy country. For a time, this left the field army dangerously exposed as well as necessitating the significant effort and expense to raise and transport an entirely new host of volunteers to Mexico to replace the first lot.[30]

Politics created the conditions for discord between Polk and his generals, though personalities also played a large role in creating the distrust that would hinder the American effort. Shortly after war was declared, Polk called Scott, the commanding general of the army since 1841, to the White House to discuss strategy. Scott urged a methodical approach of thoroughly training the volunteers before attacking into Mexico. Polk, far more confident in the prowess of the volunteers and eager for the end of a controversial war, wanted a quick victory. This disagreement caused Polk to reconsider his decision to give Scott command of the armies in Mexico. Moreover, Scott was a Whig with presidential aspirations. Allowing him the opportunity to become a national hero was tantamount to creating a rival. Yet Polk also had doubts about the abilities of the commander already in Texas, Brevet Brigadier General Zachary Taylor. An impertinent letter from Scott to the secretary of war provided Polk with a pretext to leave Taylor in command. The reversal left Scott bitter. Meanwhile, scraps of gossip and rumor reached the distant Taylor, causing him to suspect that the famously ambitious Scott had some scheme to unseat him. Thus began a self-perpetuating cycle of distrust, as the president and his two principal generals all fell prey to their fears and faults—Taylor's prickly insecurity, Scott's arrogance, and Polk's duplicity and paranoia.[31]

This unfortunate confluence of personalities was sufficient cause for mischief, but it also occurred against the background of decades of civil-military distrust. The president was heir to a tradition that saw officers as arrogant martinets so beholden to the Old World that they lacked the virility of the New. Scott's condescending lectures, which Polk disapprovingly described in his diary as "rather scientific and visionary," conformed to this stereotype.[32] The regulars, meanwhile, regarded themselves as the long-suffering victims of undeserved hostility from ungrateful civilians. Thus, the perceived betrayals by the president fit into what the generals regarded as a broader pattern of denigration and neglect of the army by craven politicians.[33]

One consequence of the regulars' collective insecurity was a desire to limit the contributions of the volunteers. Just weeks before the first battles in Texas, Captain Philip Barbour agonized that the regulars under Taylor would not secure a victory before the volunteers arrived: "This *must* be done before the arrival of volunteers, or the army is *disgraced*."[34] Though Taylor and his small band of regulars won two victories before the arrival of the volunteers, these fears remained. Regulars were reluctant to admit that

American military policy ensured that citizen-soldiers would figure prominently in any war of significant scale. Taylor could not advance into Mexico without reinforcements, and subsequent events would demonstrate that even when volunteers made up most of the force, they depended on the regulars' administrative, logistical, technical, and tactical expertise.[35]

Despite their fractious leaders, by the end of 1846, the Americans had conquered nearly all of the territory that would eventually be ceded under the Treaty of Guadalupe Hidalgo. The "Army of the West," a mixed force of approximately 2,500 regulars and volunteers under Brigadier General Stephen Watts Kearny, marched overland taking present-day New Mexico and Arizona before uniting with the navy's Pacific Squadron and a small army of anglos under the adventurer Captain John C. Frémont. These combined forces captured the principal settlements in California. Meanwhile, with the arrival of the volunteers, Taylor's army doubled in strength to about 7,000 officers and men—still a frightfully small force to invade a country as large as Mexico. Nevertheless, Taylor marched on the northern Mexican city of Monterrey and took the city in a three-day assault that tested the mettle of regular and volunteer alike. The hard fight, at times a room-to-room brawl, cost 523 American casualties but did not yield any concessions from the Mexican government.[36]

Polk now understood that only a direct threat to Mexico City would yield a settlement. An advance overland from Monterrey was too difficult logistically, so the president decided to open a new front with an amphibious landing at Vera Cruz. Yet he was reluctant to name either of his top generals to command. From Washington, it seemed that Taylor had been too generous in negotiating a truce that allowed the Mexican army at Monterrey to retire from the city with almost all of its equipment, thus rekindling the president's doubts about Taylor's judgment. Moreover, Taylor was also a Whig and his popularity was growing. But Polk's objections to Scott still pertained. Desperate to avoid giving either regular the opportunity to command, Polk hoped to manufacture a politically reliable general by commissioning Senator Thomas Hart Benton as a lieutenant general. Though Benton was a veteran of 1812, even congressional Democrats balked at conferring on a novice the rank that had previously been held only by Washington. Polk finally acceded to giving Scott command of the new army.[37]

The new American strategy presented the Mexican president and general Antonio López de Santa Anna with an opportunity. In order to outfit Scott's army, Taylor was stripped of his dependable core of regular infantry. The weakened Taylor pushed even farther south to an exposed position past Saltillo. Santa Anna then made a daring march across the desert, nearly surprising Taylor, who was able to withdraw just in time to a strong position in the hills near the village of Buena Vista. There he deployed his outnumbered army on good ground and adeptly used his several batteries of regular artillery to shore up the volunteers' line wherever it seemed ready to buckle in the face of the Mexicans' superior numbers. Santa Anna, having impaled his poorly trained conscript army on the Americans' regular artillery and volunteer infantry, retreated. Several weeks later, Scott would land at Vera Cruz and regain the strategic initiative. With that, Santa Anna lost his chance to take advantage of the Americans' great weakness: a too-small regular army that could concentrate in significant numbers only at a single point.[38]

Like New Orleans in 1815, Buena Vista was widely hailed as proof of the natural prowess of the American citizen-soldier, a view that slighted the contributions of the regulars. Yet the unusual strategic circumstances that led to Taylor's army being composed of almost entirely volunteer infantry and regular artillery made the battle an unusually stark example of the complementary relative advantages of citizen and professional soldiers: The volunteers provided the manpower, the regulars provided military and technical expertise. Taylor was not brilliant; but he was a seasoned commander who knew how to lead men and remain calm in a crisis, while the well-trained batteries tore great gaps in the Mexican ranks. With the benefit of regular leadership and artillery, the volunteers were able to hold the line.[39]

Professional expertise could be married even more intimately with citizen-soldiers when they were combined within a volunteer unit, though during the Mexican-American War this powerful combination occurred only haphazardly. One of the most famous examples of this cooperation was Colonel Jefferson Davis and the First Mississippi Regiment (also known as the Mississippi Rifles.) Davis was actually only a former regular. After graduating from West Point, he served for seven years before resigning his commission in 1835. Yet that experience was only one of several factors that led to his command. When war was declared, Davis was serving in Congress; but there were other influential citizens who also wanted to command the regiment, including two generals of the state militia. Perhaps to avoid antagonizing any of the candidates, the governor left it to the soldiers to select their colonel. Davis argued that his West Point education and military experience made him best fitted for command, a point with which at least one friendly newspaper agreed. Yet Davis received just the second-highest number of votes on the first ballot and eventually prevailed only after the most popular candidate—one of the militia generals—withdrew his name from consideration. So even among those who had a direct stake in the colonel's proficiency, Davis's military pedigree was not decisive. Furthermore, it is not evident whether those who voted for him did so because of his military knowledge or out of regard for his social and political status. At least twenty-six other West Point graduates served in the volunteers, and ten of those commanded regiments; so there seems to have been some general recognition of the value of prior training and experience, but this was far from universal during a time when many regarded general managerial competence, good character, and innate ability as being more important than any specifically military expertise.[40]

The selection of Davis proved fortuitous, for under his command the Mississippi Rifles came to be known as one of the best volunteer regiments. Taylor's chief of staff offered the backhanded compliment that the Mississippians had "perfect discipline, for volunteers."[41] This was largely due to Davis's qualities. To be a successful colonel in the volunteers, it was not enough to be a good tactician; the commander also had to be drillmaster, teacher, and charismatic leader to a greater extent than was necessary in a regular regiment, in which he could rely on officers and noncommissioned officers with years of service. A volunteer colonel presided over a fractious cast of subordinates of widely varied experience. Davis insisted on a West Point–like regimen of drill and discipline that many of his subordinates thought unnecessary, so he was required to impose his will nearly alone through the application of extraordinary energy and determination. Even then, his command was never absolute. On the morning of the Battle of Buena Vista, Davis was stymied by the commander of the company detailed to guard the supply train. The captain demanded a place in the line of battle and only agreed to stay behind when Davis convinced him that in case of disaster (a real possibility) the rear guard would have the opportunity for the most glory. Several months before, Davis had overcome an even more serious and extended dispute with his second-in-command. The lieutenant colonel, a prominent Whig, claimed credit for having directed the capture of a key position at Monterrey. In Mexico, the regiment broke into factions, while in Mississippi proxies for the two men carried out their own fight in the newspapers and parlors. The matter only subsided when the lieutenant colonel was invalided home due to a wound that was fortunate for the regiment if not for the individual.[42]

If the volunteers' proud moment was at Buena Vista, then the regulars' glory came on the road to Mexico City. That campaign began in March 1847 with a highly successful landing at Vera Cruz. The Mexican commander hesitated, allowing Scott to land his forces without incident in a meticulously planned operation. Yet the Americans still faced the formidable defenses of Vera Cruz, which by Scott's estimate could be taken by assault only at the cost of about two thousand casualties. Rather than weaken his army at the outset of a campaign and provoke Mexican resistance, Scott relied on his West Point-trained engineers and artillerymen to lay siege to the city. They were able to take the city in just three weeks and at the cost of only thirteen American and perhaps two hundred Mexican lives.[43]

Nevertheless, at least one of Scott's subordinates, Major General William J. Worth—a former protégé of Scott—ridiculed this approach as too cautious. Worth's division had been part of Taylor's army at Monterrey, so he fully understood the implications of a frontal assault, but he still advocated the same for Vera Cruz. In his *Memoirs,* Scott claimed that when a crowd in the United States heard of the low casualties at Vera Cruz, one bystander called out, "That won't do. Taylor always loses thousands. He is the man for my money."[44] Though we might question Scott as a source, there is some evidence that at a least a portion of the public might have been perversely disappointed with low casualties.[45]

On the march from Vera Cruz to Mexico City, Scott continued to spare life through elegant generalship. At the Battle of Cerro Gordo, he routed the Mexican army from a strong defensive position by sending a column to the enemy rear along a dangerously constricted route. He won a decisive victory with only moderate casualties that would have been still fewer if not for mistakes by impetuous subordinates. With a tiny army of never more than 12,000, Scott understood the need to husband his forces. On two later occasions, Scott again spared blood through the skillful use of maneuver, although neither of these victories was quite so complete as that at Cerro Gordo.[46]

Scott handled his army as skillfully on the march as in battle. In contrast to Taylor, he exercised unusual restraint and sensitivity toward the Mexicans. In each occupied city, he paid careful attention to matters of governance so

STORMING OF PALACE HILL AT THE BATTLE OF MONTEREY.

Eng'd by H.S. Sadd.

Painted by T.H. Matteson.

Though the officers may not have always been so heroic and the ranks not so perfectly ordered as those depicted in this lithograph of the storming of Monterrey, due to the efforts of the foundational generation, the performance of the regulars in Mexico was far superior to that during the War of 1812. (Popular Graphic Arts Collection, LC-USZ62-62224, LC) that the citizens had no cause for complaint, attended Catholic services in occupied cities, and placed strict restrictions on the movements of American soldiers so that there would be no incidents to arouse the passions of either side. The latter was difficult in light of the racist disregard for the Mexicans (reinforced by virulent anti-Catholicism) that was prevalent throughout his army. The lax discipline of the volunteers made them particularly prone to acts of casual violence against the populace, a propensity that many regulars commented on disapprovingly. Captain Kirby Smith's description of the volunteers was typical: "They are expensive, unruly, and not to be relied on in action. Their conduct towards the poor inhabitants has been horrible."[47] As the expiration of the twelve-month enlistments drew near, Scott was so worried about the conduct of homeward-bound volunteers that he sent them home earlier than necessary in order to ensure they would be under military discipline the entire way. This left the weakened army dangerously exposed within the interior of Mexico for several weeks, but Scott understood better than most of his contemporaries that clumsy tactical victories and thoughtless behavior could undermine the larger strategic goal. That calculation made the risk worthwhile. But as the army neared Mexico City, the options for maneuver narrowed and Scott, too, had to resort to frontal assaults. He lost nearly a quarter of his army at Molino del Rey and Chapultepec. But with those victories the capital fell, effectively ending the war.[48]

Throughout the campaign, Scott varied his tactical methods according to the situation, a trait admired by Lieutenant Thomas J. Jackson—the future "Stonewall." Jackson served in combat under both Taylor and Scott and rated the latter the more capable tactician. Historians have almost universally agreed with Jackson; but generalship is also a matter of image, and in this aspect, the contrast between Scott and Taylor was even greater, if not so clearly to Scott's advantage. Even while on the battlefield, Scott's staff moved in accord with the protocol governing the arrangement of a general's entourage and was always accompanied by van riders who announced the arrival of the commanding general with due pomp. Taylor travelled with a small staff, informally grouped, and without fanfare. Scott wore a resplendent uniform at all times; Taylor often wore no uniform at all, preferring comfortable civilian attire instead. Ulysses S. Grant, who was also a lieutenant in Mexico, recalled that "both were pleasant to serve under—Taylor was pleasant to serve with."[49] Of course, a general does not need grand uniforms to perform grand maneuvers, as Grant would later demonstrate during his Vicksburg campaign in 1863: He dressed as simply as Taylor but demonstrated a strategic sense on par with Scott's. Nonetheless, there might have been some link between the form and function of generalship. The same impulse that drove Scott to dress like a European aristocrat might also have impelled him to emulate Napoleon's *maneuver sur la derriere* (movement to the enemy rear) whenever possible. Similarly, one can imagine in a period of self-congratulatory provincialism the rationalization of simple, bloody tactics as a positive manifestation of authentic American manhood. So while not an iron connection, perhaps, at least within Scott, the love of ostentatious display came from the same well that fed his martial brilliance.

The collective performance of the more junior regulars was one of consistent competence, a marked contrast to the War of 1812. Many officers attributed this improvement to the Military Academy. After the first battles in Texas, Thayer proudly wrote, "The sons of West Point have covered themselves with glory."[50] Taylor was more skeptical and often denigrated what he saw as the bookish inclinations of West Pointers.[51] Scott, however, was convinced that West Point training had been essential to success. At a celebratory banquet in Mexico City in 1847, he declared, "But for the science of the Military Academy, this army, multiplied by four, could not have entered the capital of Mexico."[52] He later repeated a similar statement that was so eagerly seized upon that to this day cadets still memorize the sixty-eight words of "Scott's fixed opinion." Yet it is unclear to what extent these successes were specifically due to the training given at West Point and what was simply the product of years of experience within a well-ordered army.

The performance of young West Pointers was particularly critical to the American victory because so many of the senior officers were incapable of performing their duties. This problem was due to the repeated refusal of Congress to allow a retirement system. Unwilling or unable to give up their pay, officers clung to their positions even when they could no longer serve. In 1843, the War Department promoted to major an infantryman who was unable to walk. Colonel John D. Walbach, commissioned in 1799, was able to continue on active service until his death in 1857, nominally commanding his regiment at the age of 93. With the upper grades littered with such relics and still others given temporary assignments, less than a third of the army's majors, lieutenant colonels, and colonels served with their units in Mexico. Three of the six regiments at the Battle of Resaca de le Palma seem to have been commanded by captains. This was just as well, for the army was probably better entrusted to more youthful hands. The previous summer, an elderly commander had decided that with war threatening he should put his assembled regiment through drill. He himself had not drilled in several years; but even the exertion of the parade ground was too much, and the colonel died. Nearly a year into the war, Congress belatedly made the limited concession of authorizing an additional major for each regiment; but this half-measure did nothing to solve the larger problem and so the logjam of decrepit senior officers continued to accumulate, blocking promotions for all those below. Though the Military Academy had been founded in 1802, no graduate would gain enough seniority to be promoted to general officer before 1860.[53]

Fortunately for the United States, this and other flaws of the military profession were not a serious impediment in Mexico or on the frontier. For while the army gave its officers little formal training, little was required. Because the organization did not change significantly in the transition from peace to war, officers prepared through the simple accumulation of experience were more than capable of meeting the martial challenges of the antebellum era. Yet in hindsight, it is obvious that this experientially based competence was brittle, because it was entirely a product of prevailing conditions. If the political and strategic context were to change, then officers would face new conditions armed only with experience that had been rendered largely irrelevant.

With the benefit of hindsight, we know that the 1860s were to bring just such a change. Richard Ewell earned distinction as a company officer in Mexico and on the Plains but is now principally remembered as a Confederate general unequal to demands of high command. In 1863, Ewell commanded a corps larger than the Mexican-American War armies of Scott and Taylor combined. From that vantage, service in "the old army" seemed quaint and tragically irrelevant to Ewell, who wryly observed that in his twenty years of service on the frontier and in Mexico, he had learned all about commanding fifty dragoons and forgotten everything else.[54] Yet Ewell's comment does not give due credit to the "old army." Through the work of Scott, Calhoun, Thayer, and others, the army had developed institutions, practices, and norms that underpinned effective small-unit operations under a variety of conditions and across a continent. The army of 1846 was the army that Scott and others wished they had in 1812. It was entirely suitable for frontier or expeditionary wars like the one in Mexico, a conflict that in terms of scale was towards the comfortable limit of the army's institutional capabilities. Yet with oceanic security, the foundational generation saw little need to prepare for war on a larger scale.

. . . . .

It is ironic in light of Jefferson Davis's role in bringing on the great political crisis of the 1860s as part of a vain effort to preserve an unsustainable societal status quo that in the 1850s he was an activist secretary of war struggling to prepare the army for a broader role in a changing world. Davis served in the administration of Franklin Pierce, with whom he had a good relationship. That strong political base, a mighty capacity for work, and the strength of his convictions allowed Davis to achieve much during his tenure: He supported large camps of instruction that represented some of the most ambitious attempts in the antebellum army to train for war; he reopened the Artillery School; and he convinced Congress to expand the army from fifteen to nineteen regiments in order to guard the territory taken from Mexico and to protect the vast frontier. Moreover, Davis ensured that some of the best positions in the new regiments went to regulars rather than political hacks and the remainder went to Democrats with at least some military qualifications.[55]

Even with his political stature, however, Davis could not persuade Congress to allow a consolidation into a few strategic posts that could be more cheaply supplied by rail or steamboat and from which "large columns" could venture out to deter or defeat hostile Native American tribes. No locality wanted to lose the economic benefits derived from a nearby post, and those settlements that were genuinely threatened clung to the protection of even small garrisons. This left the army dispersed into many small garrisons that were largely consumed by the work of sustaining themselves.[56]

Within the War Department, vested interests also frustrated Davis's efforts to reassert secretarial control over staff bureaus surrendered by his more lenient predecessors. Long tenures allowed the bureau chiefs considerable autonomy, and so Davis sought to make the positions temporary appointments held by line officers rather than by permanent staff corps. He was not only unsuccessful but was forced on to the defensive by congressmen friendly to the bureau chiefs. They questioned the secretary's motives, accusing him of nepotism and acting from personal spite.[57]

There was likely some truth in the last allegation, for Davis was famously combative. That flaw caused him to expend an inordinate amount of energy in conflict that might otherwise have been spent in more productive pursuits. Generals who might otherwise have welcomed a politically powerful former regular came into personal conflict with the secretary, even Davis's former friend and Mexican-American War comrade Brevet Major General John E. Wool. Yet the most bitter feud was with Scott. Even before Davis came to the War Department, the two had a history of personal, professional, and political antagonism. Moreover, Scott had been the Whig presidential candidate whom Pierce defeated in the 1852 election. Scott's awkward status within the administration was reflected in his self-imposed exile to New York, where he kept his headquarters for the duration of Pierce's presidency. That distance, however, proved insufficient to avoid the rapid escalation of hatred between the secretary of war and commanding general. The mail was a sufficient conduit for bile. Eventually, Scott eventually compared the secretary to an "enraged imbecile."[58] For his part, Davis claimed that the general's "petulance, characteristic egoism and recklessness of accusation have imposed upon me the task of unveiling some of your deformities, marked by querulousness, insubordination, greed of lucre and want of truth."[59] When the 254 printed pages of correspondence became public, even allies of the respective figures were embarrassed by the vindictive pettiness. One editorial described the feud simply as "disgraceful." Thus, personality prevented collaboration between two of the most quarrelsome, but also most capable, figures in American military history.[60]

Yet it is not clear that Scott and Davis could have found common intellectual ground even as friends. As already discussed, Scott delighted in setting forth administrative detail and expanding his own professional knowledge but did not feel compelled to dictate how officers should command or to try to shape the profession through education. Davis's plans for West Point suggest that he had a more expansive view of the military profession. The academy of the 1850s still bore Thayer's imprint, preserved by long-serving professors like Mahan. The academic curriculum remained technical, emphasizing math, science, drawing (essential for both topographic work in the field and technical design in ordnance foundries), and civil and military engineering. Davis was not necessarily opposed to those subjects, but his experience with the infantry led him to believe that the academy needed more military training and courses in the humanities. Others had lobbied for similar changes; but as a senator in 1860, Davis made a novel argument for why such a broad curriculum was necessary. Because the country relied on citizen-soldiers in any large war, Davis argued, it was necessary to provide regular officers "with elementary and practical knowledge of the science of war and service of the three arms, so as to be fit for all the duties of the staff and for the command of troops in all the combinations and contingencies which belong to the vicissitudes of war."[61]

Events would soon prove Davis correct, but there was little precedent for his argument. Until that time, the bulk of wartime growth was diverted into new units of citizen-soldiers distinct from the regulars. Even the ten regiments created by Polk in 1847, though regular in name, were largely officered by recent civilians. Thus, contrary to Davis's claims, the country's reliance on citizen-soldiers had little effect on the majority of regulars, such as Captain Braxton Bragg or Lieutenant Ulysses S. Grant. Their duties in war were not much different than those they held in peace. Davis was apparently thinking of his own transformation from former first lieutenant of dragoons to colonel of infantry, but this was hardly typical. His colonelcy was made possible by a political and social status that few, if any, regular officers could match; so there was no reason to believe that Davis's role with the Mississippi Rifles was going to be an archetype for the next war. The professors at West Point were unmoved by Davis's quixotic vision and refused to sacrifice any of the time devoted to technical subjects. The eventual compromise came at the expense of cadets who had to suffer an additional fifth year that allowed more military training and humanities while preserving Thayer's curriculum.[62]

Davis won some measure of revenge by appointing a protégé, Lieutenant Colonel William J. Hardee, as commandant of cadets. Hardee then wrested instruction in the "science of war" from Mahan. The commandant and the professor were a great contrast. An 1838 graduate, Hardee was a veteran of the Second Seminole and Mexican-American Wars, twice brevetted for "gallantry and meritorious conduct." He had also just returned from a coveted assignment as a student at the French cavalry school at Saumur. One cadet remembered being "mortally afraid of Hardee," a war hero who seemed "a greater man than any one of the professors." Certainly, he was more impressive than Mahan, who cadets mocked as "Old Cobbon Sense," a reference to the sound of his favorite phrase and chronically infected sinuses. The same cadet who was terrified of Hardee regarded Mahan as nothing but "an old mathematical cinder, bereft of all natural feeling."[63] This was not entirely true; Mahan had the capacity to be deeply hurt by the loss of his beloved course to Hardee. In 1860, he rather naively petitioned a congressional commission led by Davis to restore the course to the engineering department; Mahan argued that the frequent change of commandants meant that the position would not always be filled by "a reading man . . . prepared by previous study" to teach strategy.[64]

But although the shift of responsibility for "strategical" instruction from the engineering to the tactics department irritated Mahan and presumably pleased cadets, there seems to have been little change to the intellectual content of the course. Cadets still read Jomini and *Out-Post,* for, as one of the commandant's assistants noted, there was a "scarcity of good text-books on the subject [of strategy]."[65] This intellectual continuity between such contrasting figures as Hardee and Mahan underscores the extent to which the academy and the American military profession as a whole had reached an equilibrium with its environment; even with as impractical a figure as Mahan, the limited instruction in the art of high command was enough to prepare West Pointers for their duties in the antebellum army.

Even in the midst of this stasis, there were indications of change. Davis sensed that technological innovations such as steamships, railroads, and telegraphs would change warfare, but how remained unclear. When France and Great Britain went to war with Russia in the Crimea, he dispatched three officers with a detailed list of questions on European organization, methods, and equipment. What became known as the Delafield Commission—named after its senior member, Major Richard Delafield—returned with a vast amount of data that was then published in several volumes. Those published reports were so popular that additional copies were soon printed. Hardee and Mahan incorporated portions into their courses at West Point. Even the pragmatic Ulysses S. Grant found them so useful that while taking command of a regiment in the early days of the Civil War, he asked his wife to forward his copy to camp. Both the War Department and a great many individual officers were actively seeking to adapt to a changing world.[66]

But the army had excelled for so long at doing small things in the fashion of others that even its brightest minds became accustomed to limited professional horizons. Davis did not ask the commissioners to address broad issues of strategy or policy; and aside from a plea for continued work on seacoast defenses and a general reaffirmation of the importance of professional soldiers, they showed little interest in those topics. Instead, they continued the American tradition of looking for useful artifacts and procedures to reproduce at home, such as the French artillery piece that inspired the twelve-pound "Napoleon," mainstay of Civil War armies. Captain George B. McClellan used his observations to design a new saddle so good that it served with only minor changes until the end of the horse cavalry nearly a century later. Less successful was his adoption of the Russian cavalry regulations. McClellan kept so closely to the original that he even included the section on combined operations with Cossacks, an irrelevance that he turned surreal by translating the term as "friendly Indians."[67]

Part of the problem in the U.S. Army was that it lacked an organization equivalent to the Prussian General Staff, and so the development of solutions to new problems was left to temporary expedients—boards and commissions—that by their nature could produce only piecemeal responses. Such was the case with the conoidal bullet invented by French captain August Minié in 1845. The "Minié ball" combined the (relative) ease of loading a smoothbore musket with the accuracy of a rifle, eliminating the need to choose between a high rate of fire and long-range accuracy. A trained soldier could still deliver 5 to 7 shots a minute, but the effective range of the standard infantry weapon increased from 50 to 100 yards to 500 to 600 yards. Having commanded a rifle-armed regiment in Mexico, Davis was enthusiastic about the potential of the Minié system, and he closely monitored the development of its American application—the 1855 Springfield rifle musket.

But it was not clear how to best employ the new weapons. Davis directed Hardee to devise new tactics for the rifle musket based on the new French regulations. But the French were even then struggling themselves to determine how to best make use of the rifle musket. Initially, they sought to extend the rigorous physical and tactical training of the elite colonial *tirailleurs* (sharpshooters) to the standard line infantry. Despite the evocative name given to the *chasseurs à pied* (hunters on foot), the results were disappointing. The average recruit was unable (and perhaps unwilling) to master the demands of two antagonistic traditions: the iron discipline of linear tactics still necessary in Europe and the skilled individualism of the skirmisher. By the late 1850s, the French began to move away from the *chasseurs à pied* concept, implicitly conceding that it was an impossible standard for the entire army.[68]

Meanwhile in the United States, Hardee's *chasseurs à pied*–inspired tactics were published in 1855. These were not meant to replace the entirety of Scott's 1835 *Drill Regulations* but only that portion that pertained to light infantry. The Americans were also learning that it was difficult to accommodate both the battle line and the new style of skirmishing. Silas Casey, the president of the board that reviewed Hardee's manual, told Davis that the manual was well-suited to frontier warfare; but he presciently cautioned that in a larger war, "not one half of our Army as at present constituted, could do it justice."[69]

The problem was not so much in the tactics as in the technology; the rifle musket required a much different method of training than was practiced at the time. All that was expected of a soldier in a massed line of battle was to level his weapon in order to hit a similarly massed enemy a short distance away. Even when soldiers were acting as skirmishers, the inherent inaccuracy of the musket meant that there was little gain in anything more than rudimentary marksmanship training. But using the rifle musket to its potential required more advanced training. The bullet had improved, but the development of propellants lagged, and so the Minié ball followed a pronounced parabola trajectory when fired at a distant target. Thus, hitting a target at any distance required an accurate estimation of the range; otherwise, the bullet would fall harmlessly well to the front or rear of the target. Hardee's *chasseurs à pied* assumed that common infantrymen would be proficient in range estimation and other skills, but the army had not yet developed the training techniques to achieve this aspiration. With no organization dedicated to such work, it was left to the initiative of individuals like Captain Henry Heth and Lieutenant Cadmus Wilcox to develop a system of marksmanship training for the rifle musket, but their efforts received little official support. When the Civil War began, the regulars had still not developed the practices required to use rifle muskets to their full potential. Thus, they had nothing to pass on to the volunteers who soon swelled their ranks, and the hectic swirl of war was hardly conducive to deliberate experimentation.[70]

The Prussian General Staff was adept at addressing such issues, but it was the product of a context quite different than that of the United States. The Prussians had been shocked by their humiliating defeat at the hands of Napoleon in 1806. Their victories under Frederick the Great had bred a complacency that was shattered as the Junker aristocracy learned that they did not have a genetic monopoly on great commanders. From this, a group of reformers concluded that it was folly to trust that in a future war the military genius of the day would be on their side. Instead, they hoped to organize and educate ordinary men who could collectively match, if not even best, an individual genius like Napoleon. From this idea came the general staff and war college.[71]

Several factors made it unlikely that the antebellum army would adopt similar institutions. The habit of looking to the French for inspiration was ingrained, and it would be several decades before the Prussian system was proven superior. Moreover, Winfield Scott and many of his contemporaries wholeheartedly believed in the Napoleonic model of military genius, and would have likely resisted any external effort to impose it on them, an unlikely possibility in a generally anti-intellectual United States. Finally, the strategic situation of the two countries was quite different. Prussia was a recently defeated midsize state without natural borders to protect it from powerful neighbors. This situation provided the General Staff with an urgent, large, and complex problem for study and planning. With oceanic security, the United States had nothing so pressing to occupy a general staff.

This same problem applied more generally to the officer corps as a whole. Conditions were such that officers could be both competent and intellectually lazy. As one West Point tactics instructor told a commission led by then-Senator Davis in 1860, "As a general rule I do not think that officers pursue their professional studies after graduating. They are sent to small isolated posts on our frontiers, where there are no facilities for study, and especially on the Indian frontier. Each is changed from one post to another so frequently and so suddenly, that even when he has succeeded in collecting a few books, he may at any time be obliged to abandon them."[72] Many other responses corroborated this assessment. But this lassitude seemed to have few practical consequences within an army broken into small detachments and plagued with slow promotion. The average officer had more than enough training from West Point that was then further honed over years and decades of experience. Yet one of Scott's protégés worried that the "expansion of science and the extension of the art of war" would soon render the existing system of postgraduate education focused on low-level technical skills inadequate. He proposed something like the Prussian war college, for in the future, Lieutenant Colonel Robert E. Lee wrote, officers would also need an education in the "the higher branches of the art of war."[73]

CHAPTER THREE

The First Upheaval

WITH THE SURRENDER of Fort Sumter, President Abraham Lincoln faced the same dilemma as did Madison in 1812 and Polk in 1846: How to raise an army while balancing the demands of politics and military effectiveness? Like his predecessors, Lincoln had three broad options: increase the regulars, raise volunteers, or call out the militia. Initially, he chose the latter. On 15 April 1861, he called on the states to provide 75,000 militia for the three months allowed by the Militia Act of 1792, the antiquated but still extant law governing those matters. As during the Mexican-American War, the state forces of 1861 were not the mythic universal militia of all able-bodied men but voluntary companies that were generally of more social than military character. With a force of such doubtful utility, ninety days was a woefully inadequate period to field an effective army. Mobilization, however, is a political as well as a military act, and the inadequacy of the initial call was a deliberate effort to signal restraint. Regulars marching into the South would evoke images of the Redcoats of the Revolution; the militia was less likely to be regarded as a tool of oppression. Lincoln, still hoping to win over non-slave-owning moderates in the South and border states, had to show determination without further inflaming opposition. With so much at stake, it would have been difficult for the president not to take the gamble of fielding an army of dubious military value if that would bring about political reconciliation.[1]

The public view was not so nuanced. Tales of Bunker Hill, New Orleans, and Buena Vista convinced most that Americans were natural fighters. This jingoistic confidence coupled with an ignorance of the time required to muster and use armies as well as a regional chauvinism that expected the other side to quickly capitulate led to a common belief that three months would be all that was required to prevail in a single grand battle that would decide the war. Emblematic of this shallow amateurism was the 12th New York Militia, one of the first units to depart for war. The regiment had been formed as part of the New York militia in 1847. The collection of independent companies such as the "Tompkins Blues" and "Italian Guard" into regiments brought a modicum of organizational order to the militia, but the practical effectiveness of the units was limited by the sporadic interest. The regiment of ten companies could muster only 380 members for an inspection in 1860. This disinterest fell away with the fall of Fort Sumter, and the regiment soon had 981 officers and soldiers on the rolls. Thus, the unit was overwhelmingly made up of new recruits. Even the regiment's commander was new to the unit; Colonel Daniel Butterfield was a scion of a notable New York family with only limited military experience in prewar militia societies and a few weeks of service as an enlisted soldier in the Clay Guards of Washington, DC. The rapid expansion of the regiment outstripped whatever supply of equipment was available. In a fit of patriotic charity, the citizens of New York City donated over $10,000 for the purchase of smart French *chasseur*-like uniforms, but these had not arrived by the time the regiment debarked for Virginia. The "guerilla-like" appearance of the regiment still in civilian clothes did not diminish the enthusiasm of the crowd seeing them off to Virginia. So many packed the streets that the intended route to the transports was blocked, and the regiment had to detour down side streets.[2]

As the 12th New York and other units came together in camps near Washington, the inefficiency of American military policy was manifest in the varied and often impractical uniforms of the volunteers that William T. Sherman later recalled were "as various as the States and cities from which they came"—blue, gray, green, and even bright red breeches imitating French Zouaves.[3] This panoply reflected the provincial belief that "our boys" were superior to those from elsewhere and thus should easily be recognized as distinct. Some would soon suffer for such localist pride as they were either mistakenly fired upon by other Union troops or were unable to discern an enemy in time. An even more serious problem was the lack of standardization in equipment. Because every attempt to update the Militia Act had foundered on the intense politics and emotions of the issue, the official specification for militia equipment was still that of 1792: By law, each citizen was required to maintain "a good musket or firelock . . . two spare flints . . . [and] a pouch with a box therein to contain not less than twenty-four cartridges, suited to the bore of his musket or firelock."[4] Even when the law was written, those with practical experience in warfare such as Secretary of War Henry Knox had urged Congress to require the states to furnish the militia with a common weapon in order to ease supply. But neither the federal government nor the states were willing to bear the cost of stockpiling weapons in the requisite quantities; and so when the Civil War began, both sides scrambled to amass weapons from armories, domestic producers, and Europe. The result was, as described by Sherman, an army with weapons "of every pattern and calibre."[5] It would be many months before this could be rectified; in the meantime, many troops carried obsolete weapons and the army's logisticians struggled to supply the various kinds of ammunition in proper quantities. This element of improvisation applied to the early war effort as a whole. Decades earlier, John C. Calhoun had cautioned that "at the commencement of hostilities there should be nothing either to new model or to create."[6] The failure of Congress to heed this warning left Calhoun's successor, Secretary of War Simon Cameron, without a framework to build upon; so details that might easily have been arranged beforehand were done in haste or left to each locality, creating inefficiency and confusion. Thus, the great reservoir of patriotic enthusiasm was imperfectly tapped for want of an effective system to translate it into useful military force.[7]

By early May, Lincoln realized that the attempt to cow the South into submission by calling on the 75,000 three-month militia would not work. He then abandoned the pretense of relying upon the militia and began to raise a true army. The president called for 42,000 three-year volunteers and authorized the regular army to increase by 23,000 officers and soldiers.[8] Thus, in a span of just a few weeks, Lincoln called out the militia, requested the creation of volunteers, and expanded the regulars. Thus, he drew upon all three of the traditional elements of American armies. But though all would play a part throughout the next four years of war, by far the greatest contribution in terms of numerical strength would come from the volunteers. This would distinguish the Civil War from earlier conflicts. By the end of the War of 1812, the Madison administration had come to rely upon the creation of new regular regiments to expand the country's land forces. During the Mexican-American War, though Polk created far more volunteer than regular regiments, the bulk of the fighting was left to the regulars. The Civil War was to be a war fought primarily by volunteers.

The aged Winfield Scott—nearing the completion of two decades as commanding general—resisted this development with all the prestige accorded to the conqueror of Mexico. He insisted that the War Department follow the precedent of the Mexican-American War and keep the regular army intact and separate from the volunteers. The regulars, Scott argued, would be best used as a dependable core of a field army that could turn the tide in a battle, much as they had several times on the road to Mexico City. Scott did not want to dilute the regulars' effectiveness by allowing officers to leave their regiments in order to seek higher rank with the state troops.[9] This reasoning, however, was inconsistent with Scott's shrewd strategic appraisal that contrary to popular opinion the war would not be won at a stroke. This was the rationale for his "Anaconda Plan," which assumed a long war and strove to avoid bloodshed that he feared would enflame passions and prolong the war rather than end it.[10]

It is unclear why, in light of this appraisal of the situation, Scott thought it important to keep the regular army intact, when it was too small to play a significant role in a conflict of the scale and duration that he envisioned. Though in hindsight it is obvious that an unprecedented strategic challenge would require equally unprecedented methods of organizing armies, only a few individuals, such as Jefferson Davis, had foreseen the widespread use of regular officers to leaven volunteer regiments, as Davis had done with the Mississippi Rifles in Mexico. That would become the archetype for the Civil War, but perhaps Scott was simply too traditional to follow his own strategic views to their novel but logical conclusion. Perhaps Scott cynically expected the volunteers of 1861 to fail as badly as the militia of 1812, forcing Lincoln to order a massive expansion of the regular army, as Madison had done in 1813. Alternatively, after five decades of insisting on the superiority of professionals over citizen-soldiers, the old regular simply might not have been able to contemplate destroying the integrity of the regular army for the benefit of the volunteers.

Whatever the basis of Scott's reasoning, the Union was in crisis and yet the regular army refused to disseminate its badly needed military expertise.

This had the ironic benefit of catapulting West Pointers who had left the service before the war past many of their old comrades who had remained in uniform, giving them an advantage in rank and seniority that would persist through the end of the war. In 1861, the most spectacular rise was that of George B. McClellan, who had been considered a particularly promising officer when he had resigned his commission in 1857 after eleven years of service. His first opportunity came with Lincoln's initial call for 75,000 militia, which put the initial burden of organizing armies upon the states that had allowed their militia system to decay. As one advisor to the governor of Ohio put it, the state executives frantically sought qualified individuals upon whom they could "properly throw the details of military work."[11] Several desperate governors courted McClellan to take charge of organizing their state's force. During his brief time as a civilian, McClellan had become a prominent railroad business executive, working within an industry of notable organizational and technical complexity for the time. He accepted the offer from Ohio and was commissioned as a major general in that state's militia on 23 April—just over a week after the call for the militia. Lincoln's attempt at soft coercion collapsed just a few weeks later, but McClellan's luck continued. With the new focus of raising three-year volunteers, the federal government assumed a greater burden of mobilization, including filling an entire slate of vacancies for general officer positions. For reasons of administrative and political expedience, many of these commissions went to generals already selected by the governors and in the state service. McClellan was well-positioned to profit from this change, as he had the support of several prominent politicians. He also had the backing of Scott, his commander during the Mexican-American War. On 14 May, McClellan was made a major general in the regular army, making him the second-ranking officer in the U.S. Army, even though he had left the regular army four years earlier as a captain and had not yet fought a single battle against the rebellion.[12]

Though with less remarkable success than McClellan, other former regulars also parlayed political connections into high rank. Both Ambrose Burnside and William T. Sherman had resigned their commission during the fleeting economic boom of 1853. For a time, Burnside had prospered in his native Rhode Island. He gained enough wealth and prestige to make an unsuccessful bid for Congress and to receive a commission as a major general in the state militia. Though after his business failed Burnside had left the state to work for McClellan's railroad, within hours of Lincoln's call for militia the governor asked Burnside to return and help organize the state forces. Sherman owed his fortune to a father-in-law who was a former senator and secretary of the Treasury and a brother just elected to the Senate. With those connections and a foreboding sense that it would be a long, unpleasant war, Sherman rejected offers to head the pro-Union Missouri militia, serve as a high-ranking civilian in the War Department, and take a high-ranking position in the Confederate army. He resolved to serve only as a regular, and held out until offered the colonelcy of the new 13th Infantry in May.[13]

In contrast to the good fortune of McClellan, Burnside, and Sherman, their classmates who had remained in uniform spent the first months of the war as mere captains. After several months, McClellan would replace Scott as commanding general, as the old titan was shuffled off to a cantankerous retirement in New York. With Scott's influence diminished, the War Department allowed regulars to seek higher rank in the volunteers. So many did so that Sherman and Burnside each had only one classmate commissioned into their arm—the artillery—remain with the regular army throughout the war; at war's end, those individuals were still only a major and captain, respectively.[14]

In the first weeks of the war, the problem of organizing the militia and volunteers was so great that Scott did allow regulars to temporarily assist in the training of citizen-soldiers. One indicator of the desperation of that early time was that even the army's newest second lieutenants were a precious reservoir of military expertise. West Point gave cadets little preparation for strategy or staff work, but it did prepare them to teach drill. The class of 1861 was graduated a month early in May and ordered en masse to Washington to serve as drillmasters for the militia. Among that group was twenty-one-year-old Emory Upton, who was sent to assist Colonel Butterfield and the 12th New York.[15]

Born in 1839, Emory was raised in the area of western New York known as the "Burned-over District" for its religious fervor during the Second Great Awakening. The Uptons were a part of this movement, subscribing to a millennialist belief that it was one's duty to God to strive for moral purity. They fulfilled this calling, in part, through fervent abolitionism and support for the Underground Railroad. The Uptons also held education sacred and though of modest means sent several of their children to college. This environment and Emory's natural intelligence and energy produced an unusually driven teenager, whom one friend remembered as "always in a hurry; spoke like lightning; very quick of perception, for he often cut a person off in the middle of a remark with his own reply, which was always to the point."[16] Emory came to believe that his calling was to help end slavery as a soldier and so applied to West Point at about the time of his fifteenth birthday. He was so certain of his life's course that he wagered a friend that by the age of forty-five he would be a general officer and slavery would be abolished. If successful, Upton was to receive an engraved revolver. Though the academy rejected his first application, Emory was undeterred and went to Oberlin College for further preparation. Like West Point, Oberlin was strict, deliberately spartan in accommodations, and dedicated to building character through work. But quite unlike the secular conservatism of the Military Academy, Oberlin was governed by a religious radicalism that led it to admit both women and African-Americans as full students. Yet even at Oberlin, Emory was notable for his dedication to abolition. To be ready to play a role in its demise, he studied military history and slept without a pillow in order to prepare himself for a soldier's life.[17]

A year older and better prepared, Upton was accepted into the West Point class of 1861—the last to suffer the five-year curriculum imposed by Jefferson Davis. Though he was not brilliant, one classmate remembered Upton as a "laborious student" who through diligence was able to steadily improve his academic standing from the middle of the class to eighth of forty-five. That rank allowed him entry into any branch, even the prestigious Corps of Engineers. Upton found Mahan's course in military engineering "very interesting" but opted for the artillery, the most technical and cerebral of the three arms of the line.[18]

For Upton, the academy proved to be more of a social than an intellectual challenge. Physically isolated, it was claustrophobically intimate, with classes typically beginning with less than a hundred cadets and counting only forty or fifty by the time of graduation. His strait-laced religiosity fit poorly within a cadet culture that exalted in officially prohibited drinking, gambling, and unauthorized trips off the academy grounds. He likely found some solace in the bible studies and prayer meetings led by Captain Oliver O. Howard but did confess to family that West Point was "a hard place to practice religion."[19] But what really set Upton apart was his abolitionism; he might even have been the first cadet to openly oppose slavery. This was a courageous stand as sectional tensions grew more intense at West Point. In late 1859, Cadet

Wade Hampton Gibbes, a South Carolinian, told a gathering of friends that Upton had had sex with an African-American woman while at Oberlin. Although likely nothing more than a rumor coming from the loose, vicious talk found in gatherings of young men, when Upton learned of Gibbes's gossip, he challenged the older cadet to a "fisticuffs duel." Following an evening formation, the two cadets and their "seconds" entered the darkened barracks, while the remainder of the Corps of Cadets urged them on from the central square outside. Decades later, one of the onlookers, certainly influenced by the subsequent events, remembered the fight as the "the most thrilling event in my life as a cadet."[20] The symbolism of the fight as precursor to civil war was heightened by the twin coincidences that Gibbes claimed to have fired the first shot on Fort Sumter and Upton similarly opened the First Bull Run campaign.[21]

As demonstrated by the Gibbes affair, Upton was ready—even eager—to fight for his beliefs. As the crisis worsened, he enthusiastically wrote about the coming reckoning, casting it as divine wrath for a full suite of societal sin: "Mormonism, spiritualism, intemperance, slavery, [and] corruption in politics."[22] With such an array of causes, the abolition of slavery alone would not satisfy Upton's desire for an ideal society; his morality was sufficiently all-encompassing to ensure that he would never want for a cause. Two sentences written in January 1860 define Upton's lifelong drive: "We must have reform. We must return to reason and virtue."[23] Throughout his life, Upton would continue to conflate reason and virtue, making those who acted contrary to his logic not just wrong headed but malign as well. This trait led to narrow-mindedness but also provided the moral imperative that drove Upton to pursue reform with a ferocious tenacity. The Civil War served as a bridge for Upton, taking him from one life mission to the next. For in the process of ending slavery, he witnessed military incompetence that cost hundreds of thousands of lives by his reckoning. That blood-letting lent the improvement of military policy and professionalism a moral aspect that allowed it to replace the abolition of slavery as the paramount cause in the young crusader's life.

* * * * *

Though in comparison to later battles of the Civil War, the First Bull Run campaign was only a middling affair—lacking the strategic significance of Vicksburg, the scale of Gettysburg, or the ferocity of Spotsylvania—but it nevertheless became a totem for the military profession, a synonym for failing to prepare for war. The development of this deeper meaning would be, in part, due to the influence of Upton's postwar writings on later generations of soldiers.

As the Union's principal army formed around Washington, Lincoln searched for someone to lead it. He had few good choices. Early in that first summer of the war, the *New York Herald* tersely editorialized, "You cannot improvise a general."[24] Though intended as criticism of the many "political generals" appointed by Lincoln—four members of Congress were commissioned as brigadiers during the war's first months—it was uncomfortably true for the regulars as well. The seventy-one-year-old Scott was no longer capable of field command; gout-ridden and obese, he could not even ascend stairs without assistance, much less mount a horse. The other three generals of the line were also well past their best days, with an average age of sixty-nine years. The lions of the foundational generation, now at their withered end, had done little to prepare successors for high command; with no retirement system, they had clung to their positions, depriving younger officers of what little opportunity for directing large bodies of troops the small peacetime army afforded. Compounding this, Scott and the others had done little to foster the professional education that might have at least provided junior officers with intellectual preparation for high command. When Robert E. Lee, Scott's preferred choice, declined to fight against Virginia, the commanding general recommended Colonel Joseph K. F. Mansfield, a fifty-seven-year-old engineer who had entered West Point the same year that Thayer became superintendent. But Scott's influence was already waning, and the command went instead to a slightly younger man, Major Irvin McDowell, who had been championed by Treasury Secretary Salmon Chase, a fellow Ohioan. McDowell was a bright, diligent engineer who had served as a staff officer in Mexico, but he had never actually commanded troops.[25]

Scott, however, did prevail in winning the appointment of Robert Patterson as a major general of volunteers and commander of the army gathering for a push into western Maryland and the Shenandoah Valley. Unlike Lee, Mansfield, or McDowell, Patterson was not a regular, though he was a veteran of both the War of 1812 and the Mexican-American War. During the latter, he had been one of Scott's most capable division commanders. But many years had elapsed in the meantime, and the sixty-nine year-old general lacked his old strength. Thus, the twin prongs of the initial effort to take

Richmond fell to McDowell and Patterson: One had vigor but no experience, the other experience but no vigor.[26]

Odd juxtapositions extended throughout the echelons of the Union Army. Sherman, despite his efforts to avoid association with unruly citizen-soldiers, found himself in command of a brigade of volunteers soon after reporting for duty in Washington. The combination of regular (for that is how Sherman regarded himself, despite his resignation six years before) and volunteer was difficult. The colonel disparaged his untrained troops as "rabble" and a "pack of . . . loafers and thieves." The volunteers, believing they would easily prevail in battle, returned the contempt by jeering Sherman's attempts to drill and discipline them.[27]

But many of the regulars and former regulars who found themselves in such positions of responsibility were as unready for battle as their charges. Few young enough to still fight possessed much knowledge—practical or theoretical—of high-level organization. As previously noted, Dennis H. Mahan had casually dismissed staff duties in Out-Post as being of no particular interest to junior officers. Just the year before First Bull Run, the Davis Commission had noted that cadets received "little practical instruction in the duties of the engineer and staff officer."[28] Inexperience piled upon inexperience, as commanders learning their positions received little help from staff officers who were just as ignorant of their own work. A British observer was amused to see General McDowell personally meeting arriving units and leading them to their bivouac sites, a task that could have been given to a capable junior staff officer if there had been one available. After his time drilling the 12th New York Militia was complete, Upton reported to the staff of Brigadier General Daniel Tyler, a West Point graduate who had resigned his commission as a first lieutenant in 1834 before making his fortune in business. In addition to looking after the general and carrying dispatches, Lieutenant Upton and the two other aides were supposed to assist the four officers of Tyler's small, improvised staff with their duties. The staff officers were all lieutenants when the war began, with between five and twelve years of commissioned experience. The two with the most seniority were given the principal posts of adjutant general and quartermaster general, but neither had ever served on even a regimental staff much less that of a division on campaign. The engineer and topographical engineer each had relevant experience but were far more junior.[29]

As McDowell struggled to form the army, the president sought to maintain political support for the war. The border states precariously wavered between support, neutrality, and rebellion. It was still uncertain whether Democrats would follow the precedent of the political opposition in past wars and seek to stymie the administration in the same manner as did the Federalists during the War of 1812 and the Whigs during the Mexican-American War; indeed, as a Whig congressman in the 30th Congress of 1847–1848, Lincoln witnessed firsthand how the legislative opposition could frustrate the executive. Amid high expectations for a quick war ending in a "single grand victory," the president could scarcely allow the ninety-day enlistments to expire without a battle. In April, the call for the militia had been a reasonable, perhaps necessary, gamble; by July, it was a liability forcing action before McDowell felt he was ready. When called to the White House, the general protested that his men were unseasoned. "You are green, it is true," Lincoln admitted, "but [the Confederates] are green also; you are all green alike."[30]

The matter settled, McDowell embarked upon what would become the First Bull Run campaign. A rebel army under Major General Pierre G. T. Beauregard lurked somewhere west of Washington. As the Union army crept forward, McDowell directed Tyler, whose division was in the lead, to avoid an engagement. But Tyler, the lieutenant-turned-businessman, thought little of the much younger McDowell and determined that he should test the Confederate strength around Blackburn's Ford, a crossing over Bull Run. He allowed his senior aide, Upton, the honor of firing the first shot of the campaign. In the ensuing fight, commanders on both sides struggled to manage their raw troops. The Union advance caused a brief panic among the Southern troops that Brigadier General James Longstreet steadied only through a combination of gallant example and threat. Tyler and his subordinates were not able to restore order when a Confederate volley turned Union exhilaration to flight; an entire regiment fled amid cries of "We are all cut to pieces!" Longstreet's brief pursuit ended when he was nearly killed by Confederate reinforcements who mistook his men for the enemy. The inability of commanders to coordinate even small offensive movements and the volunteers' unpredictability were precursors to the larger battle two days later.[31]

Meanwhile, farther to the west near Harpers Ferry, the other arm of the Union thrust stalled, as Patterson demonstrated that even the trustiest old war horses can be ridden only so far. The aged general was kept back by little more than feints, rumors, and a thin screen of cavalry even though his forces outnumbered those of the Confederates. Patterson's timidity allowed his opponent, Major General Joseph E. Johnston, to move nearly his entire army by railroad to Manassas Junction, where it combined with Beauregard's army. Despite Scott's repeated assurances that Patterson would not fail, McDowell would face two Confederate armies at Bull Run.[32]

Though chastened by Tyler's setback at Blackburn's Ford and weary from several days of campaigning in the July heat, McDowell's volunteer army shuffled on toward Richmond. In their way stood a Confederate army arrayed along Bull Run. Though the creek was not particularly formidable, it meandered through rolling countryside that presented many opportunities for defense. McDowell decided to send his main body on a flank march by way of an unguarded ford to the west of the Confederate line. This scheme echoed Scott's tactics in Mexico, but there were several important differences between the two campaigns. Most obviously, McDowell was not Scott, who was already an experienced commander in 1847. Scott's daring flank marches were also made possible by his outstanding staff of engineers, such as McDowell and Beauregard. In 1861, McDowell did not have such capable assistants, and, as a consequence, he discovered only on the morning of the battle that the critical route was a far more difficult passage than he had been told. Also, Scott could rely upon a large, dependable core of regulars within his army; despite the commanding general's attempts to keep the regulars together for the climactic battle, McDowell had but a single battalion of professional soldiers.[33]

Nonetheless, McDowell's plan was reasonable and clearly communicated. This contrasted favorably with the efforts of his opponent, who on the strength of his sparkling prewar reputation should have been the superior general. Scott had repeatedly praised Lieutenant Beauregard for his daredevil reconnaissance forays in Mexico. In January 1861, Beauregard had briefly held the prestigious post of West Point superintendent before a new secretary of war thought better of putting a likely secessionist at the head of a national symbol. But the difference in the qualities demanded at the various echelons of command made success as a junior officer an imperfect predictor of success at much higher rank. At Manassas, Beauregard initially proposed a grand maneuver that would carry the Confederates to Washington, but the more realistic Johnston demurred. They then agreed upon a far less ambitious plan for a counterattack near Blackburn's Ford, but even this was far beyond Beauregard's ability to plan and oversee. He personally wrote the order, but it reached the units too late for them to act on and was so poorly written that, if followed literally, would have resulted in one Confederate brigade attacking another. Moreover, Beauregard failed to coordinate actions personally or through his staff; on the morning of the battle, he contentedly waited for victory in his headquarters, oblivious to the situation that the Confederate line was quiet, the units immobilized by confusion.[34]

McDowell was more successful in willing his army into movement; despite a delay caused by the poor reconnaissance conducted by his staff, with Burnside's brigade in the lead the Union gained the initial advantage. As the Confederates retreated in disarray, McDowell—exhausted after several weeks of enormous personal exertion—exulted that he had won the battle and let the advance stall. But the prospect of victory faded as the morning's delay had allowed Johnston's army—the same army that Patterson was supposed to pin in the Shenandoah—to arrive. Among these unexpected reinforcements was the brigade of Thomas J. Jackson, which formed the basis of a new line blocking a further Union advance. Once McDowell realized that the battle was not yet won, he resumed the advance; but at each level of command from army to brigade, the Northern generals failed to coordinate the actions of their subordinate units. Sherman's performance was typical: He sent his regiments piecemeal up the hill toward Jackson's position rather than bringing them together as an entire brigade or coordinating his movements with adjacent commanders. The Confederates held fast against these disjointed attacks, prompting Brigadier General Barnard E. Bee to shout to his men, "Yonder stands Jackson like a stone wall!"[35] In time, "Stonewall" Jackson would demonstrate a genius for offensive action, but his nickname and first experience in command came on the defensive. Ironically, the Confederates likely benefited from Beauregard's ineptness, for it would have been much more challenging for them to fight the offensive battle that he intended.

Even with the surprising Confederate resistance, the battle hung in the balance until the arrival of a final column from the Shenandoah broke the brittle will of the Northern volunteers, who until that time had performed better than their leaders. When a pair of Confederate guns fired upon the retreating column, panic took hold and the Union army disintegrated into a mob clad in a variety of interesting uniforms. Significantly, the only unit that maintained its discipline throughout was the battalion of regulars. When called upon to do what they had done so well for decades, the regulars' discipline and experience prevailed even in the midst of a rout. Beauregard and Johnston, however, could not capitalize on this opportunity, for their armies were nearly as disorganized, if not so disheartened.[36]

First Bull Run exposed the limits of the antebellum American military profession. The performance of the regulars (and former regulars, such as Burnside, Sherman, and Jackson) was not uniformly bad, but it was inconsistent. The difference between leading a company and leading a division was more than a matter of scale. A general officer required skills beyond those necessary for a commander who could assemble all his men with a shout: the ability to communicate intent through written orders and couriers, the visualization of actions across a large battlefield, the delegation of critical actions to subordinates and staff, and the management of large-scale logistics. The consistent competence of the antebellum army at the company level came from an experientially based system of professional training in small-unit leadership that had done nothing to give officers such skills. When they were suddenly cast into positions of responsibility, they had to rely largely on their individual talent.

The regulars' explanation for the defeat at First Bull Run would evolve over time, eventually placing most of the blame on politicians who forced them into battle with poorly trained troops. At the time, many realized that the professional soldiers had made numerous mistakes before the volunteers were routed. Upton, who was wounded during the fight and had a horse killed underneath him, wrote just after the battle, "I regret to say we are defeated. Our troops fought well, but were badly managed."[37] The commanders seem to have agreed. Sherman recalled a gathering of dispirited brigade commanders several days after the battle. As they sat brooding over their imminent dismissal, a messenger arrived in the headquarters with the news that most were to be promoted to brigadier general. The stunned silence was broken by Samuel Heintzelman, a grizzled veteran of thirty-five years of service, "By———, it's all a lie! Every mother's son of you will be cashiered." According to Sherman, "we all felt he was right, but, nevertheless, it was true."[38]

Though the regulars did deserve censure for First Bull Run, the battle also made it apparent that the North would need larger armies. Despite criticism from Congress, the press, and public, the War Department could not do without Sherman and his peers; for the same shortage of military expertise that had prompted governors to fight for the services of former captains still prevailed. Moreover, as opposed to the bewildering challenge of commanding armies on the march, the work of organizing and drilling recruits was familiar. Generals who would later demonstrate little aptitude for the battlefield, such as McClellan and Burnside, excelled in the mundane work of assembling the new Army of the Potomac.

But in the first half of 1862, Union generalship again failed. McClellan capably organized the movement of the Army of the Potomac to the Virginia coast but could not take advantage of the opportunity that he had created with the maneuver. His slow advance was in marked contrast to the slashing movements of Confederate leaders like Stonewall Jackson and J. E. B. Stuart. Eventually, McClellan's ill-fated Peninsular Campaign culminated in a series of battles—the Seven Days—just east of Richmond. During those battles, First Lieutenant Upton commanded an artillery battery with some distinction, and so he was soon thereafter made the chief of artillery for the First Division, Sixth Corps. In the Mexican-American War, entrusting the direction of several batteries to an officer just a year out of West Point would have been considered impossible. But with the reversal of Scott's prohibition against regulars seeking volunteer appointments, Upton's advancement lagged behind that of some of his peers who were already colonels commanding regiments. Upton hoped to escape the artillery before his technical skills made him too valuable to release, thereby trapping him in a junior rank for the rest of the war.[39]

By the summer of 1862, the demands of the war compelled Lincoln to request an additional 300,000 volunteers. He turned to the governors, allocating each a quota of regiments. In time, Upton would be rewarded with command of one of these. But the skills required to lead a unit on the field of battle were quite different than those necessary to bring it into existence, particularly a year into the war. The most eager volunteers were already in the service or dead and the draft was still a year in the future, leaving the Union in a lull between full-throated patriotism and coercion. Tapping the country's reserves of manpower was more effectively done at the local level than by the federal government; even during the initial flush of enthusiasm in 1861, the regular army had been unable to enlist the extra 22,000 soldiers authorized after Fort Sumter, and, indeed, never met that goal throughout the war. Every state exceeded its quota in 1861.[40]

But in 1862, even the states had to rely on inducements to service. Large enlistment bounties drew recruits but at the cost of an expensive competition among localities. The individuals who organized the regiments and companies were rewarded with commissions; just as Lincoln relied on "political generals," at the local level there existed "political colonels." When the governor of New York charged the rural central counties of Otsego and Herkimer to jointly raise a regiment, Congressman Richard Franchot led the effort. For this, he was made colonel of the new 121st New York and received a fine sword presented to him by the local residents upon the unit's departure from the area. That might have been all that Franchot had ever intended to do. By one account, upon reporting to the Army of the Potomac, Franchot told the division commander that he had "a thousand of the best boys that had joined the army . . . [but] knew nothing about military matters himself" and wanted a "proper commander at an early day for his regiment."[41] But just a few days later, the 121st New York witnessed but took no active part in the battles of Crampton's Gap and Antietam. Other men alleged that even under distant fire, Franchot displayed evidence of cowardice. Perhaps that brief glimpse of warfare prompted him to return to New York, where he quit public service altogether and went into business. Nevertheless, whether through influence or perhaps even graft, Franchot was able to continue to reap the rewards of his brief military service. In March 1865, he received a brevet promotion to brigadier general for "gallant and meritorious service" despite having never served another day in uniform since 1862. After the war, "General Franchot," as he liked to be called, went on to become what one historian has called the "first paid lobbyist."[42]

The 121st New York was assigned to the division in which Upton was then serving as the chief of artillery. As a native of the state, Upton seemed a natural replacement for Franchot; but the federal government's dependence upon the states meant that Upton could not simply be placed in the position. After Antietam, he was granted leave to go to Albany in order to lobby for the command. Successful in this endeavor, Upton received his commission as a colonel of New York Volunteers on 23 October 1862, about two months after the regiment was first formed.[43]

The 121st New York had only a handful of veterans, and so the transition to camp life had been hard. In the first month alone, the regiment lost almost three hundred men to sickness or desertion. The boy colonel (he was only twenty-three years old) quickly brought it into shape by hounding the quartermasters for its full issue of camp equipment, appealing to the women of the home counties to knit mittens, ensuring proper sanitation, and forcing the resignation of the incompetent surgeon. The medical returns of the regiment improved markedly. Upton also introduced a West Point–like schedule of drill instruction. Outside of the regiment, the neatly dressed encampment and smartly executed parades impressed observers; and so the 121st New York came to be known as "Upton's regulars."[44]

Within the regiment, the marriage of regular leadership with volunteer manpower required some accommodation. Many volunteers respected the competence of their new leader. One lieutenant thought that Upton "was worth four like Franchot"; while a private wrote simply, "He is a man, every inch of him."[45] Yet Upton's youth, high-strung nature, and complete lack of personal warmth and humor made him an easy target for those who thought he was too concerned with parade ground niceties; they derisively referred to him as "the cadet." Perhaps his exaggerated solemnity was an overreaction to his intimidating predicament: Upton was a stranger cast into a group of several hundred men with an established community identity. One of his great problems was that many of the officers were prone to tolerate malingering and other acts of indiscipline out of sympathy for men whom they had known for their entire lives and, assuming that they survived, would likely again be their neighbors after the war. Yet Upton was set on imposing his standards upon the regiment. He administered written examinations for the officers to prove their proficiency and ordered harsh punishments for even minor infractions. Many officers resigned and a number of men deserted, although some of these defections were likely due to the unusually bitter winter and low morale that pervaded the Army of the Potomac.[46]

But underneath matters of standards and discipline, regulars like Upton and volunteers had fundamentally different views of the relationship between leader and led. A month into Upton's command, in a letter to the *Herkimer Journal,* a sergeant wrote that the new colonel understood that although his men "are slaves through necessity, we were once freemen by right." Thus, he continued, "the people may be assured that their sons will be dealt justly with so long as Upton commands."[47] In the regular army, it was not the place of soldiers to publicly comment upon their officers' fitness to command, however approvingly. A colonel viewed the command as "his regiment." This was not the case with the volunteers, who regarded it as a collective enterprise.

Upton's sense of ownership also led to conflict with the politicians in New York, who felt they still had a stake in the regiment and wanted to make use of it for their own purposes. The colonel made use of the same examinations that drove many of the incompetent officers to resign as a tool for meritocracy. Upton's policy was to allow any man in the regiment, whatever his rank or social standing, to take the examination and compete for a commission whenever a vacancy occurred. But when a spot opened, the governor directed Upton to promote a sergeant with strong political connections. Upton replied testily that the sergeant's friends in New York had no idea of the qualities necessary for an officer and that he would instead provide the governor with a list of ten qualified soldiers from which he could select. Upton's impatience with civilian intrusion can be readily understood, for from his vantage the selection of officers was literally a matter of life and death. Thus, he came to regard political influence in military affairs as a deadly evil. But his vantage also spared him any worries about maintaining popular and political support for a long, costly war. Volunteer regiments were rooted in local politics because most Americans trusted local politicians more than the military functionaries of the distant federal government. Individual volunteer soldiers facing the ultimate consequence of ineptitude recognized the benefit of having a professional like Upton for colonel rather than a hack, even a local one, like Franchot. But on the national level, the great exertions of the war could only be sustained if they were channeled through local political institutions trusted and accountable to the average citizen. As a regular leading volunteers, in many ways it was Upton who was the interloper.[48]

Luckily for Upton and the 121st New York, they had time to adapt to each other before being tested in battle. Less than two months after Upton assumed command, Burnside, recently made commander of the entire Army of the Potomac, attempted to cross the Rappahannock River at Fredericksburg. Though competent as a brigade commander, Burnside was hapless at the head of an army, a truth that even he realized. When Lincoln selected him to replace McClellan, Burnside protested that he was unfit for such a command; but the president felt that he had no other general ready for the position. Both were correct. The Union lost nearly 13,000 casualties in futile assaults against positions so strong that the Confederates suffered fewer than 5,000 casualties in return. At a complete loss for any alternative, the bewildered Burnside and his subordinates ordered repeated assaults up the long, open slopes towards the Confederates posted securely behind stone walls and earthen works. Astonishingly, Burnside was ready to continue the assaults the next day but was dissuaded by those with better sense. The 121st New York was fortunate to be posted on a quiet flank, from which they watched the slaughter as bystanders rather than as participants.[49]

Afterward, Upton poured out his frustrations to his sister, "We have been defeated so often when it was not the fault of the brave soldiers that I am losing all patience. There is imbecility somewhere but it does not do to breathe it." As after Bull Run, he blamed his uniformed superiors, "How I would like to see that general who would lead us to great deeds! . . . Never as yet have I seen evidence of great generalship displayed on our side. It is astonishing and depresses one's spirits to know and feel this." Though the 121st New York was largely unscathed, Fredericksburg brought Upton's anger to a high pitch. But by this point, he had come to believe that politicians were also to blame, and perhaps were even the principal villains. "Our defeats emanate from Washington, for with poor generals the courage of our troops would surmount the obstacles of the rebels opposed to our march." He concluded with a plaintive wish. "How I would like to describe one decisive victory!"[50]

It was only a few months before Upton was again disappointed. But unlike at Fredericksburg, during the Chancellorsville campaign it was the turn of the 121st New York to bleed for the mistakes of its generals. General "Fighting Joe" Hooker, the new commander of the Army of the Potomac, ordered the Sixth Corps to stage a demonstration at Fredericksburg to fix Lee's army, while the bulk of the Union army crossed the Rappahannock near Chancellorsville. Initially successful, Hooker hesitated on the cusp of victory and then had his confidence and an entire corps shattered by a Confederate counterattack. Thus as Upton's 121st New York along with the rest of the Sixth Corps began moving to aid the rest of the army, the campaign was already lost. All that followed was nothing but a bloody postscript.[51]

On a low ridge astride the road towards Chancellorsville stood Salem Church, a stout brick structure, and the Confederate brigade of Cadmus M. Wilcox, one of Upton's former tactics instructors at West Point. Though the 121st New York was toward the front of the column, at first Upton could see nothing, only hearing the sporadic firing ahead. Eager to catch the enemy who he thought was retreating, Upton urged his men on. After deploying and crossing through a wooded creek bed, the New Yorkers emerged to see an imposing (and steady) line of grey on the rise not far to their front. Quickly reforming the lines disrupted by the movements through the wooded hollow, the regiment fixed bayonets and rushed forward, only to be stopped dead by what Wilcox described as "a close and terrible fire." The ensuing firefight lasted nearly twenty minutes, with the two lines coming as close as sixty-five feet at some points. Upton was in the thick of the fray. One soldier wrote admiringly that his colonel fought "with a fearlessness that seemed to defy both injury and death." Indeed, Upton's war nearly ended when his horse, "Manassas," was wounded and charged panic-stricken toward the rebel lines. He barely avoided capture by jumping from the crazed horse.[52]

Despite his valor, the young artilleryman's first attempt at handling infantry in combat was not flawless. The more experienced regiments were not as eager and did not advance so far despite the urgent pleas of the major of the 121st New York, who Upton dispatched to request support once he realized his predicament. As a consequence, when the Confederates counterattacked, the 121st New York bore the brunt, losing approximately 60 percent of its strength in dead and wounded. The ninety-seven killed or mortally wounded (there were more than two hundred total casualties) were the tenth-highest total of any Union regiment in a single engagement during the war. In a letter to his brother, Upton noted with morbid satisfaction that the ratio of killed to wounded among his men was more than twice the norm. With presumably less pride, he admitted in his official report that only half of the regiment initially rallied around the colors after the Confederate counterattack.[53]

Though perhaps too aggressive, Upton had performed credibly. Superior officers had long noted his efficiency in camp and on the drill field, but now his brigade commander commended Upton for leading "his regiment into action in a masterly and fearless manner . . . with unflinching nerve and marked ability."[54] Civil War reports tended to florid excess, but several months later, as Lee invaded Pennsylvania, the brigade commander offered a more meaningful compliment: When he was called upon to temporarily command the division on the march to Gettysburg, he selected Upton from among the regimental commanders to take charge of the brigade.[55]

Upton, too, was gaining confidence in his abilities. The Sixth Corps was one of the last units to arrive at Gettysburg and played only a minor role; but on the last day of the battle, standing on the slopes of Little Round Top where the battle had raged the day before, Upton sensed the gravity of the moment as the enemy gathered for Pickett's famous charge. He gave a speech to his regiment; and if only for a moment, his personal reserve fell away. "For the first time in my life," he ecstatically wrote his brother, "words and actions came to me spontaneously." The soldiers responded with "a cheer that would have raised the hair of a confronting rebel"; and, at least in Upton's mind, whatever divide had earlier separated him from the volunteers disappeared. "From that instant I had as much confidence in them as in myself."[56] Not long after, he was selected to permanently command the brigade. This increase in responsibility, the cocky young officer assured his sister, was just "a half-way step between colonel and brigadier-general." He vowed to "take the full step in the next battle." In the meantime, Upton solicited recommendations for his promotion, eventually amassing a dozen from general officers, including George G. Meade, Joseph Hooker, John Sedgwick, and Butterfield, the militia commander who he had assisted in that first summer just before Bull Run.[57]

Upton's ambition went unsated for several months; but when the opportunity to prove his mettle came in November 1863, it was spectacular. The division commanded by General D. A. Russell, which included Upton's brigade, was to seize a strong Confederate bridgehead at Rappahannock Station. The position hinged upon two large earthen redoubts perched atop the river bluff, one on each side of the road. A conventional assault against such a strong position would require a force several times larger than Russell's, but he thought that a surprise nighttime assault might overwhelm the complacent defenders. It was a hazardous scheme. Linear tactics required tight control that was nearly impossible in the dark, so nineteenth-century armies tended to avoid night actions at all costs. But Russell was ready to gamble; he ordered two brigades, including Upton's, to make the attack.[58]

Under the guise of the routine evening rotation of sentinels, Russell cunningly snuck extra forces into the picket line. At dusk, this vanguard sprang from their positions and overran the Confederate outerworks, followed closely by the remainder of the two brigades. With Upton in the lead, his men pushed forward to the edge of the redoubt that was his principal objective. There, as the soldiers prepared for the final assault, Upton used his own improvised bit of deception. He loudly called upon his men to take the position before the arrival of nonexistent reinforcements. After the battle, a Confederate officer claimed that his men overheard this speech and, believing their situation hopeless, surrendered as a result. Meanwhile, the other brigade met similar success; but the honors of capturing the ultimate prize—

the pontoon bridges over the Rappahannock—went to Upton, who had made it clear to his officers before the battle that he wanted to win the race. The colonel made little effort to hide his ambition; a friend later admitted "there was no enterprise too perilous for Upton, if only he might hope to gain credit or promotion thereby."[59]

Rappahannock Station certainly added to Upton's laurels; Russell's division captured four guns and approximately 1,600 Confederates during the battle. Upton's losses were extraordinarily light for an assault on prepared works: eleven killed and fifty-two wounded. The battle also removed Lee's dangerous bridgehead, creating an opportunity that the Union generals were unable to exploit during their abortive Mine Run campaign. Nevertheless, General Meade called the officers involved in the successful *coup de main* to his headquarters for a champagne toast. As Upton savored the drink, he might have thought that he had at last won his promotion.[60]

The Army of the Potomac then settled into winter quarters, but the restless Upton took advantage of the pause in campaigning to train his brigade. Rather than repetitious drill on a flat parade ground, he sent his soldiers in ragged waves over rough terrain against mock fortifications like those at Rappahannock Station. Marksmanship instruction was also more realistic than training had been before the war. The targets were placed at various ranges and the soldiers had to estimate the range, rather than it being given by the officers. Such realistic training was the element that had been missing from the antebellum army's attempt to achieve the *chasseur à pied* ideal laid out in Hardee's tactics.[61]

Though Upton was becoming an adept brigade commander, even the spectacular success at Rappahannock Station did not bring his coveted promotion to brigadier general. In April 1864, he confided to his sister that General Meade had told him "without 'political' influence I will never be promoted."[62] Unwilling to forego advancement, Upton bitterly decided to resort to the same methods that he had tried to quash when practiced by his subordinates: He wrote to various New York politicians seeking their intercession on his behalf. Shamed by his hypocrisy, Upton verbally lashed out at the system that valued the "baneful influence of the paltry politicians" over "those officers whose lives have been periled in every battle of the war." As the Army of the Potomac readied itself for the most terrible summer in American military history, Upton resigned himself to fighting for promotion on political battlefields. "I have not fully despaired of receiving promotion, but I have despaired of receiving it in the manner honorable to a soldier. It is now solely the reward of political influence, and not of merit, and this when a government is fighting for its own existence."[63]

It was not yet apparent to Upton, or even to Meade, but the relationship between the army and the government had entered a new phase. The president granted the new commanding general, Ulysses S. Grant, unprecedented discretion in selecting general officers for promotion. Lincoln had enormous trust in Grant, in part due to his demonstrated military competence but also because the general actively worked to support the administration's policy aims. Rather than condescendingly lecture the president or insist upon a protected sphere of "military strategy" distinct from "political strategy," Grant shared his plans and was willing to moderate them as necessary to conform to the president's needs. Ironically, this submission won Grant the autonomy that other generals had sought. Because the president trusted Grant to remain within the bounds of administration policy, he allowed the general great discretion in determining how best to employ and manage his army. This included the management of general officers, which by 1864 was not so critical in building political support as it had been during the heyday of political generals early in the war. At the beginning of the 1864 campaign, Secretary of War Edwin Stanton authorized Grant to fill several vacancies for brigadier general with men of proven competence. Though Upton would soon be one of the beneficiaries of Grant's enlightened approach to civil-military relations, from his vantage he could not see the way in which deference to political needs could enhance professional expertise.[64]

In early May, Grant and the Army of the Potomac struck south, meeting Lee's army in the Wilderness, a tangled thicket near Chancellorsville. For Upton, the battle was a confusing round of marches, countermarches, and devastating Confederate attacks that suddenly emerged from the dense brush. Despite heavy casualties and tactical setbacks, Grant refused to follow the familiar pattern of withdrawing and regrouping after battle. Instead he pressed on, hoping that with a flank march he might catch Lee on more open ground farther to the south. But the Northerners were not quite quick enough, and Lee's army took refuge in a strong position near Spotsylvania Courthouse. By this time in the war, the soldiers of both armies were experts in quickly erecting field fortifications; soon the Confederates were behind manned trenches and redoubts reinforced with heavy logs, a tangle of sharpened tree limbs facing the Union lines, and cleared fields of fire. Connecting trenches allowed reinforcements and resupplies to be moved under cover. For all of its strength, in the heart of the Spotsylvania position an awkwardly placed rise posed a dilemma for the Southern engineers. Rather than cede the high ground, they elected to create a salient that became known as the "Mule Shoe." As a rule, armies avoid occupying such positions, for as a consequence of geometry they allow the attacker to concentrate fire from multiple directions. In the case of the Mule Shoe, this weakness was accentuated by the cover of concealing woods just two hundred yards in front of the defensive line and a slight crease in the ground that offered an attacker several precious seconds of protection from enfilading fire. A sharp-eyed engineer, Lieutenant Ranald S. Mackenzie, spotted this flaw during a reconnaissance. Grant, having failed to outmaneuver Lee, decided to take the position with an early-evening assault.[65]

The mission fell to Upton, who had played a leading role in the similar attack at Rappahannock Station. Grant gave him twelve regiments— approximately 5,000 men, or the equivalent of a division. Upton organized this ad hoc command into four successive lines of three regiments abreast. Each line was given a distinct mission: The first would overwhelm the defenders of the outermost trenches, then attack to either flank to widen the gap in the enemy lines; the second would occupy the positions captured by the first, then prepare to fire on any Confederate reinforcements; the third line would advance in support of the second; the fourth would remain in reserve. Even with the advantages of terrain and surprise, Upton knew that the attack would succeed only if the first line crossed the open ground with ferocious abandon. To ensure the soldiers of the first line were fully committed to the task, he ordered them to go into battle with unloaded weapons. Their only hope was to cross the deadly two hundred yards as quickly as possible and use the bayonet. Upton asked no less of himself; he was the only officer who went into the attack on horseback, making him a suicidally conspicuous target.[66]

Despite the claims of some historians, Upton's tactics were nothing more than a sound but entirely conventional response to a poorly sited enemy position.[67] The more noteworthy aspect was the unusual thoroughness of his preparations. With only several hours to prepare, he conducted a personal reconnaissance with the regimental commanders, carefully explaining his plan. He then gathered all the officers of the entire command, and repeated his instructions to them. Though such techniques are common in the best armies today, at the time few commanders were so methodical in developing and ensuring that all their subordinates understood the plan for battle.[68]

The initial assault went much as Upton intended. The Confederates could fire only two volleys before the first line of attackers crested the works, eager to exact revenge for those who had already fallen. As the remnants of the first line fought with bayonet and clubbed rifle, the second and third lines bounded across the open ground nearly unscathed. The attack stalled, however, as adjacent Union units failed to advance in support, allowing Confederate reinforcements to concentrate upon Upton's command. The opportunity squandered, Grant reluctantly ordered a withdrawal under the cover of darkness. Some of the soldiers refused to retreat from ground so painfully won; only after repeated commands did all of the Northern soldiers cross back over the narrow strip of ground, now shrouded in darkness. Rightly, they blamed the incompetence of the generals who were unable to coordinate the actions of their commands. Still, Upton's assault yielded at least a thousand Confederate prisoners and perhaps an equal number of killed and wounded for Union losses of about one thousand. Though his superiors had once again failed to control complex operations, Upton had performed his role brilliantly. The night of the assault, Grant used his new authority to promote Upton to brigadier general.[69] At the age of twenty-four, Upton had achieved his boyhood ambition by earning a general's stars in the fight against slavery.

The Army of the Potomac pounded Lee's Spotsylvania line for another eight days, including another assault on the Mule Shoe that featured some of the fiercest fighting of the war. Eventually, Grant moved around a flank and so forced Lee to retreat from that position, and then once again at yet another line along the North Anna River. But in the three weeks since the Wilderness, the Army of the Potomac had suffered tens of thousands of casualties. By the end of May, Upton's brigade, like most of the army, was a shadow of its former self. Most states preferred to fill their manpower quotas by creating new regiments, which provided a fresh source of patronage in commissions, rather than undertaking the difficult and politically unrewarding work of recruiting replacements for existing units. Upton's old regiment, for instance, received only two large infusions of replacements throughout the war. As a consequence, at the beginning of May 1864, it had only 477 officers and soldiers present for duty, and by August was down to a mere 250 men.[70] This flawed replacement policy gave Upton one more reason to question the influence of politics upon the war effort. As the losses of the summer mounted, the Union resorted to desperate expedients, such as using as infantry the heavy artillery units that had been manning fortifications around the capital. Upton's brigade received one of these units, the 2nd Connecticut Heavy Artillery, which had more men than the four original regiments of the brigade combined. Thus, the army was made up of either large bodies of inexperienced troops or small bands of weary veterans closer in size to companies than to regiments.[71]

As May drew to a close, Grant made another attempt to get around Lee. The Union cavalry seized a crucial road junction at Cold Harbor, but it was then lost as confusion among the generals meant that the infantry was slow to follow. A strong Southern line had started to congeal by the time that the Sixth Corps was finally ready to attack late on June 1st. In his sector, Upton put his exhausted veteran regiments in reserve behind the unblooded gunners of the 2nd Connecticut. Through sheer force of will and numbers, the brigade reached a position in front of the Confederate lines and was able to exchange fire for a brief period. But in the process it lost over three hundred men in the attack, nearly all from the 2nd Connecticut; and due to poor generalship, no troops came to exploit this fleeting success.[72]

Two days later, Grant—out of patience and room to maneuver—hoped that he might simply overwhelm the enemy. As the commander of the Army of the Potomac, it was Meade's responsibility to issue the detailed order. Yet his order did nothing more than direct all of the corps to attack simultaneously, a simple method that might work in a fluid battle, but that was unlikely to succeed against an established position. Major General William "Baldy" Smith, a corps commander, complained that such a simple plan "would never be adopted by a trained general."[73] Strictly speaking, however, the U.S. Army had no trained generals. Those who had succeeded had done so through talent, perhaps some self-education, and through what little experience in handling large units was available in peacetime. The Civil War generals did not even have the advantage of the latter, for most had been relatively junior when the war began. Meade, for instance, had been a captain of topographical engineers in 1861. But the lack of a retirement system had meant that when the war began many of the field grade officers were too old for active service, which combined with the vast scale of the conflict meant that junior officers were thrust into positions for which they had never been trained and had little relevant experience. Both then and now, the "school of experience" is often glorified as the best means of learning; but aside from the human cost of on-the-job training for generals, it was not so thorough an instructor as some might imagine. Days after Cold Harbor, Upton wrote a scathing letter complaining about corps commanders "not fit to be corporals." The faults he described—poor reconnaissance and planning—were not the types of unavoidable errors caused by the fog and friction of war but indicated a more general ignorance of the methods of high command.[74] Though that letter was written in anger, it represented Upton's objective belief that Union generalship was generally poor. Even with the remove of several years from the war, he still attributed the many failures of the Army of the Potomac to a "want of minute instructions, and particularly at the moment of success."[75] But what would set Upton apart from most other members of the Civil War generation was that he did not regard poor generalship as primarily a reflection of individual weakness. Instead, systemic problems were the result of an institutional failing. Years later, in response to a book critical of West Pointers' management of the Civil War, Upton asked, "[the author] lays all the blame on generals but what has our government ever done to make a general?"[76]

On the plane of strategy, Grant was battering Lee and the Confederacy into submission. At Upton's lower tactical level, the war appeared to be a horrifying slaughter made worse by the repeated failures of his superiors. In the several weeks of the Overland Campaign, the Army of the Potomac suffered just under 55,000 casualties, a staggering number that was more than half of the casualties suffered by the army from its creation in 1861 to that time—a period that encompassed the battles of Antietam, Fredericksburg, Chancellorsville, and Gettysburg. This catastrophic bloodletting left the army so exhausted that even the usually fearsome and fearless Upton, upon receiving his orders for the second Cold Harbor assault, deemed them "impracticable" and simply declined to attack.[77] That spared his brigade, for Meade's inelegant plan worked as poorly as Smith and Upton expected. The Union sustained 7,000 casualties and reached the enemy lines only at a single point. The Confederates suffered fewer than 1,500 casualties.[78]

Yet many of the skills mastered in the antebellum army were still useful. Grant recovered from the debacle of Cold Harbor by having his engineers build a bridge over the wide, tidal James River. That technical feat was then followed by an equally impressive organizational achievement of shifting with surprising quickness the entirety of the army's base of operations to a

Major General William H. French (USMA 1837) and his staff not long before his relief for incompetence in 1863. An expert on artillery training and a brevetted veteran of Mexico and the Second Seminole War, like other antebellum officers, French found that earlier service was poor preparation for high command. (Civil War Photograph Collection, LC-DIG-cwpb-04388, LC)

new location where it could be supplied by sea. But then, once again, the generals squandered opportunity by failing to seize the nearly undefended railroad hub of Petersburg. The two armies then settled into an elaborate series of trenches and fortifications where they would remain until the final days of the war.[79]

Upton was spared the misery of the trenches of Petersburg; for not long after the crossing of the James, Grant sent the Sixth Corps to the Shenandoah Valley. From there, the small but audacious Confederate army of General Jubal Early had raided into Maryland and Pennsylvania even while the Confederacy crumbled. To end these embarrassments, Grant ordered General Philip Sheridan to form the Army of the Shenandoah and crush Early. On 19 September 1864, near the town of Winchester, the two armies met at the

Battle of Opequon. Sheridan attacked, but as his forces advanced, a dangerous gap opened in the lines. General D. A. Russell rushed his division into the void but was mortally wounded, leaving command to Upton, who was soon also seriously wounded. An artillery shell nearly severed the femoral artery of the young general. These sacrifices were not in vain, and Sheridan credited Russell and Upton with saving the Union line at the battle's crucial moment. For his actions at Opequon, Upton received a brevet promotion to major general.[80]

The young general returned to Batavia for his convalescence and might have stayed at home for the remainder of the war if not for a letter from James H. Wilson, a friend from the preceding class at West Point. Originally an engineer, Wilson's work in organizing the provision of horses for the cavalry had won Lincoln's admiration and a brigadier's star in 1863. Wilson's subsequent performance as a cavalry commander brought him further promotions. In late 1864, he was ordered to end the threat of General Nathan Bedford Forrest, who had long been the scourge of the Union rear areas in the western theater. Wilson was to take the many cavalry regiments scattered throughout the region in a vain effort to counter the Confederate raids, consolidate them into the new Cavalry Corps of the Military Division of the Mississippi (CCMDM), and destroy Forrest in his sanctuary in northern Alabama. For the task, Wilson wanted the best weapons available and so armed his troops with the new seven-shot Spencer carbine. He also wanted the most aggressive subordinates and so asked his friend Upton to join him. Though Upton's leg was not yet fully healed, it was an opportunity too good to resist.[81]

It took three months of feverish activity to assemble and equip the new unit, but by late March 1865 the CCMDM was finally ready. Wilson took two divisions, including Upton's, to Selma, where the tired remnants of Forrest's army waited behind fortifications. Unlike the lazy generals whom he detested, Upton was careful with the lives of his men. He conducted a hazardous personal reconnaissance close to the Confederate lines to find an unguarded approach through swampy ground into the town. In the ensuing attack, Wilson smashed Forrest's motley force of cavalry and militia. He then proceeded to take Montgomery en route to his final objective, Columbus, Georgia. There, he ordered Upton, who was becoming something of an expert in unorthodox assaults, to capture a critical bridge leading into town. The Confederates had prepared the bridge for destruction, so

Wilson envisioned a night *coup de main*. Upton prepared with his usual thoroughness but just before the attack seemed uncharacteristically confused and irresolute. He was ready to call off the attack when Wilson intervened. The attack was a spectacular success, but Upton was likely physically exhausted and emotionally spent. If so, the end of the war several days later was perfectly timed.[82]

Upton amassed an extraordinary record during the war. Within four years of his graduation from West Point, he had risen to the rank of major general, in the process commanding at every level from battery to division and in all three of the principal arms—artillery, infantry, and cavalry. He had proven his valor on multiple occasions. But he was more than a mere "fighting general." Upton understood combat generalship in all of its facets: organizing units, training officers and soldiers, preparing for battle, and commanding in combat. In short, his reputation and breadth of experience made him unusually qualified to codify and institutionalize the lessons of the war, a task that would dominate the rest of his career.

. . . . .

Several weeks after Lee's surrender at Appomattox, Upton happened to be on the same train as William T. Sherman. Though they had likely not seen each other since the summer of First Bull Run, the two fell into an hours-long conversation concerning the lessons of the war. For at least a year, Upton had been obsessed with the problem of developing a tactical system that would avoid the slaughter attending even many successful Civil War attacks. His ideas had advanced far enough that he had begun to train his brigade in new methods that impressed others when he was wounded at Opequon. Though he had no more opportunity for practical experimentation, he continued to think about tactics, "almost to the exclusion of everything else," according to his friend Peter Michie.[83]

One problem was the often rough and forested American terrain, which precluded armies from deploying in the manner envisioned by the European tacticians from whose work previous American drill regulations were derived. "In wooded country with narrow roads," Ulysses S. Grant would recall, "we might as well have had no tactics at all, so far as the old system served us. Indeed, it was not infrequently the case that we were obliged to entirely abandon the system and depend upon plain common sense."[84] The awkwardness of applying European tactics to the United States had long been a problem, but rough terrain combined with the range and accuracy of well-handled rifle muskets resulted in Civil War armies placing much more emphasis on skirmishers in the attack and field fortifications in the defense. Sherman thought those trends had been the most important developments of the war; and Upton, having commanded a division armed with breech-loading rifles, knew that the new weapons would only lead to an even greater departure from past forms. Just a decade old, Hardee's manual written in response to the rifle muskets had already been rendered obsolete by the new weapons. Upton resolved to write a new manual.[85]

Naturally, Upton's ideas reflected his wartime experiences. Among all else, he sought to make tactics simple. In contrast to the intricate movements of Scott's manuals, which highlighted the skills of professional soldiers, Upton wanted something that could be quickly learned by volunteers like those of 1861. Simplicity did not mean that he held citizen-soldiers in low regard. Indeed, Upton wrote that officers should "constantly aim to impress each man with the idea of his individuality, and the responsibility that rests upon him."[86] The entire basis of antebellum drill had been to suppress individuality; Upton's desire to encourage individualism among the enlisted ranks would have been heresy just a few years before.

Elements of his new system were meant to take advantage of the opportunities presented by patriotic volunteers who did not have to be dragooned into line and were armed with the new breech-loading rifles. Upton imagined a strong screen of such men advancing as skirmishers ahead of the main line of battle. They could more easily navigate amid ravines, trees, and boulders in rough country; but even if the army were in more open terrain, skirmishers would offset the advantage of the defense by using their breechloaders to "derange" the enemy with fire. Though this had often been attempted during the war, the old system of tactics did not provide commanders with an adequate means of controlling the skirmish line. Upton made several modifications to Hardee's system in order to provide the finer control so that commanders could mete out their units by "small fractions" and thus more finely modulate the pace of battle. Once the defender was sufficiently weakened, the main attack could go forward.[87]

The other great change was that Upton adjusted the line of battle to reflect the change from musket- to breech-loading weapons. In the early days of firearms, cumbersome matchlock muskets required over thirty steps to reload. During that time, an individual soldier was utterly vulnerable. The solution was to array musketeers in formations several rows (or ranks) deep; soldiers with ready weapons would fire then move to the back to be protected by their comrades while they reloaded. In practice, this required an intricate ballet of coordinated, collective movement in the midst of death that could be effectively performed only by disciplined and thoroughly trained troops; hence the preoccupation with drill that characterized European-style armies until the nineteenth century.[88] The early formations were up to ten rows deep; but as weapons improved and the rate of fire became faster, fewer ranks in the formation were necessary. By the American Revolution, trained soldiers could reload their flintlock muskets so quickly that British formations commonly used just two ranks. In the antebellum U.S. Army, the great question was whether two or three ranks were preferable. Scott preferred the French three-rank formations, even though (or perhaps because) they required more intricate movements that were difficult for militiamen to replicate. But the introduction of breechloaders had eliminated the need for any form of multirank formation. "The feats of dismounted cavalry, armed with the Spencer carbine," Upton wrote, clearly thinking of his own command at war's end, "have demonstrated the fact that one rank of men so armed is nearly, if not quite, equal in offensive or defensive power to two ranks armed with the Springfield musket."[89]

Single-rank formations had several advantages. Thinner lines meant that each regiment deployed across a longer front, freeing other units to be used elsewhere or kept in reserve. Soldiers were also less vulnerable than when they were arrayed in dense formations of multiple ranks. Thus, dispersion was simultaneously a more efficient use of firepower and a counter to the presumably equally effective weapons of the enemy. Though Upton tended to emphasize the greater offensive capability, in an 1880 lecture Sherman vividly described both the offensive and defensive implications: "If Baron Steuben were to arise, he would doubtless attack one of Upton's thin lines with his old column of attack doubled on the center, and would learn in a single lesson that the world has advanced in science, if not in patriotism, courage, and devotion to duty."[90]

Though certainly an improvement over Hardee's manual, Upton went too far in boasting that his system was a "complete revolution."[91] Instead, it was nothing more than a tweak to a dying way of war, as Upton could not bring himself to depart from linear tactics even though the technological reason—the inadequacy of muzzleloaders—no longer pertained. Yet Upton believed that battle would still end in a climactic charge from which the enemy would flee or be overwhelmed in hand-to-hand combat. In either event, it was critical that commanders had absolute control over a large mass of men arranged in a line of battle, even if it was just one rank deep.[92] Linear tactics required absolute subordination from the common soldier; individual initiative would only create confusion within a unit. The ideal soldier for the line of battle was an automaton. In monarchical Europe, this was an advantage, for it reinforced the societal relationship between aristocratic officers and commoner soldiers.[93] Linear tactics did not accord so well with the political culture of the United States. Citizen-soldiers particularly tended to rebel against the subordination that characterized effective units, though Americans with more Whiggish political views, like Scott, appreciated the imposed order.

Because Upton's appreciation for the qualities of the volunteers that he led during the war was sincere, he found himself torn between the tactics that he learned as a cadet and the patterns of leadership he had developed as a commander. His attempt to reconcile them was hopelessly illogical; later in his career, he would write that the warfare of his time required "increased individuality among the men, and this individuality, it has been shown by experience, can only be developed by rigid discipline and steadiness when in ranks."[94] The absurd contention that individuality was enhanced through rigid obedience was not explained, for it could not survive closer examination.

Despite these flaws that are evident in hindsight, Upton's ideas became official tactics in a remarkably short time. With impressive speed, he submitted his draft regulations to the War Department in January 1866. That summer a reviewing board unanimously recommended its adoption by the army. General Grant endorsed the finding, noting approvingly that the manual "is no translation, but a purely American work."[95] There were many detractors, but these were generally those who either wanted their own system or took issue with some minor aspect of drill commands and movements. The officer corps as a whole was as locked into the paradigm of skirmishers and line as was Upton. Like him, everything they knew of combat was based upon that premise; it would have taken someone of extraordinary vision to break free of a mental pattern so ingrained. The most substantive criticisms of Upton's tactics related to his system of organizing skirmishers into temporary groups of "fours." Though Sherman singled out that element for special praise in his *Memoirs,* others argued—with some justification— that the fours might break down under the strain of heavy combat. To quell this discontent, Grant personally chaired a second board that compared Upton's system with several alternatives. After that group reaffirmed the earlier recommendation, Upton's manual, *A New System of Infantry Tactics, Double and Single Rank: Adapted to American Topography and Improved Fire-Arms,* became the Army's official drill regulations for infantry in 1867. Further confirming Upton's status as the army's leading tactician, the influential *Army and Navy Journal* named him its tactical editor.[96]

But if the Civil War generation was wedded to linear tactics, they also were convinced that the army of the next war would be dominated by volunteers and so require simple tactics. The Grant board noted that Upton's system could be easily learned by recruits, thus "abbreviating materially the time required to fit them for the field, and practically extending the effective term of service of the soldier. This is of great importance in its relation to the volunteer force, of which, in all great wars, our armies must be largely composed."[97] Upton even built upon this virtue by following his military *Tactics* with a simpler civil version, the descriptively titled *Tactics for Non-Military Bodies, Adapted to the Instruction of Political Associations, Police Forces, Fire Organizations, Masonic, Odd Fellows, and Other Civic Societies.* With so many former soldiers returned to society, for decades after the Civil War, "marching societies" and other civic groups had a pronounced martial tone, and Upton hoped to use those groups as a vehicle for rudimentary military training to give future volunteers a familiarity with military commands.[98]

Upton's *Tactics,* like Scott's 1815 drill regulations, provide a window into the military profession at a pivotal moment. Both appeared just after a war that while ultimately successful still exposed professional weaknesses. As such, the manuals were more than a mere catalogue of formations and commands, though that was indeed much of their substance. Inevitably embedded within these manuals is an implicit understanding of war: assumptions about where, who, and how the army will fight. The War of 1812 was a traumatic experience for the regulars, exposing their amateurish incompetence; Scott's tactics provided the blueprint for a disciplined army capable of mastering European-style warfare. The Civil War was similarly traumatic, as Scott's simple professionalism proved incapable of expansion; Upton's tactics were an attempt to devise a new means of fighting that was more consistent with the characteristics of mass volunteer armies and better suited to the weapons and terrain of late nineteenth-century America. Unable to fully unburden himself of old paradigms, Upton did not take full advantage of the opportunities presented by breech-loading rifles. Nonetheless, in stressing simplicity, flexibility, and morale, he made great strides in codifying the lessons of the war.

Both Scott and Upton, each in his own time and each in his own manner, expressed more a vision of what the army should be than what it actually was at the end of their respective wars. Scott described a thoroughly trained Napoleonic army of professional soldiers. In its essentials, this army came to fruition through the efforts of Scott, Calhoun, Thayer, and others, a process aided by the relative simplicity of Scott's vision and the degree to which conditions in antebellum America, while perhaps not conducive, were at least not entirely hostile. Upton's vision was more complex, and so even he struggled with some of its inconsistencies. He saw that modern arms meant that success in battle required more tactical flexibility, which in turn demanded greater initiative and proficiency among both officers and men. He would spend the rest of his life trying to build the institutional methods of education, training, and organization so that the next generation of soldiers would be more ready for war than he and his fellow regulars had been in 1861.

CHAPTER FOUR

The Civil War's Legacy

WHILE UPTON DEVELOPED tactics for the army of the next war, the army of the last was melting away. At its wartime peak, the Union had over one million men under arms. By 1869, the authorized strength of the army stood at just 37,313.[1] Though this left the army more than twice as large as it had been in 1860, four years of warfare followed by such a swift, dramatic contraction left a deep imprint on the regulars. As was the case after the War of 1812, the residual officer corps was in its prime and battle hardened. The fortunate survivors had experienced war on a scale unlike anything yet seen in the American military experience. A veteran army would seem to be an unalloyed good; but in some senses the Civil War had a mischievous effect on the army, for the war that defined them was an anomaly and so its lessons could be misleading. Yet the regulars could not simply return to their antebellum state after such a transformational event, even though (with the significant exception of Reconstruction) postwar conditions were in many respects similar to those that had prevailed before the war.

One immediate consequence of the postwar reduction was an infusion of former volunteers into the regular army; this abrupt demographic shift reversed the antebellum trend of an increasingly homogenized officer corps dominated by West Pointers. In 1860, they constituted nearly three-quarters of the officer corps. But in 1866, Congress stipulated that the majority of

commissions in the postwar army go to former volunteers; this democra-
tized the army while rewarding the service of many deserving citizen-soldiers
who might otherwise have been shunted aside by the regulars. In 1866 and
1867, 1,360 former volunteers received commissions; and though some left
or were forced from the service during a subsequent reduction, this group
constituted a large segment of the officer corps, which was typically about
2,100 strong throughout the 1870s.[2]

The incorporation of this large body of former volunteers obviously had
some effect on the character of the military profession, but the very nature
of the change—from uniformity to diversity—makes it difficult to charac-
terize its precise effects. Most obviously, there was no guarantee that these
new officers had the minimum academic attainment required by West Point.
Some of the volunteers had little education, and a few were illiterate. Yet
even the well-educated were likely prone to professional anti-intellectualism,
for their personal identity as officers was rooted in the school of experience
rather than in professional education. For volunteers to acknowledge the
importance of formal training would consign them to a perpetual secondary
status within the officer corps in relation to their West Point-trained colleagues. Though some would concede that they wished they had preliminary
military training, most preferred to perpetuate the traditional belief that any
American (or at least those of the right class) could leave his civilian life and
become a successful military commander.[3]

Senator John A. Logan, one of the most successful volunteer generals of
the war, took this line of reasoning further to claim that volunteers were
better than those trained at West Point. Logan sincerely believed in the qualities of the citizen-soldier, but he also had a visceral hatred for West Pointers
as a group and for Sherman in particular. The source of this animus was an
incident in 1864, when a less-deserving West Pointer had been given command of the Army of the Tennessee rather than the volunteer Logan. Thus,
he had good reason to believe that professional education bred an antimeri-
tocratic cliquishness. But Logan was also skeptical of the value of military
education. Like many of his generation, he believed that the overwhelming
determent of success as a commander was natural "genius." Logan compared
generalship to singing; just as training could aid a talented performer but
would be of no use to someone with a poor voice, so, too, Logan wrote, "No
degree of scholastic education and training can make a distinguished soldier of a man who has not the inherent qualifications of a soldier."[4] Because

military education was more likely to result in command being given to those who were good students but poor soldiers, he thought that on the balance it should receive less emphasis.

Though Logan's nemesis, Sherman, was a staunch supporter of West Point as a means for instilling general military traits of obedience and discipline, the two shared a skepticism about the value of education for command. In an 1879 graduation address at the Michigan Military Academy, Sherman noted, "I have known many an officer who knew Jomini by heart, and could demonstrate every battle of Frederick the Great and of Napoleon on the blackboard[,] who could not properly station a picket-guard, or handle a company skirmish-line, or know how to provide for his men on a ten day's scout."[5] For just as Logan had reason to deny the importance of the West Point degree that he lacked, Sherman had never received any formal preparation for generalship. Any acknowledgement that such training was important would imply that he had not been fully qualified to hold the positions on which his fame and identity rested. The same dynamic applied to all the other regulars whose reputations rested on their wartime service for which the army had given them little or no preparation.

Thus, Upton was likely in the minority, for he believed that a strong foundation in the art of war, to include strategy, logistics, law, and, above all, history, was essential knowledge for high command. To Upton, it was obvious that Civil War generals would have benefited greatly from such training. "How ignorant our generals were," he wrote "of all the principles of generalship."[6] But the war had featured both triumph and failure in sufficient quantity to allow each officer to see in it whatever lessons he desired to see. It was perhaps natural that most chose to remember that which validated, rather than diminished, their own efforts and professional identity.

Another characteristic of the late nineteenth-century officer corps was a corrosive concern with political influence as a path to rank. For most officers, the Mexican-American War resulted in only limited promotions that were largely distributed according to seniority and so produced no significant reordering of relative rank among the regulars. But such equality was not the case after the Civil War. Through a combination of influence, skill, and luck, some regulars achieved much greater gains than did their peers during the war. The policy of allocating postwar rank on the strength of wartime performance then made those disparities permanent. The postwar reduction boards granted some young officers handsome awards: Though just thirty-four years old at the war's end, Phil Sheridan was allowed to keep his general's stars; former store clerk and volunteer Nelson A. Miles—just a few weeks older than Upton—was made a colonel; Upton and his friend James H. Wilson were each granted commissions as lieutenant colonels. In the antebellum army, officers typically waited until they were fifty years old to reach that rank. Upton was still only twenty-six. More importantly, he had vaulted past hundreds of older officers, some who had also served capably. One of these, Alexander Piper, was ten years senior to Upton and had also commanded a volunteer regiment and received two brevet promotions for meritorious service, but evidently without a patron he reverted to his normal rank of captain after the war. It was not until 1882 that Piper finally was promoted to lieutenant colonel; thus, in the postwar reorganization, Upton effectively gained twenty-six years of seniority on Piper.[7] Common to the success of Sheridan, Miles, Wilson, and Upton was the good fortune of having their talent and efforts recognized with a significant promotion in 1862. But although there was a certain element of luck involved, each had already demonstrated unusual professional capacity at the lower ranks. Yet the highest positions in the postwar army went to those who had received their great opportunity in 1861. Of the army's fifteen general officers in 1869, nine had gained their first stars (either as a volunteer or a regular) within three months of First Bull Run, and another three had received that promotion by the end of 1861. Sheridan had been the latest to rise to flag rank, and even he was a brigadier general of volunteers by September 1862. Thus, most of the postwar generals had risen to prominence in the early months before anyone had a chance to amass much of a record; and so rank was distributed by some combination of political connections, apparent potential, and sheer luck. Some of these generals, such as Sherman and Winfield Scott Hancock, subsequently demonstrated their worth; but there were others, such as Henry W. Halleck, Irvin McDowell, O. O. Howard, and John Pope, who had simply persisted despite having demonstrated themselves to be, at best, mediocre generals.[8]

The lesson was clear: The greatest and most enduring gains were to be made while the armies were still organizing, perhaps even before any significant battle had been fought. Because most officers assumed that the Civil War method of raising armies would be repeated in any future war, throughout the rest of the nineteenth century and up to World War I, whenever the clouds of war seemed to be gathering, officers began their individual campaigns for rank with governors, congressmen, generals, and whoever else might be able to influence the granting of commissions. Thus, one byproduct of the Civil War was a "land-rush" mentality that would persist for the entire period up to World War I in which any sign of foreign crisis prompted many officers to look to their own prospects with the intention of deserting their regular units.[9] The glacial rate of promotion in the 1870s and 1880s only reinforced the determination to seize the opportunity for higher rank when it next presented itself. Upton would have to wait until 1880—fourteen years later—before he once again wore the shoulder straps of a colonel, a rank that he had first held in 1862.[10]

In the meantime, Upton sought to improve the quality of the military profession. After enjoying a honeymoon to Europe paid for by the royalties of *Tactics,* Upton served for several months as the acting commander of the 18th Infantry at Fort McPherson, Georgia. For a regiment with so many veterans, the unit was in a poor state. Though most of the junior officers were former volunteers, Upton found that they were collectively in need of "elementary instruction." He was dismayed that veterans should lack such basic knowledge, a fault that he attributed to the inattentiveness of their former commanders, particularly the West Pointers. "[I] have always been at a loss how to explain the indifference of our celebrated generals during the war to these two essential elements [tactical drill and discipline] of success," he complained.[11] The problem of an ill-trained regiment, however, was familiar to Upton; he readily resumed the role of drillmaster, a task made even easier now that he had literally written the book on the subject. This happy period ended when the regiment's colonel rejoined the unit, relegating Upton to second-in-command. Unless the commander was lazy or the regiment split into several detachments, neither of which was the case with the 18th Infantry, there was little for a lieutenant colonel to do in garrison.[12]

Fortunately for Upton, he escaped the doldrums of garrison duty to become the commandant of cadets at West Point. Since 1868, he and Wilson had dreamt of returning together to their alma mater, with Wilson as the superintendent and Upton as the commandant. Before he could be considered, Wilson, bored with the peacetime army and unwilling to wait decades for promotion, resigned from the army. But Grant and Sherman both approved of Upton's appointment; in the summer of 1870, just nine years after his graduation, Upton became the second-ranking officer at the academy. The posting was the perfect vehicle for him to continue the work of professionalization began in *Tactics,* for it put him in charge of the training of the generation of officers who would play a key role in the next large war. But first, he would have to address the problem of widespread indiscipline that had developed during the Civil War, when, with the best officers serving in the field armies, the school had been left to a series of caretaker superintendents. The "hazing" of first-year cadets had grown particularly brutal and pervasive.[13]

To address these problems, Upton adopted the fierce motto, "proficiency or hair"—cadets would learn to be officers or be "scalped." He vowed to "send away every trifler who does not appreciate his advantages, and meet the requirements of the profession."[14] After his first year, the lenient superintendent was replaced by Colonel Thomas H. Ruger, a Civil War hero as committed to imposing order as was Upton. "Discipline was very strict," remembered one graduate from the era. "With Gen. Ruger as Superintendent and Gen. Emory Upton as Commandant, it reached heights never seen before or since."[15]

Though Ruger and Upton were unable to eradicate hazing, they made life very difficult for cadets who took part in the practice. Though several decades later Hugh L. Scott would serve as the academy's superintendent, as a cadet he complained that Upton was "ruining the Corps [of Cadets]" because he prevented the upperclassmen from keeping the plebes in a "continual scare." Naturally, in the battle of wills between commandant and cadet, Scott was routinely the loser, spending many days in "light prison" (confinement) for various infractions before nearly being expelled from the academy for hazing. Instead, possibly through the help of an influential uncle, Scott was suspended for the remainder of the academic year and "turned back" to become a member of the following class. For a time after his return to the academy, Scott refused to wear his eyeglasses; he was convinced that Upton—who he assured his mother "looks on me with an evil eye"—would use Scott's poor sight as an excuse to dismiss him from the service. And although Scott would go on to a distinguished career, even serving as the Chief of Staff of the Army for the first months of World War I, as a cadet he might indeed have been one of the "triflers" whom Upton wished to purge.[16]

But Upton was not a mere martinet; he had a more constructive aim than to simply uphold regulations. "I have got a great field for usefulness," he wrote to Wilson, "and I hope to bring the cadets to a high sense of honor."[17]

Soon after arriving at the academy, he decided to invite the senior cadets to his quarters for fraternal conversations over dinner, even though this was contrary to the academy's tradition of separation between officers and cadets. According to one graduate, "cadets generally disliked [the officers], lampooned them in private, and gave them credit for nothing," identifying only Upton and one instructor as exceptions. Upton, he remembered, spoke to the cadets in the same way that his father tried to give advice.[18] The academy did not require the cadets' good will or consent, and Upton could have maintained discipline and imparted knowledge of tactics in a completely impersonal way. But perhaps reflecting some of what he learned as a commander of volunteers, Upton believed that graduates would be more receptive to lessons from an officer who they felt was genuine and interested in their personal development. It is impossible to determine how many of the nearly four hundred graduates who spent at least one of their cadet years under Upton's tutelage thought of him as a professional exemplar. But he did make a great effort to mold the cadets to his professional ideal, and many of those former pupils would play an important role when the army went through perhaps its greatest period of reorganization and reform.

In addition to his duties as commandant, Sherman directed Upton to undertake the task of "assimilating" the tactics of infantry, artillery, and cavalry so that all used a common set of movements and commands. Just several years after the publication of his infantry manual, Upton had no desire to revisit the subject, particularly because an earlier effort led by John M. Schofield unleashed a storm of criticism but no workable tactics. But Sherman was insistent that the work be pushed through as quickly as possible, even though it consumed nearly all of Upton's time outside of his normal duties.[19] The work, however, brought the two closer together. They corresponded regularly, and in one letter the commanding general's mock sympathy—"sorry you have had so much work, but you can stand it"—suggests a fraternal warmth toward his protégé.[20] Later, Sherman sent Upton a copy of his newly published *Memoirs,* a thoughtful gesture that seems to have meant much to Upton, particularly as Sherman praised *Tactics* in the conclusion. Moreover, Sherman aided Upton by sending one of his aides to West Point to assist the work and through expressions of support. "You are working more for yourself, than for me, as I hardly ever expect to master a new tactics [manual]," Sherman assured him. "I would much rather have you make them conform strictly to your own opinions rather than mine."[21]

Sherman probably found it easy to place such trust in Upton because, in contrast to their opinions on the quality of generalship, the two interpreted the tactical lessons of the Civil War in much the same way. In *Memoirs,* Sherman's description of the effect of breech-loading weapons on tactics coincided perfectly with Upton's views: "The only change that breech-loading arms will probably make in the art and practice of war will be to . . . still further "thin out" the lines of attack . . . . The more we improve the fire-arm the more will be the necessity for good organization, good discipline and intelligence on the part of the individual soldier and officer."[22]

The two also agreed that tactics had to conform to the composition of the wartime armies. This applied as much to the physical form of the manuals as to their intellectual content. Sherman directed that they should be small enough to fit in a coat pocket so that volunteer officers could keep them close for easy reference. He also mandated the inclusion of an appendix covering basic tasks that were familiar to regulars but would be novel for volunteers, such as guard mount, posting sentinels, and parades. But the changes were not solely for the benefit of citizen-soldiers; the principal reason for assimilated tactics was to make it easier for officers to command units of other arms, a rare occurrence in peace but something that happened frequently during the Civil War. Sherman even considered requiring line officers to buy the drill regulations of the other arms and to periodically test their knowledge of all three arms. In sum, the Civil War had taught both Sherman and Upton that clever tactics were of no use if they could not be mastered by the officers and soldiers who were to implement them.[23]

Yet Civil War veterans were prisoners as well as beneficiaries of their war experience. It was natural that such a monumental conflict would forever define war for those who lived through it. Upton was particularly prone to this, for professionally he knew little else. He had gone from West Point to the war and then spent most of his postwar career in military education and special duty. Insulated from the reality of the army's constabulary duties, he would concentrate solely on the problems of fighting another great war.

· · · · ·

In five years at West Point, Upton advanced his agenda of professional reform in several ways: He mentored several hundred cadets, improved and extended his tactics, and deepened his relationship with Sherman. His experiences prior to coming to the academy had prepared him well for his duties as commandant. But as he left the academy in 1875, Upton began a new period in his career that would take him from the familiar fields of leadership and tactics into the more treacherous and uncertain realm of politics and military policy. This new phase began when Upton approached Sherman with the request that he be sent on a tour to observe foreign militaries. The general immediately took to the idea; in the 1840s, he had hoped for a similar opportunity. The armies of Asia particularly fascinated Sherman, who imagined that these exotic locales might offer fresher insights than the oft-studied European armies. Perhaps living vicariously through Upton, Sherman drew up detailed itineraries for travels in "India, Afghanistan, Persia, Kohkand, Bokhara, Turkistan &c." With such enthusiastic high-level backing, the penny-pinching War Department allotted funds for Upton and two other officers to embark on a tour of Asia and Europe.[24]

The trio departed westward from San Francisco in August 1875. They spent approximately a month in Japan, another month in China, and then two months in India. Though Sherman imagined them traveling through the Khyber Pass, the British viceroy could not guarantee their safety and warned against trusting the "savage or semi-independent tribes who dwell in Afghanistan." The party went to Persia by sea instead, then overland through the Caucasus and into Europe. The other unplanned detour was into the Balkans, where the Serbian Army was reorganizing during an armistice in the Serbian-Turkish War. This unexpected opportunity partially compensated for the disappointment of missing the German grand maneuvers, which they could not attend due to the mistake of an inexperienced ambassador. They did, however, have the opportunity to study the German military education system.[25]

These observations were useful when on his return to the United States, Upton was put in charge of instruction in military history and strategy at the Artillery School. That assignment was meant to allow Upton to compile the report on his trip with access to a good library, but it also provided the opportunity to immediately apply some of what he had learned abroad to the army's woeful system of postgraduate military education. Aside from the Artillery School, there was only one other such institution, the recently reestablished Engineer School at Fort Totten. This underwhelming educational establishment was not only small but also outdated. Fort Monroe was still run in accord with the old pattern borrowed from the French military schools of the previous century. The narrow curriculum was meant to improve the technical skills of the army's most junior officers, a limited aim that was sufficient so long as the army operated in only small detachments. But as the Civil War had demonstrated, large-scale warfare required even young officers to master skills far more complex than properly siting a gun. A comparison of the early careers of the West Point classes of 1846 and May 1861—classes who graduated at the outset of a war—conveys how radically different the experience was for young officers in the Civil War. The class of 1846, which included George B. McClellan, Thomas J. Jackson, and George B. Pickett, served credibly in Mexico, with thirty-seven of its fifty-nine members receiving brevet promotions for valorous or otherwise commendatory service. Nevertheless, at war's end the surviving members of that class were all still lieutenants. In contrast, of the forty-five graduates of the class of May 1861, three—Upton, Judson Kilpatrick, and Adelbert Ames—were generals commanding divisions; another fifteen served as field grade officers; and among the remainder were seven aides-de-camp, two corps chief engineers, and one corps inspector general.[26]

At Fort Monroe, Upton wanted to replicate aspects of the European education systems that prepared officers for high command by also teaching them advanced tactics, staff operations, and strategy. The addition of a second year to the Artillery School course allowed Upton to introduce instruction in the "art of war" that included history, strategy, and law. He also ensured that the young artillerymen practiced infantry tactics as well. Upton was preparing the students to replicate his own Civil War experience, in which he commanded units from all three arms—not just the artillery— and at the higher echelons.[27]

The Artillery School curriculum, however, quickly reverted back to the earlier antebellum type following Upton's departure from Fort Monroe in 1880. Even Peter S. Michie, Upton's friend and the compiler of his posthumous papers, wanted the Artillery School to focus only on "science and art of Artillery alone." In Michie's opinion it was "neither proper nor desirable to teach there the rudiments of an academic education nor the principles of generalship."[28] There were several reasons for this rejection of Upton's vision for military education. One problem was that with only a single postgraduate course in an officer's entire career, general military education came at the expense of technical training that was still necessary, particularly for artillerymen in a time of rapid technological change. Because most officers did not share Upton's dismal appraisal of Civil War generalship, they were less inclined to sacrifice what they considered more essential training in skills necessary for more immediate needs. This was particularly true after the end of Reconstruction brought a period that was in terms of foreign affairs quite placid. Aside from brief and not entirely convincing war scares with Chile and the United Kingdom, there seemed little prospect of a large war. As such, Quartermaster General Montgomery Meigs, an unusually thoughtful officer, grumbled to Sherman that "too many men who have only an infinitesimal chance of ever commanding more than a Company spend their time in studying grand strategy instead of the duties of a Company officer."[29] There was a great deal of truth in this assertion. In 1893, an article in *United Service* magazine reported that the average age of a first lieutenant was thirty-six years, six months old.[30] Thus, many of the West Pointers who studied under Upton as cadets in the early 1870s and then again as lieutenants at the Artillery School in the late 1870s had still not even reached the rank of captain by the early 1890s. Their careers looked nothing like the meteoric rise of Upton and his contemporaries; and with exciting advances in ordnance, explosives, and electricity, it seemed far more useful for the Artillery School students and faculty to turn their attention to those fields. This pattern of favoring immediate, tangible needs rather than the esoteric, abstract demands of a future war would continually reassert itself in American military professional education.[31]

* * * * *

To that point in his career, Upton had been a commander, tactician, and educator. But at Fort Monroe, he added the role for which he would be most remembered, as an advocate for military reform. His entry into the field of military policy came by way of the official report of his trip, which through diligent effort was ready for publication in 1878 under the title *The Armies of Asia and Europe*. Naturally, the author of the army's drill regulations paid considerable attention to foreign tactics, but he eschewed the "details of arms and equipments" that had been the principal focus of other officers who had gone abroad.[32] He had no interest in finding a design for a better saddle or a new artillery piece, for he believed that minor improvements contributed little so long as the country neglected military preparations for war. In *Armies*, he hoped to draw the attention of the public and its elected representatives to the need for professional reform and a better method of raising and organizing armies.

These ambitions made *Armies* more of a polemic than a faithful record of what Upton had seen, which he privately admitted.[33] Though each of his ten chapters was putatively a description of the military institutions of one of the countries that he had visited, they all also contained elements of a morality play of military policy virtue or vice. The exotic garb clothing his arguments barely concealed the American targets of his attacks. The late Qing dynasty, for instance, served as a surrogate for the problems created by state control of the militia. It required only a substitution of *state* for *province* to apply his description of China to the United States: "The wide discretion given to the governors inevitably tends to destroy uniformity in the army. In no two provinces are the troops armed and equipped alike, and, according to the greater or less conservatism of the governors, the troops stand still or advance."[34] This was contrasted with the centralization of Meiji Restoration Japan, which he commended for "substituting a national force in the place of the undisciplined hordes, voluntarily furnished by the clans under the old *régime*."[35] Upton's purpose left little room for nuanced discussion of the political, cultural, legal, and social structures that shaped military policy both in the United States and abroad. Though he recognized the role played by local factors, he seems to have regarded them as little more than obstacles to a rationalist approach based on purely military considerations.

Upton commented favorably on many aspects of the various European armies, but in Germany he took note of those components that made it probably the most effective military in the world. He admired their reserve system, which could quickly mobilize a large, trained army. Upton was equally impressed with the German general staff, which matched the country's fine field armies with a rigorously selected and trained cadre of commanders and staff officers. He particularly admired the method of selecting officers recognized as the most proficient by their fellows rather than politicians. The elite thus selected were then given wide experience in both line and staff functions supplemented by a broad education combining practical application and theoretical study. He hoped to foster the same broad professionalism in the United States.[36]

The most novel idea in *Armies,* however, was Upton's plan for a new system of raising armies, which was largely a native concept inspired by the Civil War. Upton proposed the establishment of a federal force of citizen-soldiers to replace the state militia as the principal means of mobilization. He conceded that the regular army would not be large enough to sustain a war on its own, but he also believed that the states had proven their inability to maintain viable military forces. Unsurprisingly, Upton thus turned to the model of professional leadership and volunteer manpower that he knew so well from his Civil War experience. But he also wanted to correct what had been from his point of view the major deficiencies in the Union effort: the governors' desire to raise new regiments rather than provide replacements for those in the field; the influence of local politics on the selection and promotion of officers; the confusion owing to the creation of units once war began; and the lack of prior military training for officers and noncommissioned officers.[37]

Upton proposed to address most of these problems by creating a skeletal structure of volunteers organized by the War Department called the National Volunteers. Each regiment of the army would have one or two battalions apiece of regulars and National Volunteers, all serving under the command of a regular army colonel and sharing a regimental depot. The depot was to serve as a recruiting station for the regular battalions and an armory and training base for the National Volunteers, who would have officers selected and partly trained by the federal government in peacetime. The common regional identity of each regiment would bring regulars, volunteers, and community together in a way that Upton hoped would "nationalize and popularize" the army. When war came, Upton expected that as in 1861 there would be an early surge of enthusiasm. He thought it likely that eager recruits would quickly fill the National Volunteers battalions, but with the common depot and regional affiliation the excess could be diverted to the regular battalions. "The whole regiment would thus become volunteers," Upton wrote, and would therefore "go forth with the sympathy of the entire community, and differ only from the volunteer regiments of the late war in having at the beginning trained officers to lead every company."[38] This was the vision that linked all of his various writings and activities: The tactics manuals provided a system of fighting suited to volunteers with modern arms; the education system provided regulars ready to command large volunteer armies; and the National Volunteers plan provided a framework for bringing the two together quickly.

Upton's vision and its constituent elements of tactics, education, and policy so clearly drew on his Civil War experiences that it is worth noting just how far the war had moved the regulars from their prewar assumptions. In 1861, Winfield Scott fought desperately to preserve the integrity of the regular army, even at the cost of denying regular officers leadership of the vast host of volunteers. But in 1878, having experienced the system that so terrified Scott, Upton regarded the dissolution of the regular army within the mass of wartime volunteers as not only normal but even desirable. In the abstract, Sherman and Upton both preferred the draft and a large army to reliance on volunteers; but realizing that this was politically impossible and knowing from personal experience that volunteers could serve as the basis for capable armies, they resolved to develop the best possible organization consistent with American political and cultural realities.[39] As Upton wrote to Congressman James A. Garfield, "Whatever military record I have was won as a volunteer, and like all of our people I believe in the future we shall have to look to the volunteers whenever great emergencies arise. Only let us give them a good organization."[40] So long as that good organization put professional soldiers at its head, Upton cared little if the regular army as an institution dissolved in war.

Indeed, Upton was so focused on preparing for a large conflict that he might have been too willing to sacrifice the interests of the peacetime regular army. The National Volunteers plan would have required a peacetime authorization several thousand soldiers less than what was actually maintained throughout most of the late nineteenth century.[41] This indifference to the demands of frontier was a luxury of Upton's unusual assignments, which insulated him from the immediate concerns of the army's peacetime routine; with the exception of a few months early in 1870, Upton spent the entire decade away from troops. From this cloistered position, it was possible to take the extreme view that in peace the army was nothing "but a school of training to prepare officers and men for efficient service in time of war."[42] In fact, Congress and the public expected that the army would do much more than simply prepare for war: Keep peace on the frontier and borders, guard the coasts, police labor strikes, maintain and improve rivers and harbors, and execute other sundry tasks such as exploration. With his greater responsibilities, Sherman had a more expansive perspective. Although he agreed in principle that the army should serve as a school for war, the commanding general knew that Upton's simplistic dichotomy of distinct states of war and peace did not represent the American reality. For just as Upton was completing *Armies,* Sherman lectured a congressman that "the words 'In time of peace,' are obscure, for we are not now at peace, and never have been in my memory. There is now war, bitter cruel war, in the vast region west of

Minnesota and north of the Pacific road, and there is a condition of semi-war on our Mexican border, which will increase rather than diminish with time."[43]

Of course, Upton knew that the army was continually at work on the frontiers, but he was contemptuous of the common view within the officer corps that active service there was better preparation for conventional war than classroom education or peacetime training. "'Bush whacking,' and Indian fighting, with one or two companies, do not qualify an officer for the position of general," he scoffed. Yet Upton was aware enough to realize that this view was in the minority and so presciently predicted to a friend that "twenty years hence, in case of a great war, you will find our higher grades filled by men whose sole claim will be bravery, and success, in action which will not merit the title of a skirmish."[44]

In order for his ideas to alter policy, however, Upton realized that he had to take a more direct approach than sly criticism routed through foreign lands. Sharp critiques of the Qing Dynasty would not alter deeply entrenched public opinion. But *Armies* was sponsored by the War Department, and in an official report even Upton had to temper his arguments. Writing privately, he would have greater latitude to make his case that bad policy had made earlier wars unnecessarily costly in both money and lives. He hoped that by framing the matter as one of cost and benefit, he could appeal to the pragmatic natures of lawmakers, convincing them that skimping on military preparations made wars longer and ultimately far more expensive.[45]

In late 1877, Upton proposed a second book—*Military Policy of the United States*—which would expand on the theme that "in every civilized country success in war depends upon the organization and application of its military resources."[46] He blithely told Sherman that the new work would be complete in 1878, the same year that *Armies* was published. The commanding general had a better sense than Upton of the difficulty of the task that he was undertaking. "Now you are on delicate ground," Sherman cautioned. "This publication . . . by an army officer, who by members of Congress is construed to be their paid servant[,] arraigning Congress for a long series of foolish, extravagant, and wicked acts, will bring about your ears a clatter which you may not be able to stand."[47] Nonetheless, Sherman gave the project his blessing, for he also hoped that *Military Policy* might convince Congress to become more charitable to the army.[48]

Sherman's mixed feelings reflected his own largely unhappy experiences with politics during what was arguably the most difficult extended period in

American civil-military relations. Since 1861, regulars had been subject to continual criticism, often from multiple parts of the political spectrum. During the war, radical Republicans in Congress had been relentless in their attacks against regulars, whom they felt were as a group insufficiently zealous in prosecuting the war and in undermining slavery. Sherman was one of the generals who endured several periods of intense criticism, the last coming at the very end of the war. Despite having achieved fame with his "March to the Sea," Sherman exceeded his authorities while negotiating an ill-advised armistice with Confederate General Joseph E. Johnston in North Carolina. The excitable secretary of war, Edwin Stanton, shaken by Lincoln's assassination, suggested publicly that Sherman might have accepted Confederate bribes in exchange for such generous terms. Sherman retaliated by refusing the secretary's outstretched hand on the reviewing stand of the grand victory parade in the capital several days later. This public snub brought the affair to a close, but it was a portent of the tempestuous years to come.[49]

The politics of victory were complex; as President Andrew Johnson and Congress dueled for control of policy, Republicans sought to build a political base in the South by displacing local whites who wanted to maintain their social and political dominance under the standard of the Democrats. As the principal agent of Reconstruction in the South, the army found itself in the midst of both of these national feuds and many smaller local ones as well. Every action seemed to bring approbation and enmity from some quarter.[50]

For Grant and Sherman, the greatest difficulty was navigating a safe course between the president and Congress. In 1867, congressional Republicans desiring a harsher policy toward the South passed several laws that limited the president's authority over both Secretary of War Stanton and Commanding General Grant. When Johnson defied the law by attempting to remove Stanton from office, Grant and Sherman were plunged unwillingly into the midst of a constitutional crisis. Grant hoped to evade a break with either side, but when forced to choose sided with Congress. After Sherman made several ill-judged comments, Johnson hoped that he might win Sherman's support even if he had lost Grant and so proposed placing Sherman at the head of a new military command in the capital. Only with some difficulty was Sherman able to avoid being swept up in the president's vaguely menacing Praetorian scheme. Though the crisis eventually passed without an irredeemable rupture of civil-military relations, the extraordinary

correspondence between Grant and Sherman as they were forced to selec-
tively defy the president documents one of the lowest points in civilian control of the military in America.[51]

Sherman naturally believed that Grant's election to the White House in
1868 meant a reprieve for him and the army, but he was disappointed. Grant
allowed successive secretaries of war to marginalize his old comrade to such
an extent that in a fit of frustration Sherman removed his headquarters to
St. Louis. He spent most of his nineteen months of self-imposed exile engaged
in writing his memoirs. Even after Secretary of War William W. Belknap was
removed from office for corruption, the petulant general returned to Washington only after repeated pleas from his brother, other generals, and the
new secretary of war.[52]

The presidential election of 1876 ensnared Sherman in yet another constitutional crisis. Both parties resorted to manipulation and intimidation
where they could, putting the legitimacy and outcome of the election in
doubt for several months. Extremists threatened to install their favorite candidate by force, an act that would have essentially resumed the Civil War.
Sherman quietly prepared to maintain order in the capital in case of violence, even while resisting calls for him to serve as a forceful arbiter. Eventually, the crisis was averted with the quintessential backroom deal that brought
President Rutherford B. Hayes to office, the army out of the last two occupied states in the South, and the Republicans ceding political control of the
South to the Democrats.[53]

But although the "Bargain of '77" avoided a catastrophic political frac-
ture, it also created the conditions in which neither party could prevail; from
1874 until 1896, government was divided except for three two-year inter-
vals. One consequence of extended political stalemate was that the evolution
of the federal government as a whole was stymied.[54] But the army was particularly prone to being used as a pawn in larger political games, or as the
Army and Navy Journal lamented, to be "ground between the upper and
nether millstones of Democratic and Republican struggles for power."[55]

During the election of 1876, federal troops guarding Southern polling
places had prevented the widespread intimidation employed against African-
Americans elsewhere. Thus, one of the Democrats' chief aims was to restrict
the use of the regular army in law enforcement. Failing to win any concessions from Republicans, the Democrats blocked the 1877 appropriations
bill. This left officers and soldiers without pay during what happened to be

one of the army's busiest summers of the late nineteenth century, with the pursuit of Chief Joseph and his Nez Perce across the Northwest and the use of thousands of soldiers to maintain order throughout the Midwest and East during the Great Railroad Strike. Though the middle and upper classes approved of the use of troops against "anarchists" and "communists," most officers detested domestic policing duties. When the strike began, Sherman was inspecting western forts and ignored the president's order to return, leaving Winfield Scott Hancock, commander of the forces in the East, to supervise the operation. The use of troops at home also irritated Democrats, who renewed their efforts to restrict the use of federal troops within the United States. When Congress resumed session, Henry B. Banning—the Democratic chairman of the House Military Affairs Committee and a former volunteer colonel from Ohio—proposed legislation that would have disbanded the regular army if Congress once again failed to appropriate funds. The bill was defeated; but it demonstrated that even after Reconstruction, the political situation of the army was fraught with danger.[56]

Yet the crises of 1877 yielded an unexpected opportunity for military reform in 1878. That year's army appropriations act contained two important provisions. One was the realization of the Democrats' principal aim: It severely restricted the use of federal troops as a *posse comitatus*. In the South, this meant that except under extraordinary circumstances, the maintenance of order was left to local authorities backed by white militiamen responding to a Democratic governor. The second measure of note was the provision for a joint bipartisan committee to report on military reorganization and reform. Presumably, this was the other half of a grand bargain that ceded southern whites freedom from federal interference in exchange for the possibility of reform. From the army's perspective, this compromise was hardly perfect. Both Sherman and Schofield had requested military representation on any such commission, but the one ordered would have only members of Congress. The chairman, West Pointer and former general Senator Ambrose E. Burnside, was sympathetic, but the commission also included the army's recent nemesis Representative Banning as well as two former Confederate generals.[57] "The Rebs whom we beat in the War will conquer us in politics," Sherman groused.[58]

Sherman reacted warily to this ambiguous development. Though he promptly offered Burnside assistance and sent a number of documents, including Upton's recently published *Armies,* the general seems to have had low expectations for what the commission might achieve. In the letter accompanying *Armies,* Sherman directed Burnside's attention to the chapter on the British Army in India. That was significant, for of all the military establishments that met with Upton's approval, the British army in India was most like that of the United States. In contrast to the massive continental armies preparing for cataclysmic conflict, the British forces on the subcontinent operated in accord with the imperative of maintaining white control over the vast native armies, a legacy of the great mutiny several decades before. That colonial role required only slightly more elaborate systems of education and organization than that already used by their American cousins serving as a frontier constabulary. Sherman seems to have been chiefly interested in the British practice of rotating officers between the staff and line of the army, which was the focus of the chapter that he commended to Burnside.[59] Of the many ideas contained in Upton's work, it was one of the least daring. Yet it is not clear whether Sherman would have preferred more ambitious reform but was modifying his ambitions to match political reality or whether he was simply content with the present system and wanted only minor changes.

Aside from Sherman and Upton, the Burnside committee considered the written testimony of dozens of officers and thousands of pages of documents. The result was a massive bill of 724 sections touching on nearly every aspect of army organization, administration, and military justice. As Schofield ruefully noted, with so much contained in a single piece of legislation, "it attacks or threatens everybody in the army . . . . How can anybody advocate a "reform" which may leave him out in the cold and at best will stop all chances for promotion for a long time? How many men care for sound or unsound principles of administration under such circumstances as these?"[60] Line officers cheered the provision for rotation between staff and line, but this was vehemently opposed by the staff bureaus who warned that their functions would suffer if performed by officers with insufficient expertise. Junior officers frustrated by slow promotion welcomed the proposed mandatory retirement at the age of sixty-two, but older officers protested the injustice of being cast aside after a lifetime of service. Idealistic reformers applauded the proposal for merit promotion to the field grade ranks, while cynics questioned the army's ability to measure merit in peace.[61]

From his vantage atop the army, Sherman thought the reform proposals were on the whole beneficial and complimented Burnside for his work. But the commanding general was still torn, for the bill was a grand compromise between Burnside and Banning: professional reform in exchange for a significant reduction of the army's strength in peacetime. Though he liked the reforms, Sherman feared that the army was already at the lower limit of its tolerable strength; further reductions, he felt, would seriously compromise the army's ability to guard coast, frontier, and border.[62]

Sherman solicited the opinions of his trusted advisors, but they too were split. Phil Sheridan, the general responsible for policing the frontier, gave his "most hearty approval" to the new system of administration, particularly the better delineation of powers for the commanding general—a position that he anticipated would soon be his. But Sheridan could not support the overall bill, which reduced the cavalry that he depended on for his campaigns. Those viewing the matter from vantages in the East tended to be more sanguine about the reductions. General Winfield Scott Hancock, writing from his headquarters in New York, offered cautious support. Upton seems to have been disappointed that the bill did not go as far as he hoped, but he approved of most of the reforms while also implying that Sherman should seize the fleeting political opportunity: "Congress has never shown so favorable or friendly a disposition before." From West Point, Schofield offered the strongest support, likely because Burnside had incorporated so many of Schofield's own ideas into the bill. Reversing an earlier position, by late 1878 he had come to conclude that the immediate difficulties that would result from a reduction in the army's strength were worth a reform that would "enable the country to make some adequate preparation for war."[63]

Like his generals, Sherman was torn by the choice between the demands of the present and the need to better prepare for future wars. Furthermore, his long involvement with politics left him wary of Congress. In the end, Sherman did little to help the bill. After expressing tepid support, he left the capital on a trip through the South, revisiting many of the scenes of his past glories. Sherman evidently expected that his opinion, no matter how strenuously voiced, mattered little, a cynicism resulting from decades of hard experience in politics. Though understandable, his withdrawal nonetheless reflected poorly on him as a military leader. It was ironic that he escaped his duty in Washington by touring battlefields where he had ordered men to their deaths in desperate assaults.[64]

Meanwhile in the capital, military policy once again was subordinated to other domestic issues. Many officers expressed their preferences for or against, with many in the staff bureaus lobbying particularly vigorously against the bill. Yet both parties had matters that were of far greater concern to most politicians. In the Democratic House of Representatives, the initial bill was defeated by a narrow vote. A less ambitious version passed after the inclusion of several amendments further restricting the domestic use of the army, but reopening that contentious issue might have been enough in itself to doom the measure in the Republican Senate. Yet there were many Republicans who were willing to see the military reform fail, because they were at the time locked in an internecine struggle between "Stalwarts," who clung to the Reconstruction strategy of building a political base in the South, and "Half-Breeds," who recognized the Democrats' hegemony there and wanted to reorient the party around northern industrialists. To do so, the Half-Breeds set out to break the power of the Stalwarts' political barons, state party bosses like Senator Roscoe Conkling of New York. In an era of corrupt patronage politics, these bosses derived considerable power from their control over federal officeholders, and the New York Custom House gave Conkling the richest single source of such power within the entire country. At approximately the same time that Congress was considering the Burnside bill, Secretary of the Treasury John Sherman—brother of the general and one of the leading Half-Breeds—arranged for the appointments of several reformers to important positions within the New York Custom House. Their introduction of competitive examinations for all new vacancies had the desired effect of weakening Conkling. This cynical use of merit-based reform politicized the issue just as the Burnside commission was considering making similar changes to officer promotions. The Stalwarts feared that allowing the spread of such systems elsewhere in the government would further erode their power base, so the presumably army-friendly Republican-controlled Senate stripped out many of the reforms that had passed the hostile Democrat-controlled House. So although the political rhetoric in the 1870s was still rich with the old ideological language of opposition to standing armies, the fate of military reform likely had much less to do with arcane topics that were of interest mainly to those in uniform, such as staff rotation and lineal promotion, and were instead largely determined by larger issues of federal versus state authority and the control of patronage. With such a fine balance of political power, both parties were willing to use army matters as pawns to achieve tactical advantage in the political struggle that was of far more importance to them.[65]

But underneath political deadlock, society was undergoing a profound change from traditional personalized customs to new impersonal systems. That was, in broad terms, the difference between the Gilded Age and the Progressive Era. Naturally, such a momentous transition was neither instantaneous nor absolute. The broad trend, however, manifested itself in different ways across all aspects of society: in government, the patronage of party machines slowly yielded to an impartial bureaucracy manned by civil servants; in the private sector, unregulated free practitioners were subsumed by national credentialing associations for professions such as law and medicine; in the army, individual autonomy would be slowly subordinated to a general staff dictating a centrally determined notion of professionalism.

These different elements were complementary, as each drew on a similar desire for impartial expertise and efficiency. Upton embodied the commonality among these; for even as he was a pioneer in military professionalization, he also was an ardent believer in the need for political reform. Deeply troubled by the moral degradation of the Republican Party during the Grant administration, Upton wanted term limits for elected leaders and a professional civil service in order to rid administration of political influence, just as he hoped to free military operations of the same corrupting influences. Some historians have interpreted Upton as antidemocratic, but in the 1870s one did not have to be a uniformed militarist to regard politicians as untrustworthy stewards who would betray the public interest for personal or political gain; that was the general perception. So Upton, like other good government reformers, represented the middle and professional classes' technocratic response to rampant nepotism and corruption. Whether military or civilian professionals, these reformers were applying systematic processes to improve their own spheres of activity and naturally saw the benefits of applying the same concepts to government. They achieved some early victories, such as the Pendleton Civil Service Act of 1883, but nearly two more decades would pass before the movement would burst forth in the Progressive Era. Not coincidently, that was when many of the military reforms proposed by Upton would at last be realized. But in Upton's own time, the political and cultural conditions were not yet right for sweeping change in either the military or the civilian sphere.[66]

·　·　·　·　·

Against this stormy backdrop of societal change, Upton continued his work on *Military Policy.* Unlike with *Tactics* and *Armies,* the work went slowly, even with Sherman's prodding. Upton blamed his lack of progress on his duties at the Artillery School. He said nothing of the incapacitating headaches that came with increasing frequency.[67] But there were also inherent difficulties in such an ambitious project. American military history was an unwieldy vehicle for advancing his argument that "in every civilized country success in war depends upon the organization and application of its military resources."[68] Some of the work was easy. With his extensive research, Upton found many examples of the strategic and managerial failures of presidents, secretaries of war, and political generals ignorant of the military art, and he documented them with verve. Such instances supported his claim that "all of our wars have been prolonged for want of judicious and economical preparation, and often when the people have impatiently awaited the tidings of victory, those of humiliating defeat have plunged the nation into mourning."[69] Yet Upton's purpose was to convince the public that they should entrust professional soldiers with the country's preparations for war. This meant that he could not simply make the essentially negative argument that past policies were a failure. He also had to make the positive case that giving the regulars greater control over policy and operations would have yielded better results.

The cost of his work as a polemicist was that Upton had to make arguments that were antithetical to his work as a reformer. The latter role was built on the premise that "in every military system which has triumphed in modern war . . . . generals have not been left to acquire knowledge of their profession on the field of maneuver in time of peace; they have been granted all the advantages of war academies, where they and the members of their staffs have been taught in their minutest details all the principles of the military art."[70] But more than any other officer, Upton realized that the United States had never had anything resembling the European war academies—even as he wrote *Military Policy,* he was endeavoring to create the foundation of just such a system. So, his use of American military history placed him in the awkward intellectual position of justifying policies for a professional army that did not yet exist by drawing on examples from the army of the past, which he privately thought had been professionally deficient. When Upton touted the achievements of George Washington and Winfield Scott as proof of the superiority of the regulars, he was tacitly endorsing the view that high command required no special training—a view that was antithetical to all of his work as a military educator. Indeed, Washington and Scott were better exemplars of the natural military genius touted by John A. Logan.

Upton's conflation of *professional* in the sense of a full-time soldier with *professional* in the sense of someone formally trained and educated in the art of war gave *Military Policy* an ahistoric quality. Though he hailed milestones such as the founding of West Point, Upton yet described full-time soldiers as having always been unquestionably superior to citizen-soldiers since the time of the Revolution. If so, then logically there was little to no need for professional reform. This was an obvious flaw. When *Military Policy* was at last published in 1904, President Theodore Roosevelt—a politician who was unusually sympathetic to military reform—reported being "delighted with Upton's book" even though it was "one-sided." The president noted that two generals most responsible for the failed invasion of Canada in 1813 were regulars, although the militia produced far more capable leaders like Jacob Brown and Andrew Jackson. "Upton," Roosevelt wrote, "should have remembered to qualify continually what he said by remembering that mere length of service, that mere calling troops 'regulars,' amount to nothing whatever."[71]

Yet Upton's treatment of the Civil War, the experience that was so central to his own professional identity, was even more deeply flawed. The chapters on 1861 gave a quite different account of First Bull Run than Upton portrayed in letters at the time of the battle, in which he praised the soldiers and denounced the generals. But in *Military Policy*, it was General Irvin McDowell—an "able and judicious commander"—who was let down by the untrained and undisciplined soldiers. By coyly avoiding a description of the battle itself, Upton was able to imply that the panicked retreat was the cause of the defeat, even though the battle had already been lost by that point. He even suggested that General Patterson, the feeble commander in the Shenandoah who had allowed the Confederate army to reinforce the defenders at Manassas, was blameless. Instead, Upton ascribed the defeat to the public and its "fatal delusion, that an army animated by patriotism needed neither instruction nor discipline to prepare it for battle."[72] There was truth in that assertion, for the hubris of the time had made clear-eyed strategic calculation nearly impossible. Nevertheless, as Upton knew, poor staff work, incomplete reconnaissance, and the inability of commanders to coordinate units or the different arms were more pertinent causes of the defeat; all were endemic weaknesses among the regulars throughout the war, a truth that he acknowledged in private correspondence.

But in *Military Policy,* Upton perpetuated the excuse already advanced in Sherman's *Memoirs* and likely prevalent throughout the officer corps: The politicians' long neglect of the military put regulars into an impossible position in 1861, and therefore civilians were to blame for the early defeats.[73] Historian William Skelton has noted that the "myth of victory" built on the campaigns of 1814 was the basis for an early belief in the superiority of regulars. For the Civil War generation, First Bull Run provided a "myth of defeat" that served the same function. Attributing the blame to politicians and the public allowed the regulars to avoid acknowledging that they had not been ready for the responsibilities that had suddenly been thrust on them. Though personally Upton was not blind to the many professional deficiencies of the regulars, by fostering this blinkered appraisal of the early war, he encouraged complacency among the officer corps.

Upton continued this narrative of civilian interference into his discussion of the war in 1862. Once again, this required him to interpret events in a way quite different than he had at the time. Until writing *Military Policy,* Upton had never held George B. McClellan in high regard as a commander, and the badly managed Peninsular Campaign was an unlikely example to cause Upton to alter his opinion. McClellan had undertaken a bold amphibious maneuver with great bombast only to exercise excessive caution once he arrived; the victim of a predicament that he had created. Yet throughout the campaign, McClellan continually complained that Lincoln and Secretary of War Stanton were failing to support him properly and hindering his efforts. Upton chose to accept this argument, and so unconvincingly cast Stanton as the meddling politician who undermined the competent general.[74]

This selective interpretation of the Peninsular Campaign was driven by the belief—common among regulars in the late nineteenth century—that the secretary of war should be limited to oversight of army administration and that the commanding general should be responsible for all operational matters, answering directly to the president. Such a change would diminish the secretary of war to the point that he could, in Upton's phrase, be placed in the "pocket" of the commanding general.[75] Because of such views, historian Russell Weigley has labeled Upton the single most "destructive" influence in American civil-military relations.[76] That overstates Upton's role. Generals since the time of Andrew Jackson had sought greater autonomy from the secretary of war. Moreover, there were valid grounds to question the role of the secretary of war in the military hierarchy. Most troubling, of course, was

Stanton's usurpation of the president during Reconstruction. But the case of Belknap also raised concerns, for he had created the space for corruption by marginalizing Sherman. Stanton and Belknap had different motivations, but in both instances the secretary of war—an unelected official—acted contrary to the wishes of the constitutional commander-in-chief.

Aside from the narrow issue of the authorities and powers of the secretary of war in relation to the commanding general, it was true that Upton wanted to insulate the military from civilian control. Part of this was because he shared the general contempt for politicians shared by most Americans in the Gilded Age.[77] His own experiences gave him ample reasons to conclude that politicians were willing to sacrifice military effectiveness, and by extension lives, for political gain: the inept command of the 121st New York by congressman-turned-colonel Richard Franchot; the governor's desire to promote men in the regiment whom Upton thought unworthy; the denial of his own promotion long after he had proven his worth; and the failure to keep regiments filled with replacements. This pattern continued after the war. During his brief command of the Department of the Colorado from 1865 through 1866, Upton had been disgusted by the shameless corruption of politicians and their cronies in Denver. He was also dismayed by the willingness of Grant—his former hero—to listen to "evil councils" and make appointments prejudicial to the army.[78] Thus, Upton had nothing but negative examples of the influence of politics in military affairs. Without any personal experience in high command, he had no countervailing understanding of the necessary role of politics in the forming, equipping, and sustaining of armies. This narrow perspective naturally tilted him toward a visceral mistrust of politics and politicians in a period of widespread corruption.

But there was also a fundamental tension between the assumptions of military professionalism and civilian control. Upton fervently believed that high command was a sacred responsibility that could only be mastered through a lifetime of study and experience, and he had personally suffered for the incompetence of those who lacked the requisite expertise. It is natural that those who have devoted their lives to mastering their fields will not easily accept the possibility that their carefully honed judgments might be casually disregarded by an interloper like Stanton, who, as historian Archer Jones notes, "held the very concept of strategy in contempt, believed that 'patriotic spirit, with resolute courage in officers and men, is a military combination that never failed.'"[79] Though subordination to civilian authority is a necessary component of the American system of governance, it is not hard to understand Upton's emotional response to the hard reality that his life's work might be rendered irrelevant on the whims and predispositions of a politician.

Perhaps the strain of reconciling his views of professionalism and policy took an intellectual toll on Upton, for he began an uncharacteristic retreat from a project already underway. As early as the fall of 1878, he wrote, "If I ever get through with the *Military Policy of the U.S.* I will never touch such a subject again."[80] It was not until late the following year that he finally had completed his history up to 1862, but by then he had lost his relish for the task. In February 1880, Upton wrote Sherman with a proposal to set *Military Policy* aside until political conditions were more favorable and return to the subject of tactics instead. Sherman urged him to continue with *Military Policy*, a suggestion that the younger man could not ignore. But the general could not command enthusiasm, and Upton warned Sherman that the book could not possibly appear any earlier than late 1881.[81]

Though he continued his work on *Military Policy*, Upton's mind had turned to other, more promising areas for reform. He hoped that modest changes to the personnel system would complement his work in military education by reinforcing the need for continuous professional study, creating a livelier officer corps, and providing officers with a greater diversity of experiences. He began to write others interested in military reform. In order to restore some vitality to the officer corps, Upton proposed that the mandatory retirement age be reduced from sixty-four to sixty-two years and that officers must pass an examination demonstrating competence before they could be promoted. He also suggested that promotions be made from the most senior eligible officer in the branch of service rather than just within a regiment. He hoped to reduce the comfortable cliquishness of the regimental system that confined individuals to a narrow range of experience and often bred boredom and complacency.[82]

Despite Sherman's wishes, Upton also returned to the field of tactics. Though he had long noted the power of breech-loading rifles, even he seems to have been startled by the casualties those weapons caused in the recent Russo-Turkish War. Upton considered alternatives to linear tactics, the heresy that he had firmly rejected in 1866. Perhaps lines could be replaced by skirmishers in front of fast-moving columns packed with enough men to absorb casualties and still grind through the defense.[83] But this solution of dispersed units packed with more men posed problems of its own. Larger infantry companies spread out over a greater area would be much harder to command; simply giving orders and receiving reports would be challenging, but so too it would be far more difficult for a commander to understand the situation. To partly offset these difficulties, Upton recommended the addition of two lieutenants to the wartime strength of each company, bringing the total number of officers to five. But he realized that even this was not enough. The new battlefield simply required officers to be better.[84] This made Upton's work with officer education at Fort Monroe all the more important. Just as with generals and staff officers, the army had to systematically produce regimental officers ready for the more-challenging conditions of modern war.

But without a formal military policy, improvements within the regular army could go only so far. In case of a great war, most of the junior officers would come from the militia or volunteers. A key component of Upton's National Volunteers plan had been the means for training these officers in peace. In the absence of some similar policy, it was possible that Upton's new tactics would be too complex for volunteer armies led by officers with little or no training. But although he had been unable to bring about the necessary changes, Upton did at least recognize the interrelationships of weapons technology, tactics, professional education, military policy, and politics. Not all reformers would perceive these connections or realize that a change in one aspect sent ripples throughout all the others.

Upton also began to think of drill regulations in new ways. "You are well aware," he wrote to Sherman, "that thus far in our Infantry Tactics in all arms of the service have been simply a collection of rules for passing from one formation to another. How to fight has been left to actual experience in war."[85] Upton proposed that his next manual include a chapter on "applied tactics" that would go beyond the purely mechanical aspects of fighting—formations, movements, and commands—to discuss the principles underlying the use of those tools. Upton assumed that most regulars, veterans of the Civil War, already possessed this "indispensable knowledge," and therefore he thought of it as principally benefitting militia officers. But Upton was describing something like modern doctrine—the articulation of a philosophy of "how to fight"—that has proven as useful to professionals as to citizen-soldiers, for it allows expertise to be transmitted to those who might lack direct experience. Though that was of obvious benefit when quickly creating mass armies of recent civilians—the situation that was of most concern to Upton—doctrine could also aid regulars who were suddenly required to take on new roles, such as the lieutenant promoted to colonel and placed in command of a regiment of volunteers.

Upton, however, would never finish his new tactics or *Military Policy.* The year 1880 should have been a good one. In July he was promoted to colonel, and several months later he joined his regiment, headquartered at the Presidio of San Francisco, one of the most pleasant stations in the army. But Upton's health was declining rapidly. For many years he had suffered from headaches and a strange, audible ticking noise, as if from a time bomb inside his head. A team of modern doctors speculate that Upton likely suffered from a large, slow-growing tumor in one of his frontal sinuses. This led to a number of physical and psychological problems, including the depression that was most likely the cause of his suicide on 14 March 1881.[86]

Before ending his life with his service revolver, Upton wrote three notes. The first was to his sister, telling her that he preferred to lose his own life rather than to "perpetuate [a tactical] method which might in the future cost a single man his life." The second resigned his commission. The third was apparently a note of explanation that ended in midsentence. "In my efforts to revise the tactics so that they might apply to companies over two hundred strong, I discovered that the double column and the deployment by numbers, when compared with the French method was a failure. The fours, too, I was forced to admit—"[87]

News of the suicide came as a shock to many in the army; some speculated that it was not a suicide at all but "a cowardly assassination." Grant eulogized Upton in the *New York Times:* "As a soldier his career was remarkably brilliant . . . . As a military student and author, Gen. Upton unquestionably ranked far above the average."[88] A modern biographer simply calls him "the epitome of a professional soldier."[89]

Though correct, these statements do not capture the full complexity of Upton. The origins of his worldview were entirely conventional: He inherited his reforming morality from his parents, his idealization of the military profession from West Point, and his lessons from the Civil War. But although none of these influences was unique to Upton, he combined them in a way that was distinct. Always seeking improvement, he fastened on the flaws in the American military profession revealed by the Civil War and in response devised an unusually comprehensive vision of how to prepare for war that encompassed tactics, education, assignments, organization, and military policy. His ideas were far from perfect; his narrow perspective impeded his understanding of the interaction of politics and strategy, while his single-minded focus on large wars put too much emphasis on an atypical use of American military force. Still, even with these faults, few officers saw the interconnections among the various aspects of preparing for war so clearly. As a consequence, though he left a considerable intellectual legacy, it was to be only rarely understood in its entirety, by both adherents and critics alike.

CHAPTER FIVE

Between Old and New

FROM 1869 TO 1895, the army had just three commanding generals: William T. Sherman, Philip H. Sheridan, and John M. Schofield. All three had risen quickly through the ranks during the early portion of the Civil War and so by its end were among the top tier of the Union high command. Naturally, they held a more rosy view of generalship during the war and consequently were more inclined to believe that drastic changes to the army's means of preparing officers for war were not necessary. This conservatism was in spite of the appreciation for intellectual professionalism that each of the three, in his own fashion, displayed. None were unthinking traditionalists. But the Civil War generation, perhaps like other professional generations deriving their identity from conflict, had a fairly limited conceptual horizon. Certainly, individuals disagreed on some matters, such as the efficacy of cavalry or the qualities of a good general. But all of these questions were filtered through the common prism of the Civil War, which even accounting for differences in individual experiences was quite limiting. The war thus served as an intellectual tether limiting how far the profession could stray from past forms.

Though Sherman shared Upton's appreciation for military education in the abstract, their divergent interpretations of the problems of Union command during the war led them to quite different conclusions about what professional schools should be. For instance, though both regarded West Point as essential to military effectiveness—Sherman once warned a congressman that without the academy "our armies would soon degenerate into mobs"—aside from assigning Upton as the commandant to restore discipline, the commanding general repeatedly rebuffed efforts to update the curriculum or training.[1] Yet it was on the subject of postgraduate education that the two disagreed most significantly. As previously discussed, Upton instituted a war college-like curriculum at Fort Monroe meant to instill an appreciation that generalship was a complex art that required deliberate training. Sherman disagreed. During an 1880 visit to Fort Monroe near the end of Upton's tenure there, Sherman told the students, "whoever can command his company well can equally well command a regiment, brigade, division, or Grand Army." Accordingly, he saw no need to provide anything more ambitious than that which he and his contemporaries had received in the antebellum schools of practice. The commanding general then (likely inadvertently) mocked all that his protégé hoped to achieve at Fort Monroe when he told the students, "I suppose you already know all about the duties of a General, but I am more concerned at this moment to have good soldiers, good Colonels, Captains, and Lieutenants."[2]

The next year, Sherman established the Infantry and Cavalry School of Application at Fort Leavenworth, Kansas, and naturally his preference for limited, practical military schooling prevailed there. Indeed, education might not have even been Sherman's foremost objective. He had long sought to concentrate the army along railroads, and the school provided a pretext for assembling a large garrison. He also admitted to the hope that the school might bring him some relief from "the everlasting demands of friends and families" who wanted their "boys" to "escape company duty in the Indian country," by offering a place of relative comfort and safety for those with influential or simply assertive connections.[3] Though this ill-tempered remark was likely partly in jest, Sherman's instructions demonstrated his limited objectives for the school. He thought the proposed curriculum submitted by the first commandant was "too onerous," and so wrote his own plan for the school with much less time in the classroom. Instead, the students were to concentrate on basic duties such as company administration, the posting of guards and sentinels, and making maps and schedules for a march. He also sent the commandant a copy of the remarks given at Fort Monroe the previous year, telling him that it all applied equally to Fort Leavenworth. He wanted the school to prepare subalterns for their immediate duties in a frontier constabulary, not become a *Kriegsakademie* of the prairie.[4]

With Sherman's retirement in 1883, Sheridan became the new commanding general, a post that he held for only five years before his premature death. Though known for his quick temper, aggressive generalship, and exuberant bachelor lifestyle (at least until his marriage to a woman more than twenty years his junior), "Little Phil" was a far shrewder observer of military trends than the stereotype of the dashing but unthinking cavalryman would suggest. As commanding general, he continued Sherman's policies in relation to the existing schools but also added to the education system with the creation of School of Instruction for Cavalry and Light Artillery at Fort Riley, Kansas. Steel, breechloading artillery was replacing bronze muzzle-loaders, but it was unclear how best to use the new guns. Sheridan thought that consolidating much of the light artillery in a single location would allow artillerymen to develop new tactics and procedures. Though slightly different than Sherman's intentions for Forts Monroe and Leavenworth, Sheridan's approach had some precedent within the army. Because there was no organization dedicated to the development of tactics, schools had often been used as sites for such experimentation. Throughout the nineteenth century, West Point cadets had been used to test new infantry tactics; and at the time that Sheridan created the school at Fort Riley, the Artillery School was already serving as a center for research into the larger guns and such advanced technology as electrical engineering. These technical activities were vital and demonstrated that Sherman and Sheridan both appreciated the need for technological adaptation. But neither felt the need to make any similar efforts to produce better generals. In the early 1870s, Sheridan had gone to Europe to observe the Franco-Prussian War, and though he only saw the latter stages, he reported to Sherman that the Prussians had manifested no fighting ability superior to that of the Union during the late war.[5]

Sheridan's successor was not quite so sanguine. Perhaps because Schofield's success during the war was not quite so spectacular as that of his predecessors, he was more willing to consider the possibility that the army could improve its leaders as well as its materiel. As early as 1879, he had warned that technological advances were each year making "the duties of a military officer . . . more complex and difficult to perform." Crucially, Schofield contended that this complexity had passed the point where any individual except for a genius could grasp the entirety of modern warfare. Thus, he concluded, "it is only by united and harmonious effort that the many may even approach to that degree of excellence which ensures success in war."[6]

To help foster this collective action, Schofield helped found the Military Service Institution (MSI) of the United States, a professional association initially open only to officers of the regular army; though several years later, associate membership was allowed for officers of the Marine Corps and National Guard. The MSI centered upon the *Journal of the Military Service Institution* (*JMSI*). Westward expansion meant that the army was even more widely distributed among many small installations than before the Civil War, and for many years the *JMSI* was preeminent among the few fora in which officers could share their intellectual endeavors. These efforts were largely self-directed. The MSI's executive council—which included many of the army's generals—exerted some editorial control through their selection of the subject of the annual essay-writing contest with cash prizes; most articles, however, were on a topic selected by the individual author.[7]

The MSI imitated a British counterpart, but Schofield derived his conception of the military profession from a model closer to home. As a young lieutenant, he had taught what was then known as "natural philosophy" at West Point and was on the verge of leaving the army for a career in science when the Civil War set him along a different course. Though he remained in uniform, this early academic training influenced Schofield's approach to professional problems because he regarded military science as a field governed by immutable laws and so no different than the natural sciences such as astronomy, a subject that he had particularly enjoyed teaching. At the heart of each field was a mass of unknown facts and principles, and in each case it was the duty of practitioners to make their own investigations in order to slowly reveal the hidden truth. When Schofield was considering an academic career, American science was still in its early state of organization; the American Association for the Advancement of Science, for instance, was just several years old. "Gentlemen naturalists" were still able to make discoveries and contribute to the growing expanse of knowledge by submitting papers and specimens. Whether professional or amateur, no controlling body directed these efforts, and each researcher contributed in whatever way best suited him. Because Schofield conceived of military science as a mass of universal principles awaiting discovery, he was content to let officers similarly pursue whatever element of the problem met their fancy, confident that all paths eventually led to the same truths. This was in stark contrast with the purposeful approach of the German General Staff, which was also founded upon the premise that modern warfare could be mastered only through collective action. But rather than uncoordinated inquiry, the General Staff organized officers to investigate specific problems and produce immediately useful products, such as detailed war plans, mobilization schedules, and rail movement tables.[8]

Even after becoming commanding general, Schofield remained committed to self-directed action in professional education. The service schools continued much as they had under his predecessors. By the early 1890s, junior officers on the faculty at Fort Leavenworth had succeeded—despite Sherman's original intent—in expanding the curriculum to include elements of strategy. Schofield insisted that the same would not happen at the Cavalry and Light Artillery School and so specifically prohibited the commandant at Fort Riley from engaging in any classroom instruction beyond that which occurred at any other post.[9] But rather than found a new school of application, as both Sherman and Sheridan had done, Schofield's original contribution was to require each installation to conduct something similar to the MSI, what he called the "officers' lyceum." The lyceum had no formal curriculum. Instead, each year every lieutenant and captain was required to write a research essay on some professional topic. Though the post commander had to approve each topic, Schofield directed that "as far as practicable" the preferences of the individual should be respected. The officers of the post were to periodically convene to hear and discuss the best papers. Schofield deliberately avoided the competitive, rigorous, and structured system of German professional education that Upton admired. He hoped that "the stimulus due to friendly rivalry (but without humiliating competition) in the lecture room . . . will secure all the theoretical instruction that is necessary."[10] The lyceum was the gentlest possible mandate for education and was quite traditional in the sense that rather than simply order collective action, Schofield hoped that it would spontaneously come about through voluntary action.

But in another sense, the lyceum was far more ambitious than all previous education initiatives. In contrast to the limited concerns that schools of application were meant to address—shortfalls in technical or basic knowledge among the army's most junior officers—Schofield sensed that there was a more general deficiency throughout the officer corps. He believed that the research and writing would make the army's lieutenants and captains far better high-ranking commanders in the future. Perhaps Schofield saw the need for such education while Sherman and Sheridan did not because he had not quite reached the heights that they did during the war; perhaps it was simply due to his scientist's notion of constant progress. Whatever the reason, Schofield was the first commanding general in decades to suggest that something fundamental was missing in professional education.[11]

Schofield also departed from his predecessors in his views on civil-military relations. He surrendered the view that the commanding general was equivalent to the secretary of war—an untenable position both legally and practically—and resigned himself to serving as a chief of staff assisting the secretary in his duties. This act of conviction was also extraordinarily shrewd; for the cost of abandoning the empty pretense of command, Schofield's willful subordination earned the confidence of his civilian masters, who were far more inclined to work through, rather than around, the army's senior general. Schofield's mature understanding of the prerogative and needs of civilian policymakers was grounded in his deep experience in politics. His association with the Blair family, one of the most powerful clans in the Republican Party, was the reason why he was one of the few individuals granted an exemption to Winfield Scott's ban on regulars receiving volunteer commissions. As a commander in Civil War Missouri and then after the war in Reconstruction Virginia, Schofield could not avoid being drawn into political controversy, experiences that were instructive if personally trying. In 1868 as President Andrew Johnson and Congress were embroiled in constitutional conflict, Schofield's appointment as the successor to Secretary of War Edwin Stanton was part of the compromise that ended the crisis. Though Schofield undertook no major initiatives during his nine-month tenure as secretary of war, he was one of only a handful of soldiers to hold that position while still in uniform. In addition to his depth of political expertise, Schofield had the good fortune to work with Secretary of War Redfield Proctor, a capable, energetic, and sympathetic executive. Moreover, their pairing came during the brief period when the Republicans controlled both houses of Congress and the White House—one of only two such periods between 1875 and 1895. This favorable political situation allowed Schofield to achieve several reforms that had eluded earlier commanding generals who were not so politically astute or fortunate: the adoption of lineal promotion (the calculation of seniority for lieutenants and captains within their entire arm rather than just within their regiment); the introduction of annual evaluations, and the requirement that junior officers pass an examination before promotion.[12]

Yet Schofield's reluctance to compel professional duty robbed these reforms of some of their potential power. For instance, even though he shared the conviction common among Civil War veterans that regular officers should be familiar with the drill regulations of all three of the combat arms, Schofield refused to make that a requirement for the promotion examination to major. "The acquisition of such knowledge," he wrote, "should be voluntary on the part of the officer."[13]

In assessing the contributions of Sherman, Sheridan, and Schofield, it is striking that these keen observers of contemporary developments in military thought and technology would be so conservative and conventional in their aspirations for the military profession. Yet we must remember that from their vantage, with only the past to judge against, their incremental reforms had yielded nothing but progress in a difficult, indeed often hostile, political environment. Thus, as Schofield reflected upon his final grand inspection of the army just prior to retirement in 1895, he had reason to boast that the army was better in "equipment, discipline, efficiency in military exercises and soldierly patriotic spirit" than at any time since he entered the service in 1853. He admitted the need for some improvement in "those higher requirements which are apt to fall into neglect during active campaigns, and especially against Indians" but felt that with the frontier all but vanished there would be more time for professional study, field training, and practice marches—the individual and small-unit tasks that he felt were the basis of preparing for war.[14] With the organized militia or National Guard as it was becoming known at the time also making steady progress, Schofield felt that the army had only to continue along the course that he and his predecessors had already set in order to be ready for any future war. After having vaulted to the top of their profession with the methods of the "old army," the post-war generals saw little need for the creation of new forms or to sweep away comfortable expectations.

·　·　·　·　·

Schofield's sanguine trust that the individual members of the officer corps would self-organize to produce a coherent professional structure—in the same fashion that ants instinctively know how to make a colony—was misplaced. The lyceum was indicative of his misreading of the officer corps. He imagined that with only the slightest encouragement each individual would contribute to the best of their ability. Yet there were some who objected to any requirement for education. One senior captain used the occasion of his lyceum essay to protest having "wisdom crammed down our throats like food down the necks of Strasbourg geese."[15] Even those more willing to make the effort usually lacked the intellectual foundation to produce anything worthwhile through independent research and writing. Matthew F. Steele, a regular contributor to the *JMSI* and later the author of a popular American military history text, found the lyceum essays to be hopelessly vacuous: "a constipation of ideas in a flux of words."[16] As was the case with other aspects of the late nineteenth-century army, there were local exceptions; some post commanders were able to exert the "kindly assistance" and direction to make the discussions worthwhile as Schofield had envisioned. But he had deliberately limited what such keen commanders might achieve by prohibiting them from requiring their subordinates to read anything past the handful of regulations used in promotion examinations, while the lyceum did nothing to elevate the tenor of professionalism in those pockets of the army where proud ignorance reigned.[17]

From Schofield's vantage atop the army, the institution appeared to be moving steadily away from the legacy of the Civil War and the frontier toward a future of more single-minded preparation for conventional warfare. There was truth in this, for during Schofield's tenure the Census Bureau declared the close of the frontier in 1890 and the army fought its last campaign of the Indian Wars—Pine Ridge—in December 1890 through January 1891. The precision of those dates, however, belies the prolonged period of adjustment during which the definition of military competence was less clear than Schofield realized, as was evident in his handling of the case of Thomas C. Lebo and the lyceum. Lebo represented one lingering aspect of the Civil War that the commanding general wanted to leave behind—the mass of former volunteers that Congress had compelled the regulars to retain. This was not because Lebo was a bad soldier, even though he had never risen above the grade of captain in the Pennsylvania cavalry during the war or in the regulars afterward when Schofield conceived of the lyceum. Lebo had participated in some of the army's hardest campaigns: Sheridan's winter campaigns on the southern plains and then later the long struggle against the Apaches in the Southwest. In 1880, Lebo captured the supply camp of the chief Victorio, hidden in the aptly named Sierra Diablo (Devil's Mountain) range of Texas. In 1886, Brigadier General Nelson A. Miles commended Lebo for "his usual energy, good judgment, and gallantry" during a two hundred-mile pursuit of Geronimo that began in Arizona and ended in Mexico, where Lebo lost two troopers in a "good fight" with the famed Apache chief.[18] Yet in thirty years of service, Lebo had never attended any army school. When Sherman established the school for infantry and cavalry, Lebo was too senior to attend and would have gotten little out of it. Sherman wanted the school to teach new officers to be like Lebo, not to teach Lebo to be some facsimile of an officer of the German General Staff.[19]

Despite his lack of education, Lebo seems to have been an entirely adequate officer until 1891, the year in which Schofield decreed that every lieutenant and captain should write an essay for the lyceum. Lebo, who had persevered through years of grueling plains blizzards and desert heat, was unable or unwilling to meet this challenge. His notice of surrender to the War Department stated simply: "I have never written an essay on any professional subject nor do I think I could write one that would be in the least instructive, interesting, or of any importance." Schofield agreed, noting that Lebo had given a "fair statement of the facts." He equated the captain's "total failure . . . to perform the service required of officers of the line" to a physical disability that rendered an officer unfit for further duty. But Schofield went on to explain that the purpose of the lyceum was "not to condemn those gallant and meritorious officers who by reason of the lack of early educational advantages have now reached the age when a high grade of education has become impossible to them; but rather to educate those younger men who do not labor under such disadvantage, and thus to gradually bring the line of the Army to the high standard of professional acquirement which the War Department has indicated."[20] In other words, though Lebo's past service was admirable, Schofield believed that his time was past.

The next year, however, Lebo passed the examination for promotion to major, one component of which was writing a professional essay for the commanding general's approval. Five years later, Schofield's forbearance was justified when Major Lebo, in the absence of his colonel and lieutenant colonel, commanded the Sixth Cavalry during the famous battle for San Juan and Kettle Hills in Cuba. Promoted to lieutenant colonel in 1899 and then colonel in 1901, Lebo commanded the Fourteenth Cavalry in the southern Philippines until his retirement.[21] Of course, within a seniority-based promotion system, the mere fact of command says little; and accounts of the campaign in the Philippines are strangely silent about Lebo's actions, even though his troopers were involved in numerous engagements. Nonetheless, after a lifetime of service in cavalry regiments, Lebo probably had the requisite knowledge to lead one on the battlefield, even if that was likely the limit of his competence.

Just as Schofield might have underestimated the continued relevance of the less distinguished remnants of the Civil War generation, he might have overestimated the degree to which the predominantly West Point–trained composite generation looked to the future with fresh eyes. There was a great contrast between the two groups that were consigned to an extended intimate proximity in the junior ranks because of the stranglehold on higher ranks held by Civil War veterans with more distinguished wartime records. Yet there was little widespread friction between the unadorned veterans and school-trained youngsters, for as distinct as the groups were from each other both exhibited a great deal of internal diversity, a product of the geographic and organizational fragmentation of the army in the 1870s and 1880s.[22] In short, neither generation was monolithic enough to engage in systemic generational warfare.

During his early career, George I. McIver, an 1882 graduate of West Point, experienced the best and worst of the Civil War generation. His first assignment was to a two-company post in Minnesota with a commissioned complement of only a lieutenant colonel, two captains, and a first lieutenant— all of whom were Civil War veterans but none of whom was a graduate of West Point. When one of the captains died, the newly promoted replacement was fifty-five years old and physically incapable of leading the company in the field. Yet McIver fondly remembered the fifty-year-old first lieutenant (wounded at Antietam two decades before) who taught him the customs and regulations of the army. According to McIver, two decades after the end of the Civil War, still more than half of the officers in his regiment were former volunteers or rankers. "Not all of them were well educated and some of them considered that their positions had been given them to be held as sinecures in the way of reward for past services," McIver recalled in his memoirs. "Not all of them, however, took this attitude and many were examples of efficiency and strict attention to duty."[23] A historian can add little to that characterization of the former volunteers.

Yet the empathy that McIver and others of the composite generation might have felt for their older comrades was likely tested by the knowledge that the Civil War generation was hindering the advancement of the younger men. For line officers, promotion only came through the retirement or death of a more senior officer. But the relative youth of the Civil War generation meant that there would be few vacancies. In 1885, more than a third of the officer corps were between forty-one and fifty years of age and so still a decade or two from retirement.[24] An anonymous "Lieutenant of Artillery" gave vent to the resulting frustrations in an 1893 article. Though acknowledging that he lived comfortably and had ample time for recreation, the lieutenant argued that this pleasant life was sapping his cohort's potential: "A man who arrives at the age of forty or thereabouts without holding a place of responsibility is quite likely to lack the nerve to take the responsibility when the time comes."[25]

At times prospects of promotion had been even slower in the antebellum army, but the Civil War had drastically altered regulars' expectations and this colored the way they perceived the profession. The majority of officers in the foundational generation expected nothing more than perhaps a single increase in rank in case of conflict; war was unlikely to radically alter their professional status. The composite generation, in contrast, expected to wait for decades to even achieve the rank of major if peace endured, but if there were a major war then a lieutenant could be a colonel the next year and a general the year after that. The Civil War introduced a tension between future and present that was exacerbated by the peculiar nature of the military profession. For a soldier, what is the "reality" for which they must prepare: the present peace or hypothetical war? Having already experienced a major war, the problem was not so vexing for the Civil War generation. But it was a critical question for the composite generation, with enormous implications for how the army prepared for war. During the antebellum period, frontier service as a company commander was also good preparation for duty in the same rank against a more conventional foe like the Mexicans. But small-unit frontier experience did little to prepare an officer for duty as a commander or staff officer for a division, corps, or army. With the benefit of hindsight gained by 1906, one officer rued that the "experience a large majority of our officers got at frontier posts between the Civil and Spanish Wars was pretty worthless."[26] But this was not so clear at the time, and so individuals were left to follow their personal predilections to concentrate either on the hard certainty of the present or the potential future.

This was not the only issue that divided officers of the composite generation, for the conditions of the 1870s and 1880s ensured that the cohort would encompass a wide range of professional outlooks. The geographic and organizational fragmentation of the army meant that individual experiences varied greatly according to local conditions. The army was simply too dispersed for it to impose a homogenized service culture. In 1874, a newly commissioned lieutenant stopped at the War Department to learn something of his assigned unit in Montana, but upon arrival he discovered that his company had moved to another post over a year earlier and the captain had been dead for several months. According to one officer, even the generals commanding the territorial departments "exerted absolutely no influence over the discipline, the training or the morale of the army," limited as they were by distance to only a "perfunctory annual inspection of their posts."[27] Professor Peter S. Michie of West Point complained that within the artillery even the colonels were truly only in command of that portion of their regiment stationed near their headquarters. As a consequence, he argued, rather than having "an approximately uniform system of artillery practice, and a decent standard of efficiency . . . we have instead a hydra-headed organization, as diverse in its aim, as it is scattered in extent."[28]

The enduring image of the late-nineteenth-century army is of the lonely frontier fort. Samuel Huntington even argues that isolation was central to the development of the American military profession.[29] Although it is true that in 1881 69 percent of the officer corps was stationed in isolated areas, that still left a significant minority serving in more settled areas. Moreover, by 1891 the proportions serving in remote and settled locations were about even. A more accurate characterization of the time was that there was a broad diversity of locales and types of duties. Generals and staff officers worked in the War Department or regional headquarters in New York, St. Louis, San Francisco, and other major cities. Some coastal fortifications were as isolated as any frontier stockade, yet others were in or near urban areas. The garrison of Governor's Island was only a fifteen-minute ferry ride from Manhattan, which one artilleryman recalled as "a hummer sort of place." Rather than being cut off from society, the same officer found that his military service exposed him to a broader world than he had known as the son of a provincial doctor. Many years later, he still remembered the guilty cosmopolitan delight of playing tennis on the Sabbath.[30] Another young artilleryman assigned to Fort Adams, Rhode Island, "basked in the light of . . .

the fringes of Newport high society."[31] Recruiting, teaching at civilian colleges, and managing civil engineering projects all also afforded opportunities for the interchange with civilian governmental, professional, and business elites.[32]

Even for those on the frontier, disparities in the size of garrisons led to varying experiences. Small forts offered limited opportunities for professional growth: a personal library, a subscription to the *JMSI,* and the company of anywhere from one to a half-dozen other officers, almost always of the same branch of service, were likely to be the only intellectual stimulants. "Put four companies of a regiment at an out-of-the-way frontier station, keep them there five, ten, or fifteen years (as is not unfrequent[*sic*]) and the result may easily be imagined," wrote one officer. "Cut off from the world. . . . All get tired of and pick at the other, culminating in one extreme case, some years ago, in the trial by court-martial of every officer at a post, on charges put each against the other."[33] And for the unfortunate few who were the sole officer at a station, the strict segregation from the enlisted ranks left them doomed to "a sort of Robinson Crusoe existence." Such an officer, Lieutenant James Parker wrote, "can carry on no conversation except to give instructions."[34] The small garrisons also exacerbated the problem of chronically undermanned units caused by the top-heavy expansible structure. With a greater proportion of the soldiers devoted to maintenance and guard duties, small garrisons had few men remaining for training. Within months of graduation, one lieutenant had already reached a state of despairing boredom. "The companies are so ridiculously small," he complained to a friend, "that I find it impossible to take any interest in drills or indeed in any military duties. I do what I have to do in a perfunctory way and that is all."[35] Toward the latter part of the century, larger installations became more common. By 1895, sixteen of the eighty-two garrisoned posts had at least a regiment of troops, while only nine had just a single company. Those garrisons offered a greater collection of professional experiences and views, the possibility of a professional library, and far more opportunities for advanced training.[36]

Of course, the idle could squander the opportunity of a large post just as determined individuals could overcome the challenges of a small garrison. From one such location in Texas, Lieutenant Louis C. Scherer complained, "The greatest trouble of a post of this size is the apathy one gets in no matter what is concerned. Everything is repeated over and over again and a terrible hankering for a change takes possession of a person." Yet in the same letter, he excitedly described his efforts to map the local area. Scherer was also diligently translating a German military text with the aid of his wife, who typed the manuscript on a crude typewriter while Scherer would dictate in English.[37] This odd domestic scene gives a brief glimpse into the distance between dreams and reality for the composite generation. Was it purely an intellectual exercise to pass long nights, or did Scherer believe that at some point he would take part in the kind of continental warfare that was described in his German text?

One feature of such industrialized warfare was increasingly complex coordination among the various arms, but that was a neglected field in the U.S. Army. The cavalry and infantry were often stationed together, but it was still relatively rare to have the artillery represented. In 1892, of ninety garrisons with at least one company of line troops only one—Fort Sam Houston, Texas—had units of all three arms. The light artillery mingled with one of the other arms at only three other stations.[38] Yet even in those few places where proximity was not a barrier, the fierce tribalism of the artillery impeded cooperation. The light batteries were regarded as special commands, a custom that fostered a proud independence notable even within the individualistic nineteenth-century army. These batteries were so closely associated with their captains that they were typically referred to by their names (e.g., Grimes's battery) rather than their formal designation (e.g., Battery A, 2nd U.S. Artillery). When the colonel commanding Fort Leavenworth ordered the battery commander assigned to his garrison to provide the school with instructors, the captain refused. The matter was eventually referred to Schofield, himself an artilleryman, who upheld the independence of the battery commander. Evidently, such conflicts were so common that Schofield's aide noted the "peculiar feeling of exasperation which comes over every infantry or cavalry post commander when he discovers that the light artillery is regarded as a special service governed by special regulation."[39] Not surprisingly, artillery and infantry coordination would be one of the weaknesses of the U.S. Army in both the Spanish-American War and World War I.

The independence of battery commanders was only the most exaggerated instance of the general supremacy of local commanders throughout the army. As one officer remembered, within the regiment the "colonel was the king," and "within the regulations, his word was law."[40] The extent to which each regiment and even each station had its own character and methods was strikingly captured in the annual report of the inspector general for 1892.

That year he endeavored to collect a comprehensive view of the state of the army by having each company, troop, and battery report on a vast array of subjects: the condition of barracks and horses; how much and what kind of training was conducted; the number of soldiers in confinement and on the sick list; how many attended school, and even how many could swim. The resulting 334 pages of tables document the disparity among units in all aspects of professional activity. Some companies conducted drill only once every other week; some drilled twice a day. Even in marksmanship training, one of the areas in which the War Department gave relatively specific direction, there were similarly significant differences in the frequency of training. Such variation manifested itself among the 382 companies, troops, and batteries spread among 90 installations. Even where uniformity prevailed, it was not necessarily beneficial. The three companies of the 21st Infantry that were stationed with the regimental headquarters at Fort Niagara, New York, were uniformly inactive under the leadership of Colonel Horace Jewett. The commander of far-distant D Company, at Fort Duchesne, Utah, reported three times as many drills as the companies in New York, and he even made use of an indoor shooting range for target practice during the winter months. The D Company commander might have inflated his report, as there was no effective check on the veracity of his claim, but that possibility only reinforces the larger point; with the regimental headquarters nearly two thousand miles away, it had been more than a year since his colonel had last visited the company.[41]

The cavalry troops of Captains Edward J. McClernand and George S. Anderson—two respected officers who kept their units on a lively schedule—illustrate how much independence commanders had in determining how best to prepare for war. McClernand's D Troop, Second Cavalry, was stationed at Fort Wingate, New Mexico, along with the regimental headquarters and three other troops. McClernand brought the entire unit together for drill only once or twice a week, and his soldiers engaged in relatively little saber training and physical exercise. But he conducted tactical training for smaller units daily, paid close attention to the training of horses, and took his troop out on long multiday practice marches covering up to 300 miles. Anderson's I Troop, Sixth Cavalry, was stationed by itself at Yellowstone National Park, giving Anderson even greater freedom. Unlike McClernand, Anderson was keen on mounted drill, saber training, and physical exercise, and so ensured they were done nearly every day. But his horses were only partly accustomed to bugle calls, and the troop was less ready to take the field immediately. Perhaps representative of a more common mediocrity was Captain Henry W. Wessells, Jr., and his H Troop, Third Cavalry, which conducted roughly a third less training than the other two captains.[42]

Thus, the experience of young officers, even those of the same arm, could be quite different depending upon their commander. William Lassiter, an 1889 West Point graduate, experienced both extremes. His first commander was active and kept the men of his coastal defense battery busy with both infantry and artillery drill even though the entire battery had but one gun, a Civil War relic. "I count myself lucky to have had my start under his auspices," Lassiter later wrote. "Many of my contemporaries started under captains who never expected them to do anything very much and a lot of them acquired early dry rot." The term *dry rot* was a common one found repeatedly in the diaries, letters, and memoirs of Lassiter's contemporaries. His next captain was of that very type: "Interested in chicken incubators and catamaran boats . . . military subjects had long ceased to interest him. He was a complete wash-out."[43]

Artillerymen were particularly prone to such lethargy due to the nature of fixed defenses. Ammunition was so scarce that they often fired the guns only once a year; and daily drill for static guns, as one officer remembered, consisted of a sergeant reading from the drill manual while the crews went "through certain movements at the gun by rote, each being explained in detail as we went along, although there was not a corporal in the outfit that did not know the whole thing by heart."[44] Yet the problems of coast defense were also readily reduced to mathematical equations, and so ideal for theoretical experimentation. The two corps responsible for coast defense—the artillery and engineers—also were among the first to adopt German techniques of wargaming. This allowed interested officers to play out duels between ships and shore batteries using dice and tables of probabilities of guns hitting at various ranges. It was some of the most innovative training within the U.S. Army of the late nineteenth century.[45]

Basic drill in the infantry, cavalry, and light artillery had the advantage of movement, but its purpose was to instill obedience in soldiers through repetition that required little from officers other than knowledge of the drill regulations and a strong voice. One officer of the time conceded that "official requirements as to tactical knowledge were exceedingly meager."[46] This did not preclude imaginative commanders like Generals O. O. Howard,

At an unidentified location in 1888, cavalrymen of H Troop, Third Cavalry, train their mounts to form an emergency redoubt, a tactic most likely to be used in frontier warfare. Though some officers remained committed to the necessity to prepare for high command in conventional campaigns, after decades of service with small garrisons in such locations, that prospect must have seemed remote, if not fanciful, to others. (Samuel B. M. Young Collection, AHEC)

Wesley Merritt, and Nelson A. Miles from experimenting with "camps of instruction" and "maneuvers" meant to provide more realistic training, but the degree to which participating officers commented upon the novelty of these exercises suggests that they were the exception. The norm seems to have been a lazy adherence to rote drill that quashed the initiative of subordinates who tried to break from the established routine.[47] Colonel Richard I. Dodge, a former aide-de-camp to Sherman and 1844 graduate of West Point, was dismayed that officers of his generation were so resistant to change. In an 1887 article, Dodge wrote that he hoped that the composite generation would take "comfort from the knowledge that all really valuable innovations are forced from below, [and] can bide their time with the full assurance that, sooner or later, rank will have to move with the world."[48] This prediction assumed that the composite generation would still have the zeal for change once they finally ascended to the field ranks. It was only when Miles replaced Schofield as commanding general in 1895 that the army had an unequivocal advocate for more modern forms of field training; at the end of 1896, the War Department issued a directive requiring commanders to ensure their units received a minimum of forty days of training in "minor tactics," preferably combining units of all three arms.[49]

Officers still segregated themselves along the traditional division between the line and staff. Many line officers agreed with Colonel John Gibbon that because staff officers were permanently assigned to their department, they became so isolated that "even the best . . . [have] no sympathy whatever with their brother officers of the line; no personal knowledge of their labors and wants, and no care as to lightening the first or supplying the last, except so far as they are compelled by their positions to do so."[50] Ironically, Gibbon's complaint manifested his obliviousness to the demands on the staff; they were accountable to the secretary of war, whose chief concern was most often ensuring economy. The extreme centralization of War Department business meant that commanders had little responsibility for fiscal matters; spared of the burden of weighing operational demands against cost, they naturally privileged the former and so bitterly complained when their requests for resources were denied. But although Gibbon overstated the degree to which personal indifference was to blame, he was correct that the line and staff were separated by divergent understandings of the army and its needs. Indeed, each staff department had a unique identity reflecting its functional specialty and, quite often, the idiosyncrasies of its chief.[51]

More generally, officers lived in a society that exulted in individualism and autonomy. Decades earlier this trait had impressed the French visitor Alexis de Tocqueville, who noted it as a defining natural characteristic in *Democracy in America.* Individualism was still a prevailing value in the latter part of the century, when Americans celebrated feats of self-made men such as John D. Rockefeller and Andrew Carnegie even while detesting the massive businesses that they had built. Individualism was a recurring theme in the work of Mark Twain, while historian Frederick Jackson Turner argued in his seminal essay "The Significance of the Frontier in American History" that it was an inevitable consequence of the country's geography. The irony was that this celebration of individualism occurred within a period when the exponential growth in the organization of government, business, and society was rapidly diminishing the relative importance of the individual. Nonetheless, as governmental bureaucracy, corporations, and cities all grew larger and more sophisticated, Americans, including army officers, continued to venerate individual achievement.[52]

Against this cultural predisposition to independence and the centrifugal forces of dispersion, diversity of experience, and allegiance to regiment, corps, or department, there were only weak centripetal efforts to bind the military profession together. Though the War Department exerted strict control over matters of administration, particularly fiscal matters, it made only sporadic efforts to govern how commanders trained, educated, and employed their units. This imbalance was reflected in the focus of the inspectors general who were the army's principal means of ensuring compliance with policies and directives. By 1892, Inspector General Joseph C. Breckinridge realized that his assistants needed to look beyond the "mere drill and equipment" to also examine "the wind and muscle and skill and knowledge of the officers and men."[53] But with fewer than ten inspectors for the entire army dispersed over a hundred different locations, this was more aspiration than realistic goal.

Even if there had been a more robust inspectorate, the army lacked authoritative standards against which to evaluate commanders. The chief purpose of the army's drill regulations was to provide commanders with the means to control their own units rather than to dictate how they should command; aside from a few generalities about such matters as the desirability of the offensive—more kindly advice than firm dictates—there was no effort to impart on all officers a common philosophy of tactics. Upton had realized that something more was necessary but committed suicide before completing his contemplated addendum on "applied tactics." This void remained unfilled, a fact pointed out by Lieutenant John P. Wisser in 1887: "What we call 'Tactics' no other nation in the world dignifies with that name."[54] As a consequence, in the words of one infantryman, "officers were rated not so much on their capacity as military tacticians and students as upon their ability to display to inspectors a smartly conducted review of the troops of the garrison and a well administered, clean looking post. Post administration had become the important thing and to that extent military standards had become perverted."[55] Thus, most of the standards for competence were left to the collective determination of the officer corps in accord with local conditions, regimental traditions, and the influence of the immediate commander.

The reforms introduced by Schofield went some way to creating a more cohesive American military profession; but as he was himself ambivalent about imposing change, the changes were hardly transformative. The new system of promoting the most senior lieutenant within that branch when a vacancy opened rather than whoever was most senior within the particular regiment meant that individuals would move among units far more frequently, but Schofield's principal purpose was to reduce the dissension created by disparities in promotion rates rather than to foster homogeneity.[56]

In time, evaluation reports would have a dramatic influence over the nature of the officer corps, but in the late nineteenth century they meant little. With seniority promotion still in place, neither praise nor condemnation in an evaluation had any effect upon when an officer would be promoted. Theoretically, the reports were meant to guide special assignments, such as duty at West Point or selection for a staff bureau, but it is unclear if the evaluations were ever even consulted, much less decisive, in these decisions. At best, they supplemented the existing reliance upon general reputation and personal relations.[57]

Of all Schofield's reforms, the promotion examinations had the greatest immediate impact upon the army, but the results were less dramatic than many reformers had hoped. Contrary to the assertion of Secretary of War William C. Endicott that "no men are so well fitted to determine the capacity or incapacity of a candidate for a place as those who have already filled the place and are familiar with its requirements and its duties," many officers were reluctant to cast harsh judgment on their fellows.[58] In the first eight months that examinations were given, only 17 of the 276 officers examined failed, and all but two of those failures were due to physical incapacity rather than to professional deficiency.[59]

Though there was undoubtedly benefit in removing cavalrymen who could not ride and infantrymen who could not march, the interminable pace of promotions meant that invalids might linger for years before facing the examiner. Even then, infirmities might be overlooked. In 1893, Eben Swift received a round of congratulations from friends who assumed that a senior but incapacitated first lieutenant would surely fail his examination, thereby placing Swift in line for promotion. Much to Swift's chagrin, the doctor found the other officer fit for duty. Yet it seems that the officer corps was quite tolerant of the physically unfit. One officer remembered serving with a three-hundred-pound artillery lieutenant at Saint Augustine, Florida, who in the summer heat could do little more than sit in the shade of his front porch fanning himself. Similarly, a cavalryman recalled a regimental commissary unable to wear boots or shoes who thus conducted his duties in slippers. This was no particular handicap for a staff officer in peace, but the tender-footed commissary was of limited utility in case of war.[60]

In light of this lenience for officers who were unfit in readily discernible ways, less tangible forms of competence—such as tactical judgment and technical knowledge—were subject to even less scrutiny. The physical examinations were conducted by army physicians, but the professional examinations were administered by a board of officers. Initially, these boards were made up of individuals from the same regiment as the officer being examined, leading to the widespread belief, in the words of one office of the time, that the "boards were controlled by sentiment and sympathy, and that the good of the service was not the sole criterion."[61]

Yet even after the boards became more centralized, the number of individuals found professionally deficient remained low. From the inception of the examinations in October 1890 until February 1901, only one officer was discharged for having failed the professional portion of the examination.[62] The unwillingness of officers to deem any of their peers incompetent was more than simply a matter of regimental loyalty.[63] One possible cause was skepticism that the promotion evaluations were a meaningful measure of professional ability. The utility of the practical portion of the examination was obvious. But after decades in service, there were few officers who could not satisfactorily drill a unit of their own branch. The more difficult section of the examination and the one for which officers began studying months in advance was the portion testing knowledge of regulations and textbooks. Major George Baird, a former Civil War volunteer and decorated frontier fighter, applauded the way in which promotion examination provided a "stimulus to study and investigation" during peacetime but wondered whether it was truly "a test of practical ability." If not, he worried that examinations might even be counterproductive if they were to lead officers to "unduly exalt theoretical knowledge and make the army bookish."[64]

Yet anti-intellectualism was not the sole, or even principal, source of resistance to promotion examinations. The first three generations of officers were bound by a set of values that favored loyalty, fairness, and solidarity over efficiency and effectiveness. The officer's commission was central to this value system. Most officers regarded it as akin to a contract with the government. In exchange for their service, the government was obligated to respect the rights invested in the commission, chiefly lifelong employment and the guarantee of eventual promotion (however slow). Upton was among the few dissenters. He argued that officers were "maintained for the sole benefit of the Government" and so were not entitled to automatic promotion. He thought that the effectiveness of the institution was more important than these individual "rights." Indeed, in candid moments most officers acknowledged that seniority promotion bred complacency and that the toleration of invalids and incompetents was contrary to the interests of the service; however, they were not willing to risk what they regarded as inviolate rights by taking aggressive action against the "ignorant and incompetent," as Upton urged.[65] Instead, most agreed with the view expressed by Colonel Nelson A. Miles in a letter to a congressman protesting a proposed reduction of the army: "After an officer has been duly appointed and commissioned, depriving him of his commission, without crime or fault on his part is, if not a breach of contract, at least a breach of faith on the part of the Government."[66] Against these beliefs, proposals for meritocracy and the implementation of promotion examinations both foundered.

Thus, the defining characteristic of the composite generation was diversity. The emphatic belief that the army could not hold an officer to account without infringing upon his rights as a commission holder precluded any vigorous attempts to impose professional uniformity. But aside from this ideological objection, the conditions of service encouraged the growth of many different ideas about war and how best to prepare for it. After the beginning at West Point that was common to most officers of the composite generation, they were subjected to a wide array of experiences and conditions: the uneven professionalism and zeal of their Civil War–generation superiors; the dispersal of the army into many small garrisons; and the differing nature of service among its various arms, functions, units, and geographic regions. By the 1890s, some of these centrifugal factors began to abate as the army consolidated into fewer, larger posts and the change from regimental to lineal promotion meant that line officers moved more freely among regiments and served in more varied locales. The composite generation experimented with professional education outside of the narrow conceptual bounds that most of the Civil War generation preferred. In time, army schools would become a powerful centripetal force, but this would come too late for the composite generation. In the absence of such a force, even as they created the tools for professional unity, the pioneers of the composite generation were dogged by fundamental disagreements among themselves about how best to prepare for war.

· · · · ·

The careers of Eben Swift and Arthur L. Wagner—friends since their time as cadets in the 1870s—illustrate how the complex interplay of personality, training, and experience could lead officers to quite different professional views. Their case is particularly striking, as they would go on to become two of the most influential figures in the development of professional education. In that work, each genuinely believed that they were following the example of Upton even while they pursued divergent paths. Because of their personal affinity and mutual dedication to advancing the cause of army schools, they have come to be remembered as like-minded reformers. Historian Carol Reardon described them as "kindred spirits."[67] But although they were alike in rejecting the outright anti-intellectualism that some officers still retained, Swift and Wagner had fundamentally different notions of war and what it meant to prepare for it.

Of the two, the serious, dutiful Swift was more like Upton in temperament. Swift's affinity for the older man was so strong that throughout his career he would cling to the memory of the first day that he saw Upton. As Swift's class of 1876 waited to receive their first military instruction, the commandant addressed the second-year cadets who were going to be the drillmasters. Upton told them that if they could master the art of imparting knowledge to a single "plebe," they could do so with an entire brigade. Swift never forgot that moment; and so thirty-six years later, while he was an instructor at the Army War College, Swift recalled Upton's words before telling the captains and majors of the class that if they could give an order to a patrol they could give an order to an army corps. That nonsensical variation was a particularly clear example of how Swift grasped the form but not the spirit of Upton's teachings. Still later, in 1917, when then-Major General Swift assumed command of the 82nd Infantry Division, morale was low among the soldiers who were "generally disgusted, down-hearted and cursing their luck in having been caught in the draft." Swift's remedy was to start "promptly with the West Point Drill exercises, as much as possible like those I had pounded into me at West Point forty-five years before."[68] Although Swift had a capacity for dogmatism that was notable even in the army, these incidents still illustrate the power of early lessons that could reverberate for decades, sometimes long after conditions had rendered them obsolete. The first years of his career established patterns of thought that would long persist.

The light-hearted Wagner, in contrast, was quite unlike Upton and as a cadet regularly fell afoul of the commandant's discipline. Wagner enjoyed satirizing life at the academy, whether in mock classroom lectures to the first-year "plebes" or through his self-published newspaper of cadet affairs, "The Bombshell." Other cadets delighted in these activities, with one describing Wagner as "a real wit."[69] Upton was less impressed with Wagner's comic writing. When the cadet perhaps used too much sarcasm in an explanation of one of his many transgressions, Upton imposed a further punishment of room confinement for submitting a memorandum "discourteous in tone and containing irrelevant matter."[70] He had already been "turned back" to become a member of the following class for lying to an officer. With little interest in study—Wagner preferred light novels and military history—on the eve of graduation in 1875, he ranked fortieth among his class of forty-three and was once again confined to his room. This final punishment deprived him of the ability to attend his graduation ball, so Wagner hosted his own unsanctioned gathering with illicit alcohol punch in his barracks room. The boisterous affair soon drew the attention of Lieutenant John F. Stretch—one of Upton's sternest assistants. When Stretch entered the room, the cadets all fell quiet except for Wagner, who was, as one friend remembered, "pretty well loaded." As Stretch walked around the room in silence, glaring at each cadet in turn, Wagner followed, chattering along, "Mr. Stretch, I am glad to have the call. We are having a party you see. If anything is wrong I hope you will mention it." Without saying a word, Stretch walked out of the room. He never reported the incident, knowing that if he did, many of the cadets would have been either dismissed or had their graduation delayed. If given the opportunity, Upton might well have dismissed Wagner.[71]

Therefore, it is ironic that of all of Upton's former pupils Wagner would best understand and do more to further Upton's agenda of professional reform than any other. In all, 369 graduates—including three future chiefs of staff of the army—spent at least part of their cadet careers at West Point during Upton's tenure. Thus, approximately a third of the composite generation received some of their initial professional tutelage from Upton. But as the case of Swift and Wagner demonstrates, not all would understand his lessons in the manner that he intended.[72]

After leaving West Point, Swift soon witnessed the rough-hewn life in a cavalry regiment. He was enjoying his graduation leave when he heard of the disaster at the Battle of the Little Big Horn. Swift rushed to join his cavalry regiment in the hope of avenging Custer and the Seventh Cavalry, but when he arrived the surgeon greeted him with the anticlimactic news that "the first duty of a Lieutenant is to know how to make a toddy" (an alcoholic drink). The pursuit of the Sioux ended soon after without Swift seeing any of the combat that he craved, but he did see the spectacle of a large concentration of cavalrymen at Camp Robinson, Nebraska. As they waited for transportation to their home stations, the group grew so raucous that even the officers resembled "a howling mob." Swift remembered one lieutenant who attempted to jump his horse over a saloon billiard table. Other officers simply idled away their time in poker and more sedate drinking.[73]

Yet even in this environment Swift found stimulus for professional growth. He learned the ways of cavalry in the field, discovering to his delight that West Point had prepared him to drill a troop with "full confidence." Even the lethargy of Swift's commander did nothing to dent his enthusiasm. Swift supervised all of the daily duties—roll calls, drills, and stables—while the captain did little more than sign the morning report. "As the other captains divided the duties with their lieutenants, they voted my captain as a pretty mean man," Swift later wrote. "I did not resent it at all, was glad of it and knew it did me good."[74] The earnest young officer so impressed the regimental commander, Colonel Wesley Merritt, that after only three years of duty, Second Lieutenant Swift became the regimental adjutant, a position typically reserved for the best first lieutenant in the regiment. Swift kept that position for over eight years, until his chief's promotion to brigadier general in 1887, upon which he became Merritt's aide-de-camp. Swift stayed with Merritt until the general's headquarters shifted from Fort Leavenworth to St. Louis, but Swift quickly tired of the city and asked to return to his troop, then at Fort Reno, Indian Territory, a midsized post with a high incidence of malaria. Nonetheless, Swift—still just a first lieutenant after fifteen years of service—was happy to return to his regiment.[75]

Upon his escape from the confines of West Point, Wagner was disappointed to find regimental duty only slightly less oppressive. In his first five years of commissioned service, Wagner performed capably in several frontier campaigns though he was never engaged in combat. Under similar circumstances, Swift had found fulfillment, but Wagner hated such duty. In 1880, he sought to escape by requesting duty as a professor of military science and tactics at a civilian college. The first effort was unsuccessful; but a year later, the War Department assigned Wagner to duty at the East Florida Seminary (the present-day University of Florida).[76]

The assignment was a turning point in Wagner's career. While in Gainesville, he began his professional studies in earnest, following Upton's intellectual lead as he did so. In 1884, Wagner won the *JMSI's* annual prize essay, citing Upton repeatedly while writing on the topic of "The Military Necessities of the United States, and the Best Provisions for Meeting Them." Teaching, research, and writing appealed to Wagner, and he requested a three-year extension at the school, but this was denied. In 1885, Wagner returned to his company, then stationed at Fort Douglas, Utah Territory. There he continued his scholarly pursuits, writing a second article for the *JMSI*, "The Military and Naval Policy of the United States," which in both form and content aped Upton's *Military Policy.*[77]

Yet even as he wrote this second article, Wagner contemplated leaving the army. He applied for a year's leave to work in his father-in-law's business so that he might "have an opportunity of deciding intelligently upon the acceptance or declination of a position that has been offered to me in civil life."[78] Sheridan, the commanding general at the time, denied this brash request, leaving Wagner with no choice but to soldier on or resign his commission.

Wagner was fortunate that his moment of decision corresponded with the assignment of his regimental commander, Colonel Alexander M. McCook, as the commandant of the Infantry and Cavalry School of Application at Fort Leavenworth. McCook arrived while the school was struggling to overcome the circumstances of its birth. Many difficulties stemmed from the manner of the school's founding. In order to circumvent possible congressional meddling, Sherman had established the school through a general order. Though this avoided the possibility that he confided to Sheridan of having the school being "made political & taken out of our control," it also meant that school had to operate with makeshift resources because it had no specific appropriation.[79] Sherman loaned the library books from his own collection and barred married officers from entry into the initial class for lack of sufficient quarters. The first faculty was drawn from whatever officers were available within the garrison; in some special subjects, such as military law, student-officers with particular knowledge of the field instructed their classmates.[80]

More troubling than the inevitable growing pains of a new institution was the perception that the school was for the mediocre. At its founding, Sherman had decided to give it the additional function of providing remedial general education for a group of officers recently commissioned from civilian life. Some of these new officers had stronger political connections than personal qualifications, and so Sherman directed that Fort Leavenworth run essentially two courses simultaneously. The first was the true equivalent to the Artillery School, providing a similar grounding in basic military duties. The second was for the newly commissioned officers. In addition to some military subjects, it also included courses in geometry, "writing a plain hand, easy to read," and "correct reading aloud."[81] Though perhaps a necessary expedient, this association with crude simplicity caused the school's general reputation to suffer. Moreover, even the more advanced section was plagued by the habit of some regimental commanders who were skeptical of "book-learning" to send their least capable officers. The students began referring to themselves as the "Regimental Blockheads" and the school as the "Kindergarten." Though Sherman was on the whole satisfied with the school during its first years, he was troubled enough by the cavalier attitude of many students that he felt it necessary to threaten court-martial and dismissal from the service for any who failed to apply themselves.[82]

Under Sherman's successors, the school made incremental progress. Sheridan allowed McCook to abolish the remedial class and require student to pass an entrance examination demonstrating basic proficiency in small-unit drill and tactics so that, in the words of an 1895 history of the school, it could be conducted "for the benefit of capable officers instead of continuing to be degraded to the level of a common school for the benefit of the inefficient."[83] McCook also instituted a more rigorous six-day schedule, but the school retained its emphasis on practical outdoor work. Sheridan was not so concerned with congressional involvement, and he began a campaign that was successfully concluded by Schofield to secure specific funding for the school.[84]

With the help of Sheridan, McCook also improved the faculty. One part of that effort was Wagner's transfer to Fort Leavenworth, saving him from the decision between continuing in garrison duty and leaving the army. McCook had recognized that Wagner's "attainments, experience as an instructor and his studious habits" made him "especially well fitted for an instructor in the Art of War."[85] These talents soon bore fruit with the publication of Wagner's first book, *The Campaign of Königgrätz: A Study of the Austro-Prussian Conflict in Light of the American Civil War.* The subtitle is revealing, for Wagner's purpose was not to slavishly praise the Prussians but to rebut the claims of American officers "who are wont to bestow all possible admiration upon the military operations in recent European wars, not because they were excellent, but because they were European; and to belittle the operations in our own war, not because they were not excellent, but because they were American." Wagner also aimed the book at European military intellectuals, whom he accused of being "loth to acknowledge the military excellence displayed during the War of Secession."[86] This assertiveness was a contrast to the deference to European practices of predecessors like Winfield Scott and Dennis H. Mahan. Of course, reflexive nationalism is in itself no virtue; but Wagner's analysis was sound, earning the praise of a British journal: "If the American Army of to-day contains a large proportion of officers as zealous and well-informed in their profession as Lieutenant Wagner . . . the United States may depend with confidence upon her Army in any struggle."[87]

With his sensitivity to the honor of the American military profession, Wagner found the school's dependence on foreign studies of strategy and tactics insufferable. Aside from mere pride, differences in organization, terminology, and terrain all made an indigenous military textbook desirable. Wagner remedied this need by writing two books—*The Service of Security and Information* and *Organization and Tactics*—that through their combined nineteen editions would serve as the standard American texts on those subjects for over a decade. These works were quickly incorporated into promotion examinations, essentially elevating them to sanctioned doctrine. It was no exaggeration when Swift claimed that "Wagner's books became as familiar as the drill book."[88]

In content, Wagner's textbooks were a continuation of Uptonian orthodoxies. He sought to compensate for the "murderous fire . . . of the present day" by using extended order and devolving more tactical authority to lower-level commanders, thus extending the basic tenets of Upton's tactics.[89] Wagner also shared Upton's conviction that careful preparation was the hallmark of professionalism. *The Service of Security and Information* was almost entirely taken up with the subject of how a commander should gather intelligence in preparation for battle, a task at which Upton had excelled during the Civil War. Also like Upton, Wagner rejected the dichotomy between action and study. He conceded that war remained "the best school" for an officer but argued that much could still be accomplished in peacetime. "If an officer would prepare himself to be of service to his country," Wagner wrote, "[he] must accumulate by reading and reflection a fund of military knowledge based upon the experience of others."[90]

In 1894, Wagner was made the chief tactics instructor. He was then just finishing *Organization and Tactics,* which provided a sound curriculum. The methods of instruction, however, were still modeled upon the West Point system of recitations and were as likely to crush intellectual curiosity among the student-officers as to encourage it. Hoping to "go out of the old groove somewhat," Captain Wagner brought his old friend Swift to Fort Leavenworth with orders to make the classroom more "practical."[91] There was considerable room for improvement. Classroom interaction consisted either of lectures or superficial exchanges in which the instructor quizzed students about the specific content of passages from the assigned reading. Well-suited to simple, quantifiable problems, the technique was discouragingly adversarial and drove students toward rote memorization. "The knowledge so obtained is deceptive," Swift later wrote. "It develops the memory and not the judgment."[92] As developing judgment is the essence of professional education, Swift saw that the existing system, which provided "no chance for elaboration, explanation, or for a community of thought," needed to be replaced with a method that allowed dialogue between the instructor and student.[93]

Swift developed what he called the "applicatory system," which drew upon European, particularly German, methods of military education. After a brief series of introductory lectures, students honed their ability to apply

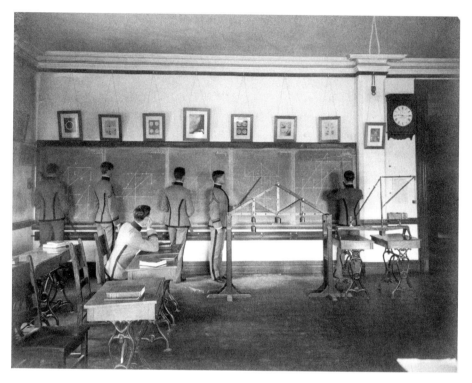

In 1903, cadets "recite" their lessons in the manner that had been customary at West Point since the early nineteenth century. Useful for some subjects—such as basic mathematics—the formality and rigidity of the educational technique was poorly suited to postgraduate military education at Fort Leavenworth. (Stockbridge Collection, USMA)

basic principles in a succession of progressively advanced tactical problems. Rather than reciting from a book, students answered these tactical problems in the form of a written order, just as they would issue in an actual campaign. Each class concluded with the instructor leading a critique of the proposed solutions. As the course progressed, the students were given the opportunity to competitively play out their solutions in *Kriegspiel* (wargame) or to solve problems outdoors in the countryside surrounding the fort. These tactical problems, wargames, and "terrain rides" allowed the students to creatively apply tactical principles while honing their skills in expressing commands verbally and in writing.[94]

Swift was rightfully proud of his work; but he came to regard it as the absolute in military education to the exclusion of other methods and subjects,

The superiority of the applicatory system over recitation is evident in this early-twentieth-century photograph of a Fort Leavenworth classroom. The students appear engrossed in the problem depicted on the large military map and are allowed easy interaction with each other and their instructor, possibly the figure wearing the cap. (Special Collections, Combined Arms Research Library, Fort Leavenworth, Kansas)

growing frustrated with what he perceived as Wagner's lack of enthusiasm. Swift later accused Wagner of being too wed to "his literary work," which Swift thought took up time that should have been given to the applicatory system.[95] Though there was likely some merit in this claim, Swift's fixation on method prevented him from seeing that the more fundamental difference between him and Wagner was in their understanding of what it meant to prepare for war. Wagner wanted Fort Leavenworth to be a European-style war college; and upon his departure in 1896, he proudly proclaimed that its curriculum was "not widely different from the War Academy at Berlin."[96] Though the assertion was overblown, the aspiration was genuine. Swift, on the other hand, wanted a school to train officers for their regimental duties and faulted Wagner for his ambition: "There was still too much military policy and institutions, strategy, grand tactics, logistics and military geography. It looked like a study of the University-Course before the primer had been mastered."[97] Wagner and Swift thus echoed the earlier disagreement between Upton and Sherman over the proper focus for the

Artillery School. For a brief period at Fort Leavenworth, Wagner ensured that the Uptonian view was ascendant; but throughout the late nineteenth century and well into the next, the Sherman-Swift view would generally prevail.

The two approaches were not mutually exclusive, but there was so little military education in the U.S. Army—just two years in a forty-year career—that the fight for curricular space became a bitter zero-sum contest, at least in the mind of Swift. Though Wagner was happy to recommend Swift as his successor, Swift would not even acknowledge the validity of Wagner's focus.[98] Instead, he averred that Wagner's failure to appreciate the applicatory system was because his "brilliant attainments were entirely literary and not in practical military matters."[99] In other words, Wagner was nothing more than a "book soldier." This was an ironic charge from Swift, who a younger officer would later deride as a "saturated solution of Civil War History."[100] But the awkwardness of the claim only underscores the depth of the bias against any semblance of theory. The great irony is that Swift considered himself to be a disciple of Upton but attacked Wagner for making the Infantry and Cavalry School curriculum resemble what Upton had hoped to institute at the Artillery School.

Swift's recourse to *ad hominem* attacks illustrates that even in intellectual matters, professional credibility ultimately derived from field service. This was not such a difficulty for members of the Civil War generation. Upton, for instance, spent virtually no time with troops during his own post war career but had built an unimpeachable reputation during the war that inoculated him against the charge of being "too theoretical." Without the opportunity to win similar battlefield distinction, officers of the composite generation could earn their reputation only through participation in the shared misery of hard duty. Wagner's aversion to service with his regiment kept him from building this credibility, and so the charge of being a "book soldier" would persist throughout his career. He dominated the army's intellectual landscape of the 1890s for lack of any alternatives, but his credentials would always be suspect.[101]

Wagner's awareness of his reputation might have contributed to the defensiveness that he displayed in a dispute arising from the *JMSI*'s 1897 essay contest on the topic of "The Proper Military Instruction for Our Officers." Swift's essay trumpeting the applicatory system received an honorable mention, but the prize went to Captain James Pettit for his essay questioning the Infantry and Cavalry School's focus on high command. Pettit noted that the curricular focus on advanced staff work did not correspond well with a student body composed of lieutenants with a median average of only four years of service at the beginning of the course. Moreover, the students were not necessarily even the best of their peers, for despite McCook's efforts some regimental commanders still regarded the school as a place to deposit the unneeded or uneducated. Pettit argued that "if [Fort Leavenworth] is to become a *War College* then the qualifications, age, rank, knowledge [etc.] of the students must be changed."[102] But rather than constructively engage with this reasonable critique, Wagner wrote a sarcastic, defensive reply. Pettit's counter was published in the May 1898 issue of the *JMSI;* but by that time the country was at war, the military schools were suspended, and there was no interest in academic debate.[103]

From its inception, Fort Leavenworth had suffered from the conflicting visions of its supporters and the skepticism or indifference of the rest of the army. Yet even without a universally accepted notion of what the school was to accomplish, it had an invigorating effect on many officers. After coming to the school as an instructor, one senior cavalryman reported, almost in wonder, "Having for the first time in my army career had access to a fine military library, I have dropped all side issues and devoted myself to an endeavor to absorb some of the professional information at hand here."[104] Similarly, Robert L. Bullard, who would go on to become one of the top American commanders in World War I, looked back at this time at Fort Leavenworth in the 1890s as a turning point in his career. Up to that assignment, the rhythms of small frontier stations had lulled Bullard into complacency: "The life with its simple duties, etc., dinners, dances, hunting, rifling, etc., was not unpleasant but it was in general unprofitable. It added little to me." But at Fort Leavenworth, even though Bullard was only part of the garrison with no official connection to the school, he was stimulated by the effort to turn "the army from mere Indian police to its true function, the art of war. Here in the school the principles of my profession were, after study, being illustrated in field practice."[105] Officers elsewhere had also taken notice; they sought the faculty's expertise in training, and some officers began to seek duty as a student or instructor.[106] The maturation of army postgraduate education coincided with Schofield's reform of the promotion system that led to more frequent transfers among the regiments. In conjunction, these changes began to erode the barriers among the various regiments and arms of service. Some hoped that in time, this would lead to greater uniformity throughout the army.[107]

In time this would come to pass, but the pioneers building the institutions necessary for a cohesive professionalism would suffer from the lack of just such institutions. Wagner, Swift, and Pettit all bore the strong imprint of Upton: Wagner most closely followed Upton's intellectual legacy in military policy, education, and tactics; Swift was an unabashed admirer of Upton; and, historian Russell Weigley cites Pettit as the epitome of a purported "Uptonian pessimism."[108] Yet for their common inspiration, the three officers fiercely disagreed as to the best form of professional education, one of the areas on which Upton wrote most clearly and extensively. This divergence among a group that should have been closely aligned in their views suggests just how diverse the composite generation was in terms of the professional experiences, enthusiasms, and outlook of its members.

CHAPTER SIX

The Second Upheaval

TENSIONS BETWEEN THE United States and Spain had been high for many months, but it was not until after an explosion that ripped through the U.S.S. *Maine* in the harbor of Havana on the night of 15 February 1898 that war preparations began in earnest. Yet President William McKinley was devoted to avoiding conflict. For two months, if the president had any thoughts on war aims or strategy in case war should occur, he did not share them with his cabinet. This left the military departments to plan for war in accord with their own hopes and fears, a process that revealed much about their relative states of institutional development.[1]

The navy was brimming with confidence. It was capably led by Secretary of the Navy John D. Long and his hyperactive assistant secretary, Theodore Roosevelt, who had been quietly readying the fleet for several months. But the foundation for success had been laid long before. During the 1880s, the navy had enjoyed a renaissance funded by unusually generous budgets to build a modern fleet, guided by the theories of Captain Alfred Thayer Mahan (son of the West Point professor Dennis and named in honor of the superintendent Sylvanus), and enabled by the professionalizing reforms of Admiral Stephen B. Luce. Ironically, the inspiration for the latter development was the army. In 1865, then-Lieutenant Commander Luce commanded a ship supporting Sherman's offensive through the Carolinas.

Coming ashore for consultations, he was amazed by the general's grasp of the many aspects of the operational situation. "The scales seemed to fall from my eyes," Luce later wrote. "It dawned upon me that there were certain fundamental principles underlying military operations."[2] Sherman might have provided the epiphany, but Upton provided the blueprint for how to develop similar capability in naval officers. Luce served at Fort Monroe during Upton's tenure there and made the Artillery School the model for the new Naval War College, even while the army (with the exception of Wagner at Fort Leavenworth) had largely abandoned the idea of a war college–like education. Meanwhile under Luce's supervision, the school flourished. Throughout the 1890s, the faculty and students examined the problems of a Caribbean war against Spain in depth. In late 1897, Roosevelt used some of these plans as a basis for his directives to the fleet. Though there was no consensus within the navy as to the proper strategy for such a war, the process of planning had fostered a common appreciation of the alternatives and the most significant considerations. Consequently, after the loss of the *Maine,* the navy developed a simple and direct plan for war: Quickly win mastery of the waters around Spain's colonies.[3]

The army was driven by doubt. To an extent, this reflected the personalities and limitations of its leaders. Secretary of War Russell A. Alger was a former Civil War regimental commander who had gone on to a successful career in business and as governor of Michigan. Though likely equal to the task of overseeing the established methods of peace, Alger lacked the drive and indomitable will necessary to take charge of the unruly War Department in a crisis. The commanding general, Nelson A. Miles, was capable and energetic but also irredeemably ambitious and vain. Though just a twenty-one-year-old clerk when the Civil War began, he recruited a company and began a spectacular rise from captain to commander of a division. After the war, Miles continued to rise through the ranks due to both his reputation as an aggressive and typically successful frontier commander and his marriage to a niece of William T. Sherman. Though Sherman was often exasperated with Miles's incessant scheming, he nonetheless aided the younger man's career. In 1895, with Schofield's retirement, Miles ascended to the army's top post, but his ambitions were not satisfied; with the possibility of a glorious war, he could not conceal his hopes that he might win enough fame to take him to the White House. As the crisis culminated, McKinley—trusting neither the inept secretary nor the scheming general—resorted to the awkward expedient of turning to the retired Schofield for military expertise. Miles's predecessor was given an office in the War Department and for several weeks conferred with McKinley daily.[4]

But the army also suffered in comparison to the navy in terms of its institutional capability. It had nothing equivalent to the war plans produced by the Naval War College nor a dedicated planning staff. The closest approximation was the Adjutant General's Office, which was responsible for issuing all orders to the army. It had long attracted some of the army's best officers, but the capacity to issue orders was a quite different matter than having the expertise to produce war plans that integrated maneuver, supply, transportation, and the many other functions of an army in campaign. The work of planning the mobilization fell to a group of just three officers, including the recently promoted Lieutenant Colonel Arthur L. Wagner, who had transferred from the infantry to the staff in 1896. Wagner was also the army representative to the joint two-man committee that Secretaries Alger and Long grandly charged with coordinating all "matters of offense and defense" that concerned both services.[5] Wagner was likely as prepared for the task as any officer of his day; in addition to his academic works, he had until his promotion in February been in charge of the army's nascent intelligence organ, the Military Information Division. Nonetheless, the small *ad hoc* committees on which he served were risibly inadequate instruments for directing the military potential of a continent-spanning industrial power in the age of steam.[6]

In contrast to the aggressive nature of the navy's plans, the War Department readied itself for a cautious war. Commanding General Nelson A. Miles dreaded the possibility of a summer campaign in disease-ridden Cuba and in the absence of any direction from the president assumed that the army's main task would be to guard the American coast. Before the autumn, no offensive action was expected aside from perhaps a small expedition to seize a remote port through which arms could be sent to the Cuban rebels. Naval superiority and rebel pressure might be sufficient to win the war. If not, only much later would a larger expedition be sent against Havana or some other strategic point.[7]

In contrast to the apprehensive pacifism of the White House, Capitol Hill was eagerly bellicose. Three weeks after the sinking of the *Maine,* Congress authorized the first peacetime expansion of the regular army since the 1850s—the creation of a sixth and seventh regiment of artillery to bolster the coast defenses. Congress also approved McKinley's reluctant request for fifty million dollars to prepare for war. In accordance with the president's wishes, the navy received most of that appropriation, with the army's share going toward defensive preparations.[8]

Despite McKinley's caution, Chairman James T. Hull of the House Military Affairs Committee hoped to use the unusual support for military readiness to achieve long-sought army reforms. Though a former volunteer officer, Hull was a strong advocate for the regular army. He introduced legislation that would have created an expansible army by reorganizing infantry regiments into a larger three-battalion structure and authorizing a greater wartime strength for companies. In conjunction, these measures would allow the army to increase in a crisis to over one hundred thousand officers and men—a nearly fourfold increase from the peacetime strength of twenty-seven thousand. With such a structure, the regulars could fight the campaign against Spain that the War Department envisioned without having to rely on either militia or volunteers. With Hull's backing, the committee reported favorably on the bill, and it was passed to the full House of Representatives for debate.[9]

The regulars' hopes that they might at last realize Calhoun's dream of an expansible regular army with the corresponding diminishment of the militia were soon dashed. The Civil War had also had a profound influence over the state soldiery. The experience of national war had caused some militiamen to create a more capable, cohesive, and centralized state force than the independent companies and regiments of the antebellum period. The leaders of this movement wanted something more than to just be a home guard for repelling invasion; if there were to be another great war, they wanted the existing state units to be able to provide the bulk of the country's armies rather than having to create new volunteer units. This heightened ambition to be recognized as the country's first-line reserve was reflected in the slow replacement of the old term *organized militia* with their preferred moniker *National Guard.* The Hull Bill threatened these dreams by rendering both the National Guard and volunteers superfluous. The guardsmen were so successful in rallying their congressional supporters that nothing remained of Hull's proposal except for the three-battalion infantry regiment organization; and even that minor concession was contingent upon the promise that in case of war the president would issue a call for sixty thousand volunteers, all of whom were to be drawn from the National Guard.[10]

In defeating the Hull Bill, allies of the National Guard had claimed that it was a trained, equipped force ready for war. Although it was indeed an improvement over the organized militia of 1861, even the best state units were far from ready for war. Moreover, there was a vast disparity between the best and the worst. Despite the implication of its title, the dominance of local personalities, priorities, and politics made the National Guard a patchwork of disparate equipment, organization, strength, and proficiency. An 1891 congressional survey found that five states allocated no funds whatsoever for their troops; units in those states supported themselves through individual and community contributions and the occasional issue of equipment from the federal government. Yet even in more generous states, guardsmen and their communities still bore a heavy burden. State governors and adjutants general (the top state military official) were thus limited in what measures they could impose. This meant that they could not upset civic pride by taking a unit that was too small to be effective and consolidating into a larger unit shared with other towns. Neither could state officials afford to lose guardsmen who were providing financial support for the local company by making service too onerous or by discharging them as physically unfit. A regular officer advising the Alabama National Guard during its 1892 summer encampment was disgusted that the opportunity to preen in uniform before admiring friends and family at the camp picnic was considered more important than training, but he grudgingly acknowledged that it was a critical inducement for the unpaid guardsmen. Despite these faults, the National Guard had ensured that it would play a significant role in any war against Spain.[11]

Once Congress approved McKinley's war resolution on 19 April 1898, events quickly overcame the strategic and political calculations of all parties: the president, the army, the navy, and the National Guard. War enthusiasm erupted across the country, completely altering the political landscape of mobilization. Governors and their adjutants general prevailed upon McKinley to ask for 125,000 volunteers instead of 60,000, thereby sparing them the duty of choosing which among their units would be selected for service. But there was even more demand from outside of the existing National Guard structure. McKinley's hometown of Canton alone was able to raise an entire regiment, while the governor of Ohio claimed that his office received pledges totaling one hundred thousand volunteers from across the state. In response to this enthusiasm, several weeks later McKinley issued a call for an additional seventy-five thousand volunteers.[12]

The Civil War experience might also have led to McKinley's call for so many volunteers. There were many, including Schofield, who believed that Lincoln had erred in not calling for more volunteers in the early days of the war. The retired general urged the president to request 400,000 volunteers, an absurdly large number with little use other than perhaps as a ploy to overawe the Spanish. Schofield also suggested a complete reorganization of the War Department and the establishment of a general staff, actions that would have been better carried out earlier while Schofield was still commanding general than in the midst of a mobilization. Such advice might have led to Schofield's gradual fall from the president's grace.[13]

Meanwhile, the initial call for 125,000 volunteers caused enough disruption. The president, however, had not consulted or even warned the War Department about his decision to double the number of volunteers that it would have to organize and equip. The military bureaucracy was ill-equipped to react to sudden change. To that point, the demands of civilian policy-makers had caused it to become tailored to the narrow task of supporting twenty-seven thousand regulars in as parsimonious a manner as possible. After decades of fiscal starvation, it was impossible to equip the massive host of volunteers as quickly as the American public expected. Surveying mobilization sites, letting contracts for food, building camps, expanding the production of military goods: All of these steps had to be taken before the task of translating manpower into armies could even begin. It took time to even acquire basic, nonmilitary supplies in the necessary quantities; one group of volunteers arrived at their mobilization camp only to be furloughed back to their homes in order to get underclothes. Within a few weeks, enough work had been done for the mobilization to begin in earnest; but many specialized items, such as large wagons rugged enough for military use, could not be fully provided to the armies before the fighting ended.[14]

The supply problems would not have been so dire if the National Guard had been as ready for service as its proponents claimed. But state units arrived at the mobilization sites with obsolete, worn, or incomplete issues of equipment. Moreover, not all guardsmen were as keen to be a first-line reserve as their leaders; many of the rank-and-file were content to serve only as traditional home guard militia. These guardsmen had no desire to fight far from their families and businesses; and because the 1792 Militia Act remained the legal foundation for bringing them into federal service, each individual had to enlist as a volunteer. A large number declined to take the oath, and still more were rejected as physically unfit. Replacements could generally be recruited, but they required a full issue of equipment. An inspection of one division in May 1898 found that none of the regiments had more than three-quarters of its authorized strength and half of the men had never even fired a military rifle. By one estimate, only a quarter of the soldiers provided by the states had any previous military training. Even the best National Guard units were under strength and ill-equipped, while the worst were of little more value than newly raised volunteer regiments.[15]

Much to the dismay of regulars who had dreamed of quick wartime promotions, virtually the only aspect of the National Guard that was at full strength was its contingent of officers. The leaders of the National Guard were generally committed to leading the units that they had built up during peace, and even commissions within the newly created regiments went to influential civilians. For just as the composite generation had sustained itself through decades of slow promotions with the hope that they would be showered with commissions by frantic governors, their civilian counterparts had been raised on tales of civilians successfully going off to fight the Civil War.[16]

One of the first to learn the realities of mobilization was Captain Eben Swift, who had left Fort Leavenworth in 1897 for a post on the staff of the governor of Illinois. When war came the next year, it seemed that fortune had placed Swift in a perfect position to win a high-ranking volunteer commission. Yet when he asked the governor for such a position, the governor turned him away with nothing. "Swift, I like you," the governor explained, "but this business is all politics, and you are not even an Illinois man." The colonel of one of the regiments offered Swift a majority, a disappointing promotion of only one grade that Swift initially refused in the hopes of something better. Yet he eventually relented when the colonel also offered to make Swift's seventeen-year-old son a first lieutenant. The father thought that was too much for such a young man, so Eben, Jr., became a second lieutenant instead. The elder Swift's fortunes improved with the second call for volunteers. Command of one of those regiments went to a congressman who requested Swift as his lieutenant colonel in order to have someone to "run the military business" of the unit. Several months later and long after the fighting with Spain was done, Swift finally became a colonel when all the field officers of another volunteer regiment were dismissed amid a barrage of charges and countercharges of "incompetence and ignorance."[17] More typical was the experience of Captain James Parker, who, despite having the advantages of a distinguished record on the frontier and a brother in Congress, was unable to secure any position with the units of his native New Jersey and only a commission as a major in a New York regiment. Because Parker was unhappy with that modest promotion, his sister, who had married into a prominent Massachusetts family, lobbied on his behalf for a higher grade in the forces of that state. The governor demurred, noting that he already had "several hundred applications . . . very many from men of large and honorable military experience in the War of the Rebellion and in the regular army, including a considerable number of graduates of West Point."[18] So although Swift was one of the most fortunate officers of the composite generation, his success paled compared to that experienced by the lucky regulars of 1861 and 1862.

The composite generation had only slightly greater luck in winning volunteer commissions controlled by the federal government. In making his selection for general officers, McKinley, though a former volunteer officer of the Civil War, was more deferential to military experience than were his predecessors Polk or Lincoln. Fifty of the eighty-three general officer appointments given in May and June of 1898 were given to regulars, and even the remaining "political generals" had experience either in the Civil War or with the National Guard. Nine were graduates of West Point, including three former Confederate generals. Yet unlike in 1861 when younger men of promise like Irvin McDowell were elevated to command, Miles ensured that the remnants of the Civil War generation took all of the high-ranking positions.[19]

This left the younger officers to vie for the staff officer commissions controlled by the War Department. Those in the higher grades of colonel and lieutenant colonel generally went to seasoned regulars, but West Pointers with just a few years of service found themselves in competition with the twenty-five thousand civilian applicants who hoped for the lower-ranking commissions. Many of these petitioners came in person, clutching letters of recommendation that they hoped would impress Secretary of War Alger or Adjutant General Henry C. Corbin. The two officials were so besieged by applicants that they could attend to the real work of mobilization only at night. Under such pressure, many of the lower-ranking volunteer commissions were given away to those with influential patrons rather than to the best qualified.[20]

Amid the frenzied preparations caused by the war resolution, McKinley at last called the military secretaries and their uniformed advisors to the White House to discuss strategy. The president favored a quick strike against Cuba. Delay entailed multiple hazards: a Spanish naval raid against the American coast, the intervention of another European power, the installation of a Cuban government hostile to American interests, and a restless public at home. The navy was eager for immediate action, but Miles argued for a delay until the fall when the threat of yellow fever had passed and the volunteers had been trained. McKinley reluctantly agreed to delay any significant invasion but ordered the blockade of Cuba and the movement of all available regular regiments to the Gulf Coast in preparation for a limited expedition in case conditions warranted.[21]

Though the pace of operations was less ambitious than the president had hoped for, the mobilization was still a massive undertaking for the small team of War Department planners. No matter how brilliant the minds devoted to the task, such movements cannot be successfully extemporized. As Wagner knew from his study of the Austro-Prussian War, the Prussian General Staff had spent decades cataloguing the capacity of every rail station and siding in their realm so that they might precisely calculate the mobilization and movement of their armies. Lacking such detailed knowledge and the time to make use of it even if it had been on hand, the War Department sent the regular regiments of the Fifth Army Corps—the country's main strike force—to Tampa. This was a fateful choice. The secondary points of embarkation, Mobile and New Orleans, were superior to Tampa in nearly every aspect. They had more robust defenses to ward off raiding Spanish ships and were closer to the interior forts from which the assembling regiments were journeying. Most importantly, both ports, but New Orleans in particular, had greater capacity and access to the national network of rail and rivers. Central Florida was on the periphery of this network, and the port of Tampa was tied to the sparse regional infrastructure by only ten miles of single-track rail. Alger claimed that the pivotal consideration was the proximity of Tampa to Cuba: It was less than half the steaming distance than that from New Orleans. Yet this was a mixed benefit. If the naval situation was such that the Americans feared the invasion force being intercepted en route, then the Spanish might just as easily make a quick raid to disrupt preparations. Corbin later hinted that Alger might have instead selected Tampa because a friend of the secretary owned the railroad leading to the port.[22]

The reasons for the selection of General William R. "Pecos Bill" Shafter as commander of the Fifth Army Corps also remain obscure. Shafter was a Civil War volunteer who had risen to the rank of colonel by the war's end. He fared well in the postwar consolidation and was made a regular lieutenant colonel in 1866. During the 1870s, Shafter's aggressive pursuit of Native American raiders in the Rio Grande valley earned him his nickname and made him one of the few federal officers popular in Texas during Reconstruction. By the time of his promotion to brigadier general in May 1897, Shafter had been either a lieutenant colonel or colonel for nearly thirty-four years. But his extraordinary depth of experience as a regimental officer was the limit of his expertise. His brief period as a brigadier was in command of the Department of California, a largely administrative post. Moreover, in his later years Shafter had become "beastly obese" in the words of one subordinate. It was uncertain whether the three-hundred-pound, gout-ridden general could effectively command. Yet in a meeting during the first days of the war, Alger, Miles, and Corbin selected him to lead the army's vanguard. Alger might have favored Shafter because of their common Michigan origins, and Corbin was an old friend from their years together in the 24th Infantry. But according to some accounts of the conference, Miles played a decisive role in Shafter's selection. The commanding general might simply have thought that Shafter was among the best of the regular army brigadiers. Alternatively, Miles might have purposefully nominated a mediocrity to ensure that Miles would eventually be sent to Cuba to take charge of the expected fall invasion.[23] It is a telling indicator of the state of the army in 1898 that historians can plausibly argue that Shafter was selected because he was either among the best or the worst of the available generals.

Shafter's subordinates were equally inexperienced: Of the twelve division and brigade commanders in the Fifth Army Corps, only Joseph Wheeler— the commander of the Cavalry Division—had any experience as a general; and that had been as a Confederate during the Civil War. The most senior regular was Jacob F. Kent, a West Point classmate of Upton who had been a midranking staff officer during the Civil War. None of these subordinate commanders had even been a colonel for more than eight years, and three were still lieutenant colonels in regular rank.[24] Due to the glacial rate of promotions in the late-nineteenth-century army, this inexperience was not even matched with its usual corrective—youthful vigor. One lieutenant of Shafter's command later remembered, "To the younger officer most of the general officers and field officers looked over-old and broken . . . . I doubt if there was a single general officer at Tampa on May 20th, 1898, who could have gone into the field and taken part in a campaign of two years or more duration as was done in the Civil War."[25]

These aged generals were supported by staffs drawn mainly from the lieutenants and captains of the regular army, a broad category that ranged from the corps adjutant general Captain Edward J. McClernand, who had twenty-eight years of service and a Medal of Honor, to a brigade assistant adjutant general, Second Lieutenant Dennis E. Nolan, who had graduated from West Point just two years earlier.[26] Yet even those who had served as staff officers during frontier campaigns found that experience to be of little benefit. Neither had training offered any preparation. Chronically understrength units, dispersion, and lean budgets had precluded the kind of large maneuvers in which European staff officers could learn their trade. These shortfalls in experience and training might have been at least partly made up through education, but the narrow preferences of Sherman and the other commanding generals for more "practical" education had limited the ability of Upton and then Wagner to provide a war college-like education.

At Tampa, Shafter and his staff were overwhelmed by the task of readying an army corps for an expedition. Even activities common to all campaigns regardless of size, and which therefore should have been familiar—establishing lines of authority, quartering and reception of new arrivals, organizing movements—were done poorly or not at all. Their task was made more difficult by the failure of the staff bureaus in Washington to coordinate their actions: The adjutant general sent units, the quartermaster general sent supplies, the commissary general sent food, and the chief of ordnance sent weapons. The steady tide of men and supplies overwhelmed the small, inexpertly run railroad to the port, leading to massive congestion that at one point extended as far away as Columbia, South Carolina. What little cargo made it through the bottleneck at Tampa was not necessarily the most important. Numerous accounts note the sense of pervasive confusion that struck those arriving in Tampa.[27]

Shafter's task was further complicated by the primacy of naval operations in the war, which made him hostage to developments at sea. Because of the uncertainty associated with fleet movements, he was subjected to a series of contradictory orders. His first orders had been to ready several thousand regulars for an immediate reconnaissance in force to Cuba, but that was soon cancelled when a Spanish fleet departed the Cape Verde Islands and disappeared into the oceanic vastness. Over the following weeks, intermittent sightings of the enemy and uncertainty about the destination of the Spanish fleet meant that the Fifth Army Corps endured a numbing succession of alerts and subsequent stand-downs. It seemed that the danger posed by the prowling enemy fleet might preclude any significant movement for several months. Then suddenly in the last days of May, the Spanish fleet appeared and then promptly sought refuge in the fortified harbor of Santiago de Cuba on the island's southern coast. With the U.S. Navy unable to get at the Spanish ships, on 31 May Corbin directed Shafter to move to Cuba, seize Santiago, capture its garrison, and force the Spanish fleet into the waiting guns of the American navy.[28]

Shafter optimistically wired that he could depart by 4 June, perhaps unaware of the severity of the problems facing his own command. The last volunteer regiments, some still without weapons, were slow in arriving from their camps in Georgia. Meanwhile, quartermasters looking for critical items wandered among waiting railcars, opening each one because the bills of lading were not posted on the outside. On the promised date of departure, supplies were still being loaded into holds and not a single soldier was aboard the transports. The embarkation would have taken even longer if there had been enough ships. As it was, only half of the tonnage required to move the entire corps was on hand. When it was at last time for the soldiers to board, a panicked rush for the ships ensued. "Found everything in the greatest confusion one can imagine, no head, no tail," one regimental commander wrote in his diary. "Confusion worse [than] confounded. No directing, no officers. Men struggling to take possession of transports."[29] Not wanting to be left behind, units crowded onto the ships. An inspector found 1,640 men aboard a ship with a stated capacity of 570 passengers. On another transport, 1,200 soldiers shared only 12 sinkholes. By the night of 7 June, Shafter had received no less than five telegrams expressing the president's impatience. Finally, on the morning of the 8th, the ships pulled into the channel carrying less than 17,000 of the approximately 25,000 officers and men of Shafter's corps.[30]

Fortunately for the Americans, once they reached Cuba the Spanish did not contest the landing at the village of Daiquirí, approximately fifteen miles east of Santiago. The several hundred Spaniards in the immediate area withdrew before the Americans came ashore. Nonetheless, the debarkation went slowly, for Daiquirí had but a single pier and dock, and there was a severe shortage of small boats to bring men and supplies to the shore. This problem would persist throughout the campaign, as operations were hobbled for want of supplies and heavy equipment that remained just several hundred yards off the shore. It took several days just to land all the troops and the bare minimum of supplies necessary to begin operations. During this vulnerable time, Shafter naturally had no desire to prod the languid Spanish into activity, and he ordered his commanders to avoid an engagement.[31]

Disregarding this directive, Major General "Fighting" Joe Wheeler—the former Confederate general—aggressively pushed his Cavalry Division forward past the division that Shafter had designated as the lead unit. Late on 23 June, the day after the initial landing, Wheeler learned from Cuban rebels that just a few miles up the road 1,500 to 3,000 Spaniards occupied a fortified position near the village of Las Guasimas. The rebels also reported that an unguarded secondary trail led into the flank of the enemy position. Wheeler and the commander of his lead brigade, Brigadier General Samuel B. M. Young, did not take the time to confirm this information with their own reconnaissance but rushed to attack an entrenched enemy possibly twice as strong as their own force. Advancing on foot (nearly all of the horses had been left behind in Tampa), Young and two regular regiments attacked up the main road while Colonel Leonard Wood's 1st U.S. Volunteer Cavalry, "The Rough Riders," attempted to flank the Spanish by way of the trail. Fortunately for the Americans, there were only 1,500 Spaniards in the rear guard that was already under orders to retreat. But the purportedly unwatched trail followed by the Rough Riders was in fact well defended, and the volunteers suffered about two-thirds of the Americans' sixty-eight casualties—approximately five percent of the force engaged. This costly skirmish provided Shafter with no tactical advantage, but Wheeler, Young, and Wood had gotten the fight that they wanted.[32]

Wood had particular cause to seek battle, for in the regular army he was not even a line officer but a surgeon with the rank of captain. Though he had earned a reputation as an unusually fearsome doctor for his role in the grueling pursuit of the Apache chief Geronimo, it was his friendship with Assistant Secretary of the Navy Theodore Roosevelt that led to his selection for command. Wood badly wanted a transfer from the Medical Department to the line, and Las Guasimas was his first opportunity to prove himself worthy. Wood was so intent on displaying his indifference to enemy fire that he seemed to forget about directing the assault; after the skirmish, Young gently chided Wood for exposing himself so conspicuously.[33]

Yet at most, Wood was guilty of taking a behavior common throughout the officer corps to excess. During the Spanish and Philippine Wars, regulars often exposed themselves to enemy fire more than effective tactics or leadership might have demanded. The cultlike emphasis on individual courage within the officer corps was a complex phenomenon both in its causes and its effects. Armies have a clear functional reason to encourage valorous acts; but when taken to excess, the demands of bravado can overwhelm calculation and lead to military disaster, as might easily have happened at Las Guasimas. But from an early age, officers of Wood's age had been steeped in romanticized memories of the Civil War. These norms were then reinforced by Victorian notions of gentlemanly honor and other imitated European aristocratic norms to create intense pressure for officers to risk their lives in order to meet personal and collective expectations. The experience of the Civil War generation demonstrated that battlefield reputation could yield more tangible benefits as well. The relative difference in seniority decided by the retention boards in 1866 and 1867 continued to manifest itself on a daily basis over the following decades in the form of better quarters and pay, greater deference, and the prerogatives of command.[34]

In an army of men eager to prove themselves worthy, perhaps no regular felt a greater burden in that regard than Wagner. "[As an] instructor in, the Art of War, and the author of officially recognized works on military subjects," he wrote to his superior, Adjutant General Corbin, "I should be placed in a humiliating position if I were confined to office duties when my comrades and many of my former pupils were actively engaged in war."[35] This plea left unstated that Wagner already suffered from the reputation of being a "book soldier." Though Corbin was regarded as particularly icy and had great need for Wagner in Washington, he granted his assistant permission to form a "Bureau of Military Intelligence in the Field." The small party consisting of Wagner, a lieutenant, an interpreter, and a clerk was soon off to Tampa, where Shafter initially welcomed the assistance. But Wagner erred by not disclosing that his bureau was not formally under the general's command until they were underway for Cuba. Shafter suspected that this unusual arrangement was some sort of unfriendly ploy of Miles's, and so he declared Wagner to be only an "observer" and eventually commandeered his three assistants. Desperate to find some employment in the campaign,

Wagner found a place as a volunteer aide to General Henry W. Lawton, commander of the Second Division. Though a poor use of Wagner's talents, the position allowed him to roam freely and witness operations at the army's front, accompanying scouts and inspecting sentinels.[36]

Though many in Shafter's army were eager to come to grips with the Spaniards, after Las Guasimas the campaign moved forward slowly. Despite the opening of a second landing site closer to Santiago, bringing supplies ashore was still a slow process. But heavy rains and poor roads were the biggest obstacle. Supplies began to mount on the beach, as there were only enough mule trains available to bring the minimum essential amount of ammunition, food, and medical supplies to the forward troops.[37]

A week after the initial landing, reports of a Spanish relief column marching to Santiago forced Shafter to action. Though the supply situation was still dire, he had the bulk of his command ashore. The Spanish had withdrawn to the fortifications around the city, which on the eastern side facing the American advance consisted of a series of trenches and blockhouses centered upon two successive ridges running perpendicular to the main road coming into the port. Shafter set 1 July for the day of the attack on the outermost ridge consisting of San Juan and Kettle hills. Behind the barbed wire running along most of the ridge, several hundred Spaniards waited for the Americans in blockhouses and trenches. Aside from the main road, there were a few lesser trails leading through thick vegetation; but the Spanish had fortified key points along that network, making any flanking movement difficult. Yet Shafter hoped that Lawton's division could use one of these trails, take the strongpoint at the village of El Caney a few miles to the northeast of San Juan, and then take the Spanish main position from the flank just as the other two divisions attacked along the main road. Buoyed by the success at Las Guasimas, Shafter anticipated an easy fight lasting only a few hours. He conducted no thorough reconnaissance and issued no written order, believing that his subordinates had enough experience to act properly. Thus, the Americans attacked with a hazy scheme based on only a vague notion of the terrain and enemy dispositions.[38]

The plan came undone immediately. Though the more than five thousand soldiers of Lawton's division were opposed by just five hundred Spanish infantrymen at El Caney, the defenders kept the Americans pinned down several hundred yards away. The Spaniards had no artillery, but Lawton frittered away his advantage by placing his battery of guns too far from the enemy and then scattering its fire across the enemy lines for most of the day. Though given two hours to take El Caney, Lawton allowed the desultory fight to last for ten. Lawton had not only failed to assist the main effort, but his predicament compelled Shafter to commit the corps reserve to support what was meant to be a secondary effort.[39]

The action at El Caney disproved Sherman's earlier assertion that a good company commander would be a good general, for during the Civil War and then again on the frontier Lawton had been an excellent company commander. Indeed, even in 1898 he still possessed the attributes desired in a good regimental officer: courage, strength, and presence. Yet as Captain George McIver, who was present at El Caney in Brigadier General Adna R. Chaffee's brigade of Lawton's division, later noted, "The problem was beyond [Lawton and Chaffee]. They did not know how to use the very efficient instrument which had been placed in their hands."[40] The following year, Lawton was killed in action in the Philippines while leading a skirmish line like the good captain that he was at heart.[41]

Lawton's failure at El Caney meant that the main attack went forward without assistance. Still, the Americans had a decided advantage in mass: about 8,000 Americans with 12 field guns against just over 500 Spaniards on the heights, with another 600 soldiers and 2 guns in the immediate vicinity. The seeming American advantage in artillery was deceptive, for the Spanish had modern guns using smokeless powder while the Americans were still using black-powder weapons. The American guns opened fire from an exposed hill more than a mile from the enemy positions. The Spanish gunners, firing from concealed positions, responded with such accuracy that the American artillery was forced to retire for a time, leaving the infantry to fend for themselves. William Lassiter, one of the gunners present at San Juan, later recalled being "disgusted" with the performance, for which infantrymen taunted them as "crabs" apt to "run to the rear.[42]

Yet the problem with the field artillery was not cowardice but technological and tactical obsolescence resulting from decades of neglect and complacency. During the late nineteenth century, the Ordnance Department had invested most of its limited resources in the large coast defense guns, even while European armies were revolutionizing field guns with innovations like recoilless carriages and high-explosive shells. The tactical deficiencies arose from the peculiar subculture of light artillerymen. The best minds in the Artillery Corps were often drawn to the more prestigious and technically challenging coast guns. The light artillerymen, perhaps as a means of psy-chological defense, came to define themselves in opposition to their favored but sedentary brethren and so came to emphasize dash and aggressiveness.[43] In 1895, the artillery director of the Light Artillery and Cavalry School identified youth, activity, and "a natural fondness for horses" as the pri-mary attributes of a good light artilleryman. He made no mention of tactical skill or technical knowledge.[44] Consequently, artillery tactics envisioned quick movements and bold deployments close to the enemy, as had been done in Mexico and the Civil War. Reflecting upon the poor performance in Cuba, Lassiter realized that his battery had confined itself to the parade ground and never attempted to train under realistic conditions. "How we were to meet the varied requirements of the battle field never entered our heads," he rued.[45]

In addition to not having support from either Lawton's division or the artillery, the two divisions poised for the main attack at San Juan also lacked a commander. Though Shafter had been one of the last of the expedition to come ashore, he was already incapacitated after just a few days in Cuba. He exerted what control he could over the fighting via telegraph from a head-quarters several miles away. The two division commanders were left to push their commands forward in accord with Shafter's vague guidance. They did so clumsily, putting so many regiments forward that the compressed line was an easy target for Spanish bullets. Casualties mounted as the American force paused uncertain in the valley below the formidable heights. Finally, one of Shafter's aides, Major John D. Miley—a first lieutenant in regular rank with just eleven years of service—ordered the assault forward. With that, the fif-teen regiments—thirteen regular, one federal volunteer (the Rough Riders), and one National Guard—rushed forward. Though the Spanish fought well, they were overwhelmed by the spirited assault. Still, the struggle left the Americans in considerable disarray, and they were fortunate that the several thousand Spanish infantry in the main defenses on the next ridge were con-tent for the time being to do nothing more than skirmish from a distance.[46]

From his far perch, Shafter had so little sense of the battle that he initially reported to Washington that casualties had been light. It was not until sev-eral hours afterward that he learned the price of victory: nearly 1,400 casu-alties from a total force of about 15,000. With only the outer ring of the Spanish defenses breached, the ailing general was unnerved; and on 3 July, he wired to Washington that he was considering a withdrawal of several

This photograph of the 21st Battery Field Artillery in 1901 reveals the deficiencies of that arm: The 3.2-inch field guns are the same type as those that fared so poorly in Cuba, and the battery organization had changed little in a century. European armies were already fielding rapid-fire guns organized into larger formations capable of devastating concentrations of firepower. (Lucien G. Berry Collection, AHEC)

miles. That same day, the Spanish fleet made a desperate attempt to break through the American blockade and was destroyed. Still, it required the intervention of more stalwart subordinates to convince Shafter to hold on to the ground so dearly won. Two weeks later the Spanish garrison surrendered, effectively ending the war in Cuba. The timing was fortunate for, as Miles had feared, yellow fever, malaria, and dysentery tore through the American ranks; by late July, more than three-quarters of the men were incapacitated by disease. The War Department evacuated the battered Fifth Army Corps to a camp at Montauk Point, New York, where they were quarantined for several weeks. Thus, the gamble of hurriedly dispatching nearly two-thirds of the regular army in a single expedition under an unproven commander was only barely made good.[47]

The far more successful campaign in the Philippines suggests that not all American generals were as hapless as Shafter. Though the War Department had not envisioned any effort there, the imperialist Roosevelt badly wanted an American colony in the Far East and so had earlier directed Commodore George Dewey, commander of the American Asiatic Squadron, to move to Manila in case of war. Dewey's subsequent destruction of the Spanish fleet created the opportunity that Roosevelt had desired, but asserting American control required land forces. Major General Wesley Merritt was hastily ordered to form the Eighth Army Corps at San Francisco and embark for the Philippines. Though San Francisco was far superior to Tampa as a staging location, in other respects Merritt faced more difficulties than Shafter. As a secondary effort, Merritt was allocated only four regular regiments. The bulk of his force was composed of volunteer units from western states that tended to give meager support to their National Guard units. Moreover, Merritt was at a lower priority for supplies to make good any shortages. Nonetheless, the movement in three convoys across the Pacific was orderly, and upon arrival it required only one sharp encounter to give the weary Spanish garrison excuse to surrender.[48]

The invasion of Puerto Rico under Miles and Major General John R. Brooke was similarly successful. Brooke carried out most of the preliminary work of organization for the relatively smooth embarkation. Once landed, the Americans performed well, albeit against even more feeble resistance. It is likely no coincidence that Miles, Merritt, and Brooke were the only three regulars still on active duty who had served as general officers during the Civil War. Provided that they were in good health, the best of the Civil War generation was still formidable. But the army had done nothing to create competent replacements. As had been the case throughout the century, this was left to natural talent and the accumulation of experience, only some of which might be relevant. So like successes in earlier wars, such as Scott's amphibious landing at Vera Cruz, Merritt's movement to the Philippines owed less to the institution and more to the fortunate convergence of individual talent and circumstances.[49]

Overall, the components of the United States military functioned as well or as poorly as should have been expected. The stunning victories at sea were a just reward for the government's investment in a modern fleet and the efforts of forward-thinking sailors like Admiral Stephen B. Luce. The public had not been so generous to the army, and that too was evident. It was impossible for it to suddenly produce the vast amount of materiel necessary for a large army. The performance of the National Guard also demonstrated that armies built upon nothing more than enthusiasm and a trickle of state and federal funds could not be expected suddenly to spring into action. Though the state volunteers fought credibly against lesser opponents in the Philippines, when faced with determined Spanish resistance in Cuba they were much less effective. National Guard apologists blamed the obsolete black-powder rifles carried by the citizen-soldiers, which indeed were a severe handicap, but an inquiry into cowardice among the leaders of a New York regiment and the relatively low casualties of state units at El Caney suggest that it was not merely a question of poor equipment.[50] The strengths and weaknesses of the regular army were also predictable outcomes of political indifference and the complacency of the Civil War generation with rudimentary training and education. Well-trained infantry companies and cavalry troops, the mainstay of the frontier constabulary, performed well enough to compensate for the obsolete artillery, confused staff departments, and uneven generalship.

• • • • •

In 1899, General James H. Wilson—Upton's former commander—captured the public mood regarding the late war: "A great nation can win even with inferior tools or by the use of inferior men, through the agency of main strength and awkwardness, or the weight of superior battalions, or the wealth of a greater treasury, but one likes to see it win by the use of brains and character where it is possible."[51] By that time, many in the public had come to doubt both the brains and the character of the War Department. The mobilization had not been as fast or orderly as they expected it should be. Also, epidemics of typhoid and other diseases killed more volunteers in their staging camps within the United States than enemy bullets overseas. To assuage the public anger over this seeming incompetence, McKinley appointed a commission led by Grenville Dodge—a respected Civil War general, former congressman, and railroad executive—to investigate the War Department's conduct of the war.[52]

The Dodge Commission spent several months gathering evidence before concluding that despite some mistakes, the War Department had done as well as could be expected under the circumstances. Yet this dispassionate finding was overshadowed by the spectacle caused by Miles's testimony. For several months Miles had been openly critical of Shafter and the War Department, while hinting of knowledge of even more serious problems that had not yet come to light. Yet when Dodge asked the commanding general to testify, Miles resisted until finally presented with a written summons. But there was no coyness when he finally appeared. Miles gave a litany of complaints, but the most sensational was that the Subsistence Department had issued toxin-laced beef to soldiers. In rebutting that charge, Commissary General Charles P. Eagan expressed the desire to "force the lie back into [Miles's] throat, covered with the contents of a camp latrine."[53] Eagan was court-martialed and retired for his outburst, while Miles was censured for failing to promptly report his suspicions, which proved to be baseless. So even though the Dodge Commission found that the commissary had done well during the war, the public perception of incompetence was reinforced by the media's gleeful coverage of feuding generals.[54]

In order to place the War Department on a firmer footing, McKinley replaced the ineffectual Alger with Elihu Root, a corporate lawyer from New York with no military experience. Root later claimed to have first declined the post on account of his lack of military knowledge and relented only when assured that McKinley wanted someone capable of establishing the legal framework for governing the possessions won during the war, not "any one who knows anything about the army."[55] Though Roosevelt knew Root well—both were prominent within the New York Republican Party—and regarded him as an exceptionally competent person, Roosevelt complained that the "foolish" appointment indicated that McKinley had no desire for substantive military reform.[56] Despite Root's modesty and Roosevelt's pique, the lawyer was well qualified for what was, after all, a political post. Secretaries of war were judged on executive ability and success in securing appropriations and favorable legislation. Root's political acumen and work ethic suited him well for the post. Aside from Roosevelt, McKinley's other political advisors approved the selection. Savvy soldiers like Adjutant General Corbin also welcomed the selection. When Roosevelt complained to James H. Wilson that McKinley should have selected a "military man," Upton's old friend predicted that Root would be "as good a Secretary of War as anybody that could have been called to the office."[57]

The confidence was well placed. Root's quick start on military reform suggests that contrary to his account he knew from the beginning that it would be part of his task. In his first annual report, released a few months after coming to office in 1899, Root gave two premises that would guide his reforms: that the purpose of the army was to prepare for war and that the regular army would never fight a major war without the militia or volunteers.[58] From this, he concluded that the regulars should not waste time preparing to fight in their present state but instead should focus on their future role as the nucleus for a larger wartime army. He identified specific measures to achieve this: better military education and more realistic field training to prepare regular officers to lead large volunteer armies, the introduction of merit-based promotions, and the modernization of the army's equipment and arms. Former Secretary of War Redfield Proctor, Schofield's partner in the reforms of the early 1890s, wired his approval: "The country and Army for all time will bless you for that report. Carried into effect it creates an Army."[59]

But before Root could embark on reform or civil governance, he had to attend to the still-incomplete military and political consolidation of the Spanish-American War. In early 1899, the Filipino independence movement led by Emilio Aguinaldo began a rebellion against the United States that would eventually require the commitment of 65,000 American troops to quell—a force more than twice the size of the prewar army. The Philippine-American War caused a significant political problem for the McKinley administration. Volunteers who had enlisted to fight the Spanish could not be retained for the new war; yet anti-imperialists would block any significant increase to the regular army, taking that as an implicit indication of a desire to retain the islands. Yet most anti-imperialists were also unwilling to risk the appearance of having been forced out of the islands by the Filipinos, who were widely regarded as an inferior race, so a compromise was reached. The regular army could maintain a temporary war strength of about 65,000 troops, and the federal government would organize an entirely new body of 35,000 "U.S. Volunteers." Both measures were authorized for two years, thus postponing the question of the regular army's permanent strength until after the 1900 elections.[60]

Paradoxically, though the "volunteers of 1899" were the product of an intense political dispute, the process of their creation was largely apolitical. Root deserved some credit for this. He came to office just as the regiments were being formed and was determined that they should be filled strictly according to merit. The enlisted soldiers were drawn from among the best of the volunteers of 1898 who desired to stay in uniform for a bit longer. The company-grade officers were a mixture of high-quality regular noncommissioned officers and some of the best officers from the state volunteers. The selection of the field officers (majors, lieutenant colonels, and colonels) was the cause of Root's first clash with Miles, who wanted those positions to be distributed among regulars on the basis of seniority. Root insisted that those positions instead go to the most promising midgrade officers of the regular army, most of whom were relatively young captains with ten to twenty years of service. Due to Root's policies, many came to regard U.S. Volunteers regiments as superior to their regular army counterparts that were led by aged colonels and common recruits.[61]

Though matters of organization would have to wait until the status of the Philippines was resolved, Root hoped to start injecting some verve into an officer corps that he felt had become ossified under the deadening weight of promotion by seniority and the restrictive system of staff assignments. In early 1900, the secretary sent Congress draft legislation meant to address these problems by setting aside a limited proportion of promotions for merit selection and eliminating all permanent staff assignments; all positions—even the heads of the bureaus—would be filled by line officers serving in the staff for four years before returning to their normal branch of service.[62]

Root's bill was quashed by overwhelming resistance from within the army. Staff officers had both personal and professional reasons for objection. They feared being cast back into the line after years or decades of absence. But they also warned that Root's proposal would destroy the reservoir of technical expertise that they collectively embodied. The opposition to merit promotion was more diffuse, as it was not related to a defined constituency;

but tellingly, even some of those who were generally supportive of reform, such as William Conant Church, editor of the influential *Army and Navy Journal,* opposed the measure. Many of the familiar arguments were once again brought forth: It was impossible to gauge martial capacity in peacetime; competition would cause bad behaviors; equality was more important than efficiency. But perhaps the greatest objection came from those who did not believe that the army could insulate promotion from political influence. This was a well-founded fear; for as one of Root's principal assistants remembered years later, when he first came to the War Department he began "to learn many things that I regretted to know . . . why so many officers regard influence as more potent that merit."[63] Resistance was so strong that aside from general officer selection, Root abandoned merit promotion entirely. It was the only area of reform outlined in his 1899 report that he failed to enact in some form.[64]

But although receptiveness to reform within the army seemed to have scarcely changed since the Burnside Bill in 1878, external conditions had become far more promising for reform. The political deadlock of the Gilded Age had given way to a period of extended Republican hegemony; after McKinley's election in 1896, the Republicans would control the White House and both houses of Congress until 1910. Moreover, a shift within the party from the cautious commercialism of McKinley and Senator Mark Hanna to the aggressive expansionism exemplified by Vice President Theodore Roosevelt and Senator Henry Cabot Lodge meant that the Republicans were more willing to expend political capital to build the effective military they needed to back up their aggressive foreign policy.[65]

Greater cultural acceptance of change also aided Root. The Progressive Era was a period distinguished by the widespread conviction that misplaced adherence to old ways was hobbling society and propping up inefficient or even corrupt systems. Reformers were optimistic about their ability to impose a better world. The chief impetuses for Progressivism were urbanization and industrialization, trends that brought prosperity to many but horrid working and living conditions to far more. The prospect of a permanently unassimilated underclass of largely immigrant laborers spurred middle-class reformers to attempt to moderate the excesses of capitalism in order to preserve stability. But although the reformers' overarching goal was inherently conservative, their methods were often radical, trampling upon old customs and notions of propriety. Government grew in scale and ambition, intervening more aggressively in society in a host of ways, such as zoning ordinances, labor laws, and compulsory education. Progressives regarded individualism and old ways with suspicion, placing their faith instead in rational organization, bureaucratic specialization, and centralization. As Root told a group of officers in 1903: "This is a time of organization. Great results are produced only by that. Individual effort, individual brilliancy, individual heroism, accomplishes but little . . . . Effective and harmonious organization is the moving power of the world to-day."[66] The perception that modern vigor was synonymous with organizational complexity was reinforced by the spectacular prominence of corporate giants like American Tobacco, Standard Oil, and DuPont, even though the growth of business "trusts" had different sources and was in opposition to the spirit of social and political reform.[67]

As a corporate lawyer and progressive Republican, Root was the epitome of the more conservative strand of Progressivism. He was thus well-placed to explain to the public and their elected officials that military reform was not some foreign scheme, as previous generations had suspected. Instead, he argued that it was entirely consistent with the best elements of a dynamic America. Root effectively reversed the traditional dynamic of opinion toward military reform, placing the burden of proof on those who wanted to preserve the status quo. This shift was evident in a *New York Times* editorial that contrasted Root's "modern" ideas with those of his congressional opponents—many of them Civil War veterans—who refused "to see any use in any improvements of organization which have been introduced since they went soldiering in an amateur way in 1861–5."[68]

The last significant political barrier to military reform fell away with the election of 1900. William Jennings Bryan, the Democratic presidential candidate, campaigned on an anti-imperialist platform. McKinley's reelection and Republican gains in both houses of Congress settled the question of retaining the Philippines and consequently also meant that the army would receive a significant increase in order to defend the new possessions. With the enlistments of the volunteers of 1899 due to expire in the summer of 1901 and a friendly Congress, Root knew that the bill to enlarge the force was virtually guaranteed passage, so he also sought to use it as a vehicle for reform. He proposed a reorganization of the artillery, consolidation of several of the staff bureaus to gain efficiency, and the replacement of permanent assignments to the staff with a system of temporary assignments for line officers. The initial reception of the bill was encouraging: The Senate Military Affairs Committee accepted nearly all of Root's proposed measures. But as the bill progressed through the legislative process, the political friends of the staff chipped away at its contents. By the end, Root was left to write in exasperation, "The House has cut out all the good things that they understood, and put in all the bad things they could think of."[69]

The 1901 Army Reorganization Act might have fallen short of Root's expectations, but it was still the army's greatest legislative victory in decades. The peacetime authorization of over 88,000 officers and soldiers was adequate to meet the army's new overseas commitments. The artillery reorganization into separate coast defense companies and light artillery batteries better reflected the reality of service than did the unnatural combination of both kinds of units into regiments that could never come together in the field. Root even won a partial victory over the staff with the conversion of a portion of their junior positions to four-year details filled by line officers. Though the bureau chiefs would retain great control over their fiefdoms, the presence of many line officers at the lower levels would break down some of the traditional barrier between line and staff.[70]

Though the Reorganization Act was meant to provide the means to hold the Philippines, it was enacted in the same month in which the war against the Filipinos entered its third year. By that point, the nationalists had long since abandoned conventional battles in favor of guerilla warfare. Though that strategy preserved the struggle, waging a shadow war in an ethnically diverse archipelago splintered the independence movement. In March 1901, Colonel Frederick Funston captured the Filipino leader Aguinaldo. That provided the pretext for many groups to end the fight, but a few of the strongest and most committed bands continued the war. Still, the war seemed to be finally coming to a close when in September a surprise assault killed or wounded nearly all of the seventy-four American soldiers in the garrison of Balangiga on the island of Samar. Major General Adna R. Chaffee, the overall military commander in the Philippines, directed his subordinates to crush the insurgents in the final two pockets of resistance—Samar and Batangas province on Luzon. Over the course of the Philippine-American War, American policy had grown increasingly severe from the original "benevolent assimilation" to the harsher "Lieber Code," which had originally been developed to govern Union forces in the occupied Confederacy. The Lieber Code allowed the summary execution of guerillas and the destruction of property in retaliation for guerilla actions; but in the field, troops sometimes exceeded even those bounds with the "water cure" (waterboarding) and other brutal methods. Chaffee's orders caused a further intensification. In Batangas, Brigadier General J. Franklin Bell herded the populace into "reconcentration" camps in order to take the torch to the countryside—a method that had caused outrage in the United States when used by the Spanish. On Samar, Brigadier General Jacob H. Smith went to criminal excess with indiscriminate reprisals that led to public outrage, congressional inquiries, and courts-martial for Smith and several of his subordinates.[71]

Despite this controversy, Root decided that the moment was right to introduce his most ambitious reform legislation to date. The bill proposed to reorganize several staff bureaus and create a general staff, for decades the holy grail of military reformers. Root's military advisors had urged him to do this earlier, but McKinley would not allow it until Congress had approved the army's expansion. But with the 1901 Reorganization Act complete and Roosevelt in the White House following the assassination of McKinley, Root was free to make the attempt. If successful, the army would at last have a central planning body dedicated to preparing for war.[72]

The staff bureaus opposed Root's proposal out of a mixture of parochialism and conviction. The reorganization threatened bureaucratic fiefdoms. But most staff officers also genuinely believed that the system within which they worked was essentially sound. They argued with some justification that many of problems of the Spanish-American War had been caused by politicians who tried to mobilize too many volunteers in an unrealistically short period after decades of starvation budgets.[73] Yet some at the lower ranks of the staff bureaus accepted the need for change. Major Robert L. Bullard, a commissary officer who had transferred from the infantry just several years before, attributed "the most violent opposition" to "the old fossils of the army, among all the preponderating mediocrities. The officers of the army kill any man who has an idea, as they would kill a mad dog."[74]

The most vocal critic of the general staff was Miles, even though as the commanding general he might have been expected to welcome a counterweight to the bureau chiefs. Yet Miles was driven by hate of Roosevelt and Root more powerful than considerations of bureaucratic advantage. After McKinley's assassination, Roosevelt hoped that he might have an amicable relationship with the commanding general, but the détente lasted only a short while. In December 1901, Miles refused to recant his public criticism of the official finding in a dispute between two admirals. Root issued a formal reprimand that Roosevelt upheld after Miles unwisely appealed the matter. The great rift came several weeks later, when Miles proposed that he lead peace negotiations for the Philippine-American War. This was a doomed effort, for Roosevelt had far more confidence in the civil and military leaders already there than he had in Miles; but it was the commanding general's remarks about the cruelties perpetuated by American soldiers that goaded Roosevelt into an emotional outburst. The president dismissed him after noting that Miles had been in overall command during the Wounded Knee massacre in 1890, which he said was much worse than anything that happened in the Philippines even though the war there "had been a thousand times more difficult and the provocation to our soldiers a hundred times greater."[75] Stung by this dismissal, Miles retaliated by leaking news of his rejected bid for peace just as the impending courts-martial of officers for atrocities in the Philippines made it a politically sensitive issue.[76]

The occasion of Miles's testimony to the Senate Military Affairs Committee on the general staff bill several weeks later, however, offered an even better opportunity for revenge. Miles attacked the centerpiece of the hated secretary of war's reforms as an institution "peculiarly adapted to monarchies" and warned that such an organization would "Germanize and Russianize the small army of the United States." Contradicting his own earlier complaints as well as those of most of his predecessors, Miles defended the existing staff system as "the fruit of the best thought of the most eminent patriots and ablest military men that this country has produced." He denied that any other system would have produced a better outcome during the Spanish-American War; any faults, he said, could be attributed either to incompetent individuals or decades of inadequate budgets. Yet the erratic general crossed the line from incoherence to insubordination with the charge that the general staff was a scheme for Root and Corbin to reward toadies within the officer corps. That allegation would have been grounds for a court-martial, if not for the intercession of a senator friendly to Miles, who allowed him the opportunity to redact any testimony. Miles deleted that accusation as well as his threat to resign rather than serve as the head of a general staff. Still, Miles achieved his aim as the Senate committee declined to take action on a bill so strenuously opposed by the commanding general.[77]

Even with the corrections to the official record, Roosevelt was only dissuaded from charging Miles with insubordination by a group of senators who argued that an officer should not be punished for congressional testimony. It was thus left to Root to discredit Miles. Even though there would be no action on the general staff during that congressional session, the secretary staged an immediate rebuttal by two retired generals with military *bona fides* as impressive as Miles's: John M. Schofield and Wesley Merritt. Schofield argued particularly effectively that the general staff was not incompatible with American civil-military relations. Afterward, the *New York Times* contrasted Schofield's self-restraint and sensibility with Miles's emotional testimony. The *Times* also questioned Miles's motives in making what it considered the baseless assertion that a general staff would not have aided the mobilization of 1898: "No man's personal vanity or personal factiousness should be permitted to stand in the way of making such a scandal impossible hereafter."[78] Over the following months, Root relentlessly pressed his case, sending dozens of letters to newspaper editors around the country and taking every opportunity to persuade wavering congressmen of the need for a general staff. One of his military assistants aimed at a more general audience with a series of articles for popular publications, such as the *North American Review.*[79]

Miles unwittingly aided Root's cause by absenting himself from the capital at a crucial time. Though by the summer of 1902 Roosevelt had declared the Philippine-American War officially concluded, Miles still hoped to use it as a means to embarrass the administration. He proposed a tour to inspect the garrison in the islands with the intention of documenting abuses committed by American troops. Root saw through Miles's ploy but approved the trip and even encouraged Miles to extend the trip to a world tour. That itinerary assured the general's absence for most of the next congressional session.[80]

The general staff was not the only major reform that Root pursued in 1902. Since coming to office, he had been carefully laying the foundation for the first comprehensive militia legislation since the 1792 Militia Act. That antiquated law had long been an embarrassment. In 1878, state soldiers seeking a new law more in line with their ambitions to be a first-line reserve had founded the National Guard Association (NGA) as an organization that could lobby for such a change. The first president of the NGA proposed a fundamental restructuring of the federal-state military relationship:

State organizations would more closely pattern themselves on the regular army and would submit to closer federal oversight in exchange for a considerable increase in federal funds. Sherman and every commanding general following favored more material support to the organized militia and a new law; yet during the late nineteenth century, Congress had been as indifferent to the desires of the National Guard as to those of the regular army, and so little was done.[81]

The problems in mobilizing the National Guard during the Spanish-American War brought the issue to the fore. Also, Root's early concession that the National Guard would play a large role in any significant conflict signaled that he would not pursue the regulars' hope of an expansible army. Several months after he came to office, Root received a letter from a joint committee of the two leading organizations representing the state soldiery— the NGA and the Inter-state National Guard Association (INGA)—with a draft militia reform law that ceded some state control in return for greater resources and recognition as the "United States Reserve."[82]

Yet not all militiamen were willing to sacrifice local autonomy. Though the initial rationale for a distinct militia—to serve as a check on a tyrannical central government—had long since ceased to be a concern, for some state soldiers autonomy had become an end in itself. Submitting to federal standards for organization, commissions, and enlistments would impede their ability to adjust to the contours of local preferences and politics. These localists cared less about efficient mobilization than for the desire of a town to have its own company even if it were too small to support a full-strength unit or to have a certain individual as its captain even if he did not meet federal standards. It was unclear whether the leaders of the NGA and INGA could overcome the resistance from militiamen satisfied with the status quo.[83]

Root thus proceeded cautiously. For the preliminary work, he relied on William Carey Sanger, a longtime associate and a prominent member of the New York National Guard. Sanger was a committed reformer; in the 1880s, he had proposed completely severing state affiliation and making the National Guard a federal institution. Yet he recommended that Root first ask Congress for a commission to solicit opinions from all interested parties before making any recommendations. Root agreed and sent Sanger to Europe to study reserve systems there. He also made Sanger the chairman of the commission and then later assistant secretary of war with specific responsibility for militia affairs.[84]

Fortunately for Root, he had an ideal counterpart to drive reform from the state side. Charles W. F. Dick was a general in the Ohio National Guard eager for change. The Spanish-American War proved, he argued, that any "flattering opinions" of the National Guard's readiness were "utterly mistaken."[85] Representative Dick was also the chairman of the House Military Affairs Committee and so perfectly placed to parry counterattacks from the localists. Just before the 1902 INGA convention being held in Washington, Dick assembled a delegation of guardsmen to negotiate with Root. Meeting on a Sunday in Root's home, they came to agreement on the fundamental elements of what become known as the "Dick Act." The federal government would bear the cost of organizing and equipping the state forces to the standards of the regular army and then would provide enough funds and equipment to sustain effective units. To ensure that state units remained within federal guidelines, they would submit to annual inspections by regular officers. To ensure that money was not wasted in training men who would then decline to enlist for war, all state soldiers would be subject to regular army courts-martial as soon as their unit was called to federal service. Governors retained the valued right to grant officers' commissions. A regular who witnessed the backroom negotiations found the process distasteful. Though Root did not win all that he wished, he had calculated that the inexorable pull of federal resources would eventually bring the National Guard closer to the War Department. "We shall attain by degrees," he predicted, what "so many have sought and failed to reach at a single step—the creation of a system of well-trained citizen soldiery."[86]

In the following convention, Dick's victory over the fierce resistance of localists was signified by his election as president of the INGA for the next year. The following day, he introduced his militia reform bill in Congress. Though it would not become law during that session, Root and Dick had made extraordinary progress toward resolving an issue that had stymied politicians and soldiers for decades.[87]

In December 1902, Root was ready to act on both the general staff and militia reform. His annual report was preceded by a preliminary barrage of personal letters to influential editors that made a strenuous case for both measures. Even the *Philadelphia Inquirer*, which had previously been sympathetic to Miles, accepted Root's argument that a general staff would have prevented many of the problems experienced during the Spanish-American War. The day after the publication of the annual report, Root's congressional allies introduced the general staff bill in both legislative houses. That coincided with the delivery of Roosevelt's annual message to Congress, which highlighted the importance of both the general staff and militia bills. Shortly thereafter, three of the army's seven major generals made an appearance where they spoke in support of the general staff, a powerful riposte to the opposition of the still-absent Miles.[88] By the time that Root appeared to testify on the measure, the lobbying effort had achieved such success that one senator commented, "It is not a question whether we will have a general staff so much as what shall be the provisions made for it by this bill."[89]

The matter of specific provisions was critical, for there were many variations of how the idea could be adapted to the American context. Because the secretary regarded it as so critical to the army's future, he took an active role in drafting the new measure. He made several concessions to ease passage, such as abandoning his twice-thwarted quest to consolidate the supply bureaus though the provision to merge the Inspector General into the Adjutant General's Office remained. To negate Miles's threat to resign rather than serve on a general staff, the date for the establishment of the General Staff Corps was specified as 10 August 1903—two days after Miles's sixty-fourth birthday and mandatory retirement. The new general staff bill also accepted a recommendation made by Schofield during his April testimony. The initial legislation followed the German model by stipulating that the army's senior general would be called *Chief of the General Staff*. But Root adopted Schofield's alternative, *Chief of Staff of the U.S. Army*, a change that implied that the chief's principal duty was not to serve as head of the general staff but to serve as chief of staff to the president and the secretary of war. Furthermore, the law stated that the chief of staff would be selected by the president, not simply appointed on the basis of seniority. Root reinforced this relationship with a later directive that the chief of staff's term was to coincide with that of the president, though that measure was never implemented. Root personally wrote the most important provision, the one stipulating the authorities of the general staff. Though he gave it a broad purview to "investigate and report upon all questions affecting the efficiency of the Army and its state of preparation," it would have only the weak power to "supervise" and "coordinate" the actions of the staff and line.[90]

The general staff created by Root in legislation was quite different than that envisioned by many of his military advisors. Officers were naturally drawn to the operational effectiveness of the German General Staff and so thought of it primarily as a body devoted to professional study and planning in peacetime and directing operations in war.[91] Although Root was concerned with the effective conduct of operations, his principal focus was the proper functioning of the War Department. The secretary of war was responsible for running a complex department engaged in diverse functions: colonial governance in the Philippines, guarding the coast, patrolling the Mexican border, producing weapons in arsenals, and maintaining rivers and harbors. Under the bureau system designed by Calhoun, the coordination of these disparate activities was accomplished only at the level of the secretary; he alone had authority over the officials overseeing these varied activities. Even during the antebellum era, secretaries of war had struggled to effectively manage the War Department, and the army's work had since grown significantly in geographic scope, scale, and technical complexity. Root looked to the general staff as a repository of independent expertise free of the parochialism associated with the bureau chiefs. Thus, the principal role of the general staff was to aid the secretary to better exercise *his* authorities rather than to operate on its own. Though a wise and necessary concession to the American tradition of civilian control of the military, the weak powers of the general staff would soon cause problems. Patterns of thought produced by decades of study of the German system would persist among officers. Not all of Root's successors would or could accept the burden that his design placed upon them.

For the time, however, Root's preferences prevailed. Congress passed both bills quickly and with few changes. The Militia Act of 1903 passed just several weeks into the congressional session. The degree to which Root had won over at least the reformist faction of the National Guard was evident when Dick introduced Root to the 1903 INGA convention by saying, "The National Guard never had a better friend than Secretary Root."[92] The general staff bill had only slightly more difficulty. The inspector general was able to fend off the consolidation of his office and there were several other minor modifications made on behalf of the staff, but the greatest obstacle to speedy passage was an internecine battle within the Senate majority over an unrelated issue. The General Staff Act became law on 14 February 1903. General Miles returned to the United States from his world tour the following day. With that triumph, the Root reforms came to a close. Later in the year, Root was dispatched to London on a diplomatic mission and then shortly thereafter returned to private life.[93]

In just more than four years, Root had established governments for the Philippines and Puerto Rico, doubled the size of the regular army, reorganized the artillery, reduced the divide between staff and line, replaced the Militia Act of 1792, and created the general staff. He also directed the establishment of a compulsory system of postgraduate education and a program of realistic field maneuvers. Yet legislation and executive orders are significant only to the extent that they are successfully implemented, a truth that Root acknowledged in his final report as secretary: "Very great and radical changes have been made in many respects during the past six years, and the Army should have time to put the new laws into operation and work out the new methods under the direction of the General Staff without further disturbance."[94]

Yet even Root seems to have underestimated the time required for the army to adjust to new conditions. Indeed, the Root reforms were only part of a larger change that was already underway before the Spanish-American War. The post-frontier consolidation of the army, the growing stature of the military schools, and the abandonment of regimental promotion had all already begun to more closely knit together the geographically dispersed and organizationally divided army of the 1880s. At the same time, new entrants to the officer corps brought with them the same faith in the power of bureaucratic structures to deliver efficiency and effectiveness that characterized their Progressive Era civilian contemporaries. Yet it was not these younger officers who would implement the Root reforms but the more senior officers of the Civil War and composite generations. Their experiences in the "old army" that prized individual autonomy were poor preparation for their task of building strong institutions capable of imposing standardization upon the army. The stage was set for confusion and generational conflict as a striving younger cohort attuned to the promise of the Root reforms emerged from below while control resided with older officers who had developed in an army vastly different than the one they were supposed to create.

CHAPTER SEVEN

Old Soldiers in a New Army

HISTORIANS HAVE LABELED as "reformers" many of the officers who implemented Root's agenda in the early years of the twentieth century. In addition to Arthur L. Wagner and Eben Swift, William H. Carter, Tasker H. Bliss, and J. Franklin Bell are often characterized by this term.[1] The descriptor is accurate in the sense that all those officers sincerely attempted to create new institutions and methods in response to changing times. But the term can easily lead us to mistakenly aggregate those individuals and to assume that all were working toward a common end. That was not the case, for they had quite different notions of war, how best to prepare for it, and therefore what should be done. One "reformer" would undo the work of his predecessor only to have his successor do the same to his own efforts. Furthermore, though all these individuals genuinely believed they were instituting "modern" ideas, some were far more conservative than others. These disparities in aims and ambition came about because the reformers were driven not by a shared vision of the future but by the lessons derived from their individual pasts.

Carter was one of the most influential officers shaping the early course of the Root reforms. Though a Washington staff officer, he had an unusually rugged past. A member of the West Point class of 1873, Carter was a committed disciple of Upton—the commandant for most of his time as a cadet.

Following graduation, Carter spent fourteen of the next twenty years in the desert Southwest engaged in some of the most arduous duty in the army. The heat and geographic isolation meant that garrison life was spartan and uncomfortable in comparison to many other regions, while the searing heat, rugged terrain, and formidable Apache adversaries made the campaigns there some of the most difficult in the annals of the U.S. Army. Yet in that harsh climate, Carter excelled. He was appointed the quartermaster of the Sixth Cavalry on the very first day that he was eligible for the post and remained in that position for eight years until Congress limited such assignments to four years in order to ensure more officers had the benefit of staff experience. In 1881, Carter earned the Medal of Honor for his attempt to save two soldiers who had been mortally wounded in an ambush at Cibicu Creek, Arizona Territory. He was also twice brevetted, once for his role at Cibicu Creek and the subsequent defense of Fort Apache and then again a decade later for leading a mounted charge against Sioux warriors at the battle of White River, the last engagement of the last campaign of the Indian Wars. Carter was also one of the cavalry's foremost experts on hippology— the selection, care, and training of horses. The latter led to his assignment to the Department of Cavalry at Fort Leavenworth in 1893. He arrived at the Infantry and Cavalry School just as it was entering its peak. That same year, Wagner published *The Service of Security and Information,* and Swift began his experiments with the applicatory system. Carter added his own notable contributions. He established the course in hippology, wrote what would remain for decades the army's standard text on the subject, edited the *Cavalry Journal,* and served as a member of the board examining lieutenants for promotion. In 1897, Carter was selected for transfer into the Adjutant General's Department, an honor that also brought promotion to major and an assignment in Washington.[2]

Two beliefs formed during his cavalry years profoundly influenced Carter's later work in the War Department. The first was that the army poorly rewarded talent. All of Carter's hard work, valor, and expertise as a regimental officer brought him little more than additional responsibilities. At times, he was the regimental quartermaster, acting regimental adjutant, and troop commander, while less-capable peers loafed in easier duties. Yet the seniority system meant that all were regarded as equally deserving of promotion. There were special rewards outside of promotion, such as assignment as an instructor or to a staff bureau, and Carter's selection for both was proof that merit was sometimes recognized. But as Carter learned early in his career, influence often played a role. After waiting years for promotion to first lieutenant, Carter had the prize given instead to "a worthless political hack" with enough influence to have Congress allocate the vacancy to him rather than Carter. Though Carter eventually regained his rightful date of rank, he was able to do so only by petitioning the War Department to retire a first lieutenant who had been retained on the rolls despite being absent for several years due to a physical disability. Thus, intrigue was met with intrigue. Once in Washington, Carter's experiences in the office responsible for assignments taught him that the problem of "pull" was even worse than he had believed.[3]

Carter also came to the War Department convinced that the postgraduate education system was failing to prepare junior officers for their duties. As a member of the Fort Leavenworth promotion board, he was dismayed by the mediocre performance of lieutenants, which he attributed to the lack of direction in Schofield's lyceum. Almost immediately after his transfer to the Adjutant General's Department in 1897, Carter requested permission to replace the lyceum with a structured course linked to the content of promotion examinations. Though his plan was not adopted, Carter was successful in having tactical problems like the ones pioneered by Swift incorporated into the examinations of professional competence. But what Carter regarded as the poor quality of these submissions only reinforced his belief that the loose structure of the lyceum was a poor fit for the average officer. "Nothing but systematized study," he concluded, "would fill the measure of the department's expectations" for its young officers.[4]

It would be just a few years before Root would give Carter the opportunity to put his ideas into effect. Though the cavalryman was disappointed to remain in Washington during the Spanish-American War, his excellent work made him an indispensable assistant to Adjutant General Corbin, the most powerful figure in the War Department. This position brought Carter into close contact with the secretary of war, and the grizzled cavalryman and the corporate lawyer even developed an improbable friendship, enjoying long horseback rides together through the hills surrounding the capital. Carter later proudly claimed to have been the one to first introduce Root to the work of Upton, having presented the secretary with a copy of *The Armies of Asia and Europe*. Root began to entrust Carter with sensitive tasks and to seek his advice on a wide range of issues.[5]

The two agreed that a revised school system might remedy many of the army's problems. Like many other Progressives, Root placed great emphasis on education. Aside from its pedagogical function, he saw it as a vital tool for ordering talent within a society. In Root's view, the dynamism of the rising democratic states was due to the way in which education allowed the best minds to rise to the top of society. He contrasted this with sclerotic aristocratic cultures in which class structures limited social mobility. The secretary sensed a similar stagnation within the officer corps caused by seniority promotion, which he regarded as another form of archaic restriction on the efficient allocation of talent. Root's direct effort to introduce merit promotion was defeated in Congress, but education reform offered an alternative means of encouraging talent. The secretary soon came to regard this as one of his most important initiatives. He naturally let much of the work fall to Carter, his close aide with a deep interest in the subject.[6]

Carter submitted his plan for a reformed professional education system in late 1901. Root approved it with only minor changes, and the plan was published in November 1901 as War Department General Order Number 155 (GO #155). Carter's scheme was revolutionary in several ways. Never before had all elements of army postgraduate education—the officers' lyceum and the various service schools—been treated as part of a single education system; previously, they had all operated under separate directives with no attempt to treat them comprehensively. Reflecting Root's notion of education as a means to sift talent, GO #155 organized the schools into a pyramidal system with four tiers. All officers would attend the lowest level, but only the best would progress to the highest level of education, a newly established Army War College. GO #155 stipulated that War College graduates would receive consideration for "special service requiring a high degree of professional capacity."[7] At the time of publication, Root had not yet won congressional acceptance of a general staff, but Carter anticipated that one would be established soon. GO #155 was his effort to make the future General Staff Corps a true meritocracy unsullied by influence and nepotism. Even more grandly, he promised Root that in time War College graduates would comprise a special elite from which "future generals could be selected without fear of disaster" in war.[8] This proposed link between classroom performance and the selection of wartime commanders was a bold departure from the past, and it was far from certain that the officer corps would accept classroom performance as a valid method for selecting its wartime commanders.

Yet in many other respects, GO #155 reflected Carter's narrow understanding of professional education. Though Carter had long believed that junior officers needed more structured education than what was provided by the lyceum, he replaced it with a surprisingly unambitious substitute—what GO #155 designated as the "officers' school for elementary instruction in theory and practice." Hereafter called garrison schools, these were little more than the lyceum reformed along the lines suggested by Carter in 1897. Each garrison was responsible for staging the school for its most junior officers. Typically taught during the winter months when there was little field training, the schools had just two annual terms, each consisting of only ninety two-hour sessions devoted mainly to a review of garrison and administrative duties. Tactics instruction was limited to a few hours, and there was no training at all in advanced staff work. In order to ensure diligence, Carter stipulated that those who failed any subsection of the course twice would have that fact reported to the examiners of their next promotion board. Though many officers would continue their professional education at the service school for their branch, further schooling was not guaranteed. That was a serious omission in an army still ruled by seniority promotion. Carter's plan did little for those mediocre lieutenants who were, under the system of promotion at the time, still destined to become colonels in several decades' time.[9]

Carter was also largely indifferent to the needs of technical specialists. The curriculum and structure of four "service schools"—the Artillery School at Fort Monroe, the School of Application for Cavalry and Field Artillery at Fort Riley, the Engineer School of Application in Washington, D.C., and the School of Submarine Defense at Fort Totten, New York—were left entirely to the determination of the chiefs of the technical arms. Though leaving the details to experts was reasonable, Carter also relegated those schools to a lesser status than that of the former Infantry and Cavalry School at Fort Leavenworth, which he renamed the General Staff and Service College (GSSC). It was to retain some of its earlier character as a service school for infantry and cavalry officers but would also prepare officers of all arms for high-level command and staff positions. As such, Carter designated Fort Leavenworth as the sole conduit to the Army War College and thus, theoretically, to the General Staff and high command. That represented a significant loss of status for the Artillery School, which had always been considered equivalent or even superior to Fort Leavenworth. Indeed, in mid-1901

Carter indicated that that outstanding performance at either school would qualify an officer for the War College. Yet for an unknown reason, that was not contained in the final draft of the order. Whatever the motivation for this change, the effect was to relegate technical expertise to a lower status within the hierarchy of professional knowledge. So while GO #155 made some provision for those of average talent and specialists, its focus was on providing a mechanism for routing the elite into positions of responsibility.[10]

The first president of the Army War College, Brigadier General Tasker H. Bliss, shared Carter's opinion that the focus of education should be routing the best toward positions of special responsibility. As one of the army's most intellectual officers, Bliss had known little else. Voted the "brain" of the West Point class of 1875, Bliss returned as an instructor within a year of graduation. In his first twenty-three years of service, Bliss spent less than three years in regimental duty or as a commissary, the department to which he transferred in 1892. Instead, he was successively a student, instructor, aide to Commanding General Schofield, special assistant to Secretary of War Daniel Lamont, and military attaché in Madrid. During the Spanish-American War, Bliss was the chief of staff of a division during the brief invasion of Puerto Rico, but it was as the collector of customs in occupied Havana that he made his name. His reformation of the corrupt and inefficient customs service was essential to the success of the military government of Cuba. In recognition for that work, he was promoted from major to brigadier general in 1902.[11]

After a career of virtually nothing but rarefied assignments, Bliss did not even attempt to conceal his contempt for the common officer. In a public report, he noted the "unfortunate tendency on the part of officers" to fall into "a process of steady decadence culminating in complete dry rot." Bliss thus concluded that the army should adopt an adversarial education system to "brace up" the unwilling until they achieved professional competence. Yet what Bliss imagined as the minimum standard for regimental officers was probably even less demanding than that stipulated by Carter. The meager garrison school curriculum, Bliss sniffed, was "enough for a good second lieutenant," and even "with certain qualities of mind presupposed at the outset, for a good colonel."[12] Yet it was unwise to ignore the average, for in case of war mere regimental officers were likely to be promoted to high positions. Even in the lesser wars of the nineteenth century, many of the colonels—the same group that Bliss dismissed as needing nothing more than experience and knowledge of regulations—became general officers. That Bliss—perhaps the most intellectual officer of his generation—thought otherwise is somewhat incredible but suggests that for all of his experience as an educator he accepted the traditional belief that the qualities of command were innate and could not be taught. Thus, the purpose of professional education was not to impart knowledge but simply to serve as a means to identify and separate the elite from their more common brethren.

But as the president of the Army War College, Bliss's immediate concern was the education of general staff officers. At Carter's urging, Root had directed Bliss to make the course like the one taught at the Naval War College.[13] Bliss was uniquely well qualified to fulfill that wish, as he had been the army representative on the inaugural faculty at Newport in the 1880s; he was convinced that the unstructured approach used there was the best method with which to train the elite. In contrast to the harsh schooling that he advocated for regimental officers, Bliss held that high staff work required "scientific imagination" that could "be learned not from books and professors but only by patient and unostentatious labor in doing these things themselves."[14] The War College was to have no fixed academic year, no diplomas, and no classes. It would operate as an unstructured "collegium," in which the students would "learn things by doing things."[15] They were, in effect, probationary General Staff officers.

In adopting this approach, Bliss rejected the German-style *Kriegsaka-demie* model of structured classes and rigorous examinations. He knew that system well from his time at Fort Monroe in the period shortly after Upton's departure and from a later inspection of the professional education systems of Europe. Bliss offered two reasons for rejecting the German model. The first was that such education was already conducted at other military schools, particularly at Fort Leavenworth. As will be seen shortly, in its first years the GSSC at Fort Leavenworth had fallen far from the standard reached under Wagner in the 1890s and had become more like the "kindergarten" of the early 1880s. Bliss knew this firsthand because Root had dispatched him to Fort Leavenworth to investigate why students were doing so badly. It was therefore incredible that Bliss would assert that the garrison schools and GSSC "[exhaust] the useful possibilities of scholastic professional training."[16]

Bliss's other argument for the collegium was that the American reliance on volunteer armies meant that German practices were inappropriate for the U.S. Army. That was an equally dubious contention, if for no other reason than that by extension it also meant that the United States should not have a general staff. A more fundamental flaw with his reasoning was that a small expansible standing army was in even greater need of theoretical education because its peacetime state was so unlike that in war. Instructing general staff officers through apprenticeship was unlikely to prepare them for the type of challenges they would face in war.

In time Arthur L. Wagner would challenge the narrow elitism of Carter and Bliss, but first he was engaged in the realization of one of Root's other great projects: the introduction of maneuvers meant to replicate the scale of modern warfare. Such training—sometimes involving tens of thousands of troops—had long been a feature of European armies; but the small, dispersed, and poor U.S. Army had previously been able to bring together only a handful of regiments and batteries in the occasional "camp of instruction" organized by an enterprising regional commander. Root regarded this as a major flaw, reasoning that "officers who have never seen a corps, division, or brigade organized and on the march can not be expected to perform perfectly the duties required of them when war comes."[17] But the demands of the Philippines meant that it would be several years before the secretary could act on that observation. It was not until 1902 that conditions were more favorable: The 1901 Reorganization Act had significantly expanded the size of the regular army; the close of the frontier meant that units were more relatively concentrated; and better transportation networks made it much easier and cheaper to bring together large bodies of troops.[18]

The first experiment in maneuvers was conducted at Fort Riley, Kansas. Major General John C. Bates, the department commander responsible for the exercises, had no special qualification for overseeing maneuvers, but by coincidence Colonel Wagner had recently been assigned to Bates's staff as a working convalescence to recover from tuberculosis contracted in Manila. The two had previously worked together and Bates was happy to leave the details to Wagner, who had some experience with such training from his time at Fort Leavenworth.[19]

Wagner was eager to use the opportunity to correct many of the failings in command, staff coordination, reconnaissance, and combined arms cooperation that he had witnessed in Cuba. In a report written at the behest of Commanding General Nelson Miles, Wagner noted systemic problems in command. He noted with feigned objectivity that Shafter's attempt to ride the lines in Cuba had so prostrated the portly general that his staff feared that he might die. But Wagner also gently criticized the more vigorous Brigadier General Adna R. Chaffee, who was able to conduct a personal reconnaissance to within earshot of the Spanish pickets. Wagner observed that it would have been better if the general had overseen the efforts of many patrols led by junior officers rather than personally undertaking just one reconnaissance. Overall, Wagner concluded that the victories at San Juan and El Caney were "obtained at a cost of life that could have been more easily avoided with more skillful tactical arrangements."[20]

The purpose of maneuvers was to correct such deficiencies. Yet as an experienced educator, Wagner knew that the training must be carefully structured to be of any value. One reason why many nineteenth-century officers held peacetime training in low regard was that the practice of unmediated "sham battles" was indeed more spectacle than training. During the Fort Riley maneuvers, each day of training presented the participants with a new scenario designed to highlight a specific tactical principle or function, such as the importance of scouting in a meeting engagement or the problems of protecting a supply train. Overall, more emphasis was placed on the preliminary preparation and maneuvering than on the mock combat. To ensure realistic outcomes, Wagner and a team of assistant umpires adjudicated losses. Most importantly, following the training Wagner brought all the officers together in a large tent to review the action and draw conclusions. These "big tent" discussions, as they came to be known, were the greatest difference between Wagner's maneuvers and the earlier "sham battles." As one officer of the time later noted, the earlier avoidance of publicly airing "mistakes and errors of judgment" precluded any critical analysis.[21] In Wagner's maneuvers, honest appraisal took precedence over pride. One U.S. Navy observer was so impressed that he concluded that maneuvers were only worth the significant effort required if they included such after-action reviews.[22]

During Root's tenure as secretary of war, the format pioneered by Wagner would be expanded each successive year. In 1903, there were maneuvers at two different sites. The passage of the Dick Act, which allowed federal subsidies for state forces to attend maneuvers, also swelled the numbers of participants from the National Guard. From that year on, there would be more guardsmen then regulars involved in summer training. The 1904 maneuvers held near Manassas, Virginia, were still larger, with 26,000 regulars and guardsmen. Yet Wagner—by that time assigned to the General Staff—

harbored still grander ambitions; he dreamed of playing out a complete campaign. The General Staff had already made a similar recommendation, proposing to replicate an entire theater of war across the four hundred miles of prairie between Fort Riley and Fort Sill, Oklahoma. That study tactfully suggested that the generals had as much to learn from maneuvers as did the lower ranks. The lead author of that report, Major Edward J. McClernand, was particularly aware of the deficiencies of American generalship; he had been Shafter's adjutant general in Cuba.[23]

Yet after 1904, the emphasis of summer training shifted from high command to small-unit tactics. This was partly due to the bad publicity associated with the Manassas maneuvers, which the public viewed as extravagant. Root's successor, William H. Taft, was unable or unwilling to argue the need for grand maneuvers. But senior officers seem to have welcomed the change from one or two larger maneuvers to a number of smaller regional camps of instruction. When Brigadier General William Carter commanded one of these camps in 1906, he directed that the training scenarios should be smaller and less ambitious. He reasonably contended that simpler exercises were more appropriate for poorly trained guardsmen who made up a large portion of the camp participants, but this meant that generals and their staffs avoided uncomfortable challenges. Carter also abolished the "big tent" discussions on the grounds that senior officers should not be subject to criticism from those of lesser rank.[24] Most other general officers did the same; and so honest assessment fell victim to the belief, sarcastically described by one junior officer, that "to put a colonel on the carpet and question his ability to command his regiment was to interfere with a vested right that had been sacred through all the history of the Regular Army."[25]

Wagner's work in education followed a similar pattern of initial success that was subsequently undermined by his peers. In early 1904, his new post on the General Staff gave him the opportunity to replace Carter's education system with a more ecumenical scheme that also recognized the needs of technical specialists and regimental officers. The plan, published in June 1904 as General Order #115 (GO #115), retained the pyramidal structure and so preserved the winnowing competition that Root, Carter, and Bliss had thought so important. But to improve the proficiency of regimental officers, GO #115 added a third year to the garrison school course and created an additional postgraduate garrison course. These changes ensured that even those officers who never progressed to a service school would receive training in tactics and higher-level staff work. Wagner also restored the parity among the branches by eliminating the General Service and Staff College at Fort Leavenworth. In its place, he created two schools: the Infantry and Cavalry School and the Army Staff College. The former was once again considered to be equivalent to the service schools for the artillery and engineers. The Army Staff College was open to the best graduates of any of these service schools. Like the GSSC in Carter's system, Wagner intended that eventually the Staff College would be a perquisite for selection to the Army War College.[26]

The demands of economy, however, necessitated that the new system fit within the existing infrastructure. As a consequence, the newly created Signal School, Infantry and Cavalry School, and Army Staff College were all located at Fort Leavenworth, where they collectively formed the Army Service Schools. Wagner foresaw the danger that proximity might blur the schools' distinct functions, so he specified that the Staff College was to have a faculty separate from that of the Infantry and Cavalry School. To ensure that the infantry and cavalry did not gain "an undue share in the college," he reserved several places in each Staff College class for artillerymen and engineers.[27] Perhaps anticipating resistance, Wagner charged the General Staff with ensuring strict compliance with his directive so that the army might have "a complete system of military education, in which each [school] shall perform its proper part."[28]

But the General Staff would be no match for the Fort Leavenworth commandant, Brigadier General J. Franklin Bell, one of the army's youngest and most dynamic general officers. Though during his cadet years Bell had displayed no fondness for study—professional or academic—at some point after his graduation in 1878 he became a dedicated student of the profession. He read military history, studied law, and even became an early physical fitness enthusiast, as well as serving as the regimental adjutant—a sought-after position usually awarded to the best first lieutenant in the unit. "I have never had under my command, or even known," one superior wrote of Bell in 1895, "an officer of his grade who possessed so much energy, intelligence and military pride and enthusiasm. The latter quality he imparts to all with whom he comes in contact, and I have known many a young officer benefited through association with him."[29] Gregarious and kind, even as a junior officer Bell also demonstrated the ability "to harmonize and compact the officers" of his unit, as noted by Captain Hugh L. Scott.[30] Years later when Bell commanded a brigade in the Philippines, these same qualities buoyed his soldiers' morale even in the midst of a frustrating guerilla conflict. "The officers and men loved him personally," remembered one subordinate. "They whole-heartedly did whatever he suggested without a doubt of its correctness."[31]

Bell's good nature persisted despite his poor career prospects. He had joined the Seventh Cavalry two years after the Battle of the Little Big Horn, which had been macabre good fortune for more than a dozen young cavalrymen who received promotions to fill the vacancies left by those killed in the battle. But that sudden influx meant that afterward the regiment was atypically youthful, meaning there were fewer retirements and so slower advancement for later arrivals, such as Bell. While his contemporaries in other regiments progressed, Bell languished. By 1890, when the army switched from regimental to lineal promotion in order to eliminate such disparities, Bell had already lost several years of seniority. As it became clear that he was unlikely to even be promoted to captain by his twentieth year of service, Bell sought a transfer to the Judge Advocate's Department. In January 1898 a small bit of fortune finally came with his assignment as the acting judge advocate for the Department of the Columbia, but even that quickly turned sour when the United States went to war just a few months later. On the cusp of the greatest professional opportunity in a generation, Bell had consigned himself to a backwater. Frantic to avoid this fate, on the day that Congress declared war Bell took leave to travel to Washington to beg for a combat assignment. Adjutant General Corbin took pity on the aged lieutenant and granted him a volunteer commission as a major of engineers on the staff of the Philippines-bound Eighth Army Corps.[32]

From that moment, Bell's fortune took a remarkable turn. His work as the director of reconnaissance for Major General Wesley Merritt won Bell a reputation for fearlessness that was notable even within the aggressive army in the Philippines. He was rewarded with a temporary promotion to colonel and command of the 36th United States Volunteers, one of the two-year volunteer regiments of 1899. While in that position, he earned the Medal of Honor for single-handedly defeating a group of seven insurgents whom he stumbled across with a scouting party. Major General Elwell S. Otis endorsed Bell's nomination for the medal with the comment, "This feat and many similar ones have been performed by Colonel Bell during this war, and the wonder is that he still lives."[33] Bell was promoted to brigadier general of volunteers not long after but would have reverted to his regular rank of captain with the expiration of the authorization for the volunteers in 1901. Roosevelt and Root, however, wished to invigorate the army with more youthful generals. This was possible because seniority promotion did not apply to general officers; the president was allowed to nominate whomever he wished. Upon the recommendation of Governor General William H. Taft and Major General Arthur MacArthur, Bell was promoted past 981 more-senior officers to become a brigadier general in the regular army. He thereafter vindicated that extraordinary leap with the pacification of Batangas, a campaign that a modern U.S. Army study hails as a "masterpiece of counter-guerrilla warfare."[34]

While Bell was in Batangas, the GSSC was suffering a catastrophic first year. Carter's neat plan for identifying future general staff officers had been lost amidst the turmoil of the 1901 expansion. Political considerations and the desire to reward volunteers who had served in the Philippines led the army to establish a low standard for the examination given to prospective officers. Yet that group of former enlisted soldiers, volunteer officers, and recent civilians formed a large segment of the officer corps, over half of the approximately 2,900 officers of the line. Root directed that the first GSSC class should largely consist of non-West Pointers who were nearing promotion to a high enough rank that they might never receive any formal professional education. The school attempted to accommodate these officers by using a simplified version of the 1890s curriculum and grading on a "liberal scale," but even then there were so many failures in the midcourse examinations that it drew the attention of the national press. That had been the impetus for Root ordering Bliss to investigate the poor showing of the first class. The resulting report led to the courts-martial of several students who were deemed to have failed for "want of application." There was improvement in the spring term, but the first year of the GSSC still fell far short of the aspirations of Root and Carter.[35]

Thus, when Bell arrived in the summer of 1903, his commander's gifts for building morale and instilling esprit were perfectly matched to the needs of the GSSC. Bell roamed the campus, engaging the faculty and students with a jovial informality in class, at social gatherings, and even in athletic competitions. Faculty and students alike appreciated the manner in which the youthful general won active support by explaining his policies rather than simply demanding obedience.[36]

For several months during the fall term of that year, Wagner served as Bell's assistant commandant. That pairing was potentially awkward, for Wagner had been senior since their cadet days. Later in the 1890s when Lieutenant Bell was the secretary for the Cavalry and Light Artillery School at Fort Riley, he came to regard the curriculum developed by Captain Wagner at Fort Leavenworth as the ideal of professional education. Bell's promotion had suddenly reversed their standing in terms of rank, but Bell's eagerness for the older man's advice and Wagner's informal tone in subsequent letters suggest that the two had an amicable relationship that was relatively equal. Though there are no records of their conversations in late 1903, it appears that they agreed upon the desirability of the GSSC expanding to become a two-year course like that of the prewar Infantry and Cavalry School.[37]

Then Wagner was assigned to the General Staff in Washington, and the two friends' thinking diverged. Wagner decided that the new Infantry and Cavalry School would remain a one-year course and that the Army Staff College was to be an entirely distinct school. If not for tuberculosis, Wagner might have ensured that his plan was followed. In 1905, he was promoted to brigadier general and was meant to become the next president of the Army War College, a post that would have given him oversight of the entire education system. Yet on the day of his promotion, Wagner passed away.[38]

Bell was thus left to run the Army Service Schools in accord with his instincts as a commander. In many ways, this continued to be a good thing. Carter and Wagner had decreed that Fort Leavenworth should be the goal for all ambitious young officers, but Bell gave that aspiration substance by recruiting talented officers. He also deterred recalcitrant colonels—many still of the Civil War generation—from continuing to send their worst officers by refusing to graduate those officers who did not meet the school's standards. He genuinely regretted the embarrassment of conscientious if slow-witted officers caught in the battle of wills among their superiors, but he refused to permit the school to relapse to a "kindergarten." As a result, Fort Leavenworth became a desirable assignment in a remarkably short period of time.[39] Though there were still some regiments that regarded the school as a mere "fad," by 1906 the school's reputation had improved to such an extent that one graduate boasted that "the *real* view of progressive officers is that in a few years the officer who is not a graduate of the [Leavenworth] school will 'not be in it.' "[40]

But Bell's virtues also caused unintended harm through his desire to institute a system of absolutely objective evaluation that he called "scientific marking." His motive was worthy. Because the school was meant to be one of the chief means of identifying general staff officers, Bell feared that a fault in grading might harm a deserving officer's career. So that students with a better or more indulgent instructor might not gain undue advantage, all lectures were read verbatim and instructors were prohibited from offering any extra information. If an instructor did provide his section with any "simple or unimportant information, instruction or warning" that might affect grades, he was required to provide all the other sections with a written memorandum providing the same information.[41] Class standings, even in subjective topics like tactics, were calculated to the thousandth of a percentage point. In Spanish, stopwatches were used to determine how long it took students to translate passages. This continual fine-grained evaluation made the Infantry and Cavalry School a stressful year of long hours in pursuit of minute advantages. Instructors and students alike complained about scientific marking, and even Bell admitted that it led to a "killing pace."[42] But he regarded it as fundamental to the school's success, and so education suffered for the sake of evaluation.[43]

Bell's more serious error was to disregard Wagner's directive to maintain the components of the Army Service Schools as separate entities. Unlike his friend, he did not realize the necessity of a professional education system as complex and multifaceted as the army that it served. Instead, Bell commanded the Army Service Schools in the same fashion that he had a brigade in the Philippines. He assured his counterpart at Fort Riley that establishing the proper "professional spirit" was "almost the whole thing" in creating a successful school.[44] That attitude was inconsistent with Wagner's reorganization scheme. Commanders do not hold their subordinate units apart as isolated entities but bring them together into cohesive teams. Bell saw an opportunity to have the Army Staff College students—some of the army's best young officers—serve as mentors for the Infantry and Cavalry School class by using them as classroom assistants. This seems to have been effective in fostering "spirit" but at the cost of Staff College students essentially repeating the Infantry and Cavalry School course rather than learning how to be general staff officers. In the 1905–1906 academic year, nearly 60 percent of Staff College time allocated to the Department of the Military Art was spent in preparation for, or in, the classroom with the Infantry and

Cavalry School. This left only forty classroom days for instruction in higher staff duties. Bell thus effectively reduced the year-long training for the General Staff to a mere eight-week course, while the Army War College under Bliss had its students "learn by doing." Thus, the Staff and War College curricula had diverged, leaving a void in between in which there was little formal education in higher staff duties.[45]

It was not that Bell saw no need for staff training but that he put far more emphasis on the needs of the line than did Carter and Bliss. When a Staff College graduate complained about a poor evaluation report, Bell upbraided him for believing that "your legitimate duty as a troop officer, [is] not only a bore, but as an occupation too limited in its requirements, and too humdrum in it its opportunities, for a man of your talent, tastes, and requirements." Bliss, who had spent only three years with his regiment, would certainly have disagreed with Bell's contention that "the only way an officer can fit himself for higher command . . . is to gain a good reputation, by zealous persevering and faithful and efficient attention to his ordinary routine duties."[46] Rather than acting as a siphon to divert talent toward high staff assignments as Carter had intended, Bell reoriented the schools to the task of raising the tenor of the entire profession. His success in this was evident in a 1906 survey of graduates, in which one noted, "It is for the average man as I understand it, that the [Infantry and Cavalry] school exists."[47]

Bell's commendable pursuit of morale and fairness also had the unintended effect of reducing the representation of artillerymen and engineers at Fort Leavenworth. That odd result was also due to his desire to integrate Staff College students into the Infantry and Cavalry School. The students from the technical arms posed a problem for Bell, because they would not be as familiar with the Infantry and Cavalry School course as would their classmates. This led him to demand that artillerymen and engineers attend the Infantry and Cavalry School before attending the Staff College. But that only created a further dilemma of potential disparity. Under GO #115, artillerymen and engineers were guaranteed places in the Staff College. Bell worried that this would harm the morale of the infantrymen and cavalrymen who were in the fierce competition to win a seat to the Staff College. Rather than prompting him to question whether the pursuit of morale was undermining the purpose of the school, Bell simply ignored Wagner's provision guaranteeing each arm a fixed proportion of seats in each Staff College class. The technical branch chiefs protested this unilateral dismantling of War

Department policy; both arms were already suffering from a shortage of junior officers, and they could ill afford to lose their best for an additional year, particularly when a successful outcome depended on those officers' ability to outperform infantrymen and cavalrymen in the tactics of those arms. The technical branch chiefs appealed to the chief of staff, cavalryman Adna R. Chaffee, who upheld Bell's policy. In response, the artillery and engineers nearly halved the number of officers they sent to Fort Leavenworth each year.[48]

Captain Henry B. Clark, one of the artillerymen in the first Staff College class, foresaw the negative consequences for the school, his branch, and the army as a whole. In a letter to Bell, he pleaded for the school to remain a place of "all-round" instruction rather than to serve "merely [as] a second year course of the Infantry and Cavalry School." Though he realized that the immediate problem was Bell's policy, Clark implied that fault lay also with an Artillery Corps that prized technical knowledge but was indifferent to general professional education.[49]

The artillery had ceded important institutional ground, for Bell was successful in raising the stature of the Army Service Schools. Each summer, he sent faculty, recent graduates, and students to the army's summer training for use as aides, staff officers, instructors, and umpires. The generals responsible for the camps of instruction eagerly accepted these well-trained officers and employed them in a variety of roles: delivering lectures, teaching classes, planning training, and serving as umpires. Fort Leavenworth already occupied a prominent position in the army's intellectual landscape by virtue of the textbooks produced by Wagner, Carter, and other faculty; but the summer employment of graduates and students provided another conduit for influencing the army. Maneuvers were described as realistic portrayals of combat but in fact replicated war as imagined by the small group of officers who constructed the rules governing the training. Each umpire received a card that specified the percentage of losses that a unit would suffer under different conditions. Implicit within these calculations were many assumptions about combat, such as the relative power of infantry and artillery or the ability of troops to sustain the advance despite heavy enemy fire. On most of these issues, there was no consensus. But unlike the statements found in a textbook, such as "artillery fire alone cannot stop infantry," which were explicit, the underpinning rationale for the "reality" portrayed in maneuvers remained hidden. The thousands of such rulings that would be made in a single summer of training were thus a powerful form of subtle indoctrination.[50]

Yet under Bell, the Army Service Schools had no coherent vision of warfare to impose on the army. Though Bell personally had advanced views on tactics—he was one of the first American generals to see the potential of both airplanes and machine guns—his preoccupation with morale meant that he paid little attention to the content of the curriculum. To manage that aspect of the school, Bell had Eben Swift assigned as assistant commandant. Predictably, Swift immediately made his applicatory method the centerpiece of instruction and purged the school of Wagner's textbooks. But Swift's obsession with form had blinded him to the value of Wagner's conceptual contribution to tactics. At first, Swift believed it would be easy to fill the large void in the curriculum he had created; he directed members of the faculty and Staff College class to write a series of several dozen essays on topics previously covered by Wagner's books. The disappointing essays were of varying quality and collectively presented no coherent view of modern warfare. Some of the essays were not even internally consistent. Though Swift remained committed to the applicatory method, he grudgingly conceded that his failed experiment was "a vindication" of Wagner's work.[51]

In 1906, the direction of American professional education turned once again when Bell was again advanced past superiors to become chief of staff of the army. Soon thereafter, he asked Swift to come to Washington in order to revitalize the Army War College, which though Bliss had since left still functioned as an unstructured *collegium*. Bell disliked that model and wanted Swift to institute a curriculum like that used at Fort Leavenworth. Swift, however, resisted coming to Washington. By the time that he relented, Bell had temporarily been called away to command the reoccupation of Cuba. In Bell's absence, Swift's efforts were stymied by the college's senior director, Lieutenant Colonel Smith S. Leach, a West Point classmate of Bliss, who loyally defended the *collegium*. When Swift persisted, Leach rebuked him, writing that War College students were "not to be treated like children"—a telling indicator of how Swift's didactic methods were perceived by others.[52]

With Bell's return and Leach's departure the following year, Swift remade the War College curriculum according to his own narrow conception of professionalism. Though Swift grudgingly retained some of the "strategical" work of mobilization and campaign planning conducted in conjunction with the General Staff, he believed that it was largely wasted effort. It would take too many years of training, he wrote, before an officer was prepared to make "plans for national defense and strategical objectives in time of war."[53] Ignoring the obvious question of where, if not at the War College, such training should take place, Swift concluded that the only real purpose of military education was to teach the "art of commanding troops."[54] He therefore introduced elements more appropriate for a school of tactics, such as the proper delivery of verbal orders. Though his use of the phonograph in those classes was an innovative use of technology, it had little to do with the duties of a general staff officer in the War Department or at an operational headquarters, where all directives were of necessity written. As with the Staff College, an elitist institution had been transformed into something more pedestrian.[55]

In less than a decade, professional education had tacked wildly among several different courses. The narrow elitist system of Carter was replaced by the broad, multifaceted system of Wagner. In practice, neither the plans of Carter nor those of Wagner were fully implemented. In the end, it was the egalitarian, practical preferences of Bell that prevailed. Though in many ways superior to the initial scheme laid out in 1901, Bell's ideas triumphed not because they had the most merit but because he was the last and highest-ranking individual to influence policy.

*   *   *   *   *

In the first decade of the twentieth century, military theorists confronted a crisis produced by several decades of technological invention. A host of weapons—magazine-fed rifles, machine guns, smokeless powder ammunition, rapid-fire light guns, and high explosive rounds—seemed certain to decimate any large-scale attack. But without the ability to mass troops, how could an army overwhelm its opponents on the battlefield? Previously, it had been possible to maneuver around strong enemy positions, but industrialization and steam-driven transportation allowed the great powers to field massive conscript armies that might be too cumbersome for such movements. Some came to the conclusion that war had become a matter of attrition. Yet with industrialization and urbanization came political and social upheaval. Generals distrusted the new urban masses. Even if brittle societies could sustain a conflict, the cost of warfare and the interdependence of European economies meant that governments and industry might not. In 1899, Polish businessman Jan Bloch argued in his controversial treatise, *The Future of*

War, that offensive war could no longer produce a favorable outcome. That conclusion was unacceptable to the armies of the great powers, particularly those of France and Germany. In the former, the army hungered to regain its honor after several decades of military, political, and social shocks. In the latter, the aggressive policies of Kaiser Wilhelm II kept alive the Prussian tradition of compensating for geographic vulnerability through operational aggressiveness. Preserving the viability of the attack thus became an existential quest for military thinkers in both countries.[56]

Some theorists sought to make attackers less susceptible to the physical effects of fire through decentralized command of thin skirmish lines and small units in the attack. After Boer marksmen devastated dense British formations in the South African War (1899–1902), that idea enjoyed a short-lived popularity. But critics soon countered that on continental battlefields such dispersion would not provide sufficient mass to overwhelm a stronger adversary.[57]

An alternative approach was to provide officers with greater control over their soldiers—typically by packing them into even tighter masses—so that they might be herded to victory despite losses. In Germany, that solution soon came to dominate, even though it rested upon uncertain assertions that willpower could overcome firepower. In hindsight it is clear that with the weapons available, the size and composition of the armies, and the respective aims of France and Germany, there was no satisfactory solution to the problem of continental war. Yet unwilling to face the unpalatable truth that they sought unobtainable aims, military theorists easily picked apart the fallacies in their rivals' methods while ignoring the problems with their own.[58]

Through translation and reprints in the professional journals, American officers followed the European debate closely.[59] Perhaps too closely, for continental tactics were rooted in a much different political, strategic, and social context. Since the first edition of Upton's *Tactics,* the dominant trend in the United States had been toward dispersion to minimize the effects of fire. In North America, small armies operating across vast spaces had much greater opportunity for maneuver to avoid frontal assault. Wagner had continued this tradition in his textbooks, and the costly battles against the Spanish in Cuba seemed to confirm the wisdom of this approach.

Yet there had always been some resistance to extended-order tactics. Even Upton had not been entirely satisfied with the balance that he had struck between mass and survivability, and the European debate rekindled these doubts. Also, for many officers their extended experience in the Philippines overshadowed the short war in Cuba. The Filipinos were poorly armed, trained, and led. American units soon learned that the most effective tactic when coming under fire from trenches was immediate and audacious counterattack. The ineffectual Filipino fire caused few casualties, and they quickly abandoned their position rather than engage in a set-piece battle.[60] Though officers denied that lessons learned in the Philippines had any relevance to "civilized warfare," for many it was their only combat experience.[61] Ingrained patterns of thought could not be so neatly compartmentalized. One senior officer feared that his younger colleagues had developed "erroneous and regrettable ideas," including a "disdain" for the lethality of modern weapons.[62]

One purpose of the Root reforms had been to provide the institutional apparatus to ensure that the army adapted correctly to modern conditions. Reformers had long assumed that through the study of history and contemporary trends a General Staff would develop sound tactics. Its first attempt to do so was promising. Indeed, the 1905 *Field Service Regulations (FSR)* was the first American manual to bind the drill regulations of the various branches together with a holistic set of principles for combined arms tactics. The 1905 *FSR* also established the composition of units larger than a regiment in an attempt to harmonize tactics and organization into a comprehensive system of fighting. It was the first American military doctrine, as the term is understood today.

Though Wagner was the head of the division producing the new manual, he opposed this development. During the preparation of the 1904 *Infantry Drill Regulations (IDR)*, he had prevented the inclusion of anything beyond the traditional elements of mechanical control—formations, commands, and movements. Unlike with his textbooks, Wager argued that putting tactical principles in binding regulations would compel officers to "conform, possibly contrary to [their] own judgment, to the principles therein prescribed."[63] Though Wagner had an interest in preserving the royalties derived from his textbooks, he also seems to have genuinely feared any infringement of the professional autonomy expected by his generation. After all, doctrine and indoctrination are related words. Yet it was ironic that the individual most instrumental in developing powerful tools of indoctrination—professional schools and umpired field maneuvers—should recoil from the logical conclusion of that work. Moreover, Wagner served on the General Staff, a body charged with developing and enforcing professional standards.

The tightly packed firing line, upright officers, and general disregard of cover seen in this 1899 photograph all indicate contempt for enemy fire that was possible in the Philippines but that would have been suicidal against a better equipped and trained adversary. (Photo by Captain J. F. Case/ Hulton Archive/Stringer/Getty Images)

Yet with ailing health and possibly restrained by the conflict of interest due to his textbook sales, Wagner was unable to prevent Captain Joseph T. Dickman, the determined officer responsible for writing the 1905 *FSR,* from including a discussion of tactical principles.[64]

Despite this departure in form, conceptually the 1905 *FSR* represented continuity with the past. A committee chaired by Wagner developed the new tables of organization, but the remainder of the work was largely that of Dickman adapting European models to suit American tastes, an approach that would have been familiar to Winfield Scott or William Hardee. Dickman continued in the tradition of Upton and Wagner by emphasizing coopera-tion among the arms and a healthy respect for modern firepower. Indeed, the manual was so uncontroversial that most of the army's general officers ignored Dickman's request for comments.[65]

The 1904 *IDR* and 1905 *FSR,* however, were not the first true tests of the General Staff; for even at the time, they were regarded as only interim measures. It had been several decades since the last major war between western-style armies when in 1904 Russia and Japan went to war in the Far East. Armies around the world eagerly dispatched observers with the expectation that it would be an empirical experiment in military science against which all competing theories could be judged. Though one American officer called the observers' reports the "final arbiter of all differences of military opinion," their conclusions should have been treated with considerable skepticism due to the challenges they faced in forming an accurate appreciation of the situation in Manchuria.[66] The Russians were relatively permissive in allowing the foreigners to move about, but they shared little detailed information—plans, reports, or even maps. Across the lines, the Japanese actively sought to frustrate the observers' attempts to witness the war. There was the additional problem of language; of the eight Americans in the initial party, only one could communicate with his hosts in their operative language. Yet even those who understood the difficulties of the observers likely thought that fragmentary reports from a contemporary war were better than the well-worn experiences of the increasingly distant past. From 1906 to 1909, more than twice as many articles in the *JMSI* cited examples from Manchuria than from the American Civil War and the South African War, the next most common examples.[67]

The initial team of four officers sent to each of the contending armies included representatives from the various branches who were to report on their respective areas of expertise. Captain Carl Reichmann was the infantryman sent to observe the Russians. Reichmann was a German immigrant who had enlisted in the army out of desperation in 1881 but had within three years earned a rare commission from the ranks. Despite the prejudice against "rankers," Reichmann earned a place within the military intelligentsia through his willingness to translate German military literature. The West Point curriculum was slow to recognize the shift of European military preeminence, and so cadets still learned only French and Spanish. While attending the Infantry and Cavalry School in the late 1880s, Reichmann developed a close relationship with Wagner, with whom he shared a dislike for regimental duty. Wagner later aided Reichmann's career by arranging detached duty as an assistant tactics instructor and then later in the War Department. Reichmann returned to his regiment long enough to prove his competence in the Philippines, but then was off again in 1900 as an observer with the Boers during the South African War.[68]

Reichmann's counterpart with the Japanese Army was of roughly the same age but of quite different professional and personal outlook. Captain John F. Morrison continually resisted any service away from the Twentieth Infantry. Even a transfer to another infantry regiment caused him to protest being made to serve "among strangers." This preference for familiarity, however, did not mean that Morrison was dull. In the 1890s, one commander noted that Lieutenant Morrison was "constantly investigating some military subject."[69] One of his few periods away from the Twentieth Infantry was an assignment as a professor of military science at the Agricultural College of Kansas (present day Kansas State University) in the late 1880s. There, Morrison enrolled in chemistry and physics courses so that he might better understand explosives and propellants but became so proficient that the college soon paid him to teach those courses in addition to his military duties. Morrison was a natural instructor. An army inspector noted this skill, particularly Morrison's ability to inspire enthusiasm in his pupils. Yet once he had returned to his regiment, Morrison rejected an offer to teach tactics at the Infantry and Cavalry School. Only when his regiment was transferred to Fort Leavenworth in 1897 did Morrison relent. He replaced Swift as the chief tactics instructor, an assignment that lasted only a few months before the school closed due to the Spanish-American War. Morrison won a brevet for valor in Cuba and then later commanded a battalion in the Philippines. During that time, he once again declined to return to Fort Leavenworth as an instructor.[70] While elitists like Bliss regarded contentment with regimental duty as a sign of limited capacity, Morrison reciprocated their disdain by denouncing "quitters" who constantly sought detached duty as "a curse to the army." Such men, Morrison wrote scornfully, "should leave the service and sell ribbons."[71]

Despite their different temperaments, Reichmann and Morrison—along with the other Americans—were awestruck by the scale of the Russo-Japanese War: Each of the field armies was larger than the entire American service. Observing just a segment of the Battle of Liaoyang from a hilltop, Captain Peyton C. March, an officer known for his icy reserve, giddily paced back and forth, muttering again and again, "This is great! This is great!"[72] The superb preparation and organization of the Japanese drew praise from all the Americans. "Everything is systemized, every detail is worked out in time of peace," noted Morrison. "War with them approaches an exact science."[73] Reichmann agreed, contrasting Japanese preparedness with Russian disorder.[74]

Reichmann and Morrison disagreed, however, on what the war meant for the infantry. The General Staff had directed them to investigate the effects of artillery, machine guns, and field fortifications on infantry. With those prescient concerns in mind, they found themselves on opposite sides of the lines during the 31 August 1904 Japanese assault on Shoushanpu, a jagged Manchurian hill. From the top of Shoushanpu, Russian signal troops could observe the surrounding country for miles around. Further down the steep slopes, infantry and machine guns in fortified positions commanded a vital railway. The fields in front of this formidable position had been cleared to provide a kilometer of killing ground on which many Japanese had perished the day before. The renewed assault on the 31st was preceded by a bombardment from nearly three hundred field guns and howitzers. The intense barrage dazed the defenders, but enough of the machine guns crews survived to cut down the Japanese infantry in droves. Only a few of the attackers were able to get within the defensive lines, where the Russians prevailed in a fierce melee.[75]

Watching the battle from the Russian lines, Reichmann was struck by the power of the preliminary barrage, certain that he was witnessing a "historic instance of the use of artillery."[76] Though it paled in comparison to later bombardments in World War I, it was sufficient to convince Reichmann that the new technique of indirect fire—artillery engaging targets outside of visual range—would change warfare. Previously, the amount of fire that could be brought against a single point had been constrained by terrain; only so many guns could be assembled in the finite space with a direct view of the target. Indirect fire freed generals from this limitation, giving them an unprecedented ability to allocate firepower as they wished: So long as the guns had sufficient range and ammunition, the army's firepower could be distributed evenly along the line or concentrated and moved from point to point. To take advantage of this new feature of warfare, Reichmann recommended that the artillery be increased, reorganized, and brought into closer cooperation with the infantry.[77]

Morrison disagreed. "I do not believe that the improvements in field artillery will have much, if any, effect on changing present infantry tactics," he later wrote.[78] Instead, he concluded that the critical variable was the discipline and training of the infantry, which was not dependent on any other arm for victory. Disregarding the outcome at Shoushanpu, Morrison maintained that the eventual Japanese victory proved the efficacy of their German-inspired tactics of massed formations. Yet Morrison left Manchuria before the final Japanese victory. Lieutenant Colonel Edward J. McClernand, who was present for the later campaigns, claimed the opposite. According to McClernand, the Japanese had "broke away from their German teaching" and adopted more dispersed formations in reaction to Russian artillery and machine guns. March, too, claimed that the Japanese abandoned German tactics in favor of more open formations like those advocated by Wagner. The Russo-Japanese War had not only failed to conclusively answer the dilemma of the attack, but the American observers could not even agree upon the basic facts of what they had witnessed.[79]

This muddled understanding of warfare was reflected in the two most important pieces of American doctrine: the 1910 *FSR* and 1911 *IDR*. In contrast to the 1905 *FSR* and 1904 *IDR,* they were the products of an established General Staff and professional education system and so the first true test of whether the Root reforms had created superior institutions for preparing for war. The two manuals are also noteworthy because they established the doctrinal framework that the U.S. Army would bring into World War I. Unfortunately for the doughboys of the Great War, both were deeply flawed, though in quite different ways.

The 1910 *FSR* began at Fort Leavenworth while Bell was still the commandant. Though he had been one of the few general officers to encourage Dickman's efforts with the 1905 *FSR,* Bell was disappointed that Dickman had introduced terms different than those then in use at the Army Service Schools. Bell worried that such deviations would complicate his cherished system of scientific marking, which coped poorly with inconsistencies in authoritative texts. So while he welcomed doctrinal progress, Bell wanted it to remain tidy so as not to disrupt grading rubrics.[80]

To correct the situation, the commandant directed the chief tactics instructor, Major Daniel H. Boughton, to begin work on a new *FSR.* Boughton had earned an enviable record in combat. In the Philippines, he had been Bell's principal assistant during the Batangas campaign, and earlier in Cuba had distinguished himself as a commander of a cavalry troop alongside the Rough Riders. Theodore Roosevelt later remembered Boughton as one of the "towers of strength to the line" on the San Juan Heights.[81] In light

John Morrison (sixth from left, third row) sits among Japanese staff officers and international observers during the Russo-Japanese War. In Manchuria, Morrison believed that even bloody defeats demonstrated the power of the traditional infantry assault. (Joseph J. Kuhn Collection, USMA)

of those accomplishments, it seems strange that Swift would dismiss Boughton as "new to the subject" of tactics.[82] Yet sly references made by other officers suggest that this might have been the common opinion, for despite Boughton's unquestioned physical courage, intelligence, and energy, for much of his career he had been indifferent to the profession of arms. Upon graduation from West Point in 1881, he elected to serve in the Third Cavalry even though he had no strong love for the mounted arm. His sole concern was that the regiment offered good chances for promotion. Yet to accrue seniority Boughton did not have to be with the unit but simply belong to it. During the first twelve years of his career, Boughton was so successful at winning detached assignments that his colonel demanded the lieutenant's return so that he might "enjoy the advantages of sufficient contact with enlisted men to make him an efficient captain."[83] Much of

Boughton's energy during those early years instead went to earning a law degree and passing the bar examination. His peers appreciated his willingness to share legal advice, but evaluations from commanders were tepid. Ironically, it was this moonlighting interest that led to Boughton's assignment as Bell's staff judge advocate in the Philippines. It also was the reason for his assignment to Fort Leavenworth. Bell wanted to reward Boughton's efforts in the Philippines with an easy assignment, so he brought him to Kansas to teach military law. Boughton was transferred to the tactics department only after the chief instructor was seriously injured while riding.[84]

For Bell's purpose, however, a fighting lawyer was the perfect choice; the 1910 *FSR* was not a creative work but a reconciliation of precedents. Boughton first identified where the 1905 *FSR* deviated from materials at the school and then most often substituted the school materials to reconcile the two. By 1908, when he joined Bell in Washington, this process had already brought the manual close to its final form. Boughton did solicit comments from the staff departments, General Staff, and army at large, but only a fraction of the suggestions made in the hundreds of pages of comments that he received were incorporated into the final draft. The chief of staff was also given a chance to comment, but tellingly the final check was with the Fort Leavenworth faculty. Even though Bell had been away from the school for several years, the integrity of scientific marking remained his paramount concern.[85]

Though the 1910 *FSR* was consistent in terminology, it presented no coherent vision of warfare. The integrity of the sizeable portion remaining from Dickman's 1905 *FSR* had been compromised by editing that reordered elements and interlaced the original with much new material. There were some improvements. A more sophisticated concept of artillery integration into the maneuver of infantry and cavalry replaced the obsolete notion of an isolated artillery duel. A new table of organization developed by the General Staff provided for "artillery scouts" and communications equipment to link the infantry and artillery.[86] But elsewhere the manual contradicted these advances by proclaiming the independence of the infantry from the artillery. Even the improved discussion of infantry-artillery coordination failed to address the critical question of command between the two arms, a comfortable omission that allowed the artillery to retain its autonomy and the infantry its illusion of needing no assistance.[87] In sum, as a compilation of diverse works, the 1910 *FSR* naturally reflected the tactical confusion then afflicting the army as a whole.

The clarity and coherence of the 1911 *IDR* was in complete contrast to the muddle of the 1910 *FSR*. Unfortunately for the U.S. Army, those qualities reflected the certainty of John F. Morrison—the chief author—that machine guns were nothing more than mere "weapons of emergency" and artillery would have only a negligible effect upon defending infantry.[88] For Morrison, the only means for an attacker to achieve fire superiority over a defending force was to mass rifle fire. It therefore followed that attacking infantry should be massed as tightly as practicable in order to achieve the maximum density of rifles upon the battlefield. Consequently, the 1911 *IDR* specified the standard battlefield spacing as a yard between soldiers— the minimum distance allowing each soldier enough space to fully use his rifle. This compacted the frontage of the infantry squad to nearly half of what the 1904 *IDR* had prescribed. Indeed, the 1911 standard was closer to that used by Civil War armies than to that of the previous manual. Just three years before the beginning of World War I, Morrison had set American tactics back several decades. He then did further damage when he was charged with rewriting the chapter on combat for the 1914 *FSR*.[89]

The greater control over soldiers that such formations offered was also considered an advantage. In an article explaining the new manual, one of Morrison's assistants conceded that dense formations would likely lead to higher casualties but argued that the unit would otherwise lose even more men to shirking; he estimated that up to a quarter of soldiers were prone to becoming "skulkers." Tactics had not always been based on such a dim appraisal of the American soldier. Upton had attempted, albeit imperfectly, to harness what he regarded as the natural spirit of initiative within the common soldier. More recently, Bell had lauded the "tendency of modern military thought toward the cultivation of the soldier's intelligence and faculties as an individual."[90]

But not every officer agreed with the rosy view of Upton and Bell. In 1902, Major Robert L. Bullard urged his fellow officers to speak kindly to soldiers and appeal to their sense of duty and patriotism. In his view, the common belief among officers that speaking to enlisted soldiers "in any but the briefest possible terms" was "unmilitary" or "undignified" contributed to the high rates of desertion in peacetime and would lead to a breakdown of morale and order in battle. Bullard had twice commanded volunteer regiments, and many of the dissenting responses suggested that he had drawn false conclusions from those experiences with soldiers who were assumed to be atypically good. Such methods, these officers contended, would be disastrous with regular soldiers recruited from the immigrant and working classes. These replies were likely correct in identifying the difference in opinion as a function of past experience. Bell and Bullard were part of a small group of composite generation officers who had commanded volunteers.[91]

This was quite different than the experience of Upton and most of the Civil War generation. To that older generation it had been obvious that the army should adopt methods suited to volunteers, whom they assumed would make up the majority of the army in any large war. Though regulars in the early twentieth century intellectually acknowledged that was still the case—indeed, they welcomed the associated prospect of rapid promotion—the full implications seem not to have been internalized in the collective psyche of the composite generation. Without direct experience with volunteers, their depictions of large-scale conflict, such as that in the 1911 *IDR,* resembled something like the continental conflict described in German military theory but one waged with a professional army unlike that ever fielded by the United States in a major war. This allowed Morrison and others to ignore the central problem of preparing for war in the United States—devising the most effective means of employing hastily trained armies of citizen-soldiers.

The evasion was deliberate. Morrison disparaged "rule of thumb" tactics like those favored by Wagner as too simplistic to be effective. Some of that criticism was well-founded. The 1904 *IDR* described a schematic "normal attack" that dictated the precise number of firing halts and rounds to be fired but that assumed an implausibly inert enemy on unnaturally featureless terrain. Even Bullard, who argued that "In America above all we must assume a soldier for war who knows nothing," conceded that such absurdly pared down tactics were "doubtless defective."[92] But the 1911 *IDR* went to the other extreme, providing only a general description of principles such as one might find in a classroom at Fort Leavenworth. Morrison grudgingly conceded that it would require "much explanation" before volunteers could even begin to understand such an abstract discussion, much less put it to practical use. Nonetheless, he chose to ignore the implication and so violated his own dictum that "the best results are obtained when leaders know the capacity and traits of those whom they command."[93]

The great irony was that Bell, who disagreed with Morrison on many issues, had been the one who had brought the conservative infantryman to prominence. While still the commandant at Fort Leavenworth, Bell decided to bring one of the observers of the Russo-Japanese War to the faculty. Swift urged him to request the assignment of Carl Reichmann, who was already familiar with the applicatory method from his time as an assistant instructor in the 1890s. Swift also wanted Reichmann to help with the backlog of untranslated German military texts. Bell complied, but the War Department initially denied the request on the grounds that Reichmann had been absent from his regiment for too long. Several days later, the War Department suggested that it might reconsider, but Bell made no effort to pursue Reichmann's assignment. Not long after, he requested that Morrison be assigned to the school as Boughton's eventual replacement as the chief tactics instructor.[94]

Conceptually, Bell had more in common with Reichmann. He was one of the first general officers to actively support experiments with machine guns, a weapon that Morrison dismissed as impractical. Bell had read the observers' reports and knew their views. But conceptual matters were of secondary importance for Bell. He wanted "practical" officers like Morrison who had served under Bell in the Philippines. Conversely, Reichmann's reputation for escaping regimental duty would have won little favor with Bell, who valued workmanlike toil.[95]

Bell wanted a good role model for the student-officers, and Morrison was outstanding in that regard. The students were enthralled by his lectures enlivened with anecdotes from Manchuria. These lively talks made Wagner's textbook lessons seem stale and obsolete. Morrison's common-sense manner also contrasted favorably with the pedantic instruction of Swift, whom students suspected of caring more about the formatting of orders than their contents. Morrison's emphasis on practicality and simplicity appealed to junior officers. Some even came to revere him, proudly proclaiming themselves "Morrison Men" even years later. The most famous of these disciples was George C. Marshall, who credited Morrison with "[having] taught me all I have ever known of tactics."[96]

Bell departed Fort Leavenworth before Morrison's arrival, but he had left the institution ripe for domination by such a dynamic individual. As commandant, Bell feared that the War Department might select instructors who did not fit into his carefully crafted "Leavenworth spirit." As the chief of staff, he sought to avoid this problem by directing that the best Staff College students be retained for an additional year or two as instructors. This policy reinforced esprit, but it also created an insular and submissive faculty. Assistant instructors were typically ten to fifteen years junior to Morrison. In a year or two on the faculty, they were unlikely to evolve past their recent role of pupil and seriously challenge their former teacher. By 1910, seven of Morrison's eight assistants were recent graduates.[97]

This left the artillery instructor as the most likely voice of dissent within the tactics department. Until 1907, that officer had been a full member of the staff, teaching general tactics in addition to lecturing on topics specific to artillery. But upon becoming the department head, Morrison restricted the new artillery instructor, Captain Dwight E. Aultman, to teaching only the technical aspects of gunnery. The reasons for this demotion in duties are unclear and might have been for some purpose other than to quash a more optimistic view of the power of artillery than that of Morrison. Regardless of the reason, that was the effect; for the relative isolation of the field artillery meant that many of the students had little personal experience with it. Morrison's interpretation of the Russo-Japanese War was effectively the only source of experience within the department. When Aultman was assigned elsewhere, Morrison insisted that the artillery position be filled by a recent graduate of his choice.[98]

Though Morrison's tactical views appear to have been a matter of sincere intellectual conviction, at the time there was a faction of militant infantrymen who sought to use the army's bureaucracy to advance their parochial interests. Their angry cynicism was the product of decades of slights to the branch, such as the army's inspector general—a former cavalryman—who argued that "the thorough training of an infantry company does not demand the continuous zeal, patience, and technical knowledge required for a troop of cavalry or a light battery."[99] So although the infantry was the last of the combat arms to form an association, it was aggressive in seeking to redress perceived wrongs. Among its many complaints was an alleged pro-cavalry bias at Fort Leavenworth. In response to this charge, Bell, ever the conciliator, attempted to assign more infantrymen there.[100] The chief aim of the Infantry Association, however, was to increase the size of the branch and therefore opportunities for promotion. The regular army had an unusually large proportion of artillery and cavalry regiments, an arrangement defended by those branches as necessary due to the overwhelming preponderance of infantry within the National Guard. The Infantry Association dismissed this argument and demanded a greater proportion of the regular regiments.[101] Within that context, infantrymen had a vested interest in having someone like Morrison write the 1911 *IDR* rather than a heretic like Reichmann, who claimed that the "artillery has more nearly reached the tactical importance of infantry" and should thus receive a "substantial increase."[102] Indeed, most of the actual drafting of the manual was likely done by two assistants detailed to assist Morrison: Captain Alfred W. Bjornstad, one of Morrison's star pupils, and Captain Merch B. Stewart, a former West Point tactics instructor and a leading figure in the Infantry Association. In 1908, Stewart had been part of a cabal that opposed the first legislation in decades to increase soldiers' pay unless there was a decrease in the pay disparities between infantrymen and some specialists. In a heated meeting on the issue, Stewart vowed that "every man, woman, and child in the Infantry would rather starve to death" than allow such inequalities to continue.[103] Stewart, too, might have genuinely believed that the infantry did not require artillery support to triumph on the battlefield. But he was also particularly attuned to the implications of tactics for the bureaucratic interests of the infantry.

Bell's cavalier attitude toward the content taught within classrooms and contained in manuals suggests that he did not fully realize the extent to which the institutional capacity for indoctrination had grown or that the Army Service Schools were the hub of much of that power. One of the few points of agreement between Carter, Wagner, and Bell had been that Fort Leavenworth should play a central role in professional education. None had foreseen the potential danger inherent to this centralization. When Fort Leavenworth became the epicenter for infantry chauvinism, it had multiple channels to inject that belief deep into the tissues of the army. The army's best young officers were deliberately brought to Morrison's classroom from where they were discharged back into the army, specially marked for service as umpires, trainers, and lecturers. School materials were widely distributed through a mailing list that included over 1800 regular officers, well more than a third of the officer corps and many guardsmen as well.[104] These conduits gave Morrison greater opportunities for influence than even those available to Upton as the West Point commandant in the 1870s or to Wagner as a tactics instructor in the 1880s and 1890s. All the while, Morrison only grudgingly accepted his mantle as the army's foremost tactician. In 1910, he longed to return to his regiment, but Bell insisted that he stay at Fort Leavenworth a while longer. "If I must stay away another year then this is as good a place as any," Morrison resignedly wrote to a friend. "It certainly is interesting work." Nonetheless, he confessed, academic life was "confining and sometimes a good sized burden."[105]

CHAPTER EIGHT

The Great War

WHATEVER THE CONCEPTUAL failings of Morrison and his compatriots, they were part of a professionally vibrant institution. This was partly the product of the Root reforms, which had deliberately sought to harness the energies of the army's best officers. Even an officer who doubted that army schools taught much that was of practical use conceded that they had the effect of "arousing military zeal" throughout the army. He attributed the surprising enthusiasm of "three or four old officers who had long been addicted to liquor, idleness, and objection to education" to the influence of young school-trained officers.[1] This was the positive aspect of the "Fort Leavenworth spirit" carefully fostered by Bell.

But even before Root, the composite generation had laid an important foundation for the later professional activism through the establishment of branch association and journals. Though these were sometimes a vehicle for divisive parochialism, they also provided a venue for officers to explore new methods of commanding, organizing, and equipping armies or the possibilities offered by new technologies such as automobiles and airplanes. Branch journals also encouraged topical specialization, which, in turn, likely sharpened the sense that officers were members of a profession distinguished by expertise. The Cavalry Association particularly fostered deeper intellectual engagement by publishing monographs—many of which were not directly related to the mounted arm—that were too long for the journals but lacked the commercial potential to be published elsewhere. The post-war expansion of the service schools offered further stimulus by enlarging the pool of officers with the facilities and time for research.

Perhaps the greatest stimulus, however, was the restless spirit of Progressive Era America. Young officers raised in that milieu eagerly tapped into the conceptual currents flowing outside of the army. In contrast to leading composite generation authors like Wagner, Matthew F. Steele, and Herbert H. Sargent who favored campaign studies that offered limited opportunities to draw upon other fields, the most ambitious efforts of the progressive generation were more abstract works that borrowed civilian concepts. This had both positive and negative elements. It allowed insights impossible with traditional battle analysis but also left officers vulnerable to the prevailing fears and fetishes of their time. As a consequence, even more so than in other periods, the military works of the Progressive Era bore the imprint of their contemporary civilian society.

One common fear that particularly resonated with professional soldiers was the idea that technological advances were causing a corresponding decline in the vitality of humankind. In 1910, Morrison suggested in his brutally straightforward fashion that it might require less "killing to break a body of troops today as fifty years ago."[2] This narrative of decline was popularized in the 1880s, when Doctor George M. Beard speculated that the pace and materialism of urban life was causing a neurological disorder—"nervousness"—that particularly afflicted the middle and professional classes. Others had followed with similar theories, so that by the early twentieth century there was a general sense that modern man was diminished in comparison to earlier generations. Some individuals resorted to extraordinary measures to stave off this decline. Roosevelt, Root, and Generals Chaffee and Bell were among the prominent figures who sought to preserve body and soul at the military-style health camp of "lay clinician" William Muldoon. For a significant fee, clients submitted themselves to a regimen of verbal abuse, cold showers, strenuous exercise, and strict discipline. Relatively few individuals with such means, however, had the desire to test themselves in such a fashion, causing Roosevelt to worry that decadence was slowly destroying the virtue of his patrician class. The situation among the lower classes seemed even more dire. In the United Kingdom, the physically and mentally stunting conditions of Victorian slums became a matter of national security when the Boer War exposed the chronic poor health of the working classes; in response, the government formed a Committee on Physical Deterioration that made a number of recommendations to improve the fitness of potential soldiers. As the work of journalists and activists like Jacob Riis, Jane Addams, and Upton Sinclair made clear, conditions were no better in large American cities.[3]

The foreign-born segment of those urban masses seemed particularly menacing to the middle- and upper-classes, including army officers. A 1908 General Staff report warned that the "absorption of 19,000,000 aliens" was one of several direct threats to internal security.[4] According to the pseudo-scientific beliefs of social Darwinism and eugenics, they also posed an indirect threat through dilution of the national spirit or a degradation of the country's "racial hygiene." The supposed military implications were described by one of Morrison's assistants, Captain LeRoy Eltinge (USMA 1896), in his monograph, *Psychology in War*. Inspired by French academic and military thought, particularly the works of sociologist Gustave Le Bon and Colonel Charles Ardant du Picq, Eltinge based his study on the belief that collective morale and psychology was the most important factor in war. He argued that tactics should conform to psychological imperatives. This led Eltinge to some interesting insights. For instance, even though he shared Morrison's low opinion of the physical effects of artillery and machine guns, Eltinge valued these weapons because they could reduce the dangerous sense of isolation among dispersed riflemen; but Eltinge also subscribed to the belief in inherent national military characteristics. Though generalizations such as the supposed tendency for "the Latin" to make enthusiastic attacks but to fall "into deepest dejection and hopelessness under a reverse" had been a staple of Western military thought since at least the eighteenth century, the rise of social Darwinism and the associated specter of cataclysmic great power conflict gave the issue greater urgency.[5] This was true in Europe as well, where it influenced both operational plans and tactical doctrine.[6] But in the United States, immigration thus posed a special problem for Eltinge. He fretted that racial mixing had gone so far that it was impossible to create an ethnically pure army, making it impossible to fit tactics to temperament.[7]

The Progressive Era, however, was also a time of great optimism that the objectivity of science and engineering could be productively applied to a broad range of activity. An exemplar of this technocratic spirit was Frederick W. Taylor and his system of "scientific management." Taylor's fundamental premise was that if allowed discretion workers would invariably use inefficient methods. Better results could be achieved if engineers and managers "do the thinking for the men."[8] Through quantitative study of every stage of the production process, engineers like Taylor could determine the most efficient methods and then strictly impose them on workers. Captain Henry E. Eames (commissioned from the ranks 1897) aspired to achieve a similar control over the "workers" of an infantry company. Rather than turn to Gallic social sciences like Eltinge, Eames based his monograph *The Rifle in War* largely on Teutonic mathematics and ballistic science. European experiments had demonstrated that although it was impossible to predict the fall of a single bullet when directed against a single target, the collective fire of a group of soldiers produced a "cone of fire" of predictable size and shape. In theory, the infantry company had a machine-like reliability. The possibilities excited Eames, but realizing the theoretical benefits of the predictability required Taylorist-like control; if all the soldiers were not firing at the same target, then the mathematical effect of aggregation would be lost. Eames assured his readers that the unit director (a nonmilitary title presumably meant to convey the technical aspect of combat) working through two lieutenants and more than a dozen noncommissioned officers could achieve such absolute control. He maintained that the director could move the cone of fire around the battlefield with the ease with which one directs spray from a water hose. In practice, that required the ability to communicate a series of precise commands to nearly a hundred soldiers spread along a noisy firing line up to several hundred feet long in the midst of battle. Contemporary experiments in command under combat conditions as well as the work of colleagues like Morrison and Eltinge suggested that such precise control, which at times had been achieved in the Philippines, was impossible under more challenging conditions. Nonetheless, the *Infantry Journal* gave the monograph a favorable review, impressed by Eames's use of "mathematics and quotations from published opinions of the world's thinkers and instructors in modern military art."[9] Yet Eames invalidated all of that quantitative data with the final incongruous assertion that it was impossible to "shoot a defender out of his position" and that the bayonet was the ultimate weapon.[10] These were bizarre conclusions for a 110-page monograph on ballistics, but they were consistent with the Fort Leavenworth orthodoxy that battle was a clash of wills. Eames came to the facile conclusion that victory went to the nation able to instill "grit" so that its soldiers could "stand punishment in order to give it."[11] To that end, he suggested commanders discourage soldiers from seeking cover from enemy fire and employing summary execution when necessary on the firing line. Despite these flaws, *The Rifle in War* and Eltinge's *Psychology in War* were incorporated into the Fort Leavenworth curriculum.[12]

The intellectual preoccupations of artillerymen were quite different than those of their brethren in the infantry. The nature of the gunners' work meant that they did not share the infantry's fears of being eclipsed by machines. As Captain William J. Snow (USMA 1890) wrote in a 1908 report on the artillery, "mechanical developments" would only increase the arm's importance "for the artillery more than any other arm involves machine principles, and depends less on human emotions."[13] Yet not all was well in the artillery, for even though the obsolete black-powder weapons had been replaced in 1902, Snow warned that the artillery still lacked the organization and knowledge to use their new equipment to its potential. In response to Snow's report, Chief of Staff J. Franklin Bell ordered Major William Lassiter (USMA 1889), perhaps the leading expert on the new materiel, to conduct a thorough inspection of the field artillery. Lassiter validated Snow's findings. Seven years after the adoption of the M1902 gun, officers were still so unfamiliar with their equipment that they could not identify the causes of mechanical malfunctions and commanders were uncertain of how to employ their guns in combat.[14]

The problem was not helped by the turmoil resulting from the complete reorganization of the artillery in 1907. The army had made a great leap forward by replacing the nineteenth-century organization of individual batteries with a more sophisticated regimental structure capable of the complex tactical, technical, and logistical coordination necessary for massed fires like those that had impressed Reichmann in Manchuria. But in the short term, this was offset by the problems resulting from the split of the Artillery Corps into separate branches of coast and field artillery that left the latter without a chief to advocate for change or a branch association, journal, or service school to foster expertise. The fledgling field artillery already suffered from a dearth of officers trained in complex tactical operations, the legacy of the artillery's earlier retreat from general professional education. By mid-1908, Snow was the only field artilleryman to have graduated from the Army War College, and only six other field artillerymen had graduated from the Army Service Schools at Fort Leavenworth. The field artillery also suffered from the post-Root shift from large maneuvers to smaller camps of instruction because less-ambitious training offered fewer opportunities to practice infantry-artillery coordination at the higher echelons. This lack of theoretical and practical knowledge of combined arms was reflected in the 1908 *Field Artillery Drill Regulations (Provisional)*, which dealt only with the technical aspects of gunnery and offered no tactical principles for its employment. The situation improved somewhat when Bell created a service school for the field artillerymen—the evocatively named School of Fire at Fort Sill, Oklahoma. But for several years, the gunners were consumed with mastering technical detail rather than improving tactical coordination with the other arms. In the two years after it was established in 1911, the *Field Artillery Journal* featured only two articles about combined arms integration but had eleven on branch-specific technique and training.[15]

One of the purposes of the General Staff was to prevent such functional insularity, but it made little more than a gesture to do so. At the time of Lassiter's report, the chief of the doctrine and training section was Colonel Robert K. Evans (USMA 1875), an infantryman and one of only three members of his class to graduate with a lower standing than Arthur L. Wagner. In a 1909 lecture to the Army War College, Evans parroted the infantry-centric ideas then in vogue at Fort Leavenworth, drawing particularly on Eames's *The Rifle in War*. Though hardly a promising conceptual basis for intraservice cooperation, Evans somehow concluded that the army should increase the proportion of artillery relative to infantry and recommended the establishment of live-fire ranges large enough to allow for realistic infantry-artillery training. If realized, such experimentation might have eventually produced the vision for combined arms cooperation that the 1910 *FSR*, which Dan Boughton was then completing under Evans's supervision, failed to provide. But although some of Evans's recommendations relating to the infantry were accomplished, such as the establishment of a School of Musketry, little progress was made in improving infantry-artillery coordination.[16] Several years later, Brigadier General Clarence R. Edwards was still left to complain that "each arm or department of our service has been left to develop itself separately and to struggle, not for the whole, but for itself alone."[17]

For all of the intellectual froth produced by the expanded school system and General Staff, in hindsight the initial results were meager. Nonetheless, the efforts of progressive generation officers like Eltinge, Eames, and Snow, were proof that Root's desire to create an active, inquisitive, youthful elite had been achieved. Those who benefitted from meritocratic opportunities like the Staff College or assignment to the General Staff relished temporary relief from the routine of subaltern duties. But the insertion of pockets of meritocracy within a larger system still willfully blind to merit invariably caused problems. Those blessed with such assignments grew frustrated when they were brought back into the normal system, while those denied favored status resented the distinction given to the few. These tensions were greatest where the young and talented intersected with the old and mediocre, an unfortunate mixture in any era (such as the dispute between Captain Winfield Scott and Major General James Wilkinson a century before.) But never before had impatient junior officers such justification for believing that they had better qualifications for command than their superiors. An anonymous article published in the *Infantry Journal,* most likely written by one of Morrison's young assistants, lampooned the composite generation embodied in a fictional account of a future war. Officers of "the old school" were depicted as concerned only with peacetime administration, high scores on the target range, and a mindless adherence to Wagner's normal attack, even to the point that the training ground was cleared of "scrub and rocks" that might interfere with the artificial regularity of the scheme. The story concludes with the battalion being destroyed after an unthinking senior officer blindly attacks an enemy force.[18]

These generational differences were particularly evident during large training events. In 1906, Brigadier General William H. Carter (USMA 1873) proudly claimed that a camp of instruction under his command "taught the younger generation to think in terms of brigades and divisions, instead of companies and battalions, as was the case with the army between the Civil War and the War with Spain."[19] Though Carter's tone might have been too self-congratulatory, his assessment of the two generations was more or less correct. The gulf was particularly stark in the Twentieth Infantry, one of the units attending the camp. The regiment was commanded by Colonel Owen J. Sweet (volunteer commission 1862), who despite being much older had less experience as a field grade commander than did his subordinate Major Robert L. Bullard (USMA 1885). In 1898, Sweet had still been just a captain while Bullard raised and trained a regiment for the Spanish-American War as a volunteer colonel. The next year, Sweet was at last a major, but Bullard was once again a colonel, one of the elite selected to command a volunteer regiment in the Philippines. Even after Bullard reverted back to his permanent rank of major in 1901, he had greater operational responsibilities as a district governor in Mindanao than Sweet, who like many of the other old colonels was left to administrative work.[20] Bullard's natural resentment of having to surrender his rank and serve under a less-qualified commander was moderated somewhat while in quiet garrison duty in Minnesota, but witnessing Sweet's fumbling tactical abilities at the camp of instruction infuriated the major. "Now I see [Sweet], after the maneuvers, as I saw him three years ago on the Moro Campaign," Bullard wrote. "He is an incompetent, hopeless, and ought to be retired at once."[21]

Admittedly, few of any age could match Bullard's exceptional resume; but many more had attended advanced professional schools or served on the General Staff, and in many ways the skills gained in those assignments set the young elite even more starkly apart from their seniors. During the 1914 Philippine Division maneuvers, Colonel William C. Buttler (USMA 1876) was the nominal commander of a force of over 4,800 "invaders" simulating a landing and overland advance toward Manila. Buttler—a classmate of Eben Swift—had won the Silver Star as a captain during the early fighting in the Philippines but had neither experience nor training to prepare him for command of a brigade in such an intricate operation.[22] Fortunately for Buttler, he was assisted by two former Fort Leavenworth instructors, Captain Jens Bugge (USMA 1895) and First Lieutenant George C. Marshall (direct commission 1902), who were, respectively, his chief of staff and adjutant. Though Marshall was only in his thirteenth year of service, four of those years had been at Fort Leavenworth as a student and assistant instructor, and so he was entirely comfortable with operational problems involving forces much larger than those in the maneuvers. That theoretical knowledge was supplemented by practical experience in planning the movements and logistics of thousands of soldiers at several National Guard summer camps. Nearing retirement, Buttler made little attempt to even maintain the pretense of command. Rather than lead from horseback, he rode in a wagon with an alcohol-filled chest from which he drew throughout the day. According to historian Forrest Pogue, J. Franklin Bell, then commanding the Philippine Division, was set to relieve Buttler when Marshall intervened on the colonel's behalf. His motive was not altruism but fear that a livelier colonel would interfere with his work. Bell had taken an interest in Marshall's career since the younger man had finished at the top of his class at Fort

The jaunty pose struck by Fort Leavenworth classmates Bruce Palmer and George C. Marshall exudes the self-confidence of specially selected and trained young officers. Summer field training offered such individuals opportunities to use their talent and education, but inevitably they had to return to the frustrating reality of an army ruled primarily by seniority. (Special Collections, Combined Arms Research Library, Fort Leavenworth, Kansas)

Leavenworth, and so the lieutenant indeed might have the influence to save a colonel. Even when Bugge fell ill and was evacuated, Marshall was left to exercise effective command of the brigade, which was poised to take Manila when the exercise ended. But such exhilarating opportunities were fleeting, and the next year a frustrated Marshall considered resigning. Promotion to captain was likely years away, and in the meantime he was but second-in-command to one of his former students in a company of fewer than a hundred soldiers.[23]

Though Marshall was unusually talented, many others also chafed under the army's misaligned distribution of rank and expertise. During the 1908–1909 academic year, assistant instructors at Fort Leavenworth were on average three years *younger* than the students in the first-year course. This situation was uncomfortable for all; younger officers felt stifled, older officers felt threatened. Just a few years after his return from Manchuria, Major Carl Reichmann (commissioned from the ranks in 1884) was placed in charge of the instruction of senior captains at his post. The experience of teaching recent graduates of Fort Leavenworth led him to confess, "I found myself put to a severe test and often in doubt whether my acquirements in this direction were sufficient."[24] Just a few years earlier upon his return from Manchuria, Reichmann had been at the forefront of the profession. Less-accomplished peers were naturally even more nervous. Captain Charles Gerhardt (USMA 1887) urged senior captains to put their "pride in [their] pocket," accept the embarrassment of competing with more junior officers, and apply for Fort Leavenworth if they had not already attended. "The time is coming," he warned, "when the officer who is not possessed of the knowledge taught at this school will have to step aside to make room for the one who has it."[25]

* * * * *

In 1903, Root told the officers of the inaugural General Staff Corps that their gathering marked a new era of efficiency within the army, while *The Nation* lauded them as the "flower of the service."[26] It was indeed an exceptional group that included such promising officers as Major George W. Goethals, Captain John J. Pershing, and Captain Peyton C. March. But the War Department was already a functional bureaucracy with well-worn procedural channels fitted to peacetime needs, and there was no obvious mechanism by which General Staff plans for hypothetical wars would alter these established processes. Root had envisioned that his successors would play an active role in the reconciliation of old and new, but Secretary of War William H. Taft was an aloof manager unwilling to dip into the bureaucratic fray. Moreover, the first and third chiefs of staff served in that position for only five and three months, respectively, before retirement, and so had little influence. The second chief of staff, Adna R. Chaffee, had just over two years in the position; but without the active support of the secretary of war, the bureau chiefs were able to stymie his efforts to establish the authority of the General Staff.[27]

The selection of J. Franklin Bell as the chief of staff in 1906 was meant to be a new start; he was vigorous, progressive, and young enough to serve a full four-year term. But like his predecessors, Bell had no experience in the War

Department. His generous spirit also put him at a disadvantage when he allowed his own promotion to major general to be deferred so that it might go instead to a distinguished older officer soon to retire; this kindness meant that for the first nine months of his tenure Bell was inferior in rank to the bureau chiefs whom he was supposed to coordinate. Bell's greatest problem, however, was the lack of support from his civilian masters. Though the president's keen interest in military reform and the success of the General Staff in particular should have made him a valuable ally, Bell was found by Roosevelt to be personally irritating and so avoided interaction with the chief of staff.[28]

The chief of staff's political isolation created an opportunity for the military secretary, Major General Frederick C. Ainsworth. A former contract surgeon with no experience as a line officer, Ainsworth had nonetheless accumulated great power in the War Department as the chief of the Pension and Records Office. Ainsworth made the most of that seemingly mundane position by forming relationships with congressmen seeking benefits for their constituents. In time, he developed an informal network of power, the locus of which was a weekly poker game attended by bureau chiefs and congressmen that was reputed to be the scene of leaks, betrayals, and backroom deals. Just before Root's departure from the War Department, Ainsworth convinced the secretary to merge the records office with that of the adjutant general to form a military secretariat responsible for managing all information throughout the War Department. Perceiving no danger in this clerical function, Root unwisely agreed. Ainsworth, who one officer described as the only completely evil man he had ever known, used his control of information to curry favor with politicians and punish enemies through leaks or by denying them access to necessary information. By the time that Bell came to the War Department in 1906, the wary Taft's first direction to the new chief of staff was "no matter what, you have to get along with Ainsworth."[29] This put Bell in an impossible position, as Root had purposefully designed the General Staff to be a tool for the secretary of war with little independent authority. He had no recourse when Ainsworth simply refused to cooperate with the General Staff, which he described as "the enemy." When mobilization planners requested vital information regarding number of personnel in various units, Ainsworth refused to release the information. As one sympathetic officer reported, "Bell is doing everything on earth a man can to keep the peace, but most all his time is taken up trying to keep from stepping on other people's toes."[30]

The ambitious officers selected for the General Staff wanted to do more than avoid giving offense. Many expected something like the powerful German central General Staff and complained that Bell was not forceful enough. Frustration was particularly high within the element responsible for creating war plans, the War College Division (WCD), which its assigned officers derisively referred to as the "Water Closet Division."[31] Root had intended that it would be the focal point of the War Department, but instead the plans and planners languished on the organizational and geographic periphery in their grand building in Washington Barracks (present day Fort McNair), more than three miles away from the rest of the department.

In 1910, the exhausted and ailing Bell was replaced by Major General Leonard Wood, who was, in the words of one of his assistants, an "outlander" within the army.[32] Wood was not a West Pointer but a graduate of the Harvard Medical School who came into the army as a contract surgeon. He had always wanted to be a soldier but in an uncharacteristic act of obedience went into medicine to satisfy the wishes of his late father. The compliance was short-lived. Wood was expelled just months into his internship for repeatedly performing procedures without the assistance of an experienced surgeon. Perhaps as he had wanted all along, Wood had little alternative but to join the Army's Medical Department. Eager for adventure, he found it in his first assignment—desolate Fort Huachuca, Arizona Territory. In 1886, Wood accompanied the column of Captain Henry W. Lawton in an epic four-month, 2,000-mile pursuit of the Apache band led by Geronimo. Over the course of the arduous campaign through rugged desert, Wood's role evolved from a purely medical capacity. As a "provisional troop officer," he carried messages, led scouting detachments, and even commanded an infantry company for a time. Though Lawton never caught Geronimo, the department commander, Brigadier General Nelson A. Miles, was impressed by Wood's determination and subsequently sought to have him assigned as his surgeon whenever possible. As commanding general, Miles aided Wood's transfer to Washington in 1895. There Wood cultivated even more powerful patrons as the White House physician and friend of Assistant Secretary of the Navy Theodore Roosevelt. During the Spanish-American War, these connections led to Wood's appointment as colonel of the "Rough Riders." In that capacity, he demonstrated far more courage than skill in handling large bodies of troops; though the same was true of many of the regular colonels.[33]

Yet it was not physical stamina nor courage that brought Wood to the top of the military hierarchy but a combination of talent as an administrator and unscrupulous ambition. Both traits were manifest during his tour as a military governor in postwar Cuba. Unlike other generals who were content with limited improvements to Cuban services and government, Wood delighted in the nearly unchecked powers of a colonial overlord. He oversaw ambitious public works projects, reorganized the education system, and implemented sweeping economic, municipal, and legal reforms that excited the admiration and envy of civilian reformers. Wood's success was partly due to the lack of constraints. He enforced his sanitation decrees with invasive home inspections, mandatory quarantines, and humiliating public punishments.[34]

Wood was just as ruthless with his fellow generals. In order to be named governor of Cuba, he hired a Washington publicist to tout his success and undermine his rivals, though he was already personally adept in both pursuits. Wood was also shameless in demanding that powerful friends like Roosevelt and Henry Cabot Lodge aid his career. These efforts yielded his overall command in Cuba; and then in 1901—sixteen years after joining the army as a contract surgeon—he was promoted to brigadier general in the regular army, finally achieving his ambition of becoming a line officer.[35]

After leaving Cuba, Wood's talent, guile, and powerful patrons continued to bring him choice assignments that culminated in his selection in 1910 as Bell's successor as chief of staff of the army. Yet success and political friends also brought envy and political enemies. Wood's nomination for major general was subject to unusually hostile scrutiny in the Senate. Some of the legislative anger was an indirect assault on Roosevelt, but some was also in response to the widespread perception that "Doctor Wood" was being promoted faster than he deserved. Roosevelt dismissed these detractors as "mutton heads [*sic*]" who "naturally object to anything resembling promotion by merit."[36] There was some truth to the claim; even the promotion of the uncontroversial and well-liked Bell had been the source of some complaint. Yet Roosevelt failed to acknowledge the extent to which Wood's habitual insubordination and self-aggrandizement, as well as the obvious role of political influence in his success, were also sources of resentment. In that, Wood stood in great contrast to the self-effacing and scrupulously loyal Bell. Unsurprisingly, the two held each other in low regard.[37]

When Wood became chief of staff, he was determined to act more assertively than Bell. This foreordained a clash with Adjutant General Ainsworth (the title was restored from military secretary in 1907), whose power was at its zenith; Democratic gains in the 1910 elections brought his crony, Representative James Hay of Virginia, to the chairmanship of the Military Affairs Committee. Soon thereafter, Hay proposed a merger of the offices of the Adjutant General, Inspector General, and the General Staff with Ainsworth as the head of this super-bureau. But Wood had also gained a powerful ally when Henry Stimson, a young partner in the same law firm as Elihu Root, became the secretary of war. Stimson's support proved decisive when Wood goaded Ainsworth into writing an insulting letter over a trivial matter of administration. The secretary insisted that the rogue bureau chief be held to account. The lobbying of Ainsworth's congressional friends won only the slight reprieve of his being allowed to retire rather than face formal charges of insubordination.[38]

To junior officers frustrated with the persistence of antiquated ways, the defenestration of Ainsworth seemed to herald the dissolution of the old order. The diary of one major at the Army War College recorded that it caused "a tremendous sensation, nothing like it in years and the rejoicing in the Army is unbounded."[39] Wood received letters and telegrams of congratulations from across the army. From Manila, James G. Harbord, a member of Wood's circle, exulted that "the change of monsoon in the War Department . . . ought to give permanently better weather and smoother sailing."[40]

Harbord and other ambitious officers hoped that Wood would also rid the army of what Harbord called "military socialism," a comfortable mediocrity hostile to exceptional work. Harbord compared the common officer to a union member who shunned any worker exceeding his output quota. "This is the real basis of the opposition to promotion by selection," he concluded, "not that promotions might be made on 'pull' but that they might quite generally be made on merit, which would quicken the pace, 'bust' up the routine, [and] disturb siestas."[41] Yet even Wood could not overcome the widespread resistance to merit promotion. Several years before, William H. Carter had regretfully noted that the mere suggestion of abandoning the seniority system caused a "serious spirit of unrest" among officers.[42] Bell called it the subject "where even angels fear to tread."[43] Harbord's disdain for those who feared change to the promotion system reflected his comfortable place within the elite: He was exceptionally capable, a member of Wood's circle, and had been rewarded with a coveted position as a temporary colonel

in the Philippine Constabulary. Those with more modest abilities, connections, or luck lacked Harbord's faith in the army's ability to distribute
rewards justly. In 1909, one such officer noted a measure before Congress
that would simply have made it somewhat easier to separate unfit officers.
This proposal had everyone in his regiment "all worked up" because "nobody
in the army would be secure in his position."[44] Even the often daring *Infantry
Journal* insisted on seniority promotion during peacetime and opposed measures to retire mediocre officers.[45]

This widespread resistance limited Wood's ambitions to ridding the army
of only the most egregiously incompetent. Major Eli Helmick, a Fort
Leavenworth graduate, conducted several inspections that led to the relief of
regimental commanders, including one who failed to adhere to War Department training directives—something that would have been a trifling offense
in the old army, when commanders were largely left to run their units as they
saw fit. Wood also directed department commanders to assess their subordinates' abilities during maneuvers; but he found that it was "a mighty hard
thing to get support," even from his fellow generals, in his efforts.[46]

This indulgence and many other faults of the "Old Army" were evident in
the 1911 mobilization along the southern border. Though some military
response to the Mexican Revolution had long been expected, when President Taft ordered the concentration of a "Maneuver Division" at San
Antonio, it took over eight weeks for the division to reach its maximum
strength. Some of the delay was due to the natural unwillingness of the railroads to disrupt commercial traffic for a mere demonstration. But a more
significant problem was the lack of standing headquarters higher than the
regimental level; the consequence was that arrangements for command,
supply, and medical support all had to be improvised, causing delay, inefficiency, and confusion. Once formed, it was the largest assembly of regular
troops ever in peacetime; but junior officers complained that Assistant Chief
of Staff William H. Carter, who commanded the temporary division, squandered the opportunity. According to John M. Palmer, another member of
Wood's circle, "the principal characteristic of the Maneuver Division was
that it never maneuvered."[47] That criticism was somewhat unfair, as even
Palmer noted that each brigade had the opportunity to conduct training on
a scale rarely seen in peacetime. But he—like his mentor Wood—disliked
Carter and was quick to find fault. Nonetheless, it was striking that Carter,
who had been at the forefront of reform just a decade earlier, had come to be

regarded as an obstacle to progress. During the Maneuver Division camp, Major William Lassiter presented Colonel Lotus Niles with a tactical problem that so befuddled the old artillerymen that the regiment's guns were perpendicular to the proper direction of fire when Lassiter finally intervened. Yet Carter was inclined to overlook Niles's incompetence, and it was only Lassiter's determination to still bring charges that prompted Niles to request retirement instead.[48]

Meanwhile in Washington, Secretary of War Stimson directed the General Staff to conduct a comprehensive review of the army's organization based on strategic first principles. At last, the General Staff was undertaking the kind of work that Root had envisioned. Rather than conforming to the dictates of peace, which yielded administrative arrangements that broke down in crisis as during the border mobilization, the army would be organized to meet the likely demands of future war. The resulting report, *The Organization of the Land Forces of the United States,* recommended a modest increase of the regular army so that it could provide a full garrison for the overseas possessions, man critical coast defenses, and furnish a small expeditionary army. It also called for a redistribution of forces within the United States. Small forts scattered across the interior were to be abandoned in favor of larger installations closer to larger cities and the coasts. Also, the system of administrative regional departments that had failed during the Texas mobilization would be replaced by an organization of the peacetime army into divisions and brigades that could also serve as operational headquarters in war. National Guard units were to be similarly reorganized, but the report's most radical proposal was for the establishment of a European-style reserve that would displace the state troops as the country's second-line land force.[49]

Stimson's hope that logic and evidence would prevail proved naïve. There was considerable resistance even within the army. Although the Maneuver Division had demonstrated the deficiencies of the old command structure, many senior officers did not want to adopt a tactical organization. To win their support, Stimson convened a general officers' conference in Washington. His relentless presentation eventually won the generals' acquiescence; but William Lassiter, who recorded the conference minutes, believed that this support meant little. "The fact was that they didn't know anything about training or leading a Brigade or a Division, not to speak of a Corps or an Army, and it was too late for them to learn," he later wrote. "It was apparent that that generation would have to pass away before much could be done."[50]

Congress was even less receptive to reform. Stimson and Wood anticipated resistance to consolidating installations, but they hoped that even an unsuccessful effort would at least forestall further expansion of unwanted posts. This underestimated the risks of antagonizing Congress, a hazard made worse by self-righteous views that turned almost certain defeat into an unnecessary rout. In an article meant to win public support, Stimson complained of the "selfish opposition of the localities."[51] Wood was even more arrogant. Some time before, he had assured a subordinate that Congress was "generally pretty willing to deal with those who know what they want to do, and have good reasons to back them."[52] When he learned that this was not the case, Wood petulantly sought to apply pressure through direct lobbying and appeals to the public. Senator Francis E. Warren of Wyoming, the Republican chairman of the Military Affairs Committee, was angered by Wood's confrontational insistence on closing what the general termed a "wretched post" near the senator's hometown. Warren allied with his counterpart in the House of Representatives, James Hay, in a bipartisan, bicameral effort to crush the chief of staff. The 1912 Army Appropriations Bill mandated Wood's removal by stipulating that the chief of staff must have served for a minimum number of ten years in the army's line, a provision targeted solely at Wood. Eventually Root and Stimson convinced President Taft, who had appointed the troublesome general only at Roosevelt's insistence, to veto the bill and save Wood.[53] After the debacle, Stimson grudgingly confessed that "we have been too radical and have bitten off rather more than we can chew in the present state of opinion."[54]

Though Wood's position was preserved, the final appropriations bill carried a provision that would significantly weaken the General Staff. Commonly referred to as the "Manchu Law," the measure required that all lieutenants and captains serve with their companies for at least two of every six years. The effect was to throw the military "aristocracy" out of the capital and other places of luxury just as the Chinese dynasty of that name had been overthrown earlier that year. Scores of instructors, attachés, aides de camp, and staff officers were "Manchued"—forced to return to their regiments. Eighty-six percent of students and instructors in the army schools fell into this category. The resulting disruption was so severe that four years later the secretary of war noted that it still "seriously handicapped" the army's ability to assign qualified officers to the General Staff.[55] The political circumstances that made the law possible were a combination of lingering resentment over the Root reforms among Democrats and misgivings about executive power accumulated by Roosevelt among congressional Republicans. Staff bureau chiefs fearful of a powerful General Staff also undoubtedly added their support. Yet the chief impetus seems to have been the resentment of regimental officers for what they saw as an arrogant elite who monopolized choice assignments.[56] According to Wood's assistant for legislative affairs, Johnson Hagood, the general blamed the "Great Un-washed" within the officer corps. Hagood—himself a "Manchu"—similarly attributed the measure to "the proletariat who were determined to unseat the intelligentsia and to take their places on the Staff."[57] The arrogance evident in the reactions of Wood and Hagood partly explains the discontent that led to the law. Whether an act of justice or envy, the backlash provoked by Wood fell hardest upon the elite group of junior officers that had cheered on his aggressive approach to affairs.

The 1912 appropriations bill was a turning point for Wood. He spent the last half of his term as chief of staff on the defensive in large part due to his friend Roosevelt's decision to contest that year's presidential election as a third-party candidate. That action split the Republican Party, bringing Woodrow Wilson to the White House, ushering Stimson out of the War Department, and removing Wood's principal source of power. Reflecting upon the reign of Wood and his bright young assistants, Carter mused, "I never knew a group of able men to do such a lot of work which got them nowhere."[58] Though Wood's four years in Washington were not quite so unproductive as Carter suggested, it was true that Wood had wasted much effort in unproductive conflict. The cost would soon become evident, for Wood left office just ten weeks before the assassination of Archduke Franz Ferdinand in Sarajevo.

For his next assignment, Wood opted for command of the Department of the East, a largely administrative post with headquarters in New York harbor. It was an exciting place to be at the height of the Progressive Era, and Wood enjoyed mixing with prominent businessmen, professionals, and opinion leaders. In that environment and without practical military problems equal to his prodigious energy, Wood began to think of national defense in increasingly abstract terms. Like many imperialists, Wood was a social Darwinist who believed that the inevitable struggle among nations would be won by the fittest races. One of the leading proponents of such ideas was Homer Lea, an author whom Wood had long admired. Lea warned that the "Anglo-Saxons" would be overcome or absorbed if they could not equal the racial vigor of the "Teutons" and "Orientals." He predicted that the United States would succumb to the "Yellow Peril" if it did not reverse the tide of commercialism and materialism that eroded martial spirit. This closely paralleled the idea common within the army that battle was a contest of wills; social Darwinism simply raised the same dynamic to the higher plane of war and nations. Indeed, LeRoy Eltinge explicitly connected the tactical and strategic by asserting that the fighting capacity of an army was a function of the moral fiber of the nation. But Wood was unique among army officers in that he had the public stature to actually take action against the alleged erosion of the Anglo-Saxon spirit caused by immigration and materialism. He was joined in this quest by Roosevelt, who held the same views and following the White House was also lacking sufficient outlet for his restless energy.[59]

The cornerstone of their effort actually began in 1913, while Wood was still in Washington. The professor of military science at Cornell University proposed that the army provide training for any interested college students. Wood immediately agreed, but there was only time to organize two camps that provided five weeks of training for 222 students. That experiment fired Wood's imagination, and he personally oversaw preparations for the next year's round of what became known as the "Plattsburg camps," a name taken from one of the sites in upstate New York. Desiring to get as much backing as possible, Wood solicited the support of numerous college presidents and gave speeches to students at Harvard, Princeton, and other top colleges. His efforts worked so well that in 1915, the camps expanded once again. Spurred on by the war in Europe, a group of New York professionals led by Grenville Clark, Elihu Root, Jr., and Theodore Roosevelt, Jr., asked for similar "businessman's camps."[60]

The upper classes were overwhelmingly represented at the camps. In part, this was due to the requirement for camp attendees to pay for their uniforms and subsistence, which along with the substantial investment in time were a significant obstacle to those with limited means. But it was also partly by design, as Wood and his chief ally, Lehigh University President Henry S. Drinker, had focused their attention on the Ivy League and other premier undergraduate institutions. The idea for the businessman's camps had originated within the Harvard Club of New York, and the organizers actively sought to maintain that social standing by excluding even lesser white collar workers while drawing "the very best men." They succeeded in drawing former cabinet officials Stimson and Robert Bacon, the mayor and police commissioner of New York, the Episcopal bishop of Rhode Island, and a partner in J. P. Morgan.[61]

Historians posit that the reform impulse of the Progressive Era was driven by the desire of the middle class to impose its values upon both the decadent "top ten percent" and the immigrant-laden working classes. Thus it is noteworthy that Drinker wrote in the *New York Times* that the two classes most in need of military discipline like that offered at the Plattsburg camps were those with "well-to-do indulgent parents" and those "lacking parental control," the latter a coded reference to immigrants.[62] The popularity of the camps among the upper class thus represented an internalization of the middle class critique of the "top ten." Further evidence for this can be found in the words of Captain Courtland Nixon, a Princeton graduate and Plattsburg instructor, who boasted that for "the rich man's son this healthful simplicity is a cure to the wasteful luxury of the remaining forty-seven weeks of the year."[63]

Though Roosevelt and Wood thought that a strong patrician class was vital, they realized that voluntary camps for the rich would never be enough to revitalize the national spirit. The logical extension of the idea was to make such training compulsory for all male youth. Roosevelt first began advocating universal military service in November 1914. Wood followed with several speeches in early 1915 and then later with an exceptionally ambitious proposal described in his book, *Our Military History*. Wood wanted the country to adopt a military curriculum of calisthenics, drill, and firearms training in schools, followed by three months of intensive Plattsburg-like training after graduation, and then seven years of reserve service. He estimated that this system would train 500,000 conscripts annually, eventually yielding a reserve army of 3.5 million soldiers.[64]

The plan was an inefficient means of producing military force, but Roosevelt and Wood both admitted that their goals were more social than military. An extended period of rudimentary training did little to create cohesive combined arms units, but it was perfectly suited to the patriotic indoctrination of individuals. Indeed, civilian progressives had long sought to use education to impose "American" values on other groups; such was the purpose of the wave of compulsory education laws and the withdrawal of public support from religious schools. While still president of Princeton University, Woodrow Wilson admitted that his aim was "not merely to help the students to adjust themselves to world life . . . [but] to make them as unlike their fathers as we can."[65] If anything, Wood's ambitions were greater and more radical than those of civilian progressives. In order to instill "real Americanism," he said that it was necessary to "obliterate the sharp distinctions of race and creed, and to make us one homogenous mass."[66] Such rhetoric would seem more likely to come from a revolutionary than a general.

Wood pressed this utopian goal with an appropriately messianic fervor. He authored several books and numerous articles, corresponded with opinion leaders, and spoke to any group who would listen, even the several hundred "ultra-fashionable women" of the New York Colony Club. During a seven-month period in 1915 and 1916, Wood gave over 156 talks to an aggregate audience of over 137,000. This public advocacy brought Wood into conflict with the administration, which had banned officers from making any public comment on military policy because Wilson wanted to maintain neutrality abroad and limit military preparations at home. Despite several written admonishments from the secretary of war, Wood persisted.[67]

In May 1915, the political climate shifted significantly with the loss of 128 Americans when a German submarine sank the RMS *Lusitania*. That incident led to a steady rise of support for increased military expenditures that eventually reached its apogee in mid-1916, when a "Preparedness Parade" in New York City attracted 135,000 participants and similar demonstrations several weeks later drew 350,000 across ten cities. Yet it was not just threat of war that caused some to welcome universal military service. Many of the same groups who tended to support civilian progressive reform—editors of cosmopolitan newspapers, educators, doctors, and public health experts—believed that military service had significant societal benefits. Swayed by loud encouragement from these groups and carried away by his own ambition, Wood believed that universal military service had broader support than was actually the case.[68]

The administration was on the opposite side of the issue, lagging slightly behind the public mood. In late 1914, as Roosevelt had already begun to call for universal service, Wilson resisted his own secretary of war's request for an increase of just 25,000 additional soldiers and a modest appropriation for more munitions. The president had to heed the fierce opposition to increased military spending from the Southern wing of his own party; foremost among that group was Representative Hay, the regulars' old *bête noire*. After the sinking of the *Lusitania,* even Hay was forced to concede the need for "reasonable" military measures; but his notion of reasonable fell far short of what a group of "big army" legislators led by his counterpart on the Senate Military Affairs Committee, George Chamberlain of Oregon, considered necessary. It was not until July 1915, when he was under extreme public pressure for more robust measures, that Wilson finally asked Secretary of War Lindley M. Garrison to provide a comprehensive plan for military expansion.[69]

Several months later, Garrison responded with a proposal for a sweeping overhaul of the military establishment that was timid only in comparison to Wood's dream of universal military service. Garrison requested an increase of the regular army from approximately 90,000 to 140,000 troops and the creation of a "Continental Army" of 400,000 volunteers who would receive two months of training each year for three consecutive years. Garrison believed that state forces were irredeemably unreliable but for political reasons elected to leave the National Guard at its present strength of approximately 130,000. Though the Continental Army bore some resemblance to Wood's plan in that both centered upon short periods of intense Plattsburg-like training, Garrison pointedly retained voluntary service; he had considered requesting a draft but ultimately decided that it was not politically feasible during peacetime.[70]

For a time it appeared that Garrison had accurately gauged the political mood; most congressional leaders, including both Hay and Chamberlain, pledged their support. But over the course of the next several months, a trickle of defections turned into mass abandonment of the administration plan. Many Democrats doubted that the Continental Army could recruit 400,000 volunteers and feared that a failure would eventually lead to compulsory service. At the same time, advocates for universal military service hated the plan because it did not lead directly to a draft; Wood attacked the continued reliance upon volunteers as militarily dangerous and socially corrosive. The simultaneous opposition of the National Guard Association and "big-army" supporters underscored the degree to which Garrison's attempt to please all had pleased none.[71]

As support for the Continental Army crumbled, Chamberlain asked the recently retired William H. Carter to help craft a bill expanding the regular army and creating a substantial federal reserve. In the House, Hay, with the assistance of his friend Frederick Ainsworth, drafted a competing bill that countered Garrison's Continental Army with a plan for a larger National Guard that would be subject to greater federal control and explicitly authorized for use outside of the United States. These provisions were attempts to provide sufficient assistance so that guardsmen would not repeat past legal evasions to avoid service in a time of crisis. Though Wilson was ideologically drawn to Hay's proposal, he was uncertain whether a "federalized" National Guard was constitutional. After receiving assurances from the attorney general that it was, Wilson endorsed the Hay Bill, prompting the resignation of Garrison.[72]

Though four months of legislative negotiations followed, Hay's bill remained the basis for what became the National Defense Act (NDA) of 1916. Senator Chamberlain won Hay's agreement to increase the number of regular regiments, though the peacetime strength of just over 220,000 was less than he had hoped. The National Guard received a substantial increase to nearly 430,000 but surrendered control over the determination of standards for enlistments and commissions. The War Department also won the authority to dictate the type of units that each state would provide. Individual guardsmen would no longer be able to decline to take the federal oath; once the president called their unit into service, individuals would immediately fall under War Department judicial authority. The expansion of the army was scheduled to take five years, indicating that the 1916 NDA was meant to prepare the United States for the aftermath of the "European War."[73]

In the final stages of drafting, Hay—likely at the urging of Ainsworth—quietly introduced a measure designed to eviscerate the General Staff by reducing its presence in the War Department to just nineteen officers and eliminating its authority to engage in any business other than war planning. It was, as one officer remarked, the bureau chiefs' "Magna Carta"—the assurance of their baronial autonomy. Yet soon after, Hay accepted a position in the federal judiciary. That gave the new secretary of war, Newton D. Baker, the opportunity to ignore the restrictions on the activity of the General Staff. In a lengthy legal finding, Baker combined deft exploitation of ambiguous language in the law with a selective account of the General Staff's legislative history to come to the disingenuous conclusion that Congress had not really intended the severe restrictions that Hay had certainly meant to impose. Nevertheless, Baker shared the traditional civilian wariness of a powerful chief of staff; and so throughout much of his tenure, he granted the bureau chiefs the independence they desired.[74]

For Wood and his followers, the 1916 NDA was a great disappointment. Yet to a regular of 1896, it would have seemed a remarkable victory. In the two decades since, the 27,000-strong army had expanded fourfold and Congress had just authorized a further expansion of over 100,000 soldiers. Even the federalized National Guard and diminished General Staff would have seemed miraculous from the vantage of the late nineteenth century. Maneuvers and a system of professional education had also come to be regarded as commonplace fixtures of a modern military whose value was no longer questioned. In sum, these changes reflected the acceptance of the central idea advocated by Upton and brought to life by Root: The quality of the military resided within its institutions, not within the collective gentlemanly honor of the officer corps or the presumed martial abilities of Americans. That shift separated the old army from the recognizably modern army that came after.

• • • • •

The 1916 NDA was a reaction to the European War; but even as it was being negotiated, a quite different threat was emerging that would nearly destroy the compromise between federal and state forces at the heart of the new structure. Surprisingly, the political framework developed to meet the challenge of the Kaiser's legions was nearly undone by the coarse band of Mexican warlord Pancho Villa. In March 1916, Villistas attacked Columbus, New Mexico, killing fifteen Americans. Wilson quickly ordered a "Punitive Expedition" commanded by Brigadier General John J. Pershing into Mexico, but Villa eluded the Americans for months. Though there were no more attacks as brazen as the raid against Columbus, a few smaller incursions into Texas caused several American deaths and panic throughout the Rio Grande Valley. Guardsmen from Arizona, New Mexico, and Texas were already on the border when passage of the 1916 NDA brought Wilson greater powers over the "federalized National Guard." He used these almost immediately to issue a call to the rest of the states. By August, over 140,000 guardsmen—nearly all of the state forces—were in federal service.[75]

The National Guard soon had cause to wonder whether the defeat of the Continental Army plan had been a pyrrhic victory. Previously, militiamen with families and businesses had been able to decline service away from home. Though that freedom undermined military effectiveness, it had the political benefit of allowing the burden of military service to fall on those willing to bear it. The 1916 NDA removed these relief valves, though confusion over its implementation allowed perhaps as many as 25,000 guardsmen to avoid border duty. Those who did go soon grew angry as they endured discomfort, boredom, and, quite often, financial loss while the rest of the country went on as normal. The Guard could not even find enough recruits to fill its existing units, much less expand to the size authorized by the 1916 NDA. Moreover, fifteen years after the Dick Act, the callout demonstrated that state forces still suffered from the traditional deficiencies in equipment and training. *Schadenfreude* was rampant among regulars who felt that their warnings about the unreliability of state troops were vindicated. Some regulars hoped that the National Guard would dissolve under the strain, while some guardsmen feared that it might. Wood crowed that 90 to 95 percent of guardsmen on the border were in favor of universal military service. Though probably an exaggeration, many guardsmen had certainly come to agree with him that they bore a disproportionate burden of service. Believing that the political situation was now more favorable, Wood resumed his agitation for universal service. An exasperated Baker replaced him in New York with the reliable J. Franklin Bell and exiled the disobedient general to a new department headquartered in Charleston, South Carolina.[76]

This removed Wood from the limelight just as the diplomatic crisis with Germany was coming to its conclusion. But Wood's relentless campaigning had had an effect on the political climate around the issue of mobilization. The traditional adherence to volunteerism had meant that in previous wars conscription had been a measure of last resort. But after the Preparedness Movement, the Continental Army plan, the 1916 NDA, and the misery of the National Guard on the border, the United States entered World War I with a more mature, somewhat weary, political mood on the subject of raising armies. As conflict seemed imminent, Wood's supporters on the General Staff recommended to Baker that the country immediately adopt conscription if the country entered the war. Baker agreed and with Wilson's consent ordered the judge advocate general to prepare the necessary legislation, which was ready when Congress declared war several weeks later. After only a few days of testimony, Baker convinced Congress to reverse over a century of military policy.[77]

Before disappearing from American military policy, volunteer armies and political generals made a brief, quixotic struggle for survival. Since 1915, Theodore Roosevelt had yearned for the country to enter the war so that he could command a volunteer cavalry division in France, reprising his role with the Rough Riders on a larger scale. Not coincidentally, in the final Selective Service Act, Congress authorized the president to raise four volunteer divisions. Roosevelt had already recruited some of the army's best young officers for specific positions in his notional command. At the time it was not obvious that the practice of "political generals" and military patronage would disappear, and so most of the regulars approached by Roosevelt accepted the offer. Many others wrote hopefully to governors seeking positions in the state units that they assumed would be formed as in the past.[78]

Chief of Staff Hugh L. Scott, however, opposed allowing volunteers and insisted on full reliance on conscription in order to maintain professional military control over mobilization. Despite a long precedent of military advice being ignored in such circumstances, Baker agreed. This might have been based on political calculations, though there would have been some advantages in coopting and occupying one of the administration's fiercest critics. Yet Baker also demonstrated a consistent pattern of deference to the regulars throughout the war. He had entered politics as a municipal reformer battling corrupt party machines and so had an ingrained preference for expertise over partisanship. Wilson had much less faith in the ability of generals, but he also had little interest in military detail and so left much of that work to the secretary of war. Yet it was not simply a matter of personality, for Baker was part of a more general trend. The growth of complex urban systems made it seem prudent to leave matters like public health, transportation, and education to doctors, engineers, and academics. Warfare seemed to fit the same pattern. Unlike in the nineteenth century, when Congress had confidently dictated details like the numbers of privates in an infantry company, matters like the organization of chemical defense troops or the proper distribution of artillery among divisions, corps, and field armies seemed best left to regulars who had acquired the trappings of professional expertise in institutions like the General Staff and War College. Consequently, Baker and Congress allowed professional soldiers unprecedented control over matters of organization, personnel policy, and even strategy.[79]

Unfortunately, the War Department was also overwhelmed by modern warfare. The initial strategic advice provided by the General Staff was hopelessly unrealistic.[80] This was partly due to the restrictions imposed by the 1916 NDA and Wilson's prohibition against planning for American entry into the war, but it was also a product of the failure of the professional education system to train officers in the methods of the strategic general staff, or what the Germans referred to as the *Großer Generalstab.* Wood also bore some responsibility, for his crusade for universal military service diverted considerable institutional energy that could have been more productively applied to intellectual preparation for the war.

There were even greater difficulties in mobilizing manpower and materiel. Some of these were due to Baker's belief that the best way to use technical expertise was to allow the bureau chiefs to carry out their functions unhindered by the chief of staff. Faced with the problem of a massive expansion of the army, the bureaus had neither the time nor the inclination to coordinate their activities. In the first days of the war, the commander of one depot bought nearly all the available leather in the country; while the adjutant general secured all of the typewriters, gleefully noting that the rest of the army would have none. General Scott played only a limited role; he had only several months until mandatory retirement and spent much of that time with a diplomatic delegation to Russia. For most of 1917, Tasker H. Bliss effectively served as the chief of staff, but he was consumed with a flood of minor details and prohibited by the secretary from forcing cooperation among the bureaus. Officers visiting the War Department in that first summer were shocked by the disarray.[81]

Politicians also bore much of the blame for the problems in outfitting the army. Since 1914, reports from Europe had emphasized the massive amount of materiel consumed by modern war; but Congress had largely ignored repeated War Department appeals for money to stockpile munitions, arms, and equipment. When war came, the capacity of government arsenals fell far short of what was needed, but the administration was reluctant to manage priorities and resources within the private sector. Consequently, shortages in equipment were more severe and persistent than was necessary in a country with such rich industrial resources. There were not enough rifles until early 1918, and the production of more complex weapons lagged even further behind. These shortages hindered training. Artillerymen waited for weeks in their camps for the delivery of their guns, while mortarmen in one division left for France without ever having seen even a single example of their primary weapon. Eventually, the lack of equipment forced Baker to defer the induction of approximately 170,000 of the draftees for 1917—about a quarter of the year's class—into 1918. The cascading effects of that delay were felt late in the war when the desperate demands for fighting units meant that soldiers drafted in July were sent into battle in early October. After the draftees' induction and transport to France, so little time was left for training that some of them had to be shown how to load their rifles literally on the eve of battle.[82]

Though the nature of mobilization meant that early mistakes reverberated up to the armistice, the turning point for the War Department came on 4 March 1918. That was the day when, under pressure from Congress and the president, Baker at last brought in two forceful personalities and granted them the authority to manage the war effort. The first was Bernard Baruch, chairman of the War Industries Board. He deftly corrected the problems of priorities and bottlenecks within the private sector. The other figure was General Peyton C. March, the new chief of staff. Long known as one of the army's most capable officers, March had benefited from several instances of Root's insistence on meritocracy, having been selected for service with the volunteers of 1899, served on the inaugural General Staff which included duty as an observer in the Russo-Japanese War and several details as an umpire for maneuvers. March was also famously unsparing of others. William Lassiter described him as the "unfortunate distiller of some venom that poisoned him and all about him."[83] Yet March's ruthlessness was an asset when directed against the military bureaucracy. "He took the War Department like a dog takes a cat by the neck, and he shook it," another officer recalled.[84] Baker disliked March's adversarial approach but supported him nonetheless as the chief of staff beat the War Department into a functioning headquarters capable of sending two million men overseas.[85]

In contrast to the responsibility for mobilization, which they shared with civilian politicians and appointees, regulars had been granted virtual autonomy in the realm of employing military force. In response to the writings of Upton, Root had given regulars the apparatus for intellectually preparing for war in the form of the General Staff and military education system. Moreover, those institutions had been preparing for European conflict for years, an incidental byproduct of their reliance on German military theory. In 1909, Dan Boughton complained, "Our officers today know more about the geography of certain sections of Germany and France than they do about any equivalent area of their own or adjoining territory."[86] This seeming deficiency later proved fortuitous, for the most commonly used tactics primer featured scenarios set in what would become the American sector in France. Also meeting one of Upton's earlier demands, Baker allowed the regulars to mandate the requirements for commissioning and oversee the training for all new officers and soldiers. The regulars had been allowed the freedom to study military developments in peace and then were given the authority to imprint those lessons into the citizen-soldiers before they went into battle.[87]

Yet the regulars wasted their incidental prescience with an inexplicable failure to reassess their views in light of events in Europe. In contrast to the curiosity evidenced during the Russo-Japanese War, the prevailing mood in the U.S. Army from 1914 was smug certainty. Just months into the war, the editors of the *Infantry Journal* noted that machine guns and heavy artillery were far more effective than expected, leading them to ask hitherto unthinkable questions: "To what extent is massed attack feasible under modern fire, how such attacks should be executed, and are the results therefrom, on the whole, such as to justify their use?"[88] Those doubts, however, were soon papered over with assumptions that the European armies simply failed to apply what were still assumed to be correct tactical principles. In mid-1917, Major Harold B. Fiske, a Fort Leavenworth instructor and the future chief of training for the American Expeditionary Forces (AEF), claimed that the "principles taught in our drill regulations have been proven in the main correct."[89] The examples of the Somme and Verdun did not prompt the General Staff to revise the 1914 *Field Service Regulations* (issued before the war began), and the 1911 *Infantry Drill Regulations* underwent only slight modifications. The May 1918 update of the *IDR* came five months after the first American unit entered the trenches but provided no update to the tactical principles as they had been written by Morrison in 1911. Unlike in France, within the *IDR* machine guns were still "weapons of emergency" that merited just two pages of discussion under the heading of "Miscellaneous."[90] That was generous, however, when compared to the manual's silence regarding the new weapons of trench warfare being issued to infantry regiments, such as automatic rifles, rifle grenades, and mortars. Rather than convey any lessons of the war, the purpose of the revised *IDR* was to detail elements of ceremonial drill for units equipped with the modified Enfield rifle.[91]

When citizen-soldiers entered their training camps, they were prepared to fight the war envisioned by regulars at Fort Leavenworth in 1911 rather than the one they would encounter in France. European visitors to American training camps were dismayed to see how much time was devoted to close-order drill and stylized bayonet "fencing." That emphasis was based on the belief that such training was the best means of instilling the discipline and aggressiveness that doctrine identified as the essential elements of victory. New officers also learned that enlisted soldiers could not be trusted to move forward on their own and so took on, sometimes in an even more extreme form, the regulars' habits of strict observance of military formality and con-descension toward the enlisted ranks.[92]

The new principles-based doctrine preferred by Morrison proved to be ill-suited to the reality of a large conscripted force. Though many of the officer candidates had at least some college education, without military experience they struggled to understand the essence of the manuals. One compared studying the drill regulations to reading a dictionary, noting that it and the *FSR* were "mighty hard stuff" that the candidates had little time to digest. "I can just about read it through carefully once and it's so boiled down that's not enough. But we do the best we can."[93] The tragic irony was that with little useful guidance from manuals, many junior officers in France relied upon semiofficial versions of the schematic "normal attack" that Morrison had wished to replace. The result was that Americans often conducted assaults in rigid formations with ruler-straight lines that were as disastrous as he had feared. Yet Morrison's willful inattention to the needs of citizen-soldiers meant that there was no useful alternative. After the war, one of Morrison's former pupils admitted that the war demonstrated the entire premise of the 1911 *IDR* to be "defective."[94]

In France, Baker's deference to military expertise also had perverse effects. The secretary of war granted the commander of the AEF, John J. Pershing, virtually complete control over personnel appointments in France. The gen-eral zealously wielded his power both to promote and to relieve, but the emphasis was often on punishment. Senior officers were particularly vulner-able, for Pershing equated success with vigorous, confident action and sus-pected that most of his contemporaries were lacking in those qualities. In early 1918, he requested that the War Department make it official policy to not assign any division commander older than fifty years of age. Though exceptions to the rule were granted, it was Pershing's wish that all tactical commands go to those commissioned in 1890 or later—the progressive gen-eration. Among the leading figures of the composite generation who Pershing

Prewar doctrine reflected in World War I training: Soldiers of the 28th Division learn to leap over trenches before striking home with flashing bayonets. (World War I Signal Corps Photograph Collection, AHEC)

refused to even take command in France were Leonard Wood, J. Franklin Bell, Eben Swift, and John Morrison. In France, he relieved dozens more over the course of the war.[95]

With senior subordinates in constant fear of "the chief's" wrath, the AEF was—even more than most military organizations—extremely sensitive to the views of the commander, and Pershing firmly believed that battle was principally a test of wills. Before the war, he had followed Morrison's work through a subscription to the Staff College mailing list. The early course of the war had not caused Pershing to revise those opinions. Instead, he attributed the stalemate on the Western Front to a lack of spirit within the Allied armies caused by the infantry's reliance on artillery. That dependence, Pershing believed, had sapped the spirit of the infantry. In opposition to this artillery-centric "trench warfare," Pershing decreed that the AEF would practice "open warfare" with "self-reliant infantry" who did not wait for artillery support to attack. Though open warfare was never precisely codified, it was little more than a reiteration of prewar doctrine, particularly the 1911 *IDR*.[96]

Former students of Morrison were thus already well-versed in the way that Pershing wanted the army to fight. But this conceptual affinity only partly explains the rise of what came to be known as the "Leavenworth clique" within the AEF. Many of Pershing's composite generation peers still held the traditional notion of individual military "genius" rooted in the commander. A corollary of that view was that reliance upon junior staff officers was an indication of weakness if not incompetence. In 1902, Nelson A. Miles scoffed that generals like Grant and Sherman "did not require a corps of subordinates to dictate to them how campaigns should be conducted and victories won."[97] Pershing was far more self-confident, and so he was willing to make use of the full talents of his subordinates. As an attaché with the Japanese Army during the latter stages of the Russo-Japanese War, he had witnessed what the Germans called the *Truppengeneralstab* (general staff in field headquarters). In comparison to traditional American practices, the *Truppengeneralstab* was larger and had a more intricate organization. But what really set it apart was an ethos that in the absence of the commander the staff could independently alter the plan in light of a changing battlefield situation. Such a system relied upon a corps of highly proficient staff officers produced by a robust system of education and training. Even while most American senior officers continued to think of command in the traditional way, the Army Service Schools had been training just such a group in *Truppengeneralstab* methods. This provided Pershing with a ready pool of officers perfectly suited to his style of command. His headquarters quickly filled with Fort Leavenworth graduates working under the guidance of his trusted chief of staff, Brigadier General John G. Harbord.[98]

In contrast to the faith that Pershing placed in his youthful staff, he was inclined to believe that subordinate commanders were failing to live up to his expectations. In a revealing telegram, Pershing warned March that subordinates—even those of high rank—invariably ignored directives unless they were watched closely. He counseled March to dispatch General Staff officers to conduct probing inspections of subordinates to identify deviations from policy. In France, Pershing followed his own advice by directing that each active division have a General Headquarters (GHQ) representative to ensure compliance and report any transgressions; these liaisons were effectively doctrinal commissars sent to monitor subordinates.[99]

The manner in which Pershing used his staff naturally caused resentment among senior commanders, who were envious of the relatively junior officers who had Pershing's ear while they labored under the threat of sudden humiliating dismissal. One major general relieved by Pershing lamented, "The hard and conscientious labor of a lifetime spent by an honest solider in building for himself a clean and good record, could be smirched and ruined in an hour by a hasty or mistaken judgment of the Commander-in-Chief, or even by one of his confidential staff officers." He went on to complain that these younger staff officers expected "a certain deference."[100] For composite generation officers raised in the old, commander-centric mode of command, the younger officers' arrogance was particularly galling. Yet the Fort Leavenworth graduates whom the Root system of professional education had deliberately cultivated as elite found it natural that their power exceeded their rank. Some might have felt it just recompense for decades of frustrating subservience to an older generation lacking their hard-won professional credentials. In the midst of war, few felt the need to soothe the indignation of older officers. Hugh Drum, who as the chief of staff of U.S. First Army might have been the most influential of all Fort Leavenworth graduates, confessed after the war, "I guess all of us were too impressed with our own importance."[101]

Probably none were as guilty of this fault as Brigadier General Alfred W. Bjornstad, widely regarded as one of the brightest, if also the most abrasive, of Morrison's former pupils. By late 1918, he had risen to become chief of staff of III Corps, then under the command of Major General Robert L. Bullard. The two got along poorly, largely due to Bjornstad's insistence that the German *Truppengeneralstab* tradition justified his right to act independently of the commander. Bjornstad seems to have even pointedly withheld important information from the commander to demonstrate his own authority. Bullard meekly tolerated this insubordination, likely out of fear of the "Leavenworth clique." He had reason to be cautious. Bjornstad had once asked friends in GHQ to convince Pershing to relieve a division commander with whom he had feuded and would surely have tried to retaliate against Bullard in a similar manner. It had been just over a decade since the maneuver camp in which Bullard had been the frustrated junior laboring underneath a senior officer whom he regarded as a relic of the past. The war and Pershing had accelerated the demise of the composite generation and the rise of the progressive generation. Though Bjornstad was eventually fired, the idea that he championed prevailed. In November 1918, an AEF general order enshrined *Truppengeneralstab* practices by giving all chiefs of staff the power to approve "field orders, letters of instructions, and other orders, affecting a larger portion of the command or embodying important decisions, which modify the general plan" in the name of the commander.[102]

Noting such conflicts, historian Edward Coffman posits that there was a "generation gap" within the AEF. That would have been the case if Fort Leavenworth graduates had been representative of the progressive generation. But the resistance to merit promotion and presumably widespread resentment of elites underlying the Manchu Law indicated a divide between the elite and mass within the generation. That was hardly surprising, for creating such a division had been one of the explicit goals of professional education since Carter's plan in 1901. Bell had infused some egalitarianism into the Army Service Schools, but his cultivation of the "Fort Leavenworth" spirit had at the same time reinforced the sense of graduates being a group apart. This informal divide became an organizational reality due to the common practice of reassigning upon arrival in France graduates in troop assignments to one of the higher headquarters. Though there were only several hundred Army Service School graduates at the time, that small cadre quickly became concentrated in GHQ, field army, and corps headquarters.[103]

In many respects, the Leavenworth clique was a great asset for the AEF. The tactical focus and emphasis on esprit encouraged by Bell had created a cohesive group bound by a common lexicon and methodology remarkably appropriate for a war that was far different than anything within experience of any active member of the U.S. Army. Recalling a conference among the chiefs of staff of the U.S. First Army in October 1918, one graduate remarked that "except for an ominous rumble to the north of us, I might have thought that we were back at Leavenworth . . . . The technique and the talk were just the same."[104] This set them apart from earlier generations of officers, whose competence had been rooted in experience that was sometimes only partly applicable to new situations. In Cuba just two decades before, regulars had struggled to coordinate three dismounted divisions and a handful of guns. In September 1918, the newly created First Army headquarters conducted two offensives on separate fronts, each involving three corps, thousands of guns, and hundreds of airplanes. The second of these, the Meuse-Argonne campaign, required the relief of 200,000 French troops with more than 600,000 Americans. The intricate planning for that largely successful movement was done in less than three weeks. The consensus within the AEF—among graduates and nongraduates alike—was that this vast improvement in performance over the Spanish-American War was principally due to the professional education system.[105]

Yet along with this excellence in the process of directing armies, Fort Leavenworth graduates brought fatally erroneous ideas about the primacy of the rifleman and the ability of willpower to overcome firepower. Before the war, Bullard had complained that the pedantic methods of tactical instruction used at Fort Leavenworth and the Army War College destroyed imagination. In France, he duly found most regular officers to be intellectually "unadaptable and immovable."[106] Within Pershing's headquarters the embodiment of that trait was the Chief of Training, Harold B. Fiske, a graduate and former tactics instructor at Fort Leavenworth, whose confidence in the infantry-centric tactics taught at the school never wavered. Because the General Staff liaison officers within subordinate headquarters reported to Fiske, all lessons from operations were filtered through his doctrinaire views that had hardened long before the war. One might suppose that such rigidity can only be maintained in schools or headquarters far from the frontlines; but that was not the case with Robert Alexander, one of the few Staff College graduates to command a division. Alexander's indifference to supporting weapons was a chief cause of the mediocre performance of his 77th Division. Yet even the loss of thousands of soldiers under his command in a span of little more than ten weeks did nothing to change Alexander's opinion that machine guns, grenades, and mortars were "merely adjuncts" to the rifle.[107] It is possible that Alexander would have held such views even without having attended Fort Leavenworth. But it is likely that the affirmation of such beliefs by instructors, texts, doctrine, and like-minded peers over a period of years reinforced such views to the extent that they could not be displaced even when battlefield experience suggested otherwise.

Alexander was unusually inflexible, as most officers seem to have been more torn between prewar paradigms and present experience. This was true even for Pershing. Not long after arriving in France in 1917, he witnessed an attack by a single British army that was supported by over two thousand guns. Upon returning to his headquarters, he urged Washington to push

In May 1918, First Division soldiers go "over the top" at Cantigny. The regulars' preference for rifle and bayonet made them indifferent to "auxiliary" weapons like the rifle grenade (carried by the soldier in the center foreground), which was not even mentioned in the revised IDR issued just weeks before this attack. (World War I Signal Corps Photograph Collection, AHEC)

"our own gun construction to extreme limit without delay."[108] But his appreciation for artillery, as well as of machine guns and tanks, never quite overcame the belief that the individual rifleman was the central figure in battle. Throughout the war, Pershing and his headquarters consistently denigrated Allied habits of trench warfare, even while distributing French and British pamphlets that described it in detail. GHQ continued to insist on the correctness of prewar doctrine and the superiority of open warfare. Two directives issued in reaction to the fierce fighting in the summer of 1918, the first use of large American formations, exemplify this inconsistency. The first directive reminded commanders of the importance of maintaining tight "liaison" with the artillery. Just two weeks later, the second order instructed them to keep their command posts so far forward that they could see the fighting and restore "resolution to again advance" when the attack stalled. Pershing and his staff still believed that failure was due more to a lack of willpower than to fire support, when the case was actually the opposite. The Germans (as well as the Allies) noted that the American attacks were resolute but poorly coordinated. Yet by directing commanders so far forward, Pershing took them away from the buried communications lines that were necessary for reliable contact with headquarters and the artillery. Yet whatever problems resulted were more likely to be interpreted as more evidence of incompetent subordinates lacking in drive, rather than proof of a fundamentally flawed conception of warfare within GHQ. This dynamic was evident in the assessments conducted immediately after the war, which found that junior officers and noncommissioned officers in the AEF had performed poorly. There was considerable truth in that assertion. Division and brigade headquarters with only partially trained staff officers had also been a consistent weakness. But there was no such searching appraisal of the regulars' beliefs. A panel of senior officers convened by Pershing only went so far as to acknowledge an increased importance of machine guns, artillery, tanks, and other "auxiliary" arms, while maintaining that self-reliant infantry remained paramount. Even that was too much for Pershing, who dismissed the report as "unduly influenced" by the conditions of the Western Front. He recommended that in order for the army to be mobile enough for operations in North America it adopt an infantry-based division with fewer machine guns, tanks, and other impedimenta.[109]

Despite the role of the education system and General Staff in perpetuating such ideas and attitudes, there was nothing inherent within the Root reforms that caused these faults. Pershing, it should be noted, had had no army schooling since graduating from West Point in 1886. Just as some of his similarly untutored contemporaries held quite different opinions, so, too, there was some disagreement among the educated class of the younger generation. But although not everyone agreed with doctrine, the institutional apparatus established in the early twentieth century likely made it more difficult to dislodge the opinions of those who did. Schools, manuals, and training all pushed the official understanding of war with a persistence that had not been present in the nineteenth-century army with its more restrained drill regulations, little professional education, and limited training. The pervasiveness of doctrine made it more likely that similarly indoctrinated peers would reinforce the official view. The strong group identity of Fort Leavenworth graduates, a group deliberately chosen from among the army's best officers, was thus at once a boon and a curse. Their individual talents and common education were essential components of the ability of the AEF to function as effectively as it did. Yet that same sense of exclusivity caused them to dismiss tactical failings as the fault of the regimental officers or the citizen-soldiers that they had come to regard as inferior. This ambiguous result would likely have dismayed Upton, Root, and the other reformers who labored to create a smarter, more capable army. Their efforts had simultaneously sown the seeds of success and disaster. That outcome is a caution against hubris for any who seek to change an institution.

Epilogue

TWO LECTURES DELIVERED to the Army War College in the fall of 1922 exemplified the radical new way that the elites of the progressive generation viewed the relationship between individual officers and the army. In the first lecture, Lieutenant Colonel George C. Marshall contrasted the prewar notions of higher staff duties with what he and his contemporaries had learned in France. Marshall attributed the problems of the early General Staff to the failings of the Civil War and composite generations. "Old men . . . cannot successfully take up new activities," the forty-one-year-old Marshall judged, but can only "continue to perform functions that they have become intimately familiar with in younger days." Though hardly charitable, the diagnosis was largely correct. The "old men" that he disparaged were accustomed to a guild-like autonomy that prevented them from embracing the idea, emphatically urged on the audience by Marshall, that the General Staff had the "power and the duty . . . to indoctrinate the army" through maneuvers, army schools, and doctrine.[1] A few weeks later, Brigadier General William Lassiter—the head of the Operations and Training Division in the General Staff—described the duties of the high staff in much the same way. Lassiter even added probing inspections of field units by Washington-based General Staff officers as a fourth tool in addition to Marshall's trinity of maneuver, schools, and doctrine.[2] Both Marshall and

Lassiter saw the army as a finely crafted machine with equipment, tactics, and organization all calculated to work in harmony. Though they urged general staff officers to be sympathetic to the needs of regimental officers, ultimately it was the central staff's duty to determine how the army should work, indoctrinate the rest of the army in those methods, and enforce adherence. In this conception of professionalism were echoes of Frederick Taylor: "In the past the man has been first; in the future the system must be first."[3]

There had been no similar desire from nineteenth-century elites to impose cognitive standardization. Winfield Scott delighted in dictating small details for all aspects of army activity but made no attempt to command his subordinates' patterns of thought. Tasker H. Bliss and William H. Carter, though dismissive of regimental officers, had been content to create a protected sphere for the elite, leaving the line largely alone. Even believers in the notion that war was governed by absolute laws, such as Dennis Hart Mahan and John M. Schofield, gave little thought to methods of indoctrination; they seemed to assume that all officers would naturally follow the laws of military science once these were revealed. And for the majority of officers who believed that war was an art rather than a science, the proposition that the army could or should manufacture generals was absurd; military "genius" was understood to be an inherent quality that at best might be refined through experience and study. Marshall and Lassiter departed from these earlier views by regarding professionalism as a body of knowledge and practices that could be imparted to any suitable individual. Natural ability still differentiated the great from the merely competent, but the locus of professionalism had shifted from the character of the individual to the expertise maintained by the institution.

That shift was the culmination of a long trend toward standardization of military activity that had begun with the rise of standing armies several centuries before. Early nation-states learned that armies with units similarly organized, equipped, and trained tended to be more efficient and effective. Naturally, that insight was first applied to those areas that were most susceptible to standardization, such as administration, equipment, and small-unit drill. Early American military reforms were also of this type: John C. Calhoun's reorganization of the War Department, Scott's codification of drill and unit administration, and Sylvanus Thayer's systematization of cadet instruction. Those efforts brought the U.S. Army to a reasonable state of efficiency and effectiveness in peacetime administration and small-unit operations by the 1830s but still left a great deal to professional discretion. There were only limited attempts to codify and impart the practice of command through schools, training, or regulations.

The example of Prussia demonstrates that this did not necessarily need to be the case. Stung by defeat at the hands of Napoleon, Prussian contemporaries of Scott and Thayer established a general staff and professional education system many decades in advance of those developments in the United States, proving that there was no absolute barrier to a more standardized military professionalism in the early nineteenth century. To be sure, American political culture effectively closed the possibility of creating elaborate military institutions, but this still left the officer corps considerable latitude for professional innovation. Even at the height of Jacksonian antielitism, Congress would likely have had no objection if Scott had desired to include an extended discussion of tactical principles in a drill manual. In the 1870s, when civil-military relations were even worse, Emory Upton was still free to contemplate a doctrine-like chapter on "applied tactics" in his drill regulations. Not long thereafter, he implemented a war college-like curriculum at the Artillery School. The end of that innovation was not due to civilian ideology but to military indifference; most artillerymen preferred a narrower technical focus, and generals like William T. Sherman thought it simply unnecessary. The principal brake on further military standardization was not political opposition nor civilian neglect but the preferences of the first three generations of officers.

This reluctance was natural, for *regimentation* had a deservedly negative connotation. Acts of submission to organizational regularity, such as a staff officer compiling reports or a soldier enduring monotonous drill, were often stifling and unpleasant. The collective unwillingness of the officer corps to impose additional burdens of this sort upon itself can be easily understood, even if it sometimes led to an inconsistency between belief and policy. Schofield lectured that it was every officer's duty to "eliminate as much as possible" the " 'hazards' or 'chances' of war" through careful application of military science, but he declined to compel his subordinates to study that science.[4] Arthur L. Wagner did more than any other officer to develop the tools of indoctrination but resisted suggestions that he thought might infringe on individual autonomy.

It is therefore remarkable that attitudes toward standardization changed so rapidly in the early twentieth century. Whereas in 1903 Bliss decreed that it was impossible to teach higher-level staff skills, just seven years later one of his successors at the Army War College told the students that the structured curriculum would instill in them "uniformity of thought[,] uniformity of procedure in solving problems of war." Through such standardization, he promised, the army would gain a cadre of "safe leaders." Repudiating the earlier view that command was an innate quality, he boasted that the army was no longer dependent on the whims of fate to produce military "genius."[5] Individual talent, discretion, and autonomy had been supplanted by formal education, procedure, and centralization.

To explain such transformations, the scholarship of military adaptation offers three broad theories of change: some external impetus overcomes military conservatism; internal forces, such as competition for resources or prestige, cause change from within; or external shocks, such as defeat or a new technology, compel adaptation. Or, to reduce it to a handy if somewhat simplified shorthand, military change is caused either by politicians, generals, or events.[6]

Though elements of all are present in the case of the U.S. Army in the early twentieth century, none of the three is sufficient to explain the emergence of the new professional paradigm. Superficially, the case seems to be one of external change. A civilian (Elihu Root) took the ideas of an unconventional military thinker (Upton) and imposed them on a resistant military (embodied by Commanding General Nelson A. Miles.) But although some of Upton's ideas on how to prepare for war were idiosyncratic within his own generation, they were commonplace among the composite and progressive generations who constituted the bulk of the officer corps by Root's time. Consequently, Root was not widely considered a villain within the army and was only resisted when a specific action threatened the parochial interests of some limited portion of the army. His status as an outsider was more critical in winning public support than it was in overcoming internal inertia. Though Root left the War Department shortly after the General Staff was formed and before the War College was operational, those and other reforms were continued even though it was several years before there was another activist secretary of war, Henry L. Stimson. If the Root reforms had been a civilian imposition on a resistant military, the changes could have been easily undermined in that interim. So although the agent of change happened to be a civilian, that status was incidental rather than necessary.

But the enthusiasm for Root's specific initiatives did not mean that military reformers foresaw or welcomed the fundamental transformation of professional views that eventually occurred. Wagner, Carter, Bliss, Bell, and others thought they were making improvements to the professional identity that they knew, not accelerating the arrival of some alien understanding of the individual officer's role. Indeed, Wagner explicitly rejected the proposition that tactical views be standardized through official doctrine. So although the transformation was partly the work of internal forces, the full extent of the change was inadvertent rather than deliberate.

Finally, events in the form of the Spanish-American War certainly served as a catalyst for change. Public outrage after the Dodge Commission report brought Root to office, and he skillfully translated that unrest to public acceptance of his agenda. The country's new status as a colonial power also created more favorable political conditions for military reorganization. Yet, the trials that the secretary of war faced in Congress proved that public indignation was not so great as to compel reform.

So the profound change seen within the officer corps was to an extent the work of politicians, generals, and events; but even in conjunction they were not sufficient. It was also driven by deeper forces that lay outside of the realm of what human agency could direct. New ideas infiltrated the institution from civilian society, either wholesale in the form of younger officers just commissioned into the service or as individual concepts that modified the views of more senior officers on an issue-by-issue basis. Fundamental change in any large organization will always likely be the product of multiple intellectual strands and individual efforts coming from both within and without. One consequence of this complexity is to minimize the effect of idiosyncratic thinkers, even those Cassandras whose views are later vindicated. That is because when there are so many influences upon an organization, the efforts of those who, whether from exceptional talent or simple good fortune, perceive the future accurately are overwhelmed by the mass who are responding to what is known to all—the present and the recent past.

Armies might be too complex and subject to too many diverse forces to allow for a definitive model for change, but we can create conceptual order by grouping those influences into three broad categories: institutional mechanisms (e.g., policies governing the selection of new officers, school curricula, and doctrine); the conditions and experiences of military service that are outside of formal control (unwritten standards and norms, regimental subcultures, attitudes bred by peacetime routine); and the values, concepts, and outlooks inherited from civilian society.

These categories—summarized as institutions, experience, and culture—allow us to differentiate between deliberate efforts to shape the military profession (institutions) and the many factors that do so only incidentally (experience and culture). We can also distinguish distinctly military influences (institutions and experience) from those that emanate from the parent society (culture). This analytical trinity sheds light on why the effects of reforms fail to match the initial intentions. Institutions are the tool for reform and they provide the initial push, but experience and culture exert their own gravitational pulls that alter the intended course. The corollary of this is that even if an army were to attempt to preserve the status quo by maintaining its institutions without change, the organization would still be pulled along into new forms by experience and culture.

Indeed, this was largely the case in the nineteenth-century; as once the foundational generation established the basic professional systems of West Point, schools of application, drill-based training and regulations, that general framework persisted for the rest of the century. Yet though the institutions varied little, dramatic changes in experiences and culture produced three distinct generations. The core of the foundational generation, veterans of the War of 1812 like Winfield Scott, Zachary Taylor, and Edmund Gaines, were almost entirely a product of experience and culture, for they came into an army with few institutions. Younger members of the foundational generation were raised in an army with standardized regulations and were most often the product of West Point, but there was little further in the way of deliberate professional socialization. Experience did not suggest there was need for any more than this. Seniority promotion meant that advancing in the ranks required no skill at all and satisfactory performance of garrison duties required only an easily mastered body of knowledge. Successful field command, whether in armed diplomacy with Native American tribes, active frontier warfare, or in the Mexican-American War, did require more competence than garrison routine; but the relatively small scale of operations meant that there was no need for the expertise in the coordination of complex military operations that one would learn at a staff college. Instead, the qualities of successful commanders were for the most part those that were largely inherent to the individual, such as charisma, determination, imagination, experience, and the ability to cooperate with others. In terms of culture, just as civilian society struggled to reconcile the competing desires to emulate European norms and assert distinctive American traits, so too did the army. These tensions were manifested in a number of arenas: tactics, dress, deportment, and relations with the enlisted ranks. In short, the foundational generation was attuned to the strategic and cultural context of antebellum America.

The Civil War generation thought of war in an entirely different manner. This was not due to any change in institutions; West Point had changed little. But the experience of the war had expanded the mental horizons of the officer corps from regiments and batteries to corps and divisions. The Civil War generation also had a completely different conception of their role vis-à-vis citizen-soldiers; rather than expecting to fight alongside citizen-soldiers, regulars expected to command volunteers and to receive much higher rank in the process. Due to his own anomalous experience with a volunteer regiment in the Mexican-American War, Jefferson Davis had been one of the few to anticipate this change. Yet when as the secretary of war he had tried to alter the West Point curriculum to better prepare cadets for such duties, he had met resistance from the faculty. Lacking his point of reference, they saw no need to change proven and cherished methods. Acceptance came only when a majority of the officer corps had acquired similar experiences. But although the Civil War generation had a quite different set of experiences, they were shaped by much the same cultural influences as their predecessors. The most important manifestation of this was that they had the same indifferent attitude toward professional expertise. Thus, even though they imagined a quite different kind of future war, they were content to prepare for it in the same old fashion. The great exception to this was Upton. His low opinion of the regulars' professional competence during the war and his early acceptance of new civilian notions of professionalism caused him to place far greater emphasis on expertise conveyed through formal institutions. The commanding generals for most of the late nineteenth century—Sherman, Sheridan, and Schofield—did not share his views and so were largely content with only minor modifications to professional institutions.

This meant that the composite generation was trained in essentially the same manner as the two previous generations. But they were subject to quite different influences from experience and culture. Daily life in the army was not much different than that during the antebellum era, yet the army could not simply resume its earlier state; the expanded professional ambitions caused by the Civil War could not be set aside. This left the composite generation torn between the demands of frontier constabulary and national war. Neither was entirely satisfactory as a purpose, for the area of unsettled territory was rapidly diminishing and there was no obvious Great Power foe. All the while, Gilded Age society continued to venerate the individual, even while the pattern of life was toward ever more complex forms of political, economic, and social organization. These tensions led to a diversity of views within the composite generation, with the consequence that even those who agreed on the desirability of more robust professional institutions disagreed on what changes should be made. This was evident in the divergent opinions about military education among Wagner, Swift, Carter, Bliss, and Bell. While the complacent Civil War generation sat atop the army hierarchy, these differences remained largely hidden, but they became manifest once the Spanish-American War brought the composite generation to prominence and Root granted them the opportunity to realize their ambitions.

The progressive generation came to professional maturity in a far different army than that of the previous three cohorts. The Root reforms meant that they were subject to far more intensive efforts to shape them professionally. The education system divided officers by merit while indoctrinating the best in a standard way of fighting and conducting operations, producing the Leavenworth clique of the AEF. Yet even though institutions were far more important in shaping the generation, they were still not sufficient to create the new professional views expressed by Marshall and Lassiter. That was also the product of experiences in the more concentrated post-frontier army with its slightly reduced regimental and branch tribalism. The end of the frontier also prompted a renewed focus on conventional warfare, which naturally led to more corporatist thinking. Both these trends were then powerfully reaffirmed by the experience of World War I. Most importantly, the *zeitgeist* of the Progressive Era impressed itself on the new generation. Marshall and Lassiter expressed ideas that were entirely commonplace within their time yet would have seemed foreign a century before.

In reviewing the full sweep of the period from the War of 1812 to the American entry into World War I, it is evident that the army changed less by design and more because it was pulled along by larger forces. Samuel Huntington argues that military professionalism flourished in the late nineteenth century due to its isolation from society, but the case was nearly the opposite.[7] Professionalism in the sense meant by Huntington—doctrine,

The West Point class of 1875, including Arthur Wagner (partially lying in second row, fifth from left) and Tasker Bliss (taller figure on far right of second row.) Though all members of the class underwent the same training overseen by Commandant Emory Upton, their different personalities and experiences in a dispersed and diverse army led them to widely varying ideas about how best to prepare for war. (Tasker H. Bliss Papers, USMA)

schools, organization—was more than any other factor a product of the civilian influences that were stirring as early as the 1870s but that only fully flowered in the Progressive Era. Just as that period marked the birth of the modern United States—characterized by complex economic, social, and governmental organization—so too it was the birth of the modern U.S. Army in which the preparation for war was based more upon institutions than individuals, procedures more than personalities. That the two occurred simultaneously was not a coincidence.

Abbreviations

ACP	Appointment, Commission, and Personal Branch Files, entry 297, RG 94, NARA I
AEF	American Expeditionary Forces
AGO	Adjutant General's Office
AHEC	U.S. Army Heritage and Education Center, Carlisle, Pennsylvania
ALW	Arthur L. Wagner
CMH	United States Army Center of Military History
CMHC	Harold D. Cater interviews and correspondence, Office of the Chief of Military History Collection, AHEC
ER/ERP	Elihu Root/Papers, LC
ES/ESP	Eben Swift/Papers, Special Collections, USMA
EU	Emory Upton
FLC	Fort Leavenworth Correspondence, entry 101, RG 393, NARA I
FSR	*Field Service Regulations*
GCM	George C. Marshall Library and Archives, Lexington, Virginia
GPO	Government Printing Office
IDR	*Infantry Drill Regulations*
JFB	James Franklin Bell
JGH/JGHP	James G. Harbord/Papers, LC
JHW/JHWP	James H. Wilson/Papers, LC
JMH	*Journal of Military History*
JMS/JMSLC/ JMSWP	John M. Schofield/Papers, LC/Papers, USMA

JMSI	*Journal of the Military Service Institution*
JUSIA	*Journal of the United States Infantry Association*
LC	Manuscript Division, Library of Congress, Washington DC
LW/LWP	Leonard Wood/Papers, LC
NARA I/II	National Archives and Records Administration, Washington DC/ College Park, Maryland
OR	U.S. War Department, *The War of the Rebellion: A Compilation the Official Records of the Union and Confederate Armies,* serial I, Washington DC: GPO, 1880–1901
PHS	Philip H. Sheridan
RG	Record Group
UNC	Southern Historical Collection, Wilson Library, University of North Carolina-Chapel Hill
USMA	Special Collections, United States Military Academy Library, West Point, New York
WDAR	U.S. War Department, *Annual Reports*
WD GO	War Department General Orders
WHC/WHCP	William H. Carter/Papers, AHEC
WTS/WTSP	William T. Sherman/Papers, LC

Notes

PROLOGUE

1. Thomas J. Goss, *The War Within the Union High Command: Politics and Generalship During the Civil War* (Lawrence: University Press of Kansas, 2003); Carol Reardon, *With a Sword in One Hand and Jomini in the Other: The Problem of Military Thought in the Civil War North* (Chapel Hill: University of North Carolina Press, 2012).

2. Michael E. Howard, *War in European History* (New York: Oxford University Press, 1976); Geoffrey Parker, *The Military Revolution: Military Innovation and the Rise of the West, 1500–1800* (New York: Cambridge University Press, 1988); John A. Lynn, *Battle: A History of Combat and Culture,* rev. ed. (Boulder, CO: Westview Press, 2003); Walter Millis, *Arms and Men: A Study in American Military History* (New York: Putnam, 1956).

3. Barry Posen, *The Sources of Military Doctrine: France, Britain, and Germany Between the World Wars* (Ithaca, NY: Cornell University Press, 1984); Stephen P. Rosen, *Winning the Next War: Innovation and the Modern Military* (Ithaca, NY: Cornell University Press, 1991); MacGregor Knox and Williamson Murray, *The Dynamics of Military Revolution, 1300–2050* (New York: Cambridge University Press, 2001); David E. Johnson, *Fast Tanks and Heavy Bombers: Innovation in the U.S. Army, 1917–1945* (Ithaca, NY: Cornell University Press, 1998).

4. Samuel P. Huntington, *The Soldier and the State: The Theory and Politics of Civil-Military Relations* (Cambridge, MA: Belknap Press of Harvard University Press, 1957); Morris Janowitz, *The Professional Soldier: A Social and Political Portrait*

(Glencoe, IL: Free Press, 1960); Allan R. Millett, *Military Professionalism and Officership in America* (Columbus: Mershon Center of the Ohio State University, 1977).

5. For instance, see William B. Skelton, *An American Profession of Arms: The Army Officer Corps, 1784–1861* (Lawrence: University Press of Kansas, 1992); Mark R. Grandstaff, "Preserving the 'Habits and Usages of War': William Tecumseh Sherman, Professional Reform, and the U.S. Army Officer Corps, 1865–1881, Revisited," *JMH* 62 (July 1998): 521–545.

6. Daniel T. Rodgers, "In Search of Progressivism," *Reviews in American History* 10 (December 1982): 127.

CHAPTER 1: A PROFESSION BORN IN WAR

1. Richard H. Kohn, *Eagle and Sword: The Federalists and the Creation of the Military Establishment in America, 1783–1802* (New York: Free Press, 1975), 2–88; William B. Skelton, *An American Profession of Arms: The Army Officer Corps, 1784–1861* (Lawrence: University Press of Kansas, 1992), 3–13; Marcus Cunliffe, *Soldiers & Civilians: The Martial Spirit in America, 1775–1865* (Boston: Little Brown, 1968), 31–52.

2. Kohn, *Eagle and Sword,* 91–138.

3. George Washington, "Sentiments on a Peace Establishment," 2 May 1783, in *Soldier-Statesmen of the Constitution,* ed. Robin K. Wright, Jr., and Morris J. MacGregor, Jr. (Washington, DC: CMH, 1987), 192–199.

4. Robert Wooster, *The American Military Frontiers: The United States Army in the West, 1783–1900,* pap. ed. (Albuquerque: University of New Mexico Press, 2012), 7–24; Edward M. Coffman, *The Old Army: A Portrait of the American Army in Peacetime, 1784–1898* (New York: Oxford University Press, 1986), 4–31.

5. Skelton, *Profession,* 92; Coffman, *Old Army,* 28–31.

6. Skelton, *Profession,* 95–98; Kohn, *Eagle and Sword,* 239–249.

7. Samuel J. Watson, "Trusting to 'The Chapters of Accidents': Contingency, Necessity, and Self-Constraint in Jeffersonian National Security Policy," *JMH* 76 (October 2012): 978–983; Skelton, *Profession,* 94–95; Coffman, *Old Army,* 8.

8. Watson, "Trusting," 983–987; Wooster, *American Military Frontiers,* 35–37.

9. Quoted in Skelton, *Profession,* 51.

10. Ibid., 9, 80–82; Kohn, *Eagle and Sword,* 178–182; William G. Bell, *Commanding Generals and Chiefs of Staff, 1775–1991: Portraits and Biographical Sketches of the United States Army's Senior Officer* (Washington, DC: CMH, 1992), 64, 70.

11. Skelton, *Profession,* 23–33, 48; Coffman, *Old Army,* 8–34; Kohn, *Eagle and Sword,* 240–244; Wooster, *American Military Frontiers,* 25–28, 34–35.

12. Winfield Scott, *Memoirs of Lieut.-General Scott* (New York: Sheldon & Co., 1864), 1:31, 34–35.

13. Timothy D. Johnson, *Winfield Scott: The Quest for Military Glory* (Lawrence:

University Press of Kansas, 1998), 10–12; *Register of Graduates and Former Cadets of the United States Military Academy West Point, New York* (West Point: Association of Graduates, 2005), 4:2–3.

14. John R. Maass, "'Humanity Mourns over Such a Site': The Army's Disaster at Terre Aux Boeufs, 1809," *Army History*, no. 85 (Fall 2012): 6–23; Johnson, *Scott*, 13–15.

15. Johnson, *Scott*, 15–20.

16. Donald R. Hickey, *War of 1812: A Forgotten Conflict* (Urbana: University of Illinois, 1989), 29–48; Skelton, *Profession*, 9, 25–29, 75–80; Theodore J. Crackel, "The Battle of Queenston Heights, 13 October 1812," in *America's First Battles, 1776– 1965*, ed. Charles E. Heller and William A. Stofft (Lawrence: University Press of Kansas, 1986), 33–35.

17. Hickey, *War of 1812*, 80; Crackel, "Queenston," 42–43.

18. Hickey, *War of 1812*, 80–85; Francis B. Heitman, *Historical Register and Dictionary of the United States Army*, vol. 1 (Washington, DC: GPO, 1903), 553–554.

19. Hickey, *War of 1812*, 88–90; Heitman, *Register*, 363.

20. Account of the Battle of Queenston is taken from Crackel, "Queenston," 43–48; Johnson, *Scott*, 22–27; Scott, *Memoirs*, 1:56–64.

21. Scott, *Memoirs*, 1:60.

22. Quotation from ibid., 1:63; Crackel, "Queenston," 48; "Alexander Smyth," *Biographical Directory of the United States Congress*, http://bioguide.congress.gov.

23. Hickey, *War of 1812*, 110–112.

24. Johnson, *Scott*, 28–33.

25. Ibid., 33–40.

26. Scott, *Memoirs*, 1:94, 109–111.

27. Hickey, *War of 1812*, 139–146; Scott, *Memoirs*, 1:86–114.

28. Hickey, *War of 1812*, 126–139.

29. Ibid., 183–188; Johnson, *Scott*, 41–64; Skelton, *Profession*, 114.

30. Crackel, "Queenston," 36–40, 50–56; Johnson, *Scott*, 67–69.

31. Skelton, *Profession*, 61–63, 110–117.

32. Scott, *Memoirs*, 1:112.

33. Samuel J. Watson, *Jackson's Sword: The Army Officer Corps on the American Frontier, 1810–1821* (Lawrence: University Press of Kansas, 2012), 227, 236.

34. Ibid., 116–119; John Dwiggins, "The Military Establishment and Democratic Politics in the United States, 1783–1848" (Ph.D. diss., University of Pennsylvania, 2012), 76–77.

35. Dwiggins, "Military Establishment," 72–75. See also, Cunliffe, *Soldiers & Civilians*, 46–48.

36. Allan R. Millett and Peter Maslowski, *For the Common Defense: A Military History of the United States of America*, rev. and exp. ed. (New York: Free Press, 1994), 127–128, 136–137; Cunliffe, *Soldiers & Civilians*, 186–247; Paul W. Foos, *A Short,*

Offhand, Killing Affair: Soldiers and Social Conflict During the Mexican-American War (Chapel Hill: University of North Carolina Press, 2002), 35–43.

37. John C. Calhoun, "On Reduction of the Army, Communicated to the House of Representatives, December 12th, 1820," in *The Works of John C. Calhoun,* ed. Richard C. Crallé (New York: D. Appleton and Company, 1855), 5:90.

38. Ibid., 5:82.

39. Skelton, *Profession,* 126–128.

40. Ibid., 128–129.

41. Samuel J. Watson, "How the Army Became Accepted: West Point Socialization, Military Accountability, and the Nation-State During the Jacksonian Era," *American Nineteenth Century History* 7 (June 2006): 222–228. See also, Russell F. Weigley, *History of the United States Army,* enl. ed. (Bloomington: Indiana University Press, 1984), 133–139; Daniel R. Beaver, *Modernizing the American War Department: Change and Continuity in a Turbulent Era, 1885–1920* (Kent, OH: Kent State University Press, 2006), 1–2; Skelton, *Profession,* 119–121.

42. Bell, *Commanding Generals,* 11–12; Beaver, *Modernizing,* 2–5.

43. Scott, *Memoirs,* 1:157–174; Johnson, *Scott,* 69–71.

44. *General Regulations for the Army, or Military Institutes* (Philadelphia: M. Carey and Sons, 1821); Johnson, *Scott,* 75–79; Wayne Wei-siang Hsieh, *West Pointers in the Civil War: The Old Army in War and Peace* (Chapel Hill: University of North Carolina Press, 2009), 25–27.

45. Scott, *Memoirs,* 1:259.

46. Johnson, *Scott,* 111; Hsieh, *West Pointers,* 39–46; Paddy Griffith, *Battle Tactics of the Civil War,* U.S. ed. (New Haven, CT: Yale Nota Bene Press, 2001), 99.

47. *Infantry Tactics; or Rules for the Exercises and Maneuvers of the Infantry of the U.S. Army* (Washington, DC: Davis & Force, 1825), 7–10.

48. *Register of Graduates,* 4:3.

49. JMS to James D. Cameron, 18 December 1876, letterbooks, vol. 1, JMSWP; Matthew Moten, *The Delafield Commission and the American Military* (College Station: Texas A&M University Press, 2000), 28–32; Hsieh, *West Pointers,* 19–21; Skelton, *Profession,* 122–123.

50. Watson, *Jackson's Sword,* 257–261; Theodore J. Crackel, *West Point: A Bicentennial History* (Lawrence: University Press of Kansas, 2002), 81–100; Hsieh, *West Pointers,* 24; Heitman, *Register,* 952.

51. Quoted in Coffman, *Old Army,* 43; Watson, *Jackson's Sword,* 235–248.

52. *Register of Graduates,* 4:12; Crackel, *West Point,* 124–126; Russell F. Weigley, *The American Way of War: A History of United States Military Strategy and Policy* (New York: Macmillan, 1973), 87–89.

53. Dennis H. Mahan, *An Elementary Treatise on Advanced-Guard, Out-Post, and Detachment Service of Troops* (New York: Wiley and Putnam, 1847), 30.

54. Weigley, *American Way of War,* 88; compare with Brian M. Linn, *The Echo of*

Battle: The Army's Way of War (Cambridge, MA: Harvard University Press, 2007), 45–46.

55. Mahan, *Out-Post*, 38, 93–94; Skelton, *Profession,* 172.

56. Board of Visitors, "Report of the Committee on Military Instruction," 18 June 1838, USMA; Watson, "Accepted," 223; compare with Skelton, *Profession,* 172.

57. Skelton, *Profession,* 248–254; Hsieh, *West Pointers,* 50–52.

58. Skelton, *Profession,* 243–247; Moten, *Delafield,* 59; Coffman, *Old Army,* 98; Linn, *Echo of Battle,* 12–20.

59. Skelton, *Profession,* 184.

60. Coffman, *Old Army,* 81.

61. Ibid., 63–69, 98–103; Skelton, *Profession,* 181–204; Watson, *Jackson's Sword,* 11–22, 262–266; Moten, *Delafield,* 54–72.

CHAPTER 2: TRIALS ON THE FRONTIER AND IN MEXICO

1. Quotation from Timothy D. Johnson, *Winfield Scott: The Quest for Military Glory* (Lawrence: University Press of Kansas, 1998), 145. See also William B. Skelton, *An American Profession of Arms: The Army Officer Corps, 1784–1861* (Lawrence: University Press of Kansas, 1992), 116–119, 282–299; Samuel J. Watson, *Peacekeepers and Conquerors: The Army Officer Corps on the American Frontier, 1821–1846* (Lawrence: University Press of Kansas, 2013), 420–438.

2. *General Regulations* (1821), 13–29; Skelton, *Profession,* 172–177, 260–265; Paul W. Foos, *A Short, Offhand, Killing Affair: Soldiers and Social Conflict During the Mexican-American War* (Chapel Hill: University of North Carolina Press, 2002), 16–25; Edward M. Coffman, *The Old Army: A Portrait of the American Army in Peacetime, 1784–1898* (New York: Oxford University Press, 1986), 194–205; John A. Lynn, *Battle: A History of Combat and Culture,* rev. ed. (Boulder, CO: Westview Press, 2003), 123–124.

3. Matthew Moten, *The Delafield Commission and the American Military* (College Station: Texas A&M University Press, 2000), 39–53; Wayne Wei-siang Hsieh, *West Pointers in the Civil War: The Old Army in War and Peace* (Chapel Hill: University of North Carolina Press, 2009), 41–52.

4. Quoted in Skelton, *Profession,* 236.

5. Quoted in Johnson, *Scott,* 97.

6. Ibid., 150

7. Robert Wooster, *The American Military Frontiers: The United States Army in the West, 1783–1900,* pap. ed. (Albuquerque: University of New Mexico Press, 2012), 104.

8. Samuel J. Watson, "How the Army Became Accepted: West Point Socialization, Military Accountability, and the Nation-State During the Jacksonian Era," *American Nineteenth Century History* 7 (June 2006), 226; Skelton, *Profession,* 210–212; Samuel J. Watson, *Jackson's Sword: The Army Officer Corps on the American Frontier, 1810–1821* (Lawrence: University Press of Kansas, 2012): 208–282.

9. Winfield Scott, *Memoirs of Lieut.-General Scott* (New York: Sheldon & Co., 1864), 1:318.

10. Skelton, *Profession,* 132–134, 297–325; Coffman, *Old Army,* 73–78; Watson, *Peacekeepers and Conquerors,* 1–76; Watson, "Accepted," 220–222; Wooster, *American Military Frontiers,* 63–97; Johnson, *Scott,* 132–133.

11. Watson, *Jackson's Sword,* 72–187; Watson, *Peacekeepers and Conquerors,* 240–316; Johnson, *Scott,* 106–109, 129–132.

12. Johnson, *Scott,* 112–116; Wooster, *American Military Frontiers,* 84–85.

13. Johnson, *Scott,* 116–126; Watson, *Jackson's Sword,* 137–176.

14. Scott, *Memoirs,* 1:95.

15. Johnson, *Scott,* 115.

16. Wooster, *American Military Frontiers,* 49; Robert M. Utley, *Frontier Regulars: The United States Army and the Indian, 1866–1891* (New York: Macmillan, 1974), 45–47.

17. Coffman, *Old Army,* 77–78; Skelton, *Profession,* 255–259; Watson, *Jackson's Sword,* 20–21; Watson, *Peacekeepers and Conquerors,* 384–385, 421–430; Wooster, *American Military Frontiers,* 273–274.

18. Charles E. Callwell, *Small Wars: Their Principles and Practice,* 3rd ed. (London: H. M. Stationary Office, 1906; Lincoln: Bison Books of University of Nebraska Press, 1996); Watson, *Peacekeepers and Conquerors,* 8–13. For the post-Civil War campaigns, see Utley, *Frontier Regulars.*

19. Johnson, *Scott,* 116; *General Regulations* (1821), 90.

20. Watson, *Peacekeepers and Conquerors,* 185–238; Wooster, *American Military Frontiers,* 87–89.

21. Quoted in Coffman, *Old Army,* 51.

22. Ibid., 50–54.

23. Watson, "Accepted," 221–223, 236–239; Skelton, *Profession,* 216–220.

24. Coffman, *Old Army,* 52.

25. Ulysses S. Grant, *Personal Memoirs of Ulysses S. Grant* (New York: Smithmark, 1994), 27–28.

26. Skelton, *Profession,* 137–144.

27. Johnson, *Scott,* 116–128.

28. Richard Bruce Winders, *Mr. Polk's Army: The American Military Experience in the Mexican War* (College Station: Texas A&M University Press, 1997), 8–11, 52; Skelton, *Profession,* 134–135; Watson, *Jackson's Sword,* 261–262.

29. K. Jack Bauer, *The Mexican War, 1846–1848* (New York: Macmillan, 1974), 70–75; Winders, *Mr. Polk's Army,* 191–196; Foos, *Short, Offhand, Killing Affair,* 7–9, 33; Watson, *Jackson's Sword,* 24.

30. Bauer, *Mexican War,* 69–72; Winders, *Mr. Polk's Army,* 66–82; Foos, *Affair,* 45–59.

31. Bauer, *Mexican War,* 73–74; Johnson, *Scott,* 150–161; William C. Davis,

Jefferson Davis: The Man and His Hour (New York: HarperCollins, 1991), 138–139; Winders, *Mr. Polk's Army,* 32–34.

32. Quoted in Johnson, *Scott,* 151.

33. Skelton, *Profession,* 212.

34. Quoted in ibid., 341.

35. Bauer, *Mexican War,* 83–87; Hsieh, *West Pointers,* 54–60.

36. Bauer, *Mexican War,* 85–101, 127–141, 164–196; Russell F. Weigley, *History of the United States Army,* enl. ed. (Bloomington: Indiana University Press, 1984), 177–183.

37. Bauer, *Mexican War,* 232–237; Johnson, *Scott,* 156–160; Weigley, *History,* 177–183.

38. Bauer, *Mexican War,* 201–218.

39. Skelton, *Profession,* 211–212.

40. Davis, *Davis,* 127–133; Joseph E. Chance, *Jefferson Davis's Mexican War Regiment* (Jackson: University Press of Mississippi, 1991), 12; Winders, *Mr. Polk's Army,* 74; Heitman, *Register,* 20–21, 358. For civilian views of military command, see Reardon, *Jomini,* ch. 2.

41. Quoted in Davis, *Davis,* 159.

42. Winders, *Mr. Polk's Army,* 81–84; Davis, *Davis,* 134–159; Chance, *Davis's Regiment,* 26–103. See also, Foos, *Short, Offhand, Killing Affair,* 88–94.

43. Bauer, *Mexican War,* 240–253.

44. Scott, *Memoirs,* 2:423–425 (quotation from note on 425).

45. Johnson, *Scott,* 175–179. In his study of popular notions of war during the Civil War, Gerald Linderman asserts that courage was the central value of mid-nineteenth-century American culture. If so, assault would have been a particularly attractive form of military activity, because it offered the best opportunity to display courage and the closely associated virtues of duty, honor, and manliness. Gerald Linderman, *Embattled Courage: The Experience of Combat in the American Civil War* (New York: Free Press, 1989).

46. Bauer, *Mexican War,* 259–323; Hsieh, *West Pointers,* 64–73.

47. Quoted in Johnson, *Scott,* 190.

48. Johnson, *Scott,* 165–170; Foos, *Short, Offhand, Killing Affair,* 113–127.

49. Johnson, *Scott,* 185–186; Grant, *Memoirs,* 84–85; Bauer, *Mexican War,* 96–97; Hsieh, *West Pointers,* 64; Weigley, *History,* 181; Winders, *Mr. Polk's Army,* 29–31.

50. Quoted in Skelton, *Profession,* 345.

51. Johnson, *Scott,* 153.

52. Quoted in Ethan Allen Hitchcock, *Fifty Years in Camp and Field: Diary of Major-General Ethan Allen Hitchcock, U.S.A.,* ed. W. A. Croffut (New York: G. P. Putnam's Sons, 1909), 310.

53. Coffman, *Old Army,* 57–58, 99; Watson, "Accepted," 227; Bauer, *Mexican War,* 33; Winders, *Mr. Polk's Army,* 52–54; Watson, *Peacekeepers and Conquerors,* 399–402.

54. Richard Taylor, *Destruction and Reconstruction: Personal Experiences of the Late War in the United States* (London: William Blackwood and Sons, 1879), 38.

55. Davis, *Davis,* 221–233; Wooster, *American Military Frontiers,* 134–138.

56. Davis, *Davis,* 235.

57. Ibid., 226–228.

58. Quoted in Wooster, *American Military Frontiers,* 132.

59. Quoted in Davis, *Davis,* 229.

60. Ibid., 220–230; Johnson, *Scott,* 217–219.

61. *Report of the Commission Appointed Under the Eighth Section of the Act of Congress of June 21, 1860, to Examine into the Organization, System of Discipline, and Course of Instruction at the United States Military Academy at West Point,* 13 December 1860, Senate miscellaneous documents, 34th Cong., 2d sess., no. 3, 9. [Hereafter cited as *Davis Commission*]

62. Moten, *Delafield,* 79–83.

63. Morris Schaff, *The Spirit of Old West Point, 1858–1862* (Boston: Houghton, Mifflin and Company, 1907), 59–60, 68.

64. Testimony of Dennis H. Mahan, 17 August 1860, in *Davis Commission,* 123; Moten, *Delafield,* 57; Heitman, *Register,* 499; *Register of Graduates,* 4:24.

65. Testimony of R. Williams, 26 July 1860, in *Davis Commission.* See also, letters from Hardee, 30 July 1860, and n.d., 76, 85–86, 179–180.

66. Moten, *Delafield,* 108–204; Skelton, *Profession,* 241–243.

67. Moten, *Delafield,* 111, 173.

68. Earl J. Hess, *The Rifle Musket in Civil War Combat: Reality and Myth* (Lawrence: University Press of Kansas, 2008), 20–25.

69. Quoted in Hsieh, *West Pointers,* 81.

70. Hess, *Rifle Musket,* 25–33, 68; Paddy Griffith, *Battle Tactics of the Civil War,* U.S. ed. (New Haven, CT: Yale Nota Bene Press, 2001), 99–103; Archer Jones, *Civil War Command and Strategy: The Process of Victory and Defeat* (New York: Free Press, 1992), 274.

71. Charles Edward White, *The Enlightened Soldier: Scharnhorst and the Militärische Gesellschaft in Berlin, 1801–1805* (New York: Praeger, 1989), ch. 5–6; Peter Paret, *The Cognitive Challenge of War: Prussia 1806* (Princeton, NJ: Princeton University Press, 2009), ch. 3–4.

72. Testimony of Richard I. Dodge, 24 July 1860, in *Davis Commission,* 78. See also, responses of A. M. McCook, 26 July 1860, 77; Milton Cogswell, 6 August 1860, 97; George G. Meade, 30 August 1860, 311; and T. H. Holmes, 23 July 1860, 155.

73. Letter from Robert E. Lee, 3 September 1860, in ibid., 315.

CHAPTER 3: THE FIRST UPHEAVAL

1. Ethan S. Rafuse, *A Single Grand Victory: The First Campaign and Battle of Manassas* (Wilmington, DE: SR Books, 2002), 19–23.

2. "12th Regiment, New York State Militia, New York National Guard, Civil War," New York State Military Museum and Veterans Research Center, http://dmna .ny.gov; Francis B. Heitman, *Historical Register and Dictionary of the United States Army*, vol. 1 (Washington, DC: GPO, 1903), 270–271.

3. William T. Sherman, *Memoirs of General William T. Sherman* (New York: Da Capo Press, 1984), 1:178.

4. Quoted in James A. Garfield, "The Army of the United States, Part I," *North American Review* 126 (March-April 1878): 193.

5. Sherman, *Memoirs*, 1:178.

6. John C. Calhoun, "On Reduction of the Army, Communicated to the House of Representatives, December 12th, 1820," in *The Works of John C. Calhoun*, ed. Richard C. Crallé (New York: D. Appleton and Company, 1855), 5:84.

7. Rafuse, *Single Grand Victory*, 23–25; James M. McPherson, *Battle Cry of Freedom: The Civil War Era* (New York: Oxford University Press, 2003), 322–324; Richard H. Kohn, *Eagle and Sword: The Federalists and the Creation of the Military Establishment in America, 1783–1802* (New York: Free Press, 1975), 129–130.

8. McPherson, *Battle Cry of Freedom*, 322–324.

9. Thomas J. Goss, *The War Within the Union High Command: Politics and Generalship During the Civil War* (Lawrence: University Press of Kansas, 2003), 16–17; Timothy D. Johnson, *Winfield Scott: The Quest for Military Glory* (Lawrence: University Press of Kansas, 1998), 223–233.

10. Rafuse, *Single Grand Victory*, ch. 1.

11. Goss, *High Command*, 17–18, 64 (quotation).

12. Ibid., 55–56; Heitman, *Register*, 656.

13. Goss, *High Command*, 57–62; John F. Marszalek, *Sherman: A Soldier's Passion for Order*, pap. ed. (Carbondale: Southern Illinois University Press, 2007), 143–146; Michael Fellman, *Citizen Sherman: A Life of William Tecumseh Sherman* (New York: Random House, 1995), 86–88.

14. *Register of Graduates and Former Cadets of the United States Military Academy West Point, New York* (West Point: Association of Graduates, 2005), 4:25, 31; Heitman, *Register*.

15. David J. Fitzpatrick, "Emory Upton: The Misunderstood Reformer" (Ph.D. diss., University of Michigan, 1996), 54; Stephen E. Ambrose, *Upton and the Army* (Baton Rouge: Louisiana State University Press, 1964), 16; *Register of Graduates*, 4:43–44.

16. Quoted in Peter S. Michie, *The Life and Letters of Emory Upton, Colonel of the Fourth Regiment of Artillery, and Brevet Major-General, U.S. Army* (New York: Appleton, 1885; Decatur, MI: Invictus, 2005), 5.

17. Biographical information taken from ibid., 1–9; Fitzpatrick, "Reformer," 12–27; Ambrose, *Upton*, 4–9; *Combination Atlas Map of Genesee County, New York* (Philadelphia: Everts, Ensign & Everts, 1876), 66.

18. Michie, *Letters,* 21, 32, 41; *Register of Graduates,* 4:43; Fitzpatrick, "Reformer," 42–43.

19. EU to "My Dear Sister," 23 April 1859, in Michie, *Letters,* 16.

20. Morris Schaff, *The Spirit of Old West Point, 1858–1862* (Boston: Houghton, Mifflin and Company, 1907), 144.

21. Theodore J. Crackel, *West Point: A Bicentennial History* (Lawrence: University Press of Kansas, 2002), 81–100; Skelton, *Profession,* 172–180; Schaff, *Spirit,* 143–148, 224–225; Fitzpatrick, "Reformer," 44–48; Wade H. Gibbes obituary, *Thirty-Firth Annual Reunion of the Association of the Graduates of the United States Military Academy,* 14 June 1904 (West Point, NY: Association of Graduates, 1904), 100–106.

22. EU to "My Dear Sister," 20 January 1860 in Michie, *Letters,* 18.

23. Ibid.

24. Quoted in Carol Reardon, *With a Sword in One Hand and Jomini in the Other: The Problem of Military Thought in the Civil War North* (Chapel Hill: University of North Carolina Press, 2012), 61.

25. Johnson, *Scott,* 222–226; Rafuse, *Single Grand Victory,* 47–52; Goss, *High Command,* 53–54, 221–222 n. 57; Heitman, *Register,* 664, 688.

26. Rafuse, *Single Grand Victory,* 57; Heitman, *Register,* 775.

27. Marszalek, *Sherman,* 143–151; quotation from Fellman, *Sherman,* 89.

28. *Davis Commission,* 10.

29. Report of Daniel Tyler, 27 July 1861, *OR,* 2:351; Heitman, *Register; Register of Graduates,* 4:33; Rafuse, *Single Grand Victory,* 74–75, 82–83.

30. Rafuse, *Single Grand Victory,* ch 3–5, (quotation 74); Goss, *High Command,* ch. 2.

31. Rafuse, *Single Grand Victory,* 103–110; Fitzpatrick, "Reformer," 55.

32. Rafuse, *Single Grand Victory,* 94–99, 117–118.

33. Ibid., 115–117.

34. Crackel, *West Point,* 131–132; Scott, *Memoirs,* 2:508; Rafuse, *Single Grand Victory,* 118–120, 139–142.

35. Quoted in Rafuse, *Single Grand Victory,* 165.

36. The account of First Bull Run comes from Rafuse, *Single Grand Victory,* pt. 3.

37. EU to "My Dear Sister," 22 July 1861, in Michie, *Letters,* 53; Report of Daniel Tyler, 27 July 1861, *OR,* 2:351.

38. WTS, *Memoirs,* 1:191.

39. EU to Edward D. Townsend, 11 November 1865, Upton Cullum File, USMA; James H. Wilson, "Introduction," in Michie, *Letters,* xvii-xviii.

40. Goss, *High Command,* 18, 222–223 n. 67; Jones, *Command,* 3–4.

41. Salvatore C. Cilella, Jr., *Upton's Regulars: The 121st New York Infantry in the Civil War* (Lawrence: University Press of Kansas, 2009), 23–43, quotation on 66.

42. Cilella, *Upton's Regulars,* 23-43; "Richard Franchot," *Biographical Directory*

of the United States Congress, http://bioguide.congress.gov; Heitman, *Register,* 433; Stephen E. Ambrose, *Nothing Like It in the World: The Men Who Built the Transcontinental Railroad, 1863–1869* (New York: Simon & Schuster, 2000), 193.

43. Cilella, *Upton's Regulars,* 67–86; Heitman, *Register,* 978.

44. Cilella, *Upton's Regulars,* 84–104; Fitzpatrick, "Reformer," 64–69.

45. Quotations from Cilella, *Upton's Regulars,* 84.

46. Ibid., 95–104.

47. Quoted in ibid., 84.

48. Ibid., 148–150; Mark Grimsley, "Surviving Military Revolution: The U.S. Civil War," in *The Dynamics of Military Revolution, 1300–2050,* ed. Macgregor Knox and Williamson Murray (New York: Cambridge University Press, 2001), 75–78.

49. McPherson, *Battle Cry of Freedom,* 569–574; Goss, *High Command,* 91–92; Cilella, *Upton's Regulars,* 124–128.

50. EU to "My Dear Sister Louise," 23 December 1862, Upton Cullum.

51. McPherson, *Battle Cry,* 639–645.

52. Cilella, *Upton's Regulars,* 164–176 (quotation 169).

53. Fitzpatrick, "Reformer," 76; Report of EU, 10 May 1863, *OR,* 25 (1):589–590; EU to "Dear Brother," 6 November 1863, in Michie, *Letters,* 81.

54. Report of Joseph J. Bartlett, 11 May 1863, *OR,* 25(1):583.

55. Report of EU, 6 August 1863, *OR,* 27(1):693.

56. EU to "Dear Brother," 6 November 1863, in Michie, *Letters,* 81.

57. EU to "My Dear Sister," 4 July 1863, in ibid., 75; letters of recommendation and endorsements in File 2666-ACP-1881, ACP [hereafter "Upton ACP"].

58. The account of Rappahannock Station taken from reports of David A. Russell, 16 November 1863, and EU, 11 November 1863, *OR,* 29(1):587–593; Cilella, *Upton's Regulars,* 234–243.

59. Wilson, "Introduction," in Michie, *Letters,* xii-xiii.

60. Cilella, *Upton's Regulars,* 244–245; *OR,* 29(1):590.

61. Cilella, *Upton's Regulars,* 148–150, 278–279; Wayne Wei-siang Hsieh, *West Pointers in the Civil War: The Old Army in War and Peace* (Chapel Hill: University of North Carolina Press, 2009), 146–147.

62. EU to "My Dear Sister," 10 April 1864, in Michie, *Letters,* 88–89.

63. EU to "My Dear Sister," 18 April 1864, in ibid., 89; EU to Senator Edwin D. Morgan, 11 April 1864, Upton Cullum.

64. Goss, *High Command,* 165–176.

65. Report of EU, 1 September 1864, *OR* 36(1):665–666; Mark Grimsley, *And Keep Moving On: The Virginia Campaign, May-June 1864* (Lincoln: University of Nebraska Press, 2002), 24–59.

66. Account of the Mule Shoe assault from report of EU, *OR* 36(1):667–669; Grimsley, *Keep Moving On,* 70–81.

67. David Fitzpatrick refutes the contention made by Paddy Griffith that the

292 • NOTES TO PAGES 88–95

assaults at Rappahannock Station and Spotsylvania were similar to "stormtroop" tactics of the twentieth century: Fitzpatrick, "Reformer," 103 n. 53; Griffith, *Civil War,* 66, 152.

68. Fitzpatrick, "Reformer," 102.

69. Ulysses S. Grant to Edwin M. Stanton, 13 May 1864, *OR* 36(2):695.

70. Hsieh, *West Pointers,* 161; Cilella, *Upton's Regulars,* 159, 283, 334.

71. Reardon, *Jomini,* 99–101; report of EU, *OR* 36(1):670.

72. *OR* 36(1):671; Grimsley, *Keep Moving On,* 196–221. See also, Griffith, *Civil War,* 60–66.

73. Quoted in Grimsley, *Keep Moving On,* 211. See also, Hsieh, *West Pointers,* 174–176.

74. EU to "My Dear Sister," 5 June 1864, in Michie, *Letters,* 109.

75. Quoted in Fitzpatrick, "Reformer," 102.

76. EU to JHW, 25 July 1877, box 25, JHWP.

77. EU, *OR* 36(1):671.

78. Grimsley, *Keep Moving On,* 196–224; McPherson, *Battle Cry of Freedom,* 742.

79. Edward Hagerman, *The American Civil War and the Origins of Modern Warfare: Ideas, Organization, and Field Command* (Bloomington: Indiana University Press, 1988); Hsieh, *West Pointers,* 185–188.

80. Ambrose, *Upton,* 39–41.

81. Ibid., 42–45; Heitman, *Register,* 1046.

82. Reports of George H. Thomas, 1 June 1865, James H. Wilson, 29 June 1865, and EU, 30 May 1865, *OR* 49(1):342–343, 360, 471–475; Fitzpatrick, "Reformer," 129–142.

83. Michie, *Letters,* 190; Fitzpatrick, "Reformer," 152–153.

84. Quoted in "Army Circles Astonished," *New York Times,* 17 March 1881. See also, Perry D. Jamieson, *Crossing the Deadly Ground: United States Army Tactics, 1865–1899* (Tuscaloosa: University of Alabama Press, 1994), 1–10.

85. Fitzpatrick, "Reformer,"152–159.

86. Emory Upton, *A New System of Infantry Tactics, Double and Single Rank: Adapted to American Topography and Improved Fire-Arms* (New York: D. Appleton & Co., 1868), 98; compare with William J. Hardee, *Rifle and Light Infantry Tactics for the Exercise and Manoeuvres of Troops When Acting as Light Infantry or Riflemen* (Philadelphia: J. B. Lippincott & Co. 1860), 172.

87. Upton, *Tactics* (1868), 97–124; compare with Hardee, *Tactics,* 171–213; Ambrose, *Upton,* 64–65.

88. Michael E. Howard, *War in European History* (New York: Oxford University Press, 1976), 55–57.

89. EU to Townsend, 13 January 1866, in Michie, *Letters,* 192.

90. WTS, "Address to the Class of 1880, Artillery School, Fort Monroe, Virginia," 28 April 1880, reel 45, WTSP.

91. EU to sister, 11 February 1866, in Michie, *Letters,* 194.

92. Upton, *Tactics* (1874), viii.

93. Howard, *War in European History,* 69–70; John A. Lynn, *Battle: A History of Combat and Culture,* rev. ed. (Boulder, CO: Westview Press, 2003), 120–124.

94. Emory Upton, *The Armies of Asia and Europe, Embracing Official Reports on the Armies of Japan, China, India, Persia, Italy, Russia, Austria, Germany, France, and England* (New York: Appleton, 1878), 12.

95. Quoted in Michie, *Letters,* 197.

96. Sherman, *Memoirs,* 2:401; Michie, *Letters,* 191–205; Jamieson, *Crossing the Deadly Ground,* 10–12; Ambrose, *Upton,* 61–66; Upton, *Tactics* (1868), ii.

97. Quoted in Michie, *Letters,* 203.

98. David J. Fitzpatrick, "Emory Upton and the Citizen Soldier," *JMH* 65 (April 2001): 366–367; Mark W. Summers, *Party Games: Getting, Keeping, and Using Power in Gilded Age Politics* (Chapel Hill: University of North Carolina Press, 2004), 40–41.

CHAPTER 4: THE CIVIL WAR'S LEGACY

1. Robert M. Utley, *Frontier Regulars: The United States Army and the Indian, 1866–1891* (New York: Macmillan, 1974), 15; Jerry M. Cooper, "The Army's Search for a Mission, 1865–1890," in *Against All Enemies: Interpretations of American Military History from Colonial Times to the Present,* ed. Kenneth Hagan and William R. Roberts (Westport, CT: Greenwood Press, 1986), 175.

2. Samuel J. Watson, "How the Army Became Accepted: West Point Socialization, Military Accountability, and the Nation-State During the Jacksonian Era," *American Nineteenth Century History* 7 (June 2006): 222; Edward M. Coffman, *The Old Army: A Portrait of the American Army in Peacetime, 1784–1898* (New York: Oxford University Press, 1986), 218–223.

3. Mark R. Grandstaff, "Preserving the 'Habits and Usages of War': William Tecumseh Sherman, Professional Reform, and the U.S. Army Officer Corps, 1865–1881, Revisited," *JMH* 62 (July 1998): 532–533.

4. John A. Logan, *The Volunteer Soldier of America* (Chicago: R. S. Peale, 1887), 115–121, 430 (quotation), 583; John F. Marszalek, *Sherman: A Soldier's Passion for Order,* pap. ed. (Carbondale: Southern Illinois University Press, 2007), 143–146; 277–279. On the tradition of "genius" in American thought, see Carol Reardon, *With a Sword in One Hand and Jomini in the Other: The Problem of Military Thought in the Civil War North* (Chapel Hill: University of North Carolina Press, 2012), 56–59.

5. WTS, "Address at the Michigan Military Academy, Orchard Lake, Michigan, 19 June 1879," reel 45, WTSP.

6. EU to Henry A. du Pont, 1 April 1877, in Michie, *Letters,* 418.

7. Francis B. Heitman, *Historical Register and Dictionary of the United States Army,* vol. 1 (Washington, DC: GPO, 1903).

8. *Army Register for September, 1869* (Washington DC: AGO, 1869), 3–4; Heitman, *Register.*

9. For instance, see William W. Wotherspoon to WHC, 1 July 1914, WHCP, and numerous letters throughout boxes 94–105, LWP.

10. Heitman, *Register,* 978.

11. EU to JHW, 15 May 1869, box 25, JHWP.

12. EU to JHW, 2 June 1869, box 25, JHWP.

13. EU to JHW, 4 December 1868, 12 July and 31 December 1869, 17 June 1870, box 25, JHWP; Crackel, *West Point,* 141–143.

14. EU to JHW, 21 August 1870 and 20 February 1871 (quotations), JHWP.

15. James Parker, "My Experiences as a West Point Cadet," box 3, Parker Papers, USMA, 4.

16. Hugh L. Scott to "Dear Mother," 24 May and 30 August 1874, Scott Papers, USMA; Armand LaPotin, manuscript biography of Scott.

17. EU to JHW, 21 August 1870, box 25, JHWP.

18. ES, "Personal Memoirs," ESP, 35. See also, Michie, *Letters,* 249–279; George W. McIver, "My Memoirs," UNC, I:29–32; Ernest A. Garlington to "General Smith," 25 July 1929, Garlington Papers, USMA.

19. Perry D. Jamieson, *Crossing the Deadly Ground: United States Army Tactics, 1865–1899* (Tuscaloosa: University of Alabama Press, 1994), 6–9; Michie, *Letters,* 279.

20. WTS to EU, 18 August 1873, reel 45, WTSP.

21. WTS to EU, 3 January, 18 August, and 22 September 1873, reel 45, WTSP; EU to Henry A. du Pont, 17 April 1871, in Michie, *Letters,* 208.

22. WTS, *Memoirs,* 2:395.

23. WTS to EU, 3 January 1873, reel 45, WTSP.

24. EU to WTS, 10 September 1874 and 7 May 1875, reel 20, and WTS to EU, 12 July 1875, reel 45, WTSP; David J. Fitzpatrick, "Emory Upton: The Misunderstood Reformer" (Ph.D. diss., University of Michigan, 1996), 221–223.

25. Upton, *Armies,* vi–viii; EU to JHW, 19 October 1876, box 25, JHWP.

26. *Register of Graduates,* 4:30–31, 4:43–44; Heitman, *Register.*

27. EU to Henry A. du Pont, 1 April 1877, in Michie, *Letters,* 418; Upton, *Armies,* 362–366; Fitzpatrick, "Reformer," 344–345.

28. Peter S. Michie, "The Personnel of Sea-Coast Defense," *JMSI* 8 (March 1887): 14.

29. Montgomery C. Meigs to WTS, 9 July 1879, reel 26, WTSP.

30. "A Lieutenant of Artillery," "The Lieutenant," *United Service,* 10 New Series (October 1893): 342.

31. On the later Artillery School's technical orientation, see JMS to Redfield Proctor, 9 April 1889, box 54, JMSLC; William Lassiter, "Memoirs," Lassiter Papers, USMA, 1:47–49; Royal T. Frank to Tasker H. Bliss, 3 March 1890, and James M. Ingalls to Bliss, 4 June 1892, Bliss Papers, USMA.

32. Upton, *Armies,* ix; Moten, *Delafield,* 84–87.

33. EU to Henry A. du Pont, 1 April 1877, in Michie, *Letters,* 418.

34. Upton, *Armies,* 29.

35. Ibid., 11.

36. Ibid., viii, 197–223.

37. Ibid., 367–370. See also, Emory Upton, *The Military Policy of the United States,* ed. William D. Beach, Joseph P. Sanger, and Charles D. Rhodes (Washington DC: GPO, 1904), xiii–xiv.

38. Upton, *Armies,* 368.

39. Upton, *Armies,* 323; WTS to EU, 18 November 1878, reel 45, WTSP.

40. Quoted in Fitzpatrick, "Reformer," 305.

41. Upton, *Armies,* 337–351; Russell F. Weigley, *The American Way of War: A History of United States Military Strategy and Policy* (New York: Macmillan, 1973), 287.

42. Upton, *Armies,* 318.

43. WTS to Hiester Clymer, 15 February 1878, reel 45, WTSP. See also, WTS, "Address to . . . Artillery School."

44. EU to Francis V. Greene, 3 October 1879, box 26, LWP.

45. EU to WTS, 22 November 1877, reel 24, WTSP; EU to JHW, 19 May 1877, box 25 JHWP.

46. Upton, *Military Policy,* xi.

47. WTS to EU, 9 February 1878, reel 45, WTSP.

48. WTS to James A. Garfield, 21 June 1878, reel 45, WTSP; EU to Henry A. du Pont, 6 November 1878, in Michie, *Letters,* 420.

49. James M. McPherson, *Battle Cry of Freedom: The Civil War Era* (New York: Oxford University Press, 2003), 362–365; Thomas J. Goss, *The War Within the Union High Command: Politics and Generalship During the Civil War* (Lawrence: University Press of Kansas, 2003), 154–164; Michael Fellman, *Citizen Sherman: A Life of William Tecumseh Sherman* (New York: Random House, 1995), 240–254.

50. Coffman, *Old Army,* 234–246. For an account of how both local and national politics made command during Reconstruction difficult, see Donald B. Connelly, *John M. Schofield and the Politics of Generalship* (Chapel Hill: University of North Carolina Press, 2006), 186–203.

51. Weigley, *History,* 257–264; Marszalek, *Sherman,* 369–375; WTS correspondence with Andrew Johnson and Ulysses S. Grant, January–February 1868, reel 44, WTSP.

52. For an example of Sherman's frustrations, see letter to PHS, 1 April 1871, reel 45, WTSP. On Sherman's exile to and return from St. Louis, see correspondence to William W. Belknap, 8 May 1874, reel 45, to John Sherman, March 1876, reel 22, and with PHS, April 1876, reel 22, WTSP; Fellman, *Sherman,* 277–287.

53. See WTS to Winfield Scott Hancock, 21 January 1877, reel 45, WTSP, and JMS to WTS, 8 and 26 December 1876, 3 March 1877, letterbook vol. 1, JMSWP;

Marszalek, *Sherman,* 427–429; Eric Foner, *Reconstruction: America's Unfinished Revolution, 1863–1877* (New York: Harper & Row, 1988), 569–582.

54. Stephen Skowronek, *Building a New American State: The Expansion of National Administrative Capacities, 1877–1920* (New York: Cambridge University Press, 1982), 39–41.

55. Quoted in Coffman, *Old Army,* 246.

56. Marszalek, *Sherman,* 429–430; Coffman, *Old Army,* 246–250; Skowronek, *Building,* 98–103; Wooster, *American Military Frontiers,* 240–243.

57. WTS to John A. Logan and Henry B. Banning, 5 February 1877, and to Banning, 12 February 1878, reel 45, WTSP; *The Statutes at Large of the United States* 20 (Washington, DC: GPO, 1879), 145–152; *Report of the Joint Committee on the Reorganization of the Army,* 45th Cong., 3d sess., report no. 555, 1878, [hereafter *Burnside Report*], 1–4.

58. Quoted in Utley, *Frontier Regulars,* 61.

59. WTS to Ambrose E. Burnside, 15 July 1878, reel 45, WTSP; Upton, *Armies,* 33–57.

60. JMS to WTS, 21 January 1879, letterbooks vol. 2, JMSWP.

61. For examples of opposition, see WTS to Zealous B. Tower, 24 December 1878, and to John G. Barnard, 24 December 1878, reel 45, WTSP; Francis H. Parker, untitled pamphlet, [1878], Parker Papers, AHEC. For an example of skepticism of meritocracy, see statement of Truman Seymour in *Army Staff Organization,* 42d Cong., 2d sess., report no. 74, 1873, 57.

62. WTS to Ambrose E. Burnside, 15 December 1878. See also, WTS to JMS, 6 August 1878, and WTS to Burnside, 15 July 1878, reel 45, WTSP.

63. PHS to WTS, 4 January 1879, Winfield Scott Hancock to WTS, 17 December 1878, and EU to WTS, 15 December 1878, reel 25, WTSP; JMS to WTS, 25 October 1877, letterbooks vol. 1, 20 and 24 December 1878, 21 January 1879 (quotation), vol. 2, JMSWP.

64. Marszalek, *Sherman,* 434–436.

65. Fitzpatrick, "Reformer," 362–377; Skowronek, *Building,* 59–63, 108–109; Mark W. Summers, *Party Games: Getting, Keeping, and Using Power in Gilded Age Politics* (Chapel Hill: University of North Carolina Press, 2004), 149–156.

66. EU to JHW, 19 October 1876, box 25, JHWP; Summers, *Party Games,* 229–237; Skowronek, *Building,* 42–45. For an example of the interpretation of Upton as a militarist, see Russell F. Weigley, "The Soldier, the Statesman, and the Military Historian," *JMH* 63 (October 1999): 812–815.

67. EU to JHW, 21 October 1878, box 25, JHWP; EU to Henry du Pont, 6 November 1878, in Michie, *Letters,* 420; EU to WTS, 18 October 1878, reel 25, WTSP.

68. Upton, *Military Policy,* xi.

69. Ibid., viii.

70. Ibid., 258.

71. Theodore Roosevelt to ER, 16 February 1904, box 163, ERP.

72. Upton, *Military Policy,* 243–246.

73. Sherman, *Memoirs,* 1:181–182.

74. Fitzpatrick, "Reformer," 334–335.

75. EU to JHW, 26 December 1878, box 25, JHWP.

76. Weigley, "Soldier," 812.

77. Summers, *Party Games,* 26, 248, 259.

78. Fitzpatrick, "Reformer," 155; EU to JHW, 19 October 1876, box 25 JHWP.

79. Jones, *Command,* 80.

80. EU to "My dear Friend," 24 October 1878, Upton Cullum.

81. EU to WTS, 30 January and 2 February 1880, reel 26, WTSP.

82. Upton, *Armies,* 353–354; Stephen E. Ambrose, *Upton and the Army* (Baton Rouge: Louisiana State University Press, 1964), 142–145.

83. EU to WTS, 2 February 1880, reel 26, WTSP; Michie, *Letters,* 466–473. See also, William B. Hazen to Levi Maish, 19 January 1878, in *Reorganization of the Army,* 45th Cong., 2d sess., misc. doc. no. 56, 1878, 122.

84. Michie, *Letters,* 466–473; EU to Francis V. Greene, 3 October 1879, copy in box 26, LWP.

85. EU to WTS, 30 January 1880, reel 26, WTSP.

86. John M. Hyson, Jr., et al., "The Suicide of General Emory Upton: A Case Report," *Military Medicine* 155 (October 1990): 445–452.

87. EU to Sara Upton and to Adjutant General, 14 March 1881, in Michie, *Letters,* 494–495.

88. "Army Circles Astonished," *New York Times,* 17 March 1881.

89. Ambrose, *Upton,* 3.

CHAPTER 5: BETWEEN OLD AND NEW

1. WTS to Hiester Clymer, 15 February 1878, reel 45, WTSP; John F. Marszalek, *Sherman: A Soldier's Passion for Order*, pap. ed. (Carbondale: Southern Illinois University Press, 2007), 440–442.

2. WTS, "Address at the Michigan Military Academy, Orchard Lake, Michigan, 19 June 1879," reel 45, WTSP.

3. WTS to PHS, 31 July 1881, reel 47, WTSP.

4. WTS to Elwell S. Otis, 3 and 26 January 1882, reel 47, WTSP. See also, Mark R. Grandstaff, "Preserving the 'Habits and Usages of War': William Tecumseh Sherman, Professional Reform, and the U.S. Army Officer Corps, 1865–1881, Revisited," *JMH* 62 (July 1998): 541; Marszalek, *Sherman,* 442.

5. *School of Instruction for Cavalry and Light Artillery,* 49th Cong., 1st sess., report no. 1948, 1886, 3; Richard O'Connor, *Sheridan: The Inevitable* (Indianapolis:

Bobbs-Merrill, 1953), 308–335; Brian M. Linn, *The Echo of Battle: The Army's Way of War* (Cambridge, MA: Harvard University Press, 2007), 46–47.

6. JMS, address to Military Services Institution, 11 January 1879, box 93, JMSLC.

7. Edward M. Coffman, *The Old Army: A Portrait of the American Army in Peacetime, 1784–1898* (New York: Oxford University Press, 1986), 277–278.

8. JMS, address to Military Services Institution. On early American science, see Robert V. Bruce, *The Launching of Modern American Science, 1846–1876* (New York: Knopf, 1987).

9. WD GO #80, 5 October 1891; JMS to Forsyth, 7 April 1893, box 57, JMSLC.

10. JMS to Forsyth, 7 April 1893.

11. WD GO #80, 5 October 1891; JMS memorandum, 1 April 1892, box 56, JMSLC.

12. JMS to Stephen B. Elkins, 23 February and 27 February 1892, box 57, JMSLC; Donald B. Connelly, *John M. Schofield and the Politics of Generalship* (Chapel Hill: University of North Carolina Press, 2006), 23–310.

13. JMS to Redfield Proctor, 29 September 1891, box 55, JMSLC.

14. JMS to Daniel S. Lamont, 28 September 1895, box 58, JMSLC.

15. George S. Anderson, "Practical Military Instruction," *JMSI* 47 (November–December 1910): 331.

16. Quoted in Coffman, *Old Army,* 277. See also, General Staff memorandum on military education, [1904], box 19, entry 3, RG 165, NARA II.

17. JMS to Forsyth, 7 April 1893; WD GO #80, 5 October 1891.

18. *WDAR* (1886), 1:167.

19. Francis B. Heitman, *Historical Register and Dictionary of the United States Army, vol. 1* (Washington, DC: GPO, 1903), 622; John Bigelow, Jr., "Tenth Regiment of Cavalry," in *The Army of the United States: Historical Sketches of Staff and Line with Portraits of Generals-in-Chief,* ed. Theophilus F. Rodenbough and William L. Haskin (New York: Maynard, Merrill, & Co., 1896), 290–296.

20. JMS memorandum, 1 April 1892, box 56, JMSLC.

21. Heitman, *Register,* 622; WD GO #80, 5 October 1891; William H. Carter, *From Yorktown to Santiago with the Sixth U.S. Cavalry* (Baltimore, MD: Lord Baltimore Press, 1900), 290–298; Robert A. Fulton, *Moroland, 1899–1906: America's First Attempt to Transform an Islamic Society* (Bend, OR: Tumalo Creek Press, 2007).

22. Coffman, *Old Army,* 223–224; compare with Robert Wooster, *The American Military Frontiers: The United States Army in the West, 1783–1900,* pap. ed. (Albuquerque: University of New Mexico Press, 2012), 261.

23. George W. McIver, "My Memoirs," UNC, 1:37–45 (quotation on 37).

24. Coffman, *Old Army,* 232–233.

25. "A Lieutenant of Artillery," "The Lieutenant," 341.

26. William A. Kobbé quoted in Donald Smythe, *Guerilla Warrior: The Early Life of John J. Pershing* (New York: Charles Scribner's Sons, 1973), 24.

27. Edward E. Hardin, "The Indian Frontier: An Army Lieutenant in Montana, 1874–1876," *Military Affairs* 23 (Summer 1959): 85; quotation from Matthew F. Steele, "The Evolution of Professional Culture in the American Army," box 20, Steele Papers, AHEC, 3.

28. Peter S. Michie, "The Personnel of Sea-Coast Defense," *JMSI* 8 (March 1887): 7. For similar problems in other arms, see testimony of John Gibbon, 26 April 1878, in *Reorganization of the Army*, 45th Cong., 2d sess., misc. doc. no. 56, 1878, 266.

29. Samuel P. Huntington, *The Soldier and the State: The Theory and Politics of Civil-Military Relations* (Cambridge, MA: Belknap Press of Harvard University Press, 1957), 226–230.

30. William Lassiter, "Memoirs," Lassiter Papers, USMA, 1:23–25, 42–45.

31. Johnson Hagood, "Down the Big Road," box 1, Hagood Papers, AHEC, 58.

32. John M. Gates, "The Alleged Isolation of U.S. Army Officers in the Late 19th Century," *Parameters* 10 (Spring 1980): 32–45.

33. Richard I. Dodge, "The Enlisted Soldier," *JMSI* 8 (September 1887): 297.

34. James Parker to R. Wayne Parker, 11 February 1877, Parker Papers, USMA.

35. Quoted in Coffman, *Old Army*, 262.

36. Connelly, *Schofield*, 280; Coffman, *Old Army*, 282.

37. Louis C. Scherer to ES, 23 March 1896, box 1, ESP.

38. *WDAR* (1892), 4:338–354.

39. Tasker H. Bliss to JMS, 18 September 1891, Bliss Papers, USMA. See also, JMS to William C. Endicott, 12 December 1888, box 54, JMSLC; Lassiter, "Memoirs," 1:80.

40. Eli A. Helmick, "From Reveille to Retreat," Helmick Papers, AHEC, 117.

41. *WDAR* (1892), 4:28, 338–651.

42. Ibid., 362–369, 632–635.

43. Lassiter, "Memoirs," 1:22, 27.

44. Hagood, "Down the Big Road," 56. See also, Lassiter, "Memoirs," 1:19–21.

45. Ronald H. Spector, *Professors of War: The Naval War College and the Development of the Naval Profession* (Newport, RI: Naval War College Press, 1977), 77–78; Lassiter, "Memoirs," 1:43.

46. Charles D. Rhodes, "How Best to Instruct Officers of Our Army in Tactics," *JMSI* 43 (September–October 1908): 202.

47. *WDAR* (1892), 4:29; Walter S. Schuyler to ES, 2 July 1895, box 1, ESP; Helmick, "Reveille to Retreat," 40–55; Guy V. Henry, Jr., "Brief Narrative of the Life of Guy V. Henry, Jr." box 4, Henry Papers, AHEC, 10–16; Coffman, *Old Army*, 282–283.

48. Dodge, "Enlisted Soldier," 282. See also, McIver, "Memoirs," 1:57–59.

49. WD GO #53, 29 December 1896.

50. John Gibbon to WTS, 15 March 1877, in *Burnside Report,* 126.

51. William R. Roberts, "Reform and Revitalization, 1890–1903," in *Against All Enemies,* 199–201; Daniel R. Beaver, *Modernizing the American War Department: Change and Continuity in a Turbulent Era, 1885–1920* (Kent, OH: Kent State University Press, 2006), 21–30.

52. Alan Trachtenberg, *The Incorporation of America: Culture and Society in the Gilded Age* (New York: Hill and Wang, 1982). See also, Michael E. McGerr, *A Fierce Discontent: The Rise and Fall of the Progressive Movement in America, 1870–1920* (New York: Free Press, 2003), 6–39.

53. *WDAR* (1892), 4:710–711; Beaver, *Modernizing,* 13–21.

54. John P. Wisser, "Practical Instruction in Minor Tactics," *JMSI* 8 (June 1887): 130.

55. McIver, "Memoirs," 1:63.

56. JMS to Redfield Proctor, 23 April 1890, box 55, JMSLC.

57. Harry R. Yarger, "Army Officer Personnel Management: The Creation of the Modern System to 1939" (Ph.D. diss., Temple University, 1996), 80–93.

58. Quoted in *Examinations and Promotions in the* Army, 51st Cong., 1st sess., report no. 832, 1890, 4.

59. Coffman, *Old Army,* 281.

60. Letters to ES, March–April 1893, box 1, ESP; Hagood, "Down the Big Road"; George Van Horn Moseley, "One Soldier's Journey," box 14, Moseley Papers, LC, 68.

61. WHC, "Memoirs," WHCP, 315–318.

62. AGO memorandum, 3 January 1914, box 77, LWP. See also, JFB to Jacob M. Dickinson, 10 February 1910, box 18, entry 292, RG 393, NARA I.

63. Yarger, "Army Officer Personnel Management," 74–75.

64. George W. Baird, "Recent Army Legislation," *United Service* 10 New Series (December 1893): 502–503; Heitman, *Register,* 183. See also, Edwin V. Sumner, "The Individual Soldier," *Journal of the U.S. Cavalry Association* 1 (July 1888): 180–191; WTS, "Address of General W. T. Sherman to the Officers and Soldiers Composing the School of Application at Fort Leavenworth, Kansas, October 25, 1882," reel 47, WTSP.

65. Upton, *Armies,* 319; Yarger, "Army Officer Personnel Management," 71–73. See also, "Lieutenant of Artillery", "The Lieutenant," 349.

66. Nelson A. Miles to Henry B. Banning, 8 February 1876, box 2, Miles Papers, AHEC.

67. Carol Reardon, *Soldiers and Scholars: The U.S. Army and the Uses of Military History, 1865-1920* (Lawrence: University Press of Kansas, 1990), 22. See also, Coffman, *Old Army,* 275–276; Timothy K. Nenninger, *The Leavenworth Schools and the Old Army: Education, Professionalism, and the Officer Corps of the United States Army, 1881-1918* (Westport, CT: Greenwood Press, 1978), 15.

68. ES, "Memoirs," 25, 114–115 (quotation), and "Army War College, 1908–9: Course in Military Art, Verbal and Dictated Orders," box 3, ESP.

69. Hugh L. Scott to "Dear Mother," 8 January 1875, Scott Papers, USMA.

70. Headquarters Corps of Cadets, Special Order #5, 4 February 1874, USMA.

71. Eben Swift, "An American Pioneer in the Cause of Military Education," *JMSI* 44 (January–February 1909): 67; ES, "Personal Memoirs," ESP, 38–40; T. R. Brereton, *Educating the U.S. Army: Arthur L. Wagner and Reform, 1875–1905* (Lincoln: University of Nebraska Press, 2000), 2; *Register of Graduates*, 4:56.

72. *Register of Graduates*, 4:53–61.

73. ES, "Memoirs," 68–72.

74. Ibid., 72.

75. Ibid., 72–100; Heitman, *Register*, 940.

76. Brereton, *Educating*, 5–7.

77. ALW, 1890 Efficiency Report, 2908-ACP-1882, RG 94, NARA I [hereafter "Wagner ACP"]; Brereton, *Educating*, 7–11.

78. ALW to Adjutant General, 8 July 1886, Wagner ACP.

79. WTS to PHS, 22 November (quotation) and 28 December 1881, reel 47, WTSP.

80. *Historical Sketch, Roster of Commandants, School Staff and Graduates of the U.S. Infantry and Cavalry School, Fort Leavenworth, Kansas, from Its Organization to June 30th, 1895* (Ft. Leavenworth, KS: U.S. Infantry and Cavalry School, 1895), 3–13; WTS to John Pope, 31 July 1881, reel 47, WTSP; Nenninger, *Leavenworth Schools*, 25–28.

81. Robert W. Ritchie, "A Graduate School of War," in *Army Service Schools* (Fort Leavenworth, KS: Army Service Schools Press, 1916), 31.

82. Nenninger, *Leavenworth*, 24–27; ES, "Memoirs: Fort Leavenworth 1893–7," box 7, ESP, 1; WTS to PHS, 3 October 1882, and "Address at Fort Leavenworth," reel 47, WTSP.

83. *Historical Sketch*, 6.

84. Ibid., 12; Nenninger, *Leavenworth*, 28–35.

85. Alexander M. McCook to Adjutant General, 3 October 1886, Wagner ACP.

86. Arthur L. Wagner, *The Campaign of Königgrätz: A Study of the Austro-Prussian Conflict in the Light of the American Civil War* (Fort Leavenworth, KS: U.S. Cavalry Association, 1889), 3, 4.

87. Clipping from *Army and Navy Gazette*, 12 April 1890, Wagner ACP.

88. Arthur L. Wagner, *The Service of Security and Information* (Washington, DC: J. J. Chapman, 1893); Arthur L. Wagner, *Organization and Tactics* (New York: B. Westermann, 1895); Swift, "Pioneer," 71.

89. Wagner, *Organization and Tactics* (7th ed.), 4.

90. Ibid., vi.

91. ALW to ES, 15 August 1893, box 1, ESP; ES, "Fort Leavenworth, 1893–7," 1.

92. Eben Swift, "The Lyceum at Fort Agawam," *JMSI* 20 (March 1897): 238. For a description of recitation technique, see Moseley, "One Soldier's Journey," 31–36. For the negative effects of the similar system at the Artillery School, see *WDAR* (1892), 4:774.

93. ES, "Necessity of Study of Military Subjects," n.d. [1906–1910], box 5, ESP.

94. ES, "Lyceum," 239–260.

95. ES, "Memoirs: Fort Leavenworth 1904–6," box 7, ESP, 2.

96. *Annual Report of the U.S. Infantry and Cavalry School* (Fort Leavenworth, KS: U.S. Infantry and Cavalry School, 1896), 41.

97. ES, "Fort Leavenworth, 1893–7," 3.

98. Ibid., 5.

99. ES, "Fort Leavenworth 1904–6," 2.

100. Quoted in Nenninger, *Leavenworth,* 45.

101. Brereton, *Educating,* xi–xiv. Wagner made oblique reference to this problem in a memorandum, 24 February 1905, box 15, entry 3, RG 165, NARA II. For an example of such criticism, see RLB, "Army Tendency to Theory," 19 January 1902, notebook #2, RLBP.

102. James S. Pettit to ES, 10 March 1897, box 1, ESP. Information on students taken from, *Annual Report* (1896) and Heitman, *Register.*

103. Brereton, *Educating,* 63–66; Nenninger, *Leavenworth,* 49–50.

104. WHC, Individual Service Report, 10 January 1894, 3543-ACP-1878, RG 94, NARA I [hereafter Carter ACP].

105. RLB, "Autobiography," RLBP, 20, 21.

106. John M. Jenkins to ES, 5 June 1894, and Johnathan R. Finley to ES, 20 September 1894, box 1, ESP; Nenninger, *Leavenworth,* 48–49; Smythe, *Guerilla Warrior,* 20.

107. For instance, see Edward B. Williston, Memorandum on Proposed School Regulations, n.d. [1891], Tasker H. Bliss Papers, USMA.

108. Russell F. Weigley, *Towards an American Army: Military Thought from Washington to Marshall* (New York: Columbia University Press, 1962), 156–160.

CHAPTER 6: THE SECOND UPHEAVAL

1. David F. Trask, *The War with Spain in 1898* (New York: Macmillan, 1981), 28–59; Louis A. Pérez, Jr., *The War of 1898: The United States and Cuba in History and Historiography* (Chapel Hill: University of North Carolina Press, 1998), 7–17.

2. Quoted in Ronald H. Spector, *Professors of War: The Naval War College and the Development of the Naval Profession* (Newport, RI: Naval War College Press, 1977), 17.

3. Ibid., 11–26; Trask, *War with Spain,* 72–94; Graham A. Cosmas, *An Army for Empire: The United States Army in the Spanish-American War* (College Station: Texas A&M University Press, 1998), 80–82.

4. Robert Wooster, *Nelson A. Miles and the Twilight of the Frontier Army* (Lincoln: University of Nebraska Press, 1993), 3–217; Donald B. Connelly, *John M. Schofield and the Politics of Generalship* (Chapel Hill: University of North Carolina Press, 2006), 328–330.

5. Henry C. Corbin to ALW, 29 March 1898, Wagner ACP.

6. Henry C. Corbin memorandum, 13 April 1898, WHCP; T. R. Brereton, *Educating the U.S. Army: Arthur L. Wagner and Reform, 1875–1905* (Lincoln: University of Nebraska Press, 2000), 67–74.

7. Cosmas, *Army for Empire,* 67–76.

8. Ibid., 76–82; Gerald F. Linderman, *The Mirror of War: American Society and the Spanish-American War* (Ann Arbor: University of Michigan Press, 1974), 33.

9. Cosmas, *Army for Empire,* 82–85.

10. Jerry M. Cooper, *The Rise of the National Guard: The Evolution of the American Militia, 1865–1920* (Lincoln: University of Nebraska Press, 1997), 87–98; Cosmas, *Army for Empire,* 86–93.

11. Cooper, *National Guard,* 26–43; *WDAR* (1892), 4:50–52.

12. Trask, *War with Spain,* 11–59, 157; Cosmas, *Army for Empire,* 85–86, 99–101, 127–129. See also, Linderman, *Mirror of War,* 60–90.

13. Connelly, *Schofield,* 329–330.

14. Cosmas, *Army for Empire,* 148–165; Daniel R. Beaver, *Modernizing the American War Department: Change and Continuity in a Turbulent Era, 1885–1920* (Kent, OH: Kent State University Press, 2006), 26–30; Andrew J. Bacevich, *Diplomat in Khaki: Major General Frank Ross McCoy and American Foreign Policy, 1898–1949* (Lawrence: University Press of Kansas, 1989), 7.

15. Cooper, *National Guard,* 105–107; "Report of the Inspector General," *WDAR* (1898), 10.

16. Cooper, *National Guard,* 97–104. See also, Donald Smythe, *Guerilla Warrior: The Early Life of John J. Pershing* (New York: Charles Scribner's Sons, 1973), 46.

17. ES, "Illinois National Guard," 1–4, box 7, ESP.

18. Roger Wolcott to Mrs. Henry Parkman, 10 June 1898, James Parker Papers, USMA.

19. Francis B. Heitman, *Historical Register and Dictionary of the United States Army, vol. 1* (Washington, DC: GPO, 1903), 29, 35; *Biographical Directory of the United States Congress,* http://bioguide.congress.gov.

20. Cosmas, *Army for Empire,* 141–146.

21. Cosmas, *Army for Empire,* 94–98; Henry C. Corbin, "Autobiography of Major General Henry C. Corbin, U.S. Army," box 11, Corbin Papers, LC, 87–89; Pérez, *War of 1898,* 39–48.

22. Trask, *War with Spain,* 182–184; Corbin, "Autobiography," 87.

23. Heitman, *Register,* 876; Utley, *Frontier Regulars,* 350–356; Cosmas, *Army for Empire,* 188–189; Wooster, *Miles,* 217–218; Corbin, "Autobiography," 89.

24. Heitman, *Register, passim; Correspondence Relating to the War with Spain: Including the Insurrection in the Philippine Islands and the China Relief Expedition, April 15, 1898, to July 30, 1902* (Washington, DC: CMH, 1993), 1:541–543.

25. Eli A. Helmick, "From Reveille to Retreat," Helmick Papers, AHEC, 64.

26. Heitman, *Register*, 657, 750.

27. Trask, *War with Spain*, 180–184; Charles D. Rhodes, Diary Notes, 13 May and 8 June 1898, Rhodes Papers, AHEC; Helmick, "Reveille to Retreat," 65; Smythe, *Guerilla Warrior*, 46–47.

28. Henry C. Corbin to William R. Shafter, 31 May 1898, in *Correspondence . . . War with Spain*, 1:18–19; Trask, *War with Spain*, 162–177.

29. LW Diary, 8 June 1898, box 2, LWP.

30. *Correspondence . . . War with Spain*, 1:18–40; Cosmas, *Army for Empire*, 180–193; Rhodes, Diary Notes, 10 and 12 June 1898.

31. Trask, *War with Spain*, 212–215.

32. Ibid., 217–223; LW, "Las Guasimas," undated manuscript, box 2, LWP.

33. Jack C. Lane, *Armed Progressive: General Leonard Wood* (San Rafael, CA: Presidio Press, 1978), 3–45.

34. Linderman, *Mirror of War*, 91–107; Brian M. Linn, *The Philippine War, 1899–1902* (Lawrence: University Press of Kansas, 2000), 62–64; Paul Robinson, *Military Honor and the Conduct of War: From Ancient Greece to Iraq* (London: Routledge, 2006), 2–5, 138–154, 190.

35. ALW to Henry C. Corbin, 7 May 1898, Wagner ACP.

36. ALW to J. C. Gilmore, 21 July 1898, Wagner ACP; Brereton, *Educating*, 75–79.

37. Cosmas, *Army for Empire*, 204–209.

38. Ibid., 209–214; Trask, *War with Spain*, 225–234.

39. Trask, *War with Spain*, 235–238.

40. George W. McIver, "My Memoirs," UNC, 1:107.

41. Steven L. Ossad, "Henry Ware Lawton: Flawed Giant and Hero of Four Wars," *Army History*, no. 63 (Winter 2007): 5–25.

42. Trask, *War with Spain*, 238–239; Lassiter, "Memoirs," 1:102; Helmick, "Reveille to Retreat," 79.

43. Otho E. Michaelis, "Field-Artillery Carriage Construction," *JMSI* 8 (December 1887): 414; Vardell E. Nesmith, "The Quiet Paradigm Change: The Evolution of the Field Artillery Doctrine of the United States Army, 1861–1905" (Ph.D. diss., Duke University, 1977), 71–163.

44. Wallace J. Randolph in *Annual Report of the Light Artillery and Cavalry School*, 20 December 1895, box 13, ESP.

45. Lassiter, "Memoirs," 1:56.

46. Trask, *War with Spain*, 238–246.

47. William R. Shafter to Henry C. Corbin, 1 and 2 July 1898, and Russell A.

Alger, 3 July 1898, in *Correspondence . . . War with Spain,* 1:70, 72, 74–75; Cosmas, *Army for Empire,* 218–232, 255–266.

48. Trask, *War with Spain,* 369–422; Stephen D. Coats, *Gathering at the Golden Gate: Mobilizing for War in the Philippines, 1898* (Fort Leavenworth, KS: Combat Studies Institute Press, 2006), 1–118.

49. Trask, *War with Spain,* 336–368.

50. "The 71st Regiment Inquiry," *New York Times,* 6 January 1899; *Statistical Exhibit of Strength of Volunteer Forces Called Into Service During the War with Spain* (Washington, DC: GPO 1899); Cosmas, *Army for Empire,* 146–148; Linn, *Philippine War,* 61–64.

51. JHW to William J. Sewell, 13 November 1899, box 45, JHWP.

52. Cosmas, *Army for Empire,* 278–285.

53. Quoted in ibid., 292.

54. Cosmas, *Army for Empire,* 285–298; Wooster, *Miles,* 233–237.

55. Philip C. Jessup, *Elihu Root* (New York: Dodd Mead & Company, 1938), 1:215.

56. Ibid., 1:217.

57. Corbin, "Autobiography," 98–100; JHW to Theodore Roosevelt, 31 July 1899, box 44, JHWP.

58. *WDAR* (1899), 1:45–46.

59. Redfield Proctor to ER, 2 December 1899, box 4, ERP.

60. *WDAR* (1899), 1:4–8; Graham A. Cosmas, "Military Reform after the Spanish-American War: The Army Reorganization Fight of 1898–1899," *Military Affairs* 35 (February 1971): 13–17.

61. Jessup, *Root,* 1:228–229, 244; Linn, *Philippine War,* 125–126.

62. *Letter from the Secretary of War Relative to Bill (S. 3240) to Increase the Efficiency of the Military Establishment of the United States,* 56th Cong., 1st sess., Senate doc. no. 186, 1900; ER to Paul Dana, 20 February 1900, vol. 178, pt. 2, ERP.

63. WHC, "Memoirs," WHCP, 319, 322.

64. *Increase of the Efficiency of the Army,* 56th Cong., 1st sess., hearings on S. 4300, 1900; Donald N. Bigelow, *William Conant Church and The Army and Navy Journal* (New York: Columbia University Press, 1952), 206. For examples of resistance to merit promotion, see Theodore Schwan, "The Coming General Staff—Its Importance as a Factor in the Military System of the Country," *JMSI* 33 (July–August 1903): 25–28; Evan M. Johnson, Jr., "Promotion by Selection," *JMSI* 37 (September–October 1905): 289–294; Rufus E. Longan, "What System of Promotions and Retirements Will Secure the Highest Degree of Efficiency in the Commissioned Personnel of the Army," *JMSI* 40 (May–June 1907): 326–352. Significantly, the last of these articles won the silver prize in that year's *JMSI* essay contest.

65. Stephen Skowronek, *Building a New American State: The Expansion of National Administrative Capacities, 1877–1920* (New York: Cambridge University Press, 1982), 167–173.

66. ER, remarks at General Staff dinner, 15 August 1903, box 220, ERP.

67. Robert H. Wiebe, *The Search for Order, 1877–1920* (New York: Hill and Wang, 1967); John Whiteclay Chambers, *The Tyranny of Change: America in the Progressive Era, 1890–1920,* 2nd ed. (New Brunswick, NJ: Rutgers University Press, 2000); Alfred D. Chandler, Jr., *The Visible Hand: The Managerial Revolution in American Business* (Cambridge, MA: Belknap Press, 1977).

68. "The General Staff," *New York Times,* 9 January 1903.

69. ER to LW, 2 (quotation) and 19 January 1901, vol. 179, pt. 1, ERP; WHC, "Memoirs," 424–450.

70. *WDAR* (1901), 1:79–87.

71. Linn, *Philippine War,* 185–321; David J. Silbey, *A War of Frontier and Empire: The Philippine-American War, 1899–1902* (New York: Hill and Wang, 2007), 105–206.

72. ER to Joseph R. Hawley, 3 March 1902, in *Efficiency of the Army,* 57th Cong., 1st sess., documents on S. 3917, 1902, 3–8; WHC to JGH, 2 November 1922, WHCP.

73. Beaver, *Modernizing,* 29–33.

74. RLB, 28 March 1902, diary #2, RLBP.

75. Theodore Roosevelt to ER, 18 February 1902, box 162, ERP.

76. Theodore Roosevelt to ER, 7 and 19 March 1902, box 162, ERP.

77. "Miles' Plain Talk," *Washington Post,* 21 March 1902; WHC, "Memoirs," 457–461. Quotations from Nelson A. Miles testimony, 20 March 1902, in *Efficiency of the Army* (1902), 34, 37.

78. "The General Staff," *New York Times,* 1 December 1902.

79. Wooster, *Miles,* 242–243; Jessup, *Root,* 1:252–261; WHC, "Memoirs," 460–463. For Root's correspondence in support of the bill, see vol 175, pt. 3, ERP.

80. Edward Ranson, "Nelson A. Miles as Commanding General, 1895–1903," *Military Affairs* 29 (Winter 1965–1966): 197–198; Wooster, *Miles,* 243–247.

81. Michael D. Doubler, *Civilian in Peace, Soldier in War* (Lawrence: University Press of Kansas, 2003), 113–115; Cooper, *National Guard,* 88–91; George W. Wingate to JMS, 9 November 1878, letterbooks vol. 2, JMSWP.

82. *WDAR* (1899), 1:45; Daniel Butterfield to ER, 12 December 1899, box 7, ERP.

83. Cooper, *National Guard,* 65–86.

84. William C. Sanger to ER, 19 February 1900, box 13, ERP; David J. Fitzpatrick, "Emory Upton and the Army of a Democracy," *JMH* 77 (April 2013): 486–489.

85. Charles W. F. Dick, "Our Second Line of Defense," *JMSI* 31 (September 1902): 749.

86. *WDAR* (1903): I:73–80; WHC, "Memoirs," 451–455; Louis Cantor, "Elihu Root and the National Guard: Friend or Foe?" *Military Affairs* 33 (December 1969): 366–371. Quotation from ER to J. C. Boyd, 12 April 1902, vol. 175, pt. 3, ERP.

87. "Visited by Soldiers," *Washington Post,* 23 January 1902.

88. Correspondence in vol. 176, pt. 1, ERP; "The Commander of the Army" and "The Message of the President," *Philadelphia Inquirer,* 2 and 3 December 1902; "Spoke for Staff Bill," *Washington Post,* 21 December 1902; Ronald G. Machoian, *William Harding Carter and the American Army: A Soldier's Story* (Norman: University of Oklahoma Press, 2006), 153–157.

89. Quoted in *Establishment of a General Staff Corps in the Army* (Washington DC: GPO, 1902), 42.

90. ER testimony, 17 December 1902, in *Establishment,* 33–50; Connelly, *Schofield* 333–335; *WDAR* (1903), 1:59, 63–67.

91. For instance, Schwan, "General Staff," 1–30. See also, Edgar S. Raines, "The Field Soldier and the Bureaucrat: Major General J. Franklin Bell, Major General Fred C. Ainsworth, and the Definition of the Role of the Chief of Staff of the Army, 1906–1910," Society of Military History Annual Conference, Arlington, Virginia, 11 May 2012.

92. Quoted in Elbridge Colby, "Elihu Root and the National Guard," *Military Affairs* 23 (Spring 1959): 28.

93. Machoian, *Carter,* 156–158; Wooster, *Miles,* 245.

94. *WDAR* (1903), 1:36.

CHAPTER 7: OLD SOLDIERS IN A NEW ARMY

1. For instance, see James L. Abrahamson, *America Arms for a New Century: The Making of a Great Military Power* (New York: Free Press, 1981), xiv–xv, 51; Edward M. Coffman, *The Regulars: The American Army, 1898–1941* (Cambridge, MA: Belknap Press, 2004), 176–183; Timothy K. Nenninger, *The Leavenworth Schools and the Old Army: Education, Professionalism, and the Officer Corps of the United States Army, 1881–1918* (Westport, CT: Greenwood Press, 1978), 4, 54–58; Russell F. Weigley, *The American Way of War: A History of United States Military Strategy and Policy* (New York: Macmillan, 1973), 325–236.

2. WHC personnel file, 3543-ACP-1878, RG 94, NARA I [hereafter "Carter ACP."]; WHC, "Memoirs," 48–314.

3. WHC, "Memoirs," 195–197; Ronald G. Machoian, *William Harding Carter and the American Army: A Soldier's Story* (Norman: University of Oklahoma Press, 2006), 47–48.

4. WHC to George D. Ruggles, 4 February 1897, Carter ACP; WHC to Henry C. Corbin, 25 May 1901, in William H. Carter, *Creation of the American General Staff: Personal Narrative of the General Staff System of the American Army,* 68th Cong., 1st Sess., Senate doc. no. 119, 1924, 5; WHC, "Memoirs," 314–319 (quotation 319).

5. Carter, *General Staff,* 1–2; WHC, "Memoirs," 486–489; Machoian, *Carter,* 101–120. For an example of Carter's advice to Root, see WHC to ER, n.d. [1903], document 940, box 8, entry 288, RG 165, NARA II.

6. ER to Benjamin I. Wheeler, 10 December 1901, vol. 175, pt. 2, and to Andrew Carnegie, 10 February 1902, vol. 180, pt. 1, ERP; WHC, "Memoirs," 400–412.

7. WD GO #155, 27 November 1901.

8. WHC to ER, n.d. [1901] in Carter, *General Staff*, 21.

9. WD GO #155, 1901, and WD GO #102, 22 September 1902; WHC to ER, 14 October 1901, WHCP.

10. WHC, "Memorandum No. 1," [1901], in Carter, *General Staff*, 6.

11. Frederick Palmer, *Bliss, Peacemaker: The Life and Letters of General Tasker Howard Bliss* (New York: Dodd Mead & Company, 1934), 5–80; Statement of Service, 3525-ACP-1880, RG 94, NARA I.

12. *WDAR* (1903), 4:91, 92.

13. ER to Paul Dana, 20 February 1900, vol. 178, pt. 2, and WHC to ER, n.d. [1900], box 11, ERP.

14. THB to Adna R. Chaffee, 15 January 1904, box 1, entry 294, RG 165, NARA II.

15. Harry P. Ball, *Of Responsible Command: A History of the U.S. Army War College* (Carlisle, PA: Alumni Association of the United States Army War College, 1984), 85–96.

16. THB memorandum, 14 August 1903, box 8, entry 292, RG 165, NARA II; *WDAR* (1903), 4:90–93.

17. *WDAR* (1899), 1:49.

18. Charles D. McKenna, "The Forgotten Reform: Field Maneuvers in the Development of the United States Army, 1902–1920" (Ph.D. diss., Duke University, 1981), 14–42; Edward M. Coffman, *The Old Army: A Portrait of the American Army in Peacetime, 1784–1898* (New York: Oxford University Press, 1986), 282–283.

19. T. R. Brereton, *Educating the U.S. Army: Arthur L. Wagner and Reform, 1875–1905* (Lincoln: University of Nebraska Press, 2000), 90–97.

20. Ibid., 80–87; Arthur L. Wagner, *Report of the Santiago Campaign, 1898* (Kansas City: Franklin Hudson, 1908), 51–88, 105–121 (quotation on 109).

21. George W. McIver, "My Memoirs," UNC, 1:63.

22. Arthur L. Wagner, "The Fort Riley Maneuvers," *JMSI* 32 (January–February 1903): 70–93; Charles D. McKenna, "The Forgotten Reform: Field Maneuvers in the Development of the United States Army, 1902–1920" (Ph.D. diss., Duke University, 1981), 55–66; Charles S. Sperry, memorandum [1904–1905], Tasker H. Bliss Papers, AHEC.

23. *WDAR* (1904), 1:36; Wagner, "Fort Riley Maneuvers," 71–72; Edward J. McClernand, Benjamin Alvord, and Peyton March to Samuel B. M. Young, 31 October 1903, box 19, entry 3, RG 165, NARA II; Brereton, *Educating*, 98–100, 112–116.

24. McKenna, "Forgotten Reform," 87–106; William H. Carter, "National

Camps of Instruction," *JMSI* 39 (November–December 1906): 464–466; WHC, "Memoirs," 658–671. See also, Francis J. Kernan, "Field Training for the United States Army," *JMSI* 38 (May–June 1906): 387–388; RLB, "Small Maneuvers," October 1905, notebook #7, RLPB; Charles Morton to Adjutant General, 26 December 1908, GCM.

25. Eli A. Helmick, "From Reveille to Retreat," Helmick Papers, AHEC, 191.

26. WD GO #115, 27 June 1904.

27. General Staff memorandum on draft WD GO #115, [1904] box 19, entry 3, RG 165, NARA II. The head instructors of the academic departments were the only faculty allowed to teach in both the Staff College and the other schools.

28. WD GO #115.

29. John M. Bacon to Adjutant General, 26 June 1895, File 937-ACP-1879, Entry 297, RG 94, NARA I [hereafter "Bell ACP"].

30. Hugh L. Scott recommendation, 27 August 1895, Bell ACP.

31. Quoted in Robert D. Ramsey III, *A Masterpiece of Counterguerrilla Warfare: BG J. Franklin Bell in the Philippines, 1901–1902,* Long War Occasional Paper 25 (Fort Leavenworth, KS: Combat Studies Institute Press, 2007), 3. See also, William Lassiter, "Memoirs," Lassiter Papers, USMA, 2:17–19.

32. Personnel file, Bell ACP; JFB to Henry C. Corbin, 17 May 1901, box 1, Corbin Papers, LC; *Register of Graduates,* 4:60; *Army Register* (1890), 74–75; Francis B. Heitman, *Historical Register and Dictionary of the United States Army,* vol. 1 (Washington, DC: GPO, 1903), 74; Edgar F. Raines, "Major General J. Franklin Bell and Military Reform: The Chief of Staff Years, 1906–1910" (Ph.D. diss., University of Wisconsin, 1976), 5–9.

33. Elwell S. Otis, endorsement, 7 October 1899, Bell ACP.

34. Personnel file, Bell ACP; Raines, "Bell," 9–11; Arthur MacArthur to ER, 3 February 1901, and William H. Taft to ER, 6 February 1901, vol. 174, pt. 3, and JFB to ER, 17 May 1901, box 15, ERP; Samuel B. M. Young to Russell A. Alger, 29 December 1903, LWP; Brian M. Linn, *The Philippine War, 1899–1902* (Lawrence: University Press of Kansas, 2000), 96, 106, 300–305; Ramsey, *Masterpiece of Counterguerrilla Warfare.*

35. *WDAR* (1902), 1:30 and (1903), 1:11; "Proceedings of the Staff of the GSSC," 2 January 1903, box 4, entry 288, RG 165, NARA II; Nenninger, *Leavenworth,* 56–62; Forrest C. Pogue, *George C. Marshall: Education of a General* (New York: Viking Press, 1963), 65–66.

36. "Summary of Reports by Inspectors, &c" 29–31 October 1904, Bell ACP; Nenninger, *Leavenworth,* 69.

37. JFB to ES, 10 December 1893, box 1, ESP; ALW recommendation, 4 July 1895, Bell ACP; ALW to JFB, 10 June 1904, FLC; J. P. Clark, "The Many Faces of Reform: Military Progressivism in the U.S. Army, 1866–1916" (Ph.D. diss., Duke University, 2009), 201–202.

38. Brereton, *Educating,* 118–119; Adna R. Chaffee to WHC, 8 June 1905, WHCP.

39. Guy V. Henry to "Mother," 10 January 1904, box 3, Henry Papers, AHEC; Milton F. Davis to George Van Horn Moseley, 22 November 1903, box 46, Moseley Papers, LC; "Memoranda for Colonel Wagner," 31 October 1904, file 1286, and JFB to William W. Wotherspoon, 6 July 1905, file 4163, FLC; Nenninger, *Leavenworth,* 77–79; Brereton, *Educating,* 109–111.

40. George A. Wieczorek to Milton F. Davis, 20 September 1906, file 5341, FLC. See also George Van Horn Moseley to Milton F. Davis, 31 December 1908, box 46, Moseley Papers, LC; Paul B. Malone, "The Army School of the Line," *JUSIA* 6 (January 1910): 512, 527.

41. "Memorandum for Instructors and Assistant Instructors," n.d., box 6, ESP.

42. JFB to Adna R. Chaffee, 25 March 1904, file 2145, FLC.

43. JFB, "Suggestions Regarding Instruction, Criticism, and Marking . . . ," n.d., file 400, and letter to Charles B. Hall, 5 September 1907, file 685, FLC; Helmick, "Reveille to Retreat," 169–172; Richard H. McMaster diary, 6 April 1909, McMaster Papers, South Caroliniana Library, University of South Carolina; ES to Stephen H. Elliott, 24 June 1908, box 2, ESP; JFB to William H. Taft, 18 August 1906 in George P. Ahern, *A Chronicle of the Army War College,* AHEC.

44. JFB to James Parker, 3 January 1906, file 685, FLC.

45. JFB to President, War College Board, "Report Containing Suggestions for Future Development of the GSSC," 31 July 1903, AGO #525015, entry 25, RG 94; Appendix B, *Annual Report of the Army Service Schools, 1905* (Ft. Leavenworth, KS: Staff College Press, 1905); Army Staff College 1905–6 Course of Instruction, box 6, ESP.

46. JFB to Charles S. Haight, 2 December 1905, file 596, FLC.

47. Robert M. Brambilia to Milton F. Davis, 14 September 1906, file 5341, FLC.

48. JFB to Military Secretary, 16 March 1905, with endorsement by J. P. Story, 23 May 1905, document 990754, entry 25, RG 94, NARA I; Alexander Mackenzie to JFB 28 April 1905, and JFB to Mackenzie, 2 May 1905, file 2327 FLC; JFB to Robert Shaw Oliver, 11 January 1907, box 1, entry 300, RG 165, NARA II; *WDAR* (1905), 2:251.

49. Henry B. Clark to JFB, 4 April 1905, file 3550, FLC.

50. JFB, circular letter, 29 June 1906, file 4628, and Edward K. Massee to Milton F. Davis, 15 March 1906, file 5341, FLC; Frederick D. Grant, *Report of the Camp of Instruction . . . Mount Gretna, Pa., July 27th to September 17th, 1906* [n.p.], box 13, ESP; Nenninger, *Leavenworth,* 112–114; *Provisional Instructions for Maneuvers* (Washington DC: GPO, 1904), 6–10.

51. Adna R. Chaffee to JFB, 22 March 1904, JFB to Chaffee, 24 and 25 March 1904, file 2145, FLC; *Annual Report of the Army Service Schools, 1905,* B-9; ES, "Fort Leavenworth 1904–6," box 7, ESP.

52. ES, "The Army War College, Course of 1906–7," box 7, ESP.

53. ES to Thomas H. Barry, 5 October 1906, box 3, ESP.

54. Ibid.

55. ES, "War College, 1906–7"; ES to Thomas H. Barry, 17 April 1907, box 3, ESP; Ball, *Responsible Command,* 105–111.

56. Azar Gat, *A History of Military Thought: From the Enlightenment to the Cold War* (New York: Oxford University Press, 2001), 294–440; Jan Bloch, *The Future of War: In Its Technical, Economic, and Political Relations,* trans. R. C. Long (Boston: World Peace Foundation, 1914).

57. "Major Jette," Richard H. Wilson, tr., "The Dread of Incurring Losses on the Battle-field and the Essential Elements of the Offensive," *JMSI* 51 (November–December 1912): 330–340.

58. Michael E. Howard, "Men Against Fire: The Doctrine of the Offensive in 1914," in *Makers of Modern Strategy from Machiavelli to the Nuclear Age,* ed. Peter Paret (Princeton, NJ: Princeton University Press, 1986), 510–526; Timothy Travers, *The Killing Ground: The British Army, the Western Front, and the Emergence of Modern Warfare, 1900–1918* (Boston: Allen & Unwin, 1987), 37–72; Dennis E. Showalter, "From Deterrence to Doomsday Machine: The German Way of War, 1890–1914," *JMH* 64 (July 2000): 679–710; Antulio J. Echevarria II, *After Clausewitz: German Military Thinkers Before the Great War* (Lawrence: University Press of Kansas, 2000), 1–120; Eric D. Brose, *The Kaiser's Army: The Politics of Military Technology in Germany During the Machine Age, 1870–1918* (New York: Oxford University Press, 2001), 4–118; Steven D. Jackman, "Shoulder to Shoulder, Close Control, and 'Old Prussian Drill' in German Offensive Infantry Tactics, 1871–1914" *JMH* 68 (January 2004): 73–104.

59. The Military Service Institution and Cavalry Association published a number of translations of the works of influential European thinkers, such as Julius von Verdy du Vernois, Heinrich Rohne, Friedrich von Bernhardi, and Wilhelm Balck.

60. James Parker, "Some Random Notes on the Fighting in the Philippines," *JMSI* 27 (November 1900): 317–340; Jonathan M. Field to Joseph R. Hawley, 22 September 1900, box 9, ERP; Linn *Philippine War,* 62–64; David J. Silbey, *A War of Frontier and Empire: The Philippine-American War, 1899–1902* (New York: Hill and Wang, 2007), 85–88.

61. For instance, see Louis M. Hamilton, "Jungle Tactics," *JMSI* 37 (July–August 1905): 23; RLB, "Small Maneuvers: Our Philippine service could not teach us all of Minor Tactics," n.d. October 1905, notebook #7, RLBP.

62. Quoted in Linn, *Echo of Battle,* 87.

63. ALW to JFB, 28 September 1904, file 3790, FLC.

64. Brereton, *Educating,* 111–112; ALW to JFB, 28 September 1904, file 1168, FLC.

65. Raines, "Bell," 471; Joseph T. Dickman to JFB, 2 November 1904, file 1168, FLC.

66. William J. Snow, "The Functions of Field Artillery", 12 September 1908, entry 299, RG 165, NARA II, 112.

67. David Jones, "Military Observers, Eurocentrism, and World War Zero," in *The Russo-Japanese War in Global Perspective: World War Zero,* ed. David Wolff, et al. (Boston: Brill, 2007), 135–177; John T. Greenwood, "The American Military Observers of the Russo-Japanese War (1904–1905)" (Ph.D. diss., Kansas State University, 1971), 124–275.

68. Biographical material from 4119-ACP-1888, RG 94, NARA I [hereafter "Reichmann ACP"].

69. John C. Bates, 31 December 1891, 1953-ACP-1887 [hereafter "Morrison ACP"].

70. Biographical material from Morrison ACP and AGO correspondence, microfilm, M698, roll 813, RG 94, NARA I.

71. John F. Morrison, *Training Infantry* (Ft. Leavenworth, KS: U.S. Cavalry Association, 1914), 186.

72. Greenwood, "Military Observers," 271.

73. "Report of John F. Morrison," in *Reports of Military Observers Attached to the Armies in Manchuria During the Russo-Japanese War* (Washington DC: GPO, 1906–1907), 1:98, 99. See also Donald Smythe, *Guerilla Warrior: The Early Life of John J. Pershing* (New York: Charles Scribner's Sons, 1973), 121–123.

74. "Report of Carl Reichmann," in *Reports of Military Observers,* 1:276–279

75. Greenwood, "Military Observers," 149–156; R. M. Connaughton, *The War of the Rising Sun and Tumbling Bear: A Military History of the Russo-Japanese War, 1904–5* (London: Cassell, 1988), 172–186.

76. Reichmann, *Reports of Military Observers,* 1:280.

77. Ibid., 1:269–271.

78. Morrison, *Reports of Military Observers,* 1:84.

79. Ibid., 1:98; "Report of Edward J. McClernand," 5:101–102, and "Report of Peyton C. March," 1:43 in *Reports of Military Observers.*

80. JFB and Joseph T. Dickman correspondence in file 1168, FLC (quotation from letter, JFB to Dickman, 18 May 1905.)

81. Theodore Roosevelt to Arthur MacArthur, 29 February 1902, file 419413, entry 25, RG 94, NARA I; GSSC and Army Service School annual reports, 1904–1906; JFB to Henry C. Corbin, 18 November 1902, and efficiency report for 1902, in 1258-ACP-1885, RG 94, NARA I, [hereafter "Boughton ACP"]; Ramsey, *Masterpiece of Counterguerrilla Warfare,* 9–10.

82. ES, "Fort Leavenworth 1904–6."

83. Anson L. Mills to Adjutant General, 19 May 1893, Boughton ACP.

84. *Register of Graduates,* 4:62; Charles D. Rhodes, obituary, Boughton Cullum File, USMA; "Efficiency Reports," Boughton ACP; John D. L. Hartman to ES, 18 August 1907, box 2, ESP.

85. JFB to Daniel H. Boughton, 16 July, 1906, Boughton ACP; Ewing E. Booth to Department Heads, 26 August 1907, file 4564, FLC; *FSR* revision working documents in file AWC 1283, and William W. Wotherspoon to JFB, 16 January 1908, box 14, entry 292, RG 165, NARA II; Nenninger, *Leavenworth,* 127–128.

86. *FSR* (1910) 24–25, 162; compare with *FSR* (1905), 20, 106; Raines, "Bell," 477.

87. *FSR* (1910), 159–167.

88. *Infantry Drill Regulations, United States Army, 1911* (Washington, DC: GPO, 1911), 108–115, 123. In a later publication, Morrison admitted that artillery might play a role in achieving fire superiority, Morrison, *Training Infantry,* 32–43.

89. *IDR* (1911), 101; LW, diary, 19 February 1914, box 8, LWP.

90. Alfred W. Bjornstad, "The Infantry Drill Regulations (Part 1)," *JMSI* 50 (March–April 1912): 228–230; Upton, *Tactics* (1874), 117; J. Franklin Bell, *Reflections and Suggestions,* AHEC, 3.

91. Robert L. Bullard, "A Moral Preparation of the Soldier for Service and Battle," *JMSI* 31 (November 1902): 779–792; James Chester, Levan C. Allen, John H. O'Connell, J. W. Powell, "Comments," *JMSI* 32 (January–February 1903): 110–123.

92. *IDR* (1904), 88–89; RLB, "Infantry Normal Attack," [1909–10], notebook 16, RLBP. See also, George B. Baltzell "Our Present Drill Regulations," and Hunter Liggett commentary, *JUSIA* 6 (July 1909): 40–41, 43–44; Robert L Hirst, "The Infantry Drill Regulations of 1911," *JUSIA* 11 (March–April, 1915), 651–656; Charles J. Crane, "Our Infantry Drill Regulations," *JUSIA* 11 (May–June 1915): 776–779; James A. Moss to LW, 1 December 1916, box 91, LWP.

93. Morrison, *Training Infantry,* 97; Morrison, *Seventy Problems: Infantry Tactics, Battalion, Brigade and Division* (Ft. Leavenworth, KS: U.S. Cavalry Association, 1914), 176.

94. JFB to Military Secretary, 19 June 1905, and Henry P. McCain to JFB, 23 and 28 June 1905, file 4274, ES to William D. Beach, 12 September 1905, file 1441, John F. Morrison to JFB, 6 December, and JFB to Morrison, 18 December 1905, file 4037, FLC.

95. David A. Armstrong, *Bullets and Bureaucrats: The Machine Gun and the United States Army, 1861–1916* (Westport, CT: Greenwood Press, 1982), 141; JFB, "Suggestions"; efficiency report, 1902, Morrison ACP.

96. Laurence Halstead, "Morrison," box 60, Halstead Papers, GCM; Helmick, "Reveille to Retreat," 170; Harold D. Cater interview with John M. Palmer, 15 October 1947, CMHC; Nenninger, *Leavenworth,* 89–94; quotation from Pogue, *Marshall,* 99.

97. JFB to Charles B. Hall, 21 August 1906, file 4051, FLC; JFB to LW, 7 June 1909, box 51, LWP; *Army Register* (1910), 111; Forrest Pogue interview with Charles D. Herron, 28 May 1958, GCM.

98. John F. Morrison to Milton F. Davis, 1 May 1908, file 5635, Albert E. Saxton to Charles D. Rhodes, 20 April 1911, file 2094, and Dwight E. Aultman to Adjutant General, 13 September 1910, file 5026, FLC.

99. *WDAR* (1905), 1:447.

100. JFB to Charles B. Hall, 21 August 1906, Hall to JFB, 24 August and 1 September 1906, file 4051, FLC.

101. "Editorial Department," *JUSIA* 6 (May 1910): 869–873; Helmick, "Reveille to Retreat," 176–177; I. B. Holley and John M. Palmer, *General John M. Palmer, Citizen Soldiers, and the Army of a Democracy* (Westport, CT: Greenwood Press, 1982), 187–192. For representative arguments of the various arms, see "F.O.O.T. Prints," "Knights and Ballisticians, with References to Rabbles: Some Light Reflections on Some Dark Subjects," *JUSIA* 6 (January 1910): 584–591; Snow, "Functions of Field Artillery," 152–153; WHC, "Cavalry Reorganization," *Journal of the United States Cavalry Association* 19 (July 1908): 1–10; Cavalry Association letter to members, 5 February 1912, box 3 Steele Papers.

102. Reichmann, *Reports of Military Observers,* 1:270, 271.

103. Holley and Palmer, *Palmer,* 187; Johnson Hagood to JFB, 30 January 1908, box 1, Hagood Papers, AHEC.

104. *Annual Report of the Army Service Schools, 1911* (Fort Leavenworth, KS: Staff College Press, 1911), 16–17; John M. Palmer, *Washington, Lincoln, Wilson: Three War Statesmen* (Garden City, N.Y.; Doubleday Doran & Company, 1930), 298.

105. John F. Morrison to Matthew F. Steele, 20 January 1910, box 13, Steele Papers, AHEC.

CHAPTER 8: THE GREAT WAR

1. RLB, 28 and 30 January 1915, notebook #18, RLBP.

2. John F. Morrison, *Seventy Problems: Infantry Tactics, Battalion, Brigade and Division* (Ft. Leavenworth, KS: U.S. Cavalry Association, 1914), 6.

3. Antulio Echevarria II, *Imagining Future War: The West's Technological Revolution and Visions of Wars to Come, 1880–1914* (Westport, CT: Praeger Security International, 2007), 8–11; Alan Trachtenberg, *The Incorporation of America: Culture and Society in the Gilded Age* (New York: Hill and Wang, 1982), 42–48, 126–129; Michael E. McGerr, *A Fierce Discontent: The Rise and Fall of the Progressive Movement in America, 1870–1920* (New York: Free Press, 2003), 86–104; Paul Robinson, *Military Honor and the Conduct of War: From Ancient Greece to Iraq* (London: Routledge, 2006), 140–142; *Report of the Inter-Departmental Committee on Physical Deterioration,* Cd. 2175 (1904); Michael Pearlman, "Leonard Wood, William Muldoon, and the Medical Profession," *New England Quarterly* 52 (September 1979): 338–344. See also William J. Snow, "The Functions of Field Artillery," 12 September 1908, entry 299, RG 165, NARA II, 206–207; Brian M. Linn, *The Echo of Battle: The Army's Way of War* (Cambridge, MA: Harvard University Press, 2007), 110–111.

4. JFB to Jacob M. Dickinson, 20 April 1910, box 7, entry 299, RG 165, NARA II.

5. LeRoy Eltinge, *Psychology of War*, rev. ed. (Ft. Leavenworth, KS: Press of the Army Service Schools, 1915), 44; John A. Lynn, *Battle: A History of Combat and Culture*, rev. ed. (Boulder, CO: Westview Press, 1988), 127.

6. Michael E. Howard, "Men Against Fire: The Doctrine of the Offensive in 1914," in *Makers of Modern Strategy from Machiavelli to the Nuclear Age*, ed. Peter Paret (Princeton, NJ: Princeton University Press, 1986), 513–524.

7. Eltinge, *Psychology of War*, 40–45, 70–71.

8. Quoted in McGerr, *Fierce Discontent*, 129; Steven J. Diner, *A Very Different Age: Americans of the Progressive Era* (New York: Hill and Wang, 1998), 35–40. See also, Hugh G. J. Aitken, *Taylorism at Watertown Arsenal: Scientific Management in Action, 1908–1915* (Cambridge, MA: Harvard University Press, 1960).

9. Review of "*The Rifle in War*," *JUSIA* 6 (March 1910): 772.

10. Henry E. Eames, *The Rifle in War* (Ft. Leavenworth, KS: Staff College Press, 1908), 78.

11. Ibid., 64.

12. Ibid., 85, 98–99; Alfred W. Bjornstad, "The Infantry Drill Regulations (Part 1)," *JMSI* 50 (March–April 1912): 226–229; John F. Morrison, *Training Infantry* (Ft. Leavenworth, KS: U.S. Cavalry Association, 1914), 35–36; Eltinge, *Psychology of War*, 88–90, 116–117.

13. Snow, "Functions of Field Artillery," 193.

14. Ibid., 191–216; William Lassiter, "Memoirs," 2:31–36, and Lassiter to Inspector General, 21 June 1909, box 1, Lassiter Papers, USMA.

15. Snow, "Functions of Field Artillery," 194; *WDAR* (1908), 2:253–257; Steven A. Stebbins, "Indirect Fire: The Challenge and Response in the U.S. Army, 1907–1917," (MA thesis, University of North Carolina-Chapel Hill, 1993), 47–91.

16. *Register of Graduates*, 4–56; Robert K. Evans, "Infantry Fire in Battle," *JUSIA* 5 (May 1909): 819–853.

17. Clarence R. Edwards, "It Lacks Organization," in *What is the Matter with Our Army?*, 62d Cong., 2d sess., doc. no. 621, 1912, 20.

18. "Looking Backward: The Narrative of Lieutenant X," *JUSIA* 6 (July 1909): 49–62.

19. WHC, "Memoirs," 662.

20. Francis B. Heitman, *Historical Register and Dictionary of the United States Army*, vol. 1 (Washington, DC: GPO, 1903), 261, 940.

21. RLB, 15 September 1906, diary #3, RLBP.

22. "William C. Buttler," *Biographical Register of the Officers and Graduates of the United States Military Academy*, http://penelope.uchicago.edu/Thayer/E/Gazetteer/Places/America/United_States/Army/USMA/Cullums_Register/2618*.html.

23. Forrest C. Pogue, *George C. Marshall: Education of a General* (New York: Viking Press, 1963), 94–131.

24. Carl Reichmann to Adjutant General, 9 July 1909, Reichmann ACP.

25. Charles Gerhardt, "Senior Officers and the School of the Line," *JUSIA* 6 (September 1909): 238, 239.

26. Quoted in Edward M. Coffman, *The Hilt of the Sword: The Career of Peyton C. March* (Madison: University of Wisconsin Press, 1966), 26; ER, "Speech by Elihu Root," 15 August 1903, box 220, ERP.

27. Dennis E. Nolan interviews, 17 November 1947 and 19 March 1948, CMHC; William H. Carter, *The Life of Lieutenant General Chaffee* (Chicago: University of Chicago Press, 1917), 267–269; Edgar S. Raines, "The Field Soldier and the Bureaucrat: Major General J. Franklin Bell, Major General Fred C. Ainsworth, and the Definition of the Role of the Chief of Staff of the Army, 1906–1910," Society of Military History Annual Conference, Arlington, Virginia, 11 May 2012; James E. Hewes, Jr., *From Root to McNamara: Army Organization and Administration* (Washington DC: CMH, 1975), 13; William G. Bell, *Commanding Generals and Chiefs of Staff, 1775–1991: Portraits and Biographical Sketches of the United States Army's Senior Officer* (Washington, DC: CMH, 1992), 96–101.

28. Raines, "Field Soldier" and "Bell," 2–5; Jesse M. Lee to George Van Horn Moseley, 13 May 1907, box 46, Moseley Papers, LC; Frank R. McCoy, interview 15 October 1947, CMHC.

29. Quoted in Raines, "Field Soldier."

30. ER to WHC, 19 August 1904, WHCP; Daniel R. Beaver, *Modernizing the American War Department: Change and Continuity in a Turbulent Era, 1885–1920* (Kent, OH: Kent State University Press, 2006), 34–35; Raines, "Bell," 202; George Van Horn Moseley, "One Soldier's Journey," box 14, Moseley Papers, LC, 99–100; Frank R. McCoy to LW, 4 Mary 1907, box 39, and Clarence R. Edwards to LW, 17 April 1907, box 40, LWP (quotation).

31. JFB to ES, 25 April 1910, box 2, ESP; John M. Palmer interview notes, 28 April 1948, CMHC; Francis J. Kernan, "Memoirs," Kernan Papers, USMA, 179.

32. Johnson Hagood, "Down the Big Road," box 1, Hagood Papers, AHEC, 124.

33. Bell, *Commanding Generals,* 106; Jack C. Lane, *Armed Progressive: General Leonard Wood* (San Rafael, CA: Presidio Press, 1978), 1–54; Robert M. Utley, *Frontier Regulars: The United States Army and the Indian, 1866–1891* (New York: Macmillan, 1974), 386–391.

34. Howard Gillette, Jr., "The Military Occupation of Cuba, 1899–1902: Workshop for American Progressivism," *American Quarterly* 25 (October 1973): 410–425.

35. Lane, *Armed Progressive,* 55–113. For examples of Wood's use of political connections, LW to Henry Cabot Lodge, 12 May 1900, and LW to Theodore Roosevelt, 7 July 1900, box 28, LWP; Roosevelt to ER, 4 September 1899, box 19 ERP.

36. Theodore Roosevelt to LW, 4 June 1904, box 35, LWP.

37. LW diary, 24 May and 2 June 1909, box 4, LWP; Raines, "Bell," 156. For a representative sample of opinions on Wood, see Eli A. Helmick, "From Reveille to Retreat," Helmick Papers, AHEC, 80–81, 99; RLB, 17 September–29 November

1903, diary #2, RLBP; Stephen C. Mills to James G. C. Lee, 9 October 1907, Mills Papers, AHEC; Lassiter, "Memoirs," IX:9–10.

38. Russell F. Weigley, *The American Way of War: A History of United States Military Strategy and Policy* (New York: Macmillan, 1973), 328–333; Lane, *Armed Progressive,* 157–167; WHC, "Memoirs," 730–735.

39. RLB, 18 February 1912, diary #5, RLBP.

40. JGH to LW, 9 April 1912, vol. 4, JGHP.

41. JGH to Frank McIntyre, 16 April 1913, vol 5, JGHP. See also, RLB, "Political Influence in Merit Appointment and Promotion, 25 March 1904, notebook #4, RLBP; George Van Horn Moseley to LW, 17 February 1914, box 75, LWP.

42. *WDAR* (1906), 3:93.

43. JFB to Jacob M. Dickinson, 10 February 1910, box 18, entry 292, RG 165, NARA II.

44. Ernest Gose to "My Dear Folks," 12 December 1909, Gose Papers, AHEC. See also, Matthew F. Steele to William Richardson, 20 April 1912, Steele Papers, AHEC.

45. "Promotion," *JUSIA* 11 (July–August 1914): 130; "As to 'Plucking Boards,' *JUSIA* 11 (September–October 1914): 292.

46. Helmick, "Reveille to Retreat," 189–191; LW to JGH, 9 June 1914, box 77, LWP.

47. I. B. Holley and John M. Palmer, *General John M. Palmer, Citizen Soldiers, and the Army of a Democracy* (Westport, CT: Greenwood Press, 1982), 197.

48. *WDAR* (1911), 1:238–242; Tasker H. Bliss, "Mobilization and Maneuvers," *JMSI* 50 (March–April 1912): 175–180; Ronald G. Machoian, *William Harding Carter and the American Army: A Soldier's Story* (Norman: University of Oklahoma Press, 2006), 230–238; Lassiter, "Memoirs," 3:64–67, and Lassiter to division adjutant, 27 April 1911, box 1, Lassiter Papers, USMA.

49. John M. Palmer, *Washington, Lincoln, Wilson: Three War Statesmen* (Garden City, N.Y.; Doubleday Doran & Company, 1930), 313; Lassiter, "Memoirs," 9:6–10; *WDAR* (1912), 1:69–128.

50. Lassiter, "Memoirs," 9:7–9 (quotation on 9); Holley, *Palmer,* 204–212.

51. Henry L. Stimson, "What Is the Matter with Our Army?" in *What Is the Matter with Our Army?,* 43.

52. LW to Hugh L. Scott, 3 April 1907, box 39, LWP.

53. Lane, *Armed Progressive,* 171–173; Lassiter, "Memoirs," 9:10–11; LW to Johnson Hagood, 27 June 1912, box 60, and correspondence regarding formation of Army League, box 66, LWP; Stephen Skowronek, *Building a New American State: The Expansion of National Administrative Capacities, 1877–1920* (New York: Cambridge University Press, 1982), 223–226.

54. Quoted in John Patrick Finnegan, *Against the Specter of a Dragon: The Campaign for American Military Preparedness, 1914–1917* (Westport, CT: Greenwood Military Press, 1974), 17.

55. *WDAR* (1916), 1:54.

56. Harry P. Ball, *Of Responsible Command: A History of the U.S. Army War College* (Carlisle, PA: Alumni Association of the United States Army War College, 1984), 130; LW to Henry L. Stimson, 12 September 1912, box 56, LWP; Skowronek, *Building,* 170–174, 226–227. See also Howard Donelly response in *Command and Commanders in Modern Warfare,* ed. William Geffen (Colorado Springs, CO: United States Air Force Academy, 1971), 77–78.

57. Hagood, "Down the Big Road," 141.

58. Carter, "Memoirs," 787.

59. LW to Edwin St. John Greble, 5 February 1910, box 51, Homer Lea to LW, 26 September 1912, box 60, and LW to JGH, 9 June 1914, box 77, LWP; Homer Lea, *The Valor of Ignorance* (New York: Harper & Brothers, 1909); Homer Lea, *The Day of the Saxon* (New York: Harper & Brothers, 1912); *Address of Hon. Theodore Roosevelt, Assistant Secretary of the Navy, Before the Naval War College, Newport, R.I., Wednesday, June 2, 1897* (Washington, DC: GPO, 1897), 5, 23–24; Eltinge, *Psychology of War,* 38–40; McGerr, *Fierce Discontent,* 95–96.

60. Various correspondence relating to camps in boxes 70, 74–77, LWP; Lane, *Armed Progressive,* 180–182; Finnegan, *Specter,* 61–71.

61. Henry S. Drinker to LW, 10 August 1915, box 80, LWP; Finnegan, *Specter,* 61–71.

62. Henry S. Drinker, "The Student's Military Instruction Camp at Gettysburg," box 69, LWP; Leonard Wood, "Students' Military Instruction Camp," *Harvard Magazine* (April 1914): 349–350; McGerr, *Fierce Discontent,* 32–74.

63. Courtland Nixon, "Public Fealty," *JUSIA* 11 (May–June 1915): 821.

64. Finnegan, *Specter,* 24–25; Leonard Wood, *The Military Obligation of Citizenship* (Princeton, NJ: Princeton University Press, 1915), 35–39; Leonard Wood, *Our Military History: Its Facts and Fallacies* (Chicago: Reilly & Britton, 1916), 198–213.

65. McGerr, *Fierce Discontent,* 107–111 (quotation on 111).

66. Wood, *Military History,* 189.

67. LW, diary, 5 January 1915, box 8, and various correspondence in boxes 80–92, LWP; Lane, *Progressive,* 187–200; Finnegan, *Specter,* 57–60.

68. Finnegan, *Specter,* 92–114; Pearlman, "Wood," 331–338.

69. Finnegan, *Specter,* 25–41; George C. Herring, Jr. "James Hay and the Preparedness Controversy, 1915–1916," *Journal of Southern History* 30 (November 1964): 383–390.

70. Finnegan, *Specter,* 39–56; *WDAR* (1915): 1:12–40.

71. Herring, "Hay," 388–394; Wood, *Military History,* 177–181.

72. WHC, "Memoirs," 889–892; Finnegan, *Specter,* 80–90; Jerry M. Cooper, *The Rise of the National Guard: The Evolution of the American Militia, 1865–1920* (Lincoln: University of Nebraska Press, 1997), 114–115; Herring, "Hay," 394–401.

73. *WDAR* (1916), 1:26–29; Finnegan, *Specter,* 139–155; Cooper, *National Guard,* 153–156.

74. Holley, *Palmer,* 245–247; *WDAR* (1916), 1:49–54, 70–80; Hewes, *Root to McNamara,* 21–22.

75. *WDAR* (1916), 1:7–13.

76. Cooper, *National Guard,* 156–166; Walter Millis, *Arms and Men: A Study in American Military History* (New York: Putnam, 1956), 228–233; Lane, *Armed Progressive,* 199–212; LW, diary 20 January 1917, box 8, and Adjutant General to LW, 24 March 1917, box 97, LWP. For examples of the view of regulars and guardsmen, see John J. Pershing to WHC, 21 October 1916, WHCP; Frank Williams to "Cousin Ellen,"28 April 1917, box 3, Williams Papers, Duke University Library Special Collections; Moseley, "One Soldier's Journey," 135–143.

77. Edward M. Coffman, *The War to End All Wars: The American Military Experience in World War I* (Madison: University of Wisconsin Press, 1986), 24–28; Nolan interview, 14 November 1947, CMHC.

78. Coffman, *War,* 26–27; George W. Goethals to George R. Goethals, 18 May 1917, box 4, Goethals Papers, LC; Moseley, "One Soldier's Journey," 144–148; Bacevich, *Diplomat in Khaki,* 62–63; Malone, "School of the Line," 527. For examples of regulars expecting Civil War–like volunteer commissions, see George T. Langhorne to LW, 29 May 1914, box 78, and JGH to LW, 11 and 26 June 1915, box 85, LWP.

79. Coffman, *War,* 20–24.

80. Finnegan, *Specter,* 186.

81. Hewes, *Root to McNamara,* 21–26; Coffman, *War,* 33–37; Coffman, *Hilt,* 40–44; Kernan, "Memoirs," 26–27; McIver, "Memoirs," 2:5–6; Peyton C. March interview, 13 October 1947, CMHC; Donald Smythe, *Pershing: General of the Armies,* 1st pap. ed. (Bloomington: Indiana University Press, 2007), 9–10.

82. Coffman, *War,* 32–42, 66–67, 305; Hewes, *Root to McNamara,* 23.

83. Lassiter, "Memoirs," 13:31.

84. Quoted in Coffman, *Hilt,* 64.

85. Ibid., 19–151; Hewes, *Root to McNamara,* 30–50.

86. Dan Boughton memorandum, 11 November 1909, box 17, entry 292, RG 165, NARA II.

87. EU, *Military Policy,* 258–263; Moseley, "One Soldier's Journey," 85–86; Richard S. Faulkner, *The School of Hard Knocks: Combat Leadership in the American Expeditionary Forces* (College Station: Texas A&M University Press, 2012), 26–67, 237–286.

88. "Some General Deductions," *JUSIA* 11 (November–December 1914): 434.

89. Quoted in Faulkner, *School of Hard Knocks,* 51.

90. *IDR* (1911, corrected to 6 May 1918), 127–128.

91. Faulkner, *School of Hard Knocks,* 22–25; Mark E. Grotelueschen, *The AEF Way of War: The American Army and Combat in World War I,* 1st pap. ed. (New York: Cambridge

University Press, 2010), 13–25; James W. Rainey, "Ambivalent Warfare: The Tactical Doctrine of the AEF in World War I," *Parameters* 13 (September 1983): 35–37.

92. Faulkner, *School of Hard Knocks,* 36–86.

93. Trenevan Edwards to "Family," 5 June 1917, and to "Elizabeth," 9 June 1917, in Frederick T. Edwards Papers, Duke University Special Collections, Durham, North Carolina.

94. Helmick, "Down the Long Road," 170 (quotation); Faulkner, *School of Hard Knocks,* 258–272; Grotelueschen, *AEF Way of War,* 100–102.

95. Smythe, *Pershing,* 83–86; John J. Pershing to Newton D. Baker and Peyton C. March, 28 June 1918, AEF Confidential Cables Sent, vol. 13, JGHP; Timothy K. Nenninger, "'Unsystematic as a Mode of Command': Commanders and the Process of Command in the American Expeditionary Forces, 1917–1918," *JMH* 64 (July 2000): 748–750; Brian Neumann, "A Question of Authority: Reassessing the March-Pershing 'Feud' in the First World War," *JMH* 73 (October 2009): 1119–1128.

96. Grotelueschen, *AEF Way of War,* 30–35; Smythe, *Pershing,* 235–237.

97. Nelson A. Miles, 20 March 1902 testimony, in Senate, *Efficiency of the Army,* 57th Cong., 1st sess., documents on S. 3917, 1902, 45.

98. Timothy K. Nenninger, *The Leavenworth Schools and the Old Army: Education, Professionalism, and the Officer Corps of the United States Army, 1881–1918* (Westport, CT: Greenwood Press, 1978), 142–147; Hugh L. Drum interview, 1 December 1947, CMHC; Ball, *Responsible Command,* 105–109; Donald Smythe, *Guerilla Warrior: The Early Life of John J. Pershing* (New York: Charles Scribner's Sons, 1973), 121; Smythe, *Pershing,* 34–35.

99. John J. Pershing to Peyton C. March, 19 July 1918, AEF Confidential Cables Sent, vol. 13, JGHP; Lassiter, "Memoirs," 13:36; Nenninger, "'Unsystematic,'" 743–746; Allan R. Millett, *The General: Robert L. Bullard and Officership in the United States Army, 1881–1925* (Westport, CT: Greenwood Press, 1975), 318–324.

100. Kernan, "Memoirs," 63.

101. Quoted in Nenninger, "Unsystematic," 766.

102. Millett, *General,* 378–388; John L. Hines to Harold D. Cater, CMHC; GHQ, AEF GO #196, 5 November 1918, in *United States Army in the World War, 1917–1919,* vol. 16 (Washington DC: CMH, 1992), 515–519.

103. Edward M. Coffman, "The American Military Generation Gap: The Leavenworth Clique in World War I," 35–43, and William Geffen, "The Leavenworth Clique in World War I: A Military View," 48–78, both in *Command and Commanders;* Nenninger, "'Unsystematic,'" 751–753.

104. Palmer, *Washington, Lincoln, Wilson,* 340.

105. Pogue, *Marshall,* 171–179; Coffman, *War,* 270–356; Nenninger, *Leavenworth,* 134–151; Joseph T. Dickman to WHC, 20 July 1924, WHCP.

106. Quoted in Faulkner, *School of Hard Knocks,* 149; RLB, 10 November 1911, diary #5, RLBP.

107. Grotelueschen, *AEF Way of War,* 298–342; Kenneth E. Hamburger, *Learning Lessons in the American Expeditionary Forces* (Washington, DC: CMH, 1997), 10–12.

108. John J. Pershing to Tasker H. Bliss, 31 July 1917, AEF Confidential Cables Sent, vol. 13, JGHP.

109. GHQ, "Instruction of Liaison," 16 August 1918, and "Posts of Command in Open Warfare," 29 August 1918, Samuel Faison Papers, UNC; Faulkner, *School of Hard Knocks,* 237–286; Timothy K. Nenninger, "Tactical Dysfunction in the AEF, 1917–1918," *Military Affairs* 51 (October 1987): 177–181; Grotelueschen, *AEF Way of War,* 44–58, 343–355; Rainey, "Ambivalent Warfare," 41–44; David E. Johnson, *Fast Tanks and Heavy Bombers: Innovation in the U.S. Army, 1917–1945* (Ithaca, NY: Cornell University Press, 1998), 24–27.

EPILOGUE

1. George C. Marshall, Army War College lecture, 19 September 1922, Xerox #3521, GCM.

2. William Lassiter, Army War College lecture, 13 November 1922, box 3, Lassiter Papers, USMA.

3. Frederick W. Taylor, *The Principles of Scientific Management* (New York: Harper & Brothers, 1911), ii.

4. John M. Schofield, *Study of the Science of War: From a Paper Read to the U.S. Military Service Institute, West Point, October 11, 1877* (New York: Van Nostrand, 1877), 8.

5. "Introductory Remarks by President of the Army War College to the Class of 1910–1911," 1 September 1910, Army War College Curricular Files, AHEC.

6. Notable works framing this debate are Barry Posen, *The Sources of Military Doctrine: France, Britain, and Germany Between the World Wars* (Ithaca, NY: Cornell University Press, 1984); Stephen P. Rosen, *Winning the Next War: Innovation and the Modern Military* (Ithaca, NY: Cornell University Press, 1991); Theo G. Farrell and Terry Terriff, *The Sources of Military Change: Culture Politics, Technology* (Boulder, Co.: Lynne Rienner, 2002). The field is ably summarized in Adam Grissom, "The Future of Military Innovation Studies," *Journal of Strategic Studies* 29 (October 2006): 905–934.

7. Samuel P. Huntington, *The Soldier and the State: The Theory and Politics of Civil-Military Relations* (Cambridge, MA: Belknap Press of Harvard University Press, 1957), 226–269.

Acknowledgments

Though historical research and writing are inherently solitary activities, no project of this scope is possible without a great deal of assistance. It is a great joy to extend my thanks to all of those who have assisted along the way. The journey began at Duke University, where Alex Roland with the assistance of Dirk Bönker, Marty Miller, Sy Mauskopf, and John Thompson taught me the historian's craft. Dick Kohn of that other institution just a few miles down US 15–501 provided my first and best lessons in writing history. I have endeavored to obey his dictum: Be kind to the reader. Colonels Lance Betros, Mat Moten, Ty Seidule, Kevin Farrell, and Gian Gentile, along with the other members of the Department of History at the United States Military Academy, provided an invigorating, challenging, and encouraging environment in which to pursue historical studies, all while we endeavored to impart a respect for the past in a younger generation of soldiers. As anyone who has done archival research can attest, some collections are more pleasant places in which to pursue the past than others. In my journeys, I have found the most helpful and considerate to be the staff of the Manuscript Division of the Library of Congress; Timothy Nenninger of the National Archives; Valerie Dutdut and Deborah McKeon-Pogue of the West Point Library Special Collections; Joanne Hartog of the George C. Marshall Center Archives; and Louise Arnold-Friend, Conrad Crane, Michael Lynch, David Keough, Richard Sommers, and the other dedicated archivists of the Army Heritage and Education Center at Carlisle Barracks, Pennsylvania. The Coddingtons and Whitakers deserve special mention for their generosity in sharing their homes during some of those trips.

I have been blessed to receive assistance from many individuals who have given their time to comment on parts of this monograph: Mark Ackrill, Ed Coss, Mel Dealie, Jon Due, Matt Eberhart, Nate Finney, Jeremy Gray, Mikhail Grinberg, Pete Hart, Gary Kramlich, Sebastian Lukasik, Heather Marshall, Ed Raines, Dwight "Buzz" Phillips, Brian Schoellhorn, Tim Schultz, Tom Spahr, Jason Thomas, Don Vandergriff, and two anonymous reviewers. Dave Johnson, Armand LaPotin, and Rory McGovern deserve special mention for providing unwavering encouragement and penetrating criticism in equally impressive quantities. I am particularly in debt to Sam Watson, who provided detailed comments on the first two chapters. Rob Citino and Roger Spiller have interceded at key moments, providing great assistance in bringing this work to publication. Brian Distelberg and Kathleen Drummy offered kind assistance throughout production. Finally, I was fortunate to land on the doorstep of Joyce Seltzer, an accomplished editor who has through encouragement, deft advice, and a pitiless word count applied necessary discipline to what might otherwise have been a sprawling mass. Whatever errors and imperfections that remain are my own.

The greatest thanks go to my family. My father taught me determination and discipline. My mother instilled a love of learning. My lovely daughters, Faith and Abigail, have endured too many "work weekends" and time away yet have been encouraging throughout, even showing their own interest in history and writing. My wife, Kelly, has shouldered enormous burdens. As if being an army spouse were not difficult enough, she has had to be a book widow as well. Yet she has never complained. Whether using her freakish ability to decipher late nineteenth-century handwriting, taking the girls on many shopping odysseys so that I could write just a few pages (half of which were soon deleted), or just dealing with the vacant expression of a husband who was off somewhere a century past, she has once again proven that I, indeed, am the lucky one in our marriage.

Index